D0396592

THE
NEXT
AMERICAN
NATION

THE
NEXT
AMERICAN
NATION

*The New Nationalism and the
Fourth American Revolution*

MICHAEL LIND

THE FREE PRESS

New York   London   Toronto   Sydney   Tokyo   Singapore

The Free Press
A Division of Simon & Schuster Inc.
1230 Avenue of the Americas, New York, N.Y. 10020

Printed in the United States of America

printing number

1 2 3 4 5 6 7 8 9 10

Text design by Carla Bolte

Library of Congress Cataloging-in-Publication Data

Lind, Michael
    The next American nation: the new nationalism and the fourth
American revolution/ Michael Lind.
        p.   cm.
    Includes bibliographical references (p.   ) and index.
    ISBN 0-02-919103-3
    1. Nationalism—United States—History.   2. Pluralism (Social
sciences—United States.   3. Multiculturalism—United States.
4. United States—Civilization.   I. Title.
E169.1.L5432   1995
320.5′4′0973—dc20   95-13621
                                                            CIP

To My Parents

Contents

Acknowledgments

If I attempted to thank everyone who has provided helpful criticism of my ideas, I would inevitably neglect some friends and colleagues, while implicating others in any errors of fact or interpretation. I will therefore limit myself to thanking Owen Harries, Editor of *The National Interest,* and Lewis H. Lapham, Editor of *Harper's Magazine,* for their encouragement and support during the writing of this book; and also Alan Tonelson, for bringing me to the attention of the The Free Press. I am especially grateful to Adam Bellow, Editorial Director of the Free Press, for seeing the basis of a book in an unpublished essay by an unknown author, and for guiding the project to completion with enthusiasm, understanding, and skill.

THE
NEXT
AMERICAN
NATION

Introduction

Are We a Nation?

"Are we a nation?" The question was raised, in an address of that title, by Senator Charles Sumner of Massachusetts after the Civil War. At the end of the twentieth century, the question of whether America is a nation has arisen again. Unlike Sumner, that great champion of Union and racial integration, proponents of the leading schools of thought about American national identity today—multiculturalism and democratic universalism—tend to answer the question in the negative.

Are we a nation? No, say the multiculturalists, who are found predominantly though not exclusively on the left. The United States, they say, is not a nation-state. Rather, it is a nation of nations, a federation of nationalities or cultures sharing little or nothing but a common government: a miniature UN. How the cultures that compose the multinational American citizenry are to be defined is the subject of dispute among those who think of America in this way. Contemporary multiculturalists usually identify the nations or cultures of the United States with five races defined by descent: white, black or African-American, Hispanic, Asian-Pacific Islander, and American Indian/Inuit. In contrast, a small but eloquent band of old-fashioned cultural pluralists (in the tradition of the early-twentieth-century American thinkers Horace Kallen and Randolph Bourne) tends to identify the nations of America with ethnic groups, particularly white ethnic groups: English, German, Irish, Italian, Polish, and so on. Though they may disagree about how many American cultures there are, multiculturalists and cultural pluralists agree that the United States is not a nation-state like France or Poland or China or

1

even Brazil, but a multinational federation, like Canada and Switzerland and the former Soviet Union and Yugoslavia. The philosopher Michael Walzer has summarized this view, common to multiculturalists and cultural pluralists: "It isn't inconceivable that America will one day become an American nation-state, the many giving way to the one, but that is not what it is now; nor is that its destiny."

A multiculturalism of the right is conceivable, as a response by conservatives who wish to preserve cultural or racial "purity" through a policy of voluntary ethnic or racial segregation; something like this is promoted by the French right of Jean Marie Le Pen, and there are American parallels in some of the proposals of the Ku Klux Klan. To date, however, most multiculturalists and cultural pluralists in the United States have been on the political left. They have tended to share an antipathy to the mainstream culture of the American majority. Denying or ignoring the black and Latin American elements of American vernacular culture, multiculturalists tend to misdescribe it as "white" culture. Compounding the confusion, theorists of multiculturalism, like many conservatives, often identify this white middle American culture—rather implausibly, it must be said—with "western civilization."* The confusion only deepens when multiculturalists count among the supposed victims and enemies of "western civilization" immigrants from Spanish-speaking, Catholic Latin America, whose traditions exhibit greater continuity with ancient Rome and Latin Christendom than does the culture of Protestant, English-speaking North Americans. The confusion arises from the equation—as spurious in the case of Latin American mestizos as in the case of black Americans—of nonwestern with nonwhite. If one rejects this assumption, if one assumes that Americans of different races can, and in fact do, share, not only a common civilization but a common nationality, then the multicultural enterprise simply collapses.

The major opposition to multiculturalism today comes from demo-

---

*Whether the diverse societies of the ancient Mediterranean, Latin Christendom, and modern Western Europe and its lands of settlement and colonies really can be spoken of as a single civilization or culture is open to question. Even if they could, the United States, and all of the English-speaking countries, would be best understood as atypical offshoots of a continental civilization in which the cultural leaders for the longest periods were Italy and France, and which is based on a shared legacy of Roman law and Catholicism.

cratic univeralists, who are mostly, though not exclusively, on the political right. *Are we a nation?* The democratic universalists answer No as well. Universalists reject the multicultural celebration of racial-cultural identities, fearing it will encourage the "Balkanization" of America; however, they do not counter it with an inclusive American nationalism of their own. By their own theory, they cannot; for democratic universalists agree with multiculturalists that the United States is not a conventional nation-state. The United States, according to universalists, is not a nation-state at all, but an idea-state, a nationless state based on the philosophy of liberal democracy in the abstract. There is no American people, merely an American Idea. Someone who believes ardently in this founding idea (variously defined as human equality or natural rights or civil liberty or democracy or constitutional government) is a genuine American, even if he shares little or nothing of the prevalent culture, mores and historical memories of the American cultural majority. Americanness, in this view, is less akin to membership in a national community than to belief in a secular political faith—the religion of democracy. In the words of the late Theodore H. White, "Americans are not people like the French, Germans, or Japanese. . . . Americans are held together only by ideas." Another journalist, Cokie Roberts, has written, "We have nothing binding us together as a nation—no common ethnicity, history, religion, or even language—except the Constitution and the institutions it created."[1] (The fact that nowadays conservatives tend to espouse democratic universalism is surprising, inasmuch as this doctrine confuses the American *nation* with its *government*—a point lost on everyone on the right except for a few "paleoconservatives").*

The democratic universalist's characterization of the United States as a nonnational idea-state usually comes as part of a package with American exceptionalism—the belief that the United States is not only different in kind from other countries but superior in its morality and institutions. House Speaker Newt Gingrich has called for Americans to reject multiculturalism and "reassert American exceptionalism."[2] The British writer

---

*It can be argued, to be sure, that democratic universalism on the right is a rather thinly camouflaged popular nationalism, with "democracy" and "Western civilization" really understood, by advocates and audience alike, to refer to what used to be called the American way of life, not to Norwegian parliamentary procedure or Italian literature.

Paul Johnson even claims that the future of humanity depends on the geopolitical power of the United States, "a great and mighty nation which is something more than a nation, which is an international community in itself, a prototype global community, but which at the same time is a unity, driven by agreed assumptions, accepting a common morality and moral aims, and able therefore to marshal and deploy its forces with stunning effect."[3]

These, then, are the two schools of thought that have almost monopolized recent discussions of American identity. Both agree that the United States has never been a conventional nation-state, and differ only as to what kind of nonnational state it is or should be. Is the United States, as the multiculturalists claim, a federation of races, or is it—as the democratic universalists argue—a post-national idea-state?

The answer is: neither. The multiculturalists and the democratic universalists are both wrong. The United States is not, and never has been, either a multinational democracy or a nonnational democracy. The United States has been, is, and should continue to be a liberal and democratic nation-state.

The multiculturalists are mistaken in equating the conventionally defined American races with cultures, and identifying those cultures, in turn, with nationalities. By the usual criteria of nationality, most of the Americans who are labeled white, black, Hispanic, and Asian—as well as American Indians and Inuit who have assimilated to the mainstream culture—are members of a single national community, the American nation. That nation is not homogeneous; it is divided into subcultures, some of which, like the historic black American subculture, more or less correspond to race ("Hispanic" and "Asian and Pacific Islander," though, are bureaucratic categories that do not correspond to genuine ethnic subcultures). A people does not have to be as homogeneous as, say, the Japanese in order to constitute a nation; Italians are members of a single nation, in spite of their enormous regional variety, and the racial diversity of Brazil and Mexico does not mean that those countries lack distinctive national heritages and identities.

While the multiculturalists and their cousins the cultural pluralists are wrong to think of the United States as a federation of racial cultures, the democratic universalists are mistaken in thinking that American national identity can be founded on an idea. The very notion of a country based on an idea is absurd. What if two countries are founded on the same idea—say, individual rights, or the rule of law? Does that mean they are the same country? The communist states all professed to be founded on the ideas of Marx and Lenin—and yet Russian, Chinese, and Vietnamese communists remained not only distinct from each other but often mutually hostile. At best, a political or religious dogma is merely one—and not the most important—element of the culture that distinguishes one nationality from another.

A nation may be *dedicated* to a proposition, but it cannot *be* a proposition—this is the central insight of American nationalism, the doctrine that is the major alternative to multiculturalism and democratic universalism. To the question, *Are we a nation?* the American nationalist answers with a resounding and unequivocal Yes. A straightforward American nationalism, in one form or another, is *the* alternative to the fissioning that the multiculturalists celebrate as pluralism and the democratic universalists condemn as Balkanization.

A genuine nation is not a mere citizenry, a mere collection of individuals who share nothing other than common rulers and common laws. If a common government alone were sufficient, then the Soviet and Romanov and Hapsburg and Ottoman Empires would have been nations themselves, rather than "prison-houses of the nations" (as Tsarist Russia was described).* A real nation is a concrete historical community, defined primarily by a common language, common folkways, and a common vernacular culture.† Such an extrapolitical American nation exists today, and has existed in one form or another for hundreds of years. Most Americans, of all races, are born and acculturated into the American nation; most immigrants and their descendants will be assimilated into it.

---

*The language of international law confuses matters, by referring to subjects or citizens of a state as its nationals whether the state corresponds to an actual nation or not. The United Nations really should be called the United Regimes or the United States (the United States, conversely, might more accurately be called the United Nation of America).

†For the nationalist, as for some opponents of nationalism, there is a difference between patriotism and nationalism. Patriotism is allegiance to a particular government or constitution; nationalism is loyalty to the interests of the cultural nation. The nationalist is willing to sacrifice patriotic duty to national loyalty, if necessary—as in 1776, when the American Patriots decided that the needs of the American nation had to prevail over their patriotic allegiance to the British empire. Governments should serve nations, not nations governments.

The American nation is different in detail from the Chinese and Russian and Mexican and French nations. It is not, however, different in kind.

Not only does the transracial American majority constitute a single nation, but that majority is deeply nationalist in its sentiments. Few Americans are consistent liberals or conservatives; most are nationalists, by reflex if not reflection. American nationalism, however, is the political doctrine that dares not speak its name.

American nationalism is almost never represented in public discussions of American identity, which as I have noted tend to be dominated by multiculturalism and democratic universalism. Since World War II, nationalism has been considered by many to have been discredited by its association with German National Socialism, Italian Fascism, and Japanese militarism (which were of course three quite different phenomena). American intellectuals have also been deeply influenced by political philosophies hostile to nationalism. On the left, antinationalism has been fed by Marxism, which viewed nationalism as an ephemeral phase of political development destined to be superseded in the era of cosmopolitan socialism (ironically, Marxism has proven to be an ephemeral phase of nationalism in Russia and China). The antinationalists of the right tend to be nostalgic for multinational empires like the Hapsburg and the British, and to associate nationalism with the overthrow of European rule over nonwhite nations, something of which a certain kind of conservative disapproves. Although nationalism around the world has often been liberal and democratic rather than authoritarian or totalitarian, American politicians, intellectuals, and journalists continue to indulge in the old-fashioned practice of treating nationalism as a *malum in se*. The world, we are told again and again, is threatened by a resurgence of nationalism (as though there had ever been a great era of selfless internationalism). Adjectives like "aggressive" and "sinister" and "dark" are often affixed to nationalism in order to make the term seem even more frightening. The critics of nationalism in the abstract seldom trouble themselves to ask whether it makes any sense to view things as different and incompatible as the eighteenth-century philosopher J. G. Herder's tolerant aesthetic pluralism and Hitler's murderous racist imperialism as aspects of the same phenomenon—in this case, "German nationalism."

The pejorative connotations that hover around the subject of nationalism—ours and everyone else's—in conventional American public discourse do not mean that nationalism is weak or nonexistent in the American body politic. Indeed, nationalism in one form or another is probably the conception of American identity with the greatest influence among Americans as a whole, particularly among the majority who do not have college educations. Outside of a small educated elite, hardly any Americans think of their country as a miniature UN or as an abstract idea-state. Though they may be trained to repeat these formulas, most Americans do not really believe them. The patriotism of ordinary Americans is no different in kind from that of Italians or Indians or Russians; it has more to do with family, neighborhood, customs, and historical memories than with constitutions or political philosophies. It may very well be, indeed, that popular nationalism, as a sentimental attachment to people and customs and country, is much stronger in the United States than in Western Europe, where "post-patriotic" attitudes, at least among the more educated, are much more prevalent.

The American people, then, constitute a genuine nation; with its own nation-state, the U.S.A., and with its own genuine, if largely inarticulate, nationalism. The really interesting argument, it turns out, is not the stale debate between multiculturalists and democratic universalists about what kind of nonnational state the United States is: multi- or post? It is another controversy, a less familiar dispute, over how the "nation" in the American "nation-state" is to be defined. In this debate among nationalists, the two sides are nativists and liberal nationalists.

Nativists tend to impose racial and/or religious tests on membership in the national community. To be American, in the nativist view, is to be white and/or Christian or a member of "the Judeo-Christian tradition" (a euphemism that really means Christian). The racial and religious definitions of Americanness are not always joined; there are secular racists, and there are conservative nativists who envision a multiracial but pan-Christian American national community. The latter option—a pan-Christian but not white-supremacist American nativism—is the more or less overt goal of right-wing Christian political activists like Pat Robertson, leader of the Christian Coalition. Old-fashioned Anglo-American or even Euro-American nativism will have diminishing appeal in a country in which a growing percentage of the population is nonwhite;

however, the potential attractiveness of a nonracist, pan-Christian religious nativism to Americans of all races should not be underestimated.

Liberal nationalists share an unapologetic American nationalism with nativists—but that is about all that they share. The liberal nationalist rejects racial or religious tests for membership in the American nation. A nonwhite American is as genuine an American as a white American (indeed, black Americans can make a better claim for their "Americanness" than most of the descendants of European immigrants). One can despise and reject Christianity and Judaism and be not merely a fine citizen but a member in good standing of the American cultural nation. Insofar as American nationality is a matter of vernacular culture, rather than race or beliefs, a radical black lesbian atheist who grows up in Chicago is more "American" than a white English conservative who immigrates in adulthood and who, though he is an expert on the Founding Fathers, is unfamiliar with the American idiom.*

For the liberal nationalist, then, the American nation is defined by language and culture, not by race or religion. The national language is American English, in its various regional and subcultural dialects. The national culture is not the high culture of the art galleries and civics classes, but rather the vernacular culture that has evolved in the United States in the past several centuries, and continues to evolve, from the unsystematic fusion of various regional and racial customs and traditions. The liberal nationalist argument, it must be stressed, is not that a transracial American nationality is something that will emerge in the future, from the mingling of today's conventionally defined American racial and ethnic groups. Such mixing, rather, merely reinforces a common cultural nationality that already exists.

The American cultural nation, properly defined, has included Americans of different races for centuries. White supremacists and black nationalists to the contrary, black Americans were members of the

---

*Liberal nationalism and nativism tend to be found on the "liberal" and "conservative" sides of the contemporary American political spectrum. It is possible, however, to be a liberal nationalist with many conservative political views ("liberal" in liberal nationalism refers to the liberal-democratic constitution of the state, not to particular policies). It is also possible to imagine an American racial or religious nativism that is "left-wing" with respect to economics, like the populism of William Jennings Bryan.

American cultural nation for generations before they were granted U.S. citizenship. Indeed, the transracial American nation is considerably older than the United States itself; for several generations before 1776, a distinct, unique, English-speaking North American nationality, including slaves born and raised on American soil, had begun to diverge from other parts of the English-speaking world.* Even if the federal government were abolished tomorrow, the American cultural nation would endure. The American nation is older than its government, and will almost certainly outlive the United States, which like all regimes will prove mortal. States and constitutions come and go; cultural nations, though they are not eternal, last a very long time.

Of the two rival versions of American nationalism, nativism has the greatest antiquity, for the simple reason that most Americans, until well into the twentieth century, thought of the American people as a white Christian nation (something that is hardly surprising, insofar as most Americans for generations to come will be conventionally white and at least nominally Christian). Even though it rejects the venerable traditions of white supremacy and Protestant/Christian hegemony, the liberal nationalist philosophy that I set forth in this book has deep roots in the American heritage—in the strong-state nationalism of George Washington, Alexander Hamilton, Daniel Webster, Abraham Lincoln, and Theodore Roosevelt; in the New Deal liberalism of Franklin Roosevelt, Harry Truman, and Lyndon Johnson that created and sustains a middle class that would be destroyed by unchecked capitalism; and, most important of all, in the tradition of color-blind racial integrationism descending from abolitionists like Frederick Douglass to civil rights reformers like Martin Luther King, Jr. Liberal nationalism might be most simply defined as yesterday's "melting-pot" nationalism updated to favor the cultural fusion and genetic amalgamation not just of white immigrant groups but of Americans of all races.

In civil rights law, the natural corollary to the liberal nationalist conception of the American nation as a cultural and (in time) genetic melt-

---

*The linguistic and cultural definition of nationality, it should be noted, is an objective anthropological test that does not depend on subjective perceptions. If subjective beliefs defined nationality, then Swedes, say, might decide they were all really Portuguese, and the actual Portuguese would have no grounds for objecting.

ing pot is the rejection of any distinctions based on biological race. Race is an arbitrary category that is bound to grow more arbitrary, as intermarriage produces growing numbers of Americans with ancestors in several of today's officially defined racial groups. In civil rights, liberal nationalists favor a return to the original, color-blind vision that animated the leaders of the Civil Rights Revolution like Martin Luther King, Jr., Bayard Rustin, Hubert Humphrey, and Lyndon Johnson. Since the 1960s, this vision has been betrayed on the left by multiculturalists, with their defense of racial quotas and their conception of the United States as a federation of genetically defined nationalities. It is time for the American center-left to reclaim the color-blind idealism that should never have been ceded to the reactionary right.

Liberal nationalism provides not merely a different vision of the American people, but a different understanding of the American past. American exceptionalism, the belief in American uniqueness that is so important to democratic universalism, is rejected by liberal nationalists, whose American patriotism does not depend on overblown claims about American uniqueness or superiority. One should cherish one's nation, as one should cherish one's family, not because it is the best in the world, but because, with all its flaws, it is one's own.

The exceptionalist interpretation of American history holds that American politics from 1776 to the present has consisted of the gradual, painful, but progressive working out of the ideas of the Founding Fathers. Exceptionalism, in other words, is both *idealist* and *gradualist*. The liberal nationalist conception of the American past, in contrast, is *realist* and *catastrophist*. It is realist, insofar as it sees American society as the result of power struggles and inherited cultural legacies, not just abstract philosophical debates. It is catastrophist, insofar as it views American history not as the smooth and logical unfolding of an argument about liberty or democracy, but as a sequence of racial, cultural, and political regimes, each assembled by the victors in a cataclysmic and violent struggle.

Though the word "revolution" is easily tossed about today, in fact there have been only three genuine revolutions in U.S. history—the War of Independence and its violent aftermath (including the suppression of Shays' Rebellion and the Whiskey Rebellion); the Civil War and

Reconstruction; and the Civil Rights Revolution from the 1950s to the 1970s. American revolutions are violent. More Americans died in the Civil War than in all of America's foreign wars combined. During the Civil Rights era, the United States was convulsed by the most extensive domestic political violence since the end of Reconstruction. American revolutions are also disruptive. Since 1789, the French have had five republics (along with several monarchies, one directory, a consulate, and a couple of empires). By contrast, the United States, since 1789, has had only one federal constitution; the two dominant parties have had the same names since the 1860s; even the boundaries of the states, unlike political jurisdictions in other democracies, are fixed in America. The formal constitutional and political continuity that we Americans cherish disguises the fact that there have been three "republics" of the United States since the War of Independence: Anglo-America (1789–1861); Euro-America (1875–1957) and Multicultural America (1972–present).

Each of these three republics has put the basic building blocks of the nation-state—race, culture, and citizenship—together in a different way.* At the risk of oversimplification (a risk inseparable from any attempt to discuss major issues of public importance), I argue that each of these American "republics" has had its own consensus, its own threefold national formula, describing the national community, the civic religion, and the political creed. At any given time, there have been dissident views; but in every era, a particular national formula has tended to prevail.

In the national formula of the First Republic of the United States, Anglo-America, the national community was identified with the Anglo-Saxon or Anglo-Germanic element of the population; the civic religion, Protestant Christianity; and the political creed, federal republicanism. There was considerable doubt as to whether Irish-American Catholics—to say nothing of Jews or black Americans—could ever be "real Americans." The Civil War and Reconstruction created a Second Republic, Euro-America, which peaked in the middle of the twentieth century. The Euro-American national formula, redefined to accommodate the Euro-

---

*I do not deny that American history can be divided into periods on the basis of different criteria—for example, political party systems, or profound changes in the distribution of power between the state and federal governments (like the New Deal). Changes in the rules governing race and citizenship are not the only changes defining eras in American history; they are merely the most important.

pean immigrants of the late-nineteenth and early-twentieth century, was somewhat more inclusive than the Anglo-American. To be a "genuine American," according to the popular consensus in the Second Republic, was to be of European descent and to be Christian (Protestant or Catholic) in religion (the Eisenhower-era phrase "Judeo-Christian" was, in practice, a polite euphemism for pan-Christian). The antebellum elimination of most restrictions on white male suffrage and the post–Civil War nationalization of basic civil rights turned the Anglo-American political creed of federal republicanism into a creed of federal democracy; even in the 1950s, however, the U.S. remained a highly decentralized federal state.

The Third Republic is the one in which we live. Multicultural America was born in the turmoil of the Civil Rights Revolution between the 1950s and the 1970s. The New Deal liberals who led the first, color-blind stage of the Civil Rights Revolution, which dismantled white supremacy, lost control during the second phase, which saw the triumph of group-consciousness and racial preference programs. A revolution that began as an attempt to purge law and politics of racial classifications and to enlarge the middle class to include the disadvantaged ended, ironically, with a renaissance of race-conscious government and the political triumph of economic conservatism. Multicultural America is not the Third Republic that the color-blind liberals intended in the early sixties; it is the Third Republic that emerged later, from the intersection of black-power radicalism and white-backlash conservatism. Its patron saints are not Martin Luther King, Jr., and Lyndon Johnson, but Stokely Carmichael and Richard Nixon.

Unlike the First and Second American Republics, which were clearly nation-states, the Third Republic has the outward trappings of a multinational state. According to the quasi-official ideology of the Third Republic, there is no coherent American national community, but rather five national communities, defined by race—white, black, Hispanic, Asian and Pacific Islander, and Native American. The civic religion, to the extent that there is one, is a secular philosophy, an ideal of authenticity, that stresses conformity to particular racial or sexual or religious subcultures. The political creed of post-sixties America has been centralized multicultural democracy—the replacement of territorial federalism by a kind of Washington-centered racial federalism (exemplified by federally coerced racial gerrymandering of electoral districts).

The basic elements of Multicultural America came together by the early seventies; since then, its institutions and even its rhetoric ("multiculturalism," "affirmative action," "diversity") have been relatively stable. Multicultural America is built on the repudiation of white supremacy (common to the first two American republics) in favor, not of color-blind liberalism, but of an elaborate system of racial preferences for citizens who are officially designated as nonwhite by government bureaucracies. These racial preferences in education, hiring, contracting, and political redistricting are available not only to descendants of the victims of American white supremacy, but also to recent immigrants from Latin America, the Caribbean, Asia, and the Indian subcontinent. The high level of legal immigration from Latin America and Asia means that the category of Americans eligible for racial preference programs and subsidies at the expense of white Americans, whether native or naturalized, grows by almost a million every year.

Far from being a challenge to the post-sixties American power structure, or an inevitable response to changing demography, the ideology of multiculturalism is, in practice, a rationalization for the racially based tokenism that has ramified throughout American society since the 1960s. Multiculturalism is not the wave of the future, but an aftershock of the black-power radicalism of the sixties. Nor is multiculturalism, in the broadest sense, to be blamed entirely on the left. From the beginning, conservatives have been as instrumental as liberals in promoting racial preference politics, for tactical reasons. The Nixon administration pioneered the imposition of racial quotas in the workforce, in order to pit unionized white workers against black workers; with equal cynicism, the Reagan and Bush administrations promoted the ghettoization of black and Hispanic voters in racially gerrymandered congressional districts, thereby undermining Democratic Congressmen and helping the Republican party to capture the House of Representatives in 1994. While the influence of multicultural ideology on campus may appear to give credence to conservative charges that the left is in control, it can be argued that racial preference programs in politics and the workplace actually help the right. Tokenism provides a suitably "progressive" camouflage for a system of divide-and-rule politics in which the homogeneous American social and economic elite—the white overclass—benefits from racial divisions among the American majority. Without the political division of wage-earning white, black, and Hispanic Americans along racial lines—a division exacerbated, though not caused, by racial preferences and multicultural ideology—it is doubtful that the white overclass in the United States, in the last generation, would have been able to carry out its agenda of destroying unions, reducing wages, cutting worker benefits, replacing full-time workers with temps, and shifting the burdens of taxation from the rich to the middle and working classes, with so little effective popular opposition.

If Multicultural America endures for another generation or two, the future for the United States is a bleak one of sinking incomes for the transracial American majority and growing resentment against the affluent and politically dominant white oligarchy. The Balkanization of America, in the form of civil war along racial lines, is unlikely. American vernacular culture is so powerful in its appeal that it will break down even the strongest immigrant cultures, and interracial marriage is already undermining racial categories. The real threat is not the Balkanization but the Brazilianization of America, not fragmentation along racial lines but fissioning along class lines. Brazilianization is symbolized by the increasing withdrawal of the white American overclass into its own barricaded nation-within-a-nation, a world of private neighborhoods, private schools, private police, private health care, and even private roads, walled off from the spreading squalor beyond. Like a Latin American oligarchy, the rich and well-connected members of the overclass can flourish in a decadent America with Third World levels of inequality and crime.

Such a grim future cannot be averted by trivial reforms, like the pseudo-populist gimmicks of the plutocratic right (tax cuts, term limits) or the technocratic panaceas of the neoliberals (worker retraining, reinventing government). Renewing the American nation-state will require a real, not merely metaphorical, revolution in politics and society, a revolution as sweeping—though, we may hope, not as violent—as the Civil Rights Revolution. The goal of liberal nationalism, as a political movement, must be to dismantle Multicultural America and replace it with a Fourth Republic of the United States—let us call it Trans-America.

In Trans-America, a color-blind, gender-neutral regime of individual rights would be combined with government activism promoting a high degree of substantive social and economic equality. The racial and gender quotas of the left, and the educational and political privileges of the wealthy oligarchy defended by the right, would be rejected in favor of a new union of cultural and economic nationalism in the interest of the transracial middle class. A truly representative political system, purged both of racial gerrymandering and of campaign finance practices that favor corporations and the rich; a new system of middle-class-friendly capitalism, in which today's growing economic inequality has been checked and reversed by selective government intervention in the marketplace; and a color-blind society, in which cultural fusion is accompanied, in time, by racial amalgamation—these are the goals of American liberal nationalism at the end of the twentieth century and the beginning of the twenty-first.

This book is the first manifesto of American liberal nationalism. Liberal nationalism is not the only way beyond the present stalemate of a discredited multicultural liberalism and a plutocratic conservatism. It is the only path, however, that can lead to an America in which you and your descendants would want to live.

CHAPTER ONE

The First Republic

Anglo-America

Picture North America in the year 2000 A.D., as Thomas Jefferson might have imagined it in 1800. As the twenty-first century dawns, the American ethnic nation—defined as Americans of Anglo-Saxon descent, with infusions from closely related Western European groups—accounts for the overwhelming majority of the inhabitants of North and South America and the islands of the Caribbean. In 1801 Jefferson had foreseen the day "when our rapid multiplication will expand itself . . . and cover the whole northern, if not the southern continent, with a people speaking the same language, governed in similar forms, and by similar laws"—for this reason, Jefferson had opposed allowing emancipated blacks to settle in the west.[1]

Although they form a single cultural nation, united by common race, language, and Protestant religion, the 500 million Anglo-Saxons of North America, in Jefferson's vision, are divided among a number of friendly sister republics. In addition to the United States of America, which retains the dimensions it acquired during Thomas Jefferson's lifetime, there is the Republic of Canada, the Republic of Texas, the Republic of California, and the Republic of Oregon (Jefferson told John Jacob Astor that his Columbia river settlement was "the germ of a great, free, and independent empire on that side of our continent.")[2] Other North

American countries retain their former names—Mexico, Cuba—but they have been thoroughly Anglicized, with predominantly Anglo-American populations, with English as the official language, and with common-law institutions in place of the Hispanic heritage.*

Despite their great geographic diversity, the Anglo-American republics all have a family resemblance. If you take a slow-moving balloon-schooner from Mexico City to Oregon, you will see similar patterns in very different landscapes—the small, square fields of yeoman farmers, cultivated by simple and yet ingenious labor-saving devices, spread like quilts around the small towns, each the capitol of a ward, or a section of a county, modeled on the ancient Anglo-Saxon "hundreds." If you fly low enough, you might even see the militia drilling in the parks; none of the republics has significant standing armies, in this quartersphere of democracy, liberty, and peace. Each hamlet has its neoclassical town hall, in the Greek Revival style introduced by Thomas Jefferson, and its cluster of churches and temples—Congregationalist, Deist, Masonic and Unitarian. To one correspondent Jefferson had written in 1822: "The pure and simple unity of the creator of the universe is now all but ascendant in the Eastern states; it is dawning in the West, and advancing towards the South; and I confidently expect that the present generation will see Unitarianism become the general religion of the United States." In the same year he wrote to another: "I trust there is not a young man now living in the U.S. who will not die an Unitarian."[3]

Continuing your northward journey, you might join the pilgrimage of tourists to the spiritual capital of Anglo-America—Washington, D.C. (District of Cherronesus). The District of Cherronesus is the peninsula between Lakes Huron and Michigan. In 1784 Thomas Jefferson proposed to give this region its name to commemorate the original Cherronesus, the region (now encompassing Danish Jutland and German

---

*It may be that Jefferson, though publicly speaking of multiple republics, actually hoped that the United States would incorporate all of North America. The alternative, however, was not implausible. During the 1840s, there were three English-speaking countries in North America—the United States, British North America and the Republic of Texas. Even today, the United States, in terms of area, is the *second* largest English-speaking democracy in North America.

Schleswig-Holstein) from which he believed the Saxon ancestors of the American people migrated to Britain after the fall of Rome.[4]

The gleaming neoclassical city of Washington, D.C., buffeted by the cold winds from Lake Michigan, is full of monuments to Anglo-American ideals and history. One of them is American University, with its curriculum modeled on the one that Jefferson provided for the University of Virginia. Here, the "natural aristocracy" of North America, students from all classes selected by rigorous examination and admitted without any reference to family income, study in the hope of becoming leaders of their respective republics in the Pacific northwest, the California coast, the Canadian prairie. Their curriculum includes study of natural history, the hierarchy of races (with special emphasis on the hereditary mental and moral superiority of the Germanic peoples), the secular ethical philosophy of Jesus (in the edition of the Gospels prepared by Jefferson, with the miracles removed), and Anglo-Saxon laws and institutions, ancient and modern. Every graduate must be proficient in Anglo-Saxon, which, since its revival by Jefferson in the United States, has replaced Latin and Greek as the New World's learned tongue.

Many of the details in this vision are peculiar to Thomas Jefferson. However, the basic conception of the American people as a branch of the Anglo-Saxon tribe, whose members remained part of a single "race" no matter how many governments they were divided among, was the conception of American identity shared by most of the Founding Fathers of the United States and generations of later American leaders. Until the early twentieth century, for example, the major school of American history was devoted to the germ theory, which traced the evolution of American institutions through British roots to the customs of the ancient Germans. The idea that the United States is or should be "a nation of immigrants," not only non-Germanic but nonwhite, would have struck most Americans before World War II as bizarre. They would also have been puzzled by the idea that the American people was created in 1776. Eighteenth- and nineteenth-century Americans would not have confused the mere establishment of the American *government* in 1776 with the creation of the American *nation* (that is to say, the American branch of the millennia-old Anglo-Saxon race), and they would have been baffled by the mention of the "Judeo-Christian tradition," because everyone knew that the American nation was not only Christian but Protestant.

Such a way of thinking about American identity seems as alien to us today as the ideals and mores of a remote civilization. Indeed, in many ways, we modern Americans live in a new and different country. The United States of the 1990s differs far more from the United States of the 1790s than today's France does from that of Robespierre and Napoleon (for a start, the borders of France, and the composition of its population, have been far more stable than those of the United States). The continuities in the history of the French nation are disguised by the discontinuities in French constitutional history; since 1789, France has had five republics, several empires and constitutional monarchies, a directory and a fascist dictatorship (Vichy).* Americans are governed, at least on paper, under the same federal constitution that went into effect in 1789, and the name of the country has not changed since 1776. Constitutional continuity in America disguises the discontinuities in national history between what can be described as the three "republics" of the United States. We cannot understand our America, Multinational America, the Third Republic of the United States, without understanding its predecessors.

The First Republic of the United States (1789–1860) might be called Anglo-America. National identity in Anglo-America was a compound of three elements: an Anglo-Saxon national community, a common ethic of Protestant Christianity, and a federal-republican national political creed. These definitions of Americanness did not go unchallenged. Black Americans argued for a nonracial or multiracial conception of American identity. Irish immigrants and Catholic immigrants of varying ethnicities contested the equation of Americanness with Anglo-Saxon heritage and Protestant religion. The political creed of federal republicanism, particularly in its extreme Jeffersonian and Jacksonian variants, was challenged by Hamiltonian statesmen and intellectuals in the Federalist-National Republican-Whig tradition who emphasized a powerful central government actively promoting industrial and financial development. Although rivals of the prevailing formula sometimes won limited

---

*This has given rise to the joke about the French bookseller who, when asked for a copy of the French constitution, replies, "I do not sell periodical literature."

victories, the conception of the United States as a federal republic based on an Anglo-Saxon Protestant nation generally prevailed. Behind immigration law, Indian removal, black colonization, and annexation policy lay the ideal of the United States as a nation-state with a homogeneous population of Anglo-American Protestants.

THE ORIGINS OF ANGLO-AMERICA

The ultimate origins of the American nation are found in sixteenth-century England. The colonization of eastern North America by the English was a project pushed by a small circle of courtiers, businessmen and intellectuals around Sir Walter Raleigh, many of whom were also involved in the colonization of Ireland by Protestants. In his "Discourse of Western Planting" (1584) one of the leading members of this group, Richard Hakluyt, argued that colonization would increase England's military and commercial strength, as well as permit the English to unload their paupers and convert the North American Indians to true (that is, Protestant) Christianity. The visionary Hakluyt called for the settlement in eastern North America of "infinite nombers of the english nation."[5] Attempts in 1584 and 1587 by Raleigh and his associates to found colonies in the Carolina Banks and the Chesapeake failed (the latter, cut off by Spanish-English war and presumably destroyed by Indians, passed into legend as the lost colony of Roanoke). The Raleigh circle turned to other projects, including colonization in Ireland after the 1585 Munster rebellion and a doomed effort to colonize Guiana.

The Virginia Company managed to found a permanent settlement at Jamestown in 1607, but the outpost, plagued by war with the local Powhatan Indians, starvation, internal dissent, and disease, was always on the verge of collapse. The Crown assumed responsibility from the Virginia Company in 1624, making Virginia a royal province; not until late in the century, when it was reorganized as a tobacco-exporting plantation economy relying on black slave labor, did Virginia become more than a miserable wilderness outpost. (Virginia's future was shadowed in its beginning, when colonist John Rolfe, who married Powhatan's daughter Pocahantas, introduced the planting of tobacco, a Caribbean crop—and noted the arrival, in 1619, of a Dutch warship bearing twenty

African slaves).* Despite the glowing propaganda of colonization proponents, conditions were so miserable in the New World that ordinary Europeans preferred to stay at home. The Puritans of New England, who established the most successful colonies in the seventeenth century, succeeded in large part because they were motivated by religious fervor.

In the period between 1607 and 1689, when the major British colonies were established, different colonies tended to be peopled by refugees from this or that side in English struggles—Puritan refugees fleeing from Tudor absolutism populated New England, and a little later royalist gentry escaping from Cromwell's Puritan dictatorship founded some of the great dynasties of the Chesapeake. The English Americans also came from different parts of the British Isles—the Puritans tended to come from East Anglia, the Southern gentry from the southern counties of England, the Quakers of the Delaware Valley emigrated from the British midlands, and the Scotch-Irish who populated the Southern backcountry in the early eighteenth century originated in Ulster, Scotland, and North Britain. In the New World, these different immigrant groups tended to preserve the dialects, customs, and folkways of the parts of Britain from which they had come; their subcultures formed the basis of American regional cultures that persist to this day and are shared by millions of Americans with no English ancestors.[6]

The diverse mainland colonies of seventeenth-century English America began to be knit together into a greater unity only in the era that followed the Glorious Revolution. When William of Orange deposed James II in 1688–89, colonists in Boston, New York, and Maryland overthrew their proprietary governments as well. Under the new rule of William and Mary, all of the colonies became royal colonies with elected assemblies, except for Connecticut and Rhode Island (which retained their corporate constitutions) and Pennsylvania and Maryland (which remained proprietary).

This standardization of colonial government, combining royal control with a high degree of colonial self-rule, was part of a general reorganiza-

---

*Shakespeare's *The Tempest* was inspired by the 1611 wreck in Bermuda of an English ship bound for Virginia. Caliban is an anagram of "cannibal," or Carib Indian. The service of Caliban to Prospero reflects the hope of the English, soon disappointed, that Indians would provide the labor force, as they did in mainland Spanish America.

tion of the British empire by the Whig oligarchy that had come to power in the Glorious Revolution. The Whigs created Great Britain by incorporating Scotland in the Act of Union of 1701; a few years later, Ireland lost its independence from the jurisdiction of the London Parliament. The attitude of London toward the colonies tended to be one of benign neglect, an attitude the colonists elevated into a principle.

Throughout the seventeenth century, it never occurred to the Anglo-American majority in the colonies that they were anything other than Britons in America. In the first half of the eighteenth century, too, the American colonists for the most part identified themselves proudly as British Americans. In 1760, when Britain won the Seven Years' War (French and Indian War) with France, Benjamin Franklin declared, "No one can more sincerely rejoice than I do, on the reduction of Canada; and this is not merely as I am a colonist, but as I am a Briton."[7] He favored the annexation of French America, so that "all the country from the St. Lawrence to the Mississippi will in another century be filled with British people."[8] Colonial Americans like Franklin considered themselves part of the English nation, the freest people in the world, living under an enlightened Whig constitution characterized by the proper mixture of monarchy, aristocracy and democracy, antipapist Protestantism, and a kind of de facto imperial federalism. Political and religious evil was represented for them by the Catholic absolutism of France and Spain, in which they saw the pattern of the despotism that the Stuarts had tried to impose on the freedom-loving British.

The sharp regional differences between the Anglo-American colonies declined in the eighteenth century. The recurrent wars against the French and Spanish and the Indians, economic integration, migration between colonies, and the standardization of legal and governmental procedures tended to create a common Anglo-American identity, notwithstanding persistent localism. Zealous Puritans and fiery royalist cavaliers were succeeded by Northern and Southern elites whose members shared common economic interests and often a common education at colleges like Princeton.

By the mid-eighteenth century, Anglo-American leaders had come to share a common Whig ideology, absorbed from English Whig writers like John Locke, John Trenchard, and Thomas Gordon, authors of *Cato's Letters*, and Catherine Macaulay. Whig theory held that freedom and self-government originated in the tribal customs of ancient German tribes. The Angles, Saxons, and Jutes who migrated from Germany and present-day Denmark to England (formerly inhabited by licentious Celts and despotic Romans) brought free institutions with them. Under wise kings like Alfred the Great, the Anglo-Saxons perfected the institutions treasured by later Anglo-Americans: the representative assembly, the jury system, the militia. When William the Bastard conquered England in 1066, however, he imposed "the Norman yoke," consisting of the twin evils of continental feudalism and Roman Catholic Christianity. The promulgation of Magna Carta, the Protestant Reformation, and the overthrow of the Stuart monarchs brought about the restoration of Anglo-Saxon liberty in England. This view of the past was challenged from the right, as it were, by Thomas Hobbes and David Hume, who knew it was historical mythology, and from the relative left by radical Real Whigs or Commonwealthmen who argued that the Glorious Revolution had not gone far enough toward restoring the ancient Saxon constitution. (Mainstream Whigs and Real Whig dissidents agreed that the Dark Ages in England had been in fact a Golden Age.)

Since war tends to promote centralization, a collision between British imperial statecraft and extreme Whig ideology as a result of geopolitical struggles was perhaps inevitable. The English colonists in North America were swept up in the four great wars against French hegemony fought by Britain and its European allies—the War of the League of Augsburg (known in America as King William's War), 1689–1697; the War of the Spanish Succession (Queen Anne's War), 1702–1713; the War of the Austrian Succession (King George's War), 1745–1748; and the Seven Years' War (the French and Indian War), 1756–1763. The latter was a major struggle. More Americans died in the Seven Years' War, as a proportion of the population, than in any struggle apart from the Civil War and the Revolutionary War; the Seven Years' War saw the fourth-highest rate of mobilization, after World War II, the Civil War, and the Revolutionary War.[9] In the 1763 Peace of Paris, Britain gained control over all of the continent east of the Mississippi except for New Orleans, which the French transferred temporarily to their ally, Spain, along with Louisiana (then the name for the territory west of the Mississippi).

"With the triumph of Wolfe on the Heights of Abraham began the history of the United States," wrote the nineteenth-century historian

John Richard Green, noting that the American War of Independence grew indirectly out of the Seven Years' War.[10] The French foreign minister Choiseul prophetically warned the British ambassador to France that the colonies "would not fail to shake off their dependence the moment Canada should be ceded."[11] With the French military threat neutralized, the English colonists were bound to feel there was less need for imperial military protection and to resent the taxes that paid for it. When the British government, upset by the expenses of the war and colonial inefficiency, made the rational decision to create a more centralized, authoritarian empire in which the colonists would pay their fair share, the colonists grew alarmed. Soon the Anglo-Americans were seeing the signs of incipient absolutism like that of the Stuarts in every action of the imperial government, such as the series of taxes that occasioned crises in relations with the Crown. When Indians revolted against British rule in 1763–64, London decided to temporarily minimize its defense costs by forbidding its American subjects to settle beyond a line. The colonists saw the hand of royal tyranny in that decree, just as they sensed a papal conspiracy in the decision by London to allow the French Canadians to retain Roman Catholicism as the official religion of Quebec.

From an administrative, military, and financial point of view, the centralization of the British empire made a great deal of sense. It made no sense politically, however. The Anglo-American colonists had grown accustomed to a high degree of self-government during the first half of the eighteenth century. Different aspects of the strategy of centralizing authorities in London offended different groups in British America—frontiersmen were incensed by royal limits on western settlement; Protestant dissenters in New England were horrified by the prospect of the establishment of Anglicanism in their colonies; talk of an American aristocracy disturbed Southern gentry, long the masters in their region, who feared that they might be reduced to being political subordinates and social inferiors of titled fops from Britain. If the proponents of parliamentary absolutism had their way, local elites would lose not only political power, but social standing, as prestige in each colony would, they feared, be based on personal relationships to this or that English-born aristocrat. London's centralizing reforms thus managed to unite many Americans who had nothing else in common with one another into opposition to the empire.

Even so, Anglo-American leaders did not immediately envision independence as the result of their resistance to imperial innovation. Well after hostilities had begun, many Americans hoped that opponents of the regime in Britain, such as the radical Whigs, would bring about another Glorious Revolution throughout the empire, restoring local privileges in Ireland as in Massachusetts, and ending monarchical "corruption" of the London parliament. A number of Americans, including Thomas Jefferson, tried to save the empire by proposing constitutional reforms creating a bipartite empire linked by the crown. (Similarly, in the crisis leading to the Civil War, many politicans tried to save the Union by a variety of constitutional amendments mollifying the South.) British authorities in the nineteenth and twentieth centuries, having learned a lesson from the loss of their first empire, would experiment with such divisions of authority, especially with the "white dominions." In the 1770s, however, their inflexible commitment to the dogma of absolute parliamentary sovereignty gave them only two alternatives, to subordinate the colonies or lose them.

When an empire-wide revolution, replacing centralism with some form of federalism, failed to occur, the colonists opted for secession as a second-best measure. The formative era of Anglo-America can be dated from 1774, when the Articles of Association among the twelve (later thirteen) British colonies signaled a de facto state of rebellion against the British crown. The formative period ended in 1789, when the first government elected under the 1787 federal Constitution met. Between 1774 and 1789 the former British population of the Atlantic seaboard went from being a group of rebellious colonies that still might have been reconciled to imperial federalism to an independent, federal nation-state with a weak but genuine central government.

THE ANGLO-AMERICAN NATION

It is often said that after independence the American people were unsure of their national identity. This is a misperception, based on a confusion between political allegiance and ethnocultural nationality. The political allegiances of many Americans, between the Revolution and the Civil War, were frequently divided, because of the strength of state

loyalties. Weak and often conflicting *political* loyalties, however, coexist-
ed with a strong sense of common *ethnocultural* identity among the majority of Americans, a category that consisted throughout the nineteenth century of whites of British descent. Federalists and Anti-Feder-
alists, Unionists and Confederates disagreed about many matters; most,
however, shared an understanding of themselves as members of an
Anglo-Saxon diaspora in North America.

What might be called the Anglo-American national formula had
three elements, defining the national community as the Anglo-Saxon
race, the common ethic as Protestant Christianity, and the political
creed as federal republicanism. To be an American in Anglo-America,
according to the informal but established conception, was to be an
Anglo-Saxon (or Teuton) in race, a Protestant in religion, and a republican in political principles. Commitment to political principles was an
important part of Anglo-American identity, but it was less important, in
the minds of most white Americans, than membership in a particular
race and a particular religion.

THE ANGLO-AMERICAN RACE. Almost without exception, when the
framers of the federal Constitution and their successors in the first half
of the nineteenth century spoke of the American people, they meant
white Americans of English descent, or immigrants from the British Isles
and the Germanic countries who had lost their cultures and assimilated
to the Anglo-American norm. White Americans viewed themselves, in
the phrase of one historian, "as modified Englishmen rather than as a
product of a European amalgam."[12] The American geographer Jedediah
Morse used the term Anglo-American as early as 1789, writing that "the
greater part . . . are descended from the English; and, for the sake of distinction, are called Anglo-Americans."[13] The term Anglo-American
was also used by foreign observers, including Alexis de Tocqueville, who
wrote, "I consider the people of the United States as that portion of the
English people who are commissioned to explore the forests of the new
world."[14] The United States was considered to be the first (though not
necessarily the only) independent republic of Anglo-Americans in the
western hemisphere.

In the nineteenth century, the poet John Greenleaf Whittier

summed up the prevalent view of American nationality in a poem "To Englishmen":

> *O Englishmen!—in hope and creed,*
> *In blood and tongue our brothers!*
> *We too are heirs of Runnymede;*
> *And Shakespeare's fame and Cromwell's deed*
> *Are not alone our mother's.*

> *'Thicker than water,' in one rill*
> *Through centuries of story*
> *Our Saxon blood has flowed, and still*
> *We share with you its good and ill,*
> *The shadow and the glory.*

This predominant understanding of national identity in the early United States was inherited from the colonial period, when almost all of the Anglo-American colonists thought of themselves simply as Englishmen living in the New World. In 1690, Richard Eburne in *A Plain Pathway to Plantations* wrote "it be the people that makes the land English, not the land the people."[15] Indeed, one of the causes of the disputes that led to the American revolution, it should be recalled, was the insistence that the colonists had all the rights of Englishmen because they *were* Englishmen.

Like many of their British cousins, most Anglo-Americans did not doubt that they belonged to a race superior to all others, though they were not quite sure how to define it—as Anglo-Saxon, as broadly Germanic, or as even more broadly European or white. Many of the American founders believed, with Montesquieu and the Whig historians, that English liberty originated in the forests of ancient Germany. This notion of a Germanic race whose characteristics explained social and political history received an additional boost from the publication by William Jones in 1788 of his theory that the Indo-European or Indo-Aryan language families had a common ancestor in prehistory. From the fact of a widespread Indo-European language, German scholars like the brothers Grimm and Max Muller, an expert on Sanskrit, inferred the existence of an Aryan race that had long ago conquered the dark Dravidian peoples of India (where its descendants formed the upper castes). These Aryans, furthermore, were thought to be identical with the populations of Germany, Scandinavia, England, and Anglo-America.

One of the founders of American anthropology, Lewis Henry Morgan, a relatively sympathetic student of the Iroquois Indians, concluded his *magnum opus*, Ancient Society (1877) with these words expressing the consensus view:

> It must be regarded as a marvellous fact that a portion of mankind five thousand years ago, less or more, attained to civilization. In strictness but two families, the Semitic and the Aryan, accomplished the work through unassisted self-development. The Aryan family represents the central stream of human progress, because it produced the highest type of mankind, and because it has proved its intrinsic superiority by gradually assuming the control of the earth.[16]

Even Ralph Waldo Emerson, who at times held a more inclusive notion of American nationality, wrote in *English Traits* that "the Teutonic tribes have a national singleness of heart, which contrasts with the Latin races." He also wrote: "That which lures a solitary American in the woods with the wish to see England, is the moral peculiarity of the Saxon race—its commanding sense of right and wrong,—the love and devotion to that,—this is the imperial trait, which arms them with the sceptre of the globe." Like many American advocates of the Teutonic definition of Anglo-American nationality, Emerson had little use for the Celtic Irish, whose appearance—"deteriorated in size and shape, the nose sunk, the gum exposed"—was evidence of "diminished brain."[17]

This was not the view in the Anglo-American republic. The idea that white Americans, by the nineteenth century, were becoming a distinct and finished race was commonplace in the pseudoscience and popular journalism of the day. Alexander Stephens, a Georgia politician who became the vice-president of the Confederacy, described the Anglo-American inhabitants of the Texas Republic thus: "They are of the Americo-Anglo-Saxon race."[18] In 1851 *The Republic* asked, "Who ever saw an American, reared on his native soil and under his country's institutions, that could not be recognized at a glance, and distinguished, in nine cases out of ten, from the men of any other Caucasian nation on earth?" One phrenologist in 1843 wrote that "though the primitive stock is English, the American head differs materially from the English."[19] Josiah Nott, a leading anthropologist, identified an "Anglo-American nation" as a distinct race belonging to the "Caucasian Group."[20]

Anglo-American racial nationalism was reflected in a white-only immigration policy. Although the attempt of the British ministry to limit (white) emigration to the American colonies was cited as an example of royal "tyranny" in the Declaration of Independence, most of the Patriot elite were opposed to immigration of non–Anglo-Saxons to the United States; those who did call for immigrants had in mind Europeans, not blacks, Latin American mestizos, or Asians. In 1790, Congress passed the first naturalization act, which permitted the naturalization of those who had resided in the United States for more than two years and swore allegiance to the Constitution. There was a third and crucial qualification—only "free white persons" could become naturalized U.S. citizens. Alarmed by the French revolution, the Federalists who pushed the Alien and Sedition Acts through Congress got the residency period extended first to five and then to fourteen years. Under Jefferson, the five-year waiting period was restored; a seven-year period is in force today. And the restriction of naturalized U.S. citizenship to Caucasian immigrants lasted until the mid-twentieth century, making the 1790 Act one of the cornerstones of white supremacy in America.

PROTESTANT CHRISTIANITY. In addition to sharing a racial self-definition as Anglo-Saxons in America, the Anglo-American majority had a distinct common ethic. The predominant ethic in Anglo-America was the evangelical Protestant ethic, which prevailed in competition with Enlightened deism and the small but growing Catholic immigrant subculture. Although religion was formally disestablished by the federal government and all of the states by the early nineteenth century, evangelical Protestantism succeeded in becoming the informally established religion of the United States. According to Cincinnati Presbyterian evangelist Charles Boynton, "Puritanism, Protestantism, and True Americanism are only different terms to designate the same set of principles."[21]

Evangelical Protestants divided on the question of whether Christ's Second Coming would occur before or after the millennium—the thousand years of peace and justice which, according to the book of Revelation, will precede the final battle between God and Satan. Postmillennialism holds that Christ will return *after* the millennium; the implication is that without direct divine intervention (though with divine inspiration), mankind is capable of constructing a just social order and maintaining it for a thousand years. Postmillennial Protestant Christianity has therefore looked favorably on projects of social reform that will literally hasten the millennium. Premillennialism, by contrast, holds that human society is too corrupt to be redeemed by any merely human effort. Christ must return in glory and slaughter the wicked *before* the thousand-year kingdom of peace and justice is set up on earth. What is more, during the millennium Christ himself will govern the human race, organized as a theocratic monarchy.

The evangelical Protestantism of antebellum America was generally postmillennial. The New England Puritans had been premillennialists, expecting the imminent return of Christ. The American Revolution, however, was associated with postmillennialist fervor. Many American Protestants believed that North America would be the center of a new, just civilization in the millennium preceding the Second Coming. Postmillennialist Protestants in Anglo-America, as in Britain, threw themselves into projects for social reform: the abolition of slavery, temperance, philanthropy, penal reform, educational reform, the extension of suffrage to the lower classes and women, pacifism. Many postmillennialist sects experimented with what nowadays would be called alternative lifestyles—the Mormons, practicing polygamy, the Oneida community, practicing "complex marriage," and the Society of Believers in Christ's Second Appearing, or Shakers, repudiating sex and childbearing (Shaker history was necessarily brief).

Evangelical Protestants believed that their brand of Christianity was besieged from two sides, by the Enlightenment and Roman Catholicism. During the French Revolution, evangelical Protestants in the United States became convinced of a plot by Continental Illuminati, a branch of Freemasonry, to destroy the Christian republican United States. In 1798 Jedediah Morse, a Congregational minister, announced the discovery of a plot by the Bavarian Illuminati to overthrow all established religions and governments. Alarm over this supposed conspiracy contributed to the passage of the Alien and Sedition Act, which prohibited "secret machinations against the government." The real targets of Protestant suspicion were the small but influential Enlightened minority in the United States—deists, freethinkers, Unitarians, Episcopalians, liberal Congregationalists, and Masons.[22] In the 1800 election, the Federalist clergy of New England denounced Jefferson as a Jacobin and howled when, in 1801, Jefferson offered the atheist Tom Paine passage from France and received him in Washington, D.C.[23]

Enlightenment thought and evangelical Protestantism clashed again in the early nineteenth century, when the Second Great Awakening inspired attempts to re-Christianize America. This time, the source of Protestant alarm was Freemasonry. Most American Masons were members of liberal Christian sects, such as Unitarians and Episcopalians. When William Morgan, an apostate Mason in western New York, was kidnapped and possibly murdered in 1826, a national movement sought to destroy Masonry. An Anti-Masonic party even elected state legislators and governors in several Northeastern states.[24]

The Protestant evangelical worldview succeeded in defining the Anglo-American ethic during the First American Republic, despite the efforts of Enlightened dissenters. Judge Henry M. Brackenridge, arguing for repeal of a Maryland law that forbade Jews to hold elective office or practice law (it was not repealed until 1825), wrote: "Our political compacts are not entered into as brethren of the Christian faith, but as men, as members of a civilized society. In looking back to our struggle for independence, I find that we engaged in that bloody conflict for THE RIGHTS OF MAN, and not for the purpose of enforcing or defending any particular religious creed."[25] More representative, though, was the view expressed by the Supreme Court in 1844: "It is also said, and truly, that the Christian religion is part of the common law of Pennsylvania"— with "Christian" referring to "Protestant Christian" in practice.[26]

Premillennial Protestantism and Enlightenment liberalism, though often at odds, mingled to a degree in Anglo-American messianism. The sixteenth- and seventeenth-century idea of England's exceptional destiny as the homeland of Protestant reformation and political liberty, transferred to the English colonies in North America and then to the United States, became the basis for what to this day is "the American creed." In his 1583 description of Sir Humphrey Gilbert's final voyage to America, Edward Hayes wrote that "the countreys lying north of Florida, God hath reserved the same to be reduced unto Christian civility by the English nation."[27] One early history of Virginia began with the story of creation in Genesis, "to show how God had so managed the past that English colonization in the present was the fulfillment of his plan."[28] Jonathan Edwards referred to the English, both in Britain and overseas settlements, as "the principal nation of the Reformation."[29]

John Adams set forth his version of this theory in *A Dissertation on the Canon and Feudal Law,* published in 1765 in the *Boston Gazette* and later reprinted as *The True Sentiments of America.* After the fall of Rome, Adams wrote, Europeans "became more intelligent in general," awakening to the knowledge that they have "*Rights,* that cannot be repealed or restrained by human laws—*Rights,* derived from the Great Legislator of the Universe." These rights, discovered in the Dark Ages in the forests of Germany and England (not, let it be noted, in Athens or Jerusalem), were soon to be suppressed. The canon law, "the most refined, sublime, extensive, and astonishing constitution of policy that ever was conceived by the mind of man, was framed by the Romish clergy for the aggrandisement of their own order." The Catholic conspiracy was joined by a conspiracy of feudal aristocrats: "Still more calamitous to human liberty, was a wicked confederacy between the two systems of tyranny above described. . . . Thus, as long as this confederacy lasted, and the people were held in ignorance, liberty, and with her, knowledge and virtue too, seem to have deserted the earth, and one age of darkness succeeded another, till God in his benign providence raised up the champions who began and conducted the Reformation. From the time of the Reformation to the first settlement of America, knowledge gradually spread in Europe, but especially in England. . . ."[30]

Several generations later, Horace Bushnell, one of the most influential Protestant pastors of early-nineteenth-century America, set forth the theory of the providential destiny of the Anglo-American Protestant chosen people in an 1837 Phi Beta Kappa address: "Out of all the inhabitants of the world, too, a select stock, the Saxon, and out of this the British family, the noblest of the stock, was chosen to people our country; that our eagle, like that of the prophet, might have the cedars of Lebanon, and the topmost branches of the cedars, to plant by his great waters."[31]*

In the Anglo-American mind, Catholic religion and monarchic politics were thought of as the polar opposites of Protestantism and political liberty. Low-church Protestants and enlightened secularists alike tended to share a horror of Catholicism. When Irish Catholics sought to have their children excused from reading the King James Bible in public schools, evangelical Protestants concluded that there was a papist plot to remove the Bible from the schools. The anti–Irish Catholic Philadelphia Riots in May and July 1844 were among the most violent events before the Civil War.[32] Not until the middle of the twentieth century did a majority of Protestant Americans come to believe that there was no conflict between Catholicism and American identity.

FEDERAL REPUBLICANISM. The final element defining Anglo-American national identity was the political creed of federal republicanism. The United States was in effect a collection of subsidiary republics, which varied in the extent to which they granted citizenship to nonwhites and extended suffrage among whites.

Although the federal Constitution had created a central government much stronger than that of the Articles of Confederation, the federal government was still extraordinarily weak, even compared to most other contemporary states. From 1816 to 1861, the number of civilian employees of the federal executive branch grew from 4,479 to only 36,106—eighty-five percent of them in the postal service (the major source of patronage appointments). Indeed, apart from a few federal forts, the post office was practically the only federal institution that most people in the country came into contact with. The military was little more than

---

*North American Protestants were not the only ones who saw God's handiwork in the history of this hemisphere; the Jesuit theologian José de Acosta argued that Providence had planted mineral wealth in Mexico in order to enable the Spanish monarchy to defend Catholic Europe from Protestants and Muslims. On the face of it, this was no more implausible than the claim that the Mississippi Valley had been hidden from Europeans for millennia so that it could be conquered and colonized by Anglo-Saxon Calvinists. (D. A. Brading, *The First America: The Spanish Monarchy, Creole Patriots, and the Liberal State 1492–1867*, New York: Cambridge University Press, 1991, p. 2.)

the state militias; when Abraham Lincoln took office in 1860, there were fewer than 1,000 employees in the War and Navy Departments.

This extreme federalism was paralleled in the organization of the political parties, which were little more than loose coalitions of urban machines and courthouse gangs—the Richmond Junto, the Nashville Junto, the Albany Regency, Tammany Hall. Martin van Buren, the mastermind of the Jacksonian Democrats, replaced the loose factionalism of early national politics with a system of national nominating conventions and regularized patronage; even so, the adage "all politics is local" was particularly true in antebellum America. Small wonder that the planters believed the Southern states could exist as independent, loosely confederated republics; in most respects, they already were.

Between the American Revolution and the Civil War, property restrictions on suffrage and officeholding inherited from the colonial era were struck down peacefully, except in the case of Rhode Island, where the so-called Dorr revolt produced sustained political turmoil, though not bloodshed. At different rates, the states of the Union were transformed from oligarchic republics into nominal democracies with formal equality among adult white males. With few exceptions, women were denied the vote, since politics, like war, was seen as a masculine specialty in a republic.

There was no room in the Anglo-American Protestant federal republic for black Americans of either sex, except as slaves or outcasts. The American Revolution, though leading to the disappearance of slavery in the northern states, left the inherited racial caste system intact. Alexis de Tocqueville observed that racial prejudice in the United States was stronger in the North than in the South—and strongest of all in western states where there were no slaves.[33] In 1800, no northern state explicitly barred blacks from voting, if they could meet the property qualifications. Beginning with Ohio in 1803, however, every new free state admitted to the Union (except for Maine) expressly limited the franchise to white men. In older states in the antebellum North, the voting rights of free blacks were increasingly restricted. New York raised property qualifications for black voters in 1821, effectively disfranchising them, and in 1837 Pennsylvania revoked the right of blacks to vote completely. In 1860, only five states, all in New England, afforded blacks equal voting rights.[34] Disfranchisement was accompanied by many other forms of apartheid. As early as 1841 trains were being segregated in Massachusetts. Antebellum Illinois and Ohio refused to admit free blacks within their borders unless they posted large bonds to ensure their departure.[35]

Even the opponents of slavery tended to believe that most or all of the slaves, once emancipated, should be encouraged to leave the country, because (unlike Indians, perhaps) they could never be integrated into the white population. In his *Notes on the State of Virginia*, Jefferson describes the plan he submitted to the Virginia legislature for colonizing emancipated blacks outside of the United States as "a free and independent people" while importing an equal number of whites from Europe to take their place. Though he defended the idea of an extended republic, James Madison, a slave owner like Jefferson, never questioned the need for racial homogeneity in the citizenry as a precondition for republican government, and would have been astonished and probably horrified by the idea of a multiracial democracy. Indeed, Madison, in his final years after retiring from the presidency, became president of the Colonization Society, which attempted to put Jefferson's colonization proposal into practice by emancipating blacks and removing them to Liberia. Madison hoped that federal income from the sale of western lands could be used to pay for colonization—to put it crudely, the confiscation of Indian land for white settlers would pay for the permanent removal of blacks from American soil. According to another colonizationist, House Speaker Henry Clay, blacks, whether slave or free, were "aliens—political-moral-social aliens" in the United States.[36] Lincoln, too, would see colonization as the best answer to America's racial problem. Before the Civil War, the idea of political and social equality for black Americans, and acceptance of the fact of their permanent presence, was limited to a tiny fringe of radical abolitionists.

THE FIRST GRAND COMPROMISE

Most of the governments of the Latin American creole republics that won their independence from Spain after the Napoleonic wars were weak and fragile structures that eventually collapsed in civil war. The federal government of their North American neighbor was no exception; its collapse in 1860 was the bloodiest and most terrible of all the civil wars in the Western Hemisphere. That the disaster occurred is no surprise. What is really astonishing is that the U.S. did not collapse in 1850, or 1832, or 1820, or 1814.

Civil war did not break out sooner because of a compromise that was periodically reaffirmed. The republic that emerged from the War of Independence and its aftermath rested on a grand compromise between the Southern slave owners and the elites of the northern sections: the South would stay in the new union, as long as the federal government did not threaten Southern slavery. This grand compromise was manifested in three forms: constitutional guarantees for slavery; legislative compromises over the extension of slavery, like those of 1820, 1832 and 1850; and the custom of maintaining a balance of slave and free states in the Senate.

Article 1, Section 2, of the Constitution counted each slave (usually treated in the law as chattel property) as three fifths of a person in determining Southern representation in the House of Representatives (this compromise, it should be noted, served *Northern* interests; had each slave been counted as a complete person for purposes of congressional representation, the South would have had even more representatives in Congress). In Article 1, Section 9, legislation against the slave trade was proscribed until 1808. Article IV, Section 3 is a fugitive slave clause: "No person held to service or labor in one state, under the laws thereof, escaping into another, shall, in consequence of any law or regulation therein, be discharged from such service or labor, but shall be delivered up on claim of the party to whom such service or labor may be due."

The crucial element in the U.S. Constitution between 1787 and 1860 was one that was not written down: the sectional balance of political power in the federal government. This balance was maintained by two informal, extraconstitutional devices. The first was the custom of admitting one slave state for every free state. Whenever its interests were challenged, the planter-run South threatened to secede, and won compromises—in 1820, in 1832, in 1850, and in 1854. The second informal part of the grand compromise was a party system in which all national parties, because they had Southern wings, accepted the legitimacy of slavery. The electoral success in 1860 of the Republican party, the first purely sectional political party (Lincoln did not receive a single Southern electoral vote), signaled the repudiation of this bargain by a majority of Northerners. The planters, concluding accurately that the informal bargain had been violated, thereupon led the Southern states out of the union.

The Southern planters protected their interests not only by means of the grand compromise but also by their informal political predominance in the federal government from Jefferson's election in 1800 to Lincoln's in 1860. Within the South, Virginia was dominant—every president from 1800 to 1825 came from Virginia (thus "the Virginia Dynasty"). In the seventy-two years between 1789 and 1861, a Southern slave owner was president for forty-two years (ten of sixteen presidents); in the same period, Southerners accounted for twenty-three of the thirty-six House speakers and twenty-four of the thirty-six presidents pro tem of the Senate, as well as twenty of the thirty-five Supreme Court Justices.[37] From 1801 to 1861 the South had a majority on the Supreme Court; during that entire period, there were only two Chief Justices, both Southerners—John Marshall and Roger B. Taney. The South maintained its extraordinary advantage in staffing high federal posts even though, by 1860, its population had declined from 48 percent of the U.S. population in 1790 to only 39 percent in 1860.[38]

Some have spoken of the Southern genius for politics, but genius had less to do with it than aristocracy. A small number of rich landowning and slave-owning families nearly monopolized wealth, power, and prestige in the antebellum South. Many of these families were direct descendants of English royalist aristocrats and gentry whom Sir William Berkeley had invited to Virginia during the English civil war; the Southern cavalier was no myth. Although only a quarter of white families owned slaves in the South in 1860, almost every Southern governor, all of the justices of the state supreme courts, and a disproportionate number of the state legislators were slave owners.[39] The political feat of the Southern slave owners is truly remarkable—a minority within a minority section, they managed to dominate a populous nation's politics for more than half a century. The only comparable feat is the way that the Prussian Junkers, a backward landowning military caste on the Germanic-Slav frontier, managed to create and dominate the German nation-state from the Bismarck era to their annihilation as a class at the hands of Stalin's armies and Hitler's Gestapo. The Southern planters were the Junkers of North America.

THE GRAND STRATEGY OF ANGLO-AMERICA

During the early years of the First American Republic, two visions of American foreign policy and economic development came into conflict. The faction of modernizing nationalists was led by Alexander Hamilton, Washington's aide during the American Revolution, the first Secretary of the Treasury, and de facto prime minister of the Washington administration. In great state papers like his 1790 Report on Manufactures to the Congress, and in other writings and projects, Alexander Hamilton laid out a blueprint for the development of the United States into a great military and industrial power. The Bank of the United States, like the Bank of England, would link the propertied classes to the federal government, stabilize and strengthen government finances, and encourage productive investment. Federal subsidies and protective tariffs would encourage the growth of infant industries in what, in the 1790s, was an almost completely agrarian country, dependent on imports of European manufactured goods (Hamilton himself attempted to boost American industrial capitalism by organizing the ill-fated Society for Useful Manufactures, SUM, in Paterson, New Jersey, which later became a major mill town and factory center). The United States would have a strong standing army, capable of crushing internal rebellion as well as intimidating European powers in the Western Hemisphere, and a first-rate fleet that could protect American traders around the world. For the federal government to carry out these ambitious projects, its constitutional powers would have to be interpreted broadly, and American law, at both federal and state levels, would have to be purged of common-law anachronisms that inhibited large-scale industrial and financial organization.

All of these projects, now that most have been realized (the Bank of the United States, for example, has been re-created in the Federal Reserve) seem commonsensical today. They struck Jefferson, Madison, and other Southern slave owners with horror. These rich farmers, accustomed to dominating government, feared that their power would dwindle in an America with a strong centralized government and a rising class of bankers and industrial capitalists. With Jefferson's election in 1800, the beginning of a quarter-century reign of slaveholding Virginia presidents, agrarian isolationism triumphed over the modernizing, developmental nationalism promoted by Hamilton and the Federalists. The Federalists declined into a party of New England reactionaries, some of whom toyed with the idea of secession during the War of 1812. In the era of one-party Republican and then Democratic dominance that followed, the Hamiltonian program was pushed by "National" Republicans like John Quincy Adams and opposed by "Democratic" Republicans like Andrew Jackson, and later by Whigs like Henry Clay, whose American System was an updated version of the Hamiltonian scheme.

The grand strategy of antebellum America, however, was that of the Jeffersonian Republicans/Democrats. Jefferson denounced the Federalists in 1800, writing "we are running navigation mad, and commerce mad, and navy mad, which is worst of all."[40] The Jeffersonians were deeply influenced by British advocates of free trade like Adam Smith, who held that agrarian countries like the United States should abandon any thought of rivaling Britain in industry (Smith, like Jefferson, was suspicious of manufacturing, and believed that agriculture was morally and socially superior to industry). Writing in 1806, the Republican polemicist Clement C. Moore (best known today for the poem "A Visit from St. Nicholas"), argued that the United States should forego any foreign commerce other than that "which serves to promote the internal industry of the people, by affording a free vent for their surplus produce, and by bringing back, in return for it, foreign articles which could neither be so well nor so cheaply made at home."[41] The Jeffersonians made two exceptions to the rule that the United States should specialize in agricultural exports. "Coarse manufactures" for local use, like clothes and farm tools, could be produced on a small scale, without corrupting the virtuous yeoman republic. And an elaborate infrastructure—ports, canals, later railroads—was acceptable, as a necessity for the transportation of American crops to foreign markets. Antebellum Southern planters, hostile to other government expenditures, favored transportation and communications projects; before the Civil War, the South promoted the first transatlantic packet service, the country's first long-distance telegraph cable, and, by 1860, had one of the most extensive rail networks in the world.

The grand strategy of the Jeffersonians, then, presupposed a global division of labor, in which Britain, France, and a few other European countries would be the only manufacturing powers, and in which the

Americas, along with eastern Europe and the rest of the world, would serve as western Europe's agricultural hinterlands. The United States, in effect, was to have been the world's largest banana republic, with cotton and tobacco in place of bananas. As late as 1812, Jefferson was still committed to a Gandhian dream of a preindustrial America in which machinery was limited to farms and villages: "We have reduced the large and expensive machinery for most things to the compass of a private family, and every family of any size is now getting machines on a small scale for their household purposes."[42]

Though they were opposed in principle to state-sponsored industrialization, the Jeffersonians favored territorial expansion (yeoman farmers and slave owners alike could always use more land). The ideology of Jeffersonian exceptionalism prevented the United States from directly waging wars of conquest in the manner of a sinister Old World monarchy, something the antimilitary Republicans were not very good at anyway; the attempt of the Madison administration to conquer Canada by conventional military means during the War of 1812 resulted in humiliating defeats for the American forces, and the burning of Washington, D.C. The Jeffersonians therefore invented their own moral and republican equivalents of imperialism: purchase and filibustering. Jefferson doubled the area of the U.S. overnight by buying Louisiana from Napoleon for $15 million in 1803 (instead of conquering it, which might have been cheaper, and which would not have helped Napoleon in his war against Britain, the lesser threat to the United States). Later, James K. Polk, before the outbreak of the Mexican War, tried to buy California and the Mountain West from Mexico, then paid for the territories after conquering them.

Another kind of republican imperialism was the practice of filibustering.* Filibusters were Anglo-Americans who, legally or illegally, would settle in a territory claimed by Spain or one of its Latin American successor states, and then declare a revolution against the incumbent authority. Having detached the territory, they would then request annex- ation by the United States. This unique Jeffersonian kind of covert imperialism was first practiced in 1810, when President Madison sponsored the annexation of West Florida after a revolution by American settlers. (For generations thereafter, the U.S. Army would fight a savage war in the

---

*The term comes from a Spanish rendition of the Dutch word for freebooter, or adventurer.

Florida wilderness against the Seminole Indians, who, to the horror of the planters, sheltered many runaway slaves and intermarried with them.) Three years later, in 1813, the Madison administration also tried to revolutionize then-Spanish Texas, by backing the Gutierrez-Magee expedition. This first Texas revolution was suppressed by Spain in a bloody campaign that has been forgotten by most American and Mexican history books.* Further American-backed efforts to revolutionize Texas in 1819–20 also failed. Ironically, in light of the importance of the filibuster as the major Jeffersonian means of expansion, the precedent for these efforts was the attempt by Jefferson's vice-president and arch-rival, and the killer of Hamilton, Aaron Burr, to revolutionize the Spanish Southwest. The third major attempt to revolutionize Texas succeeded in 1836, under the leadership of Sam Houston, former Tennessee governor and one of Andrew Jackson's protégés. The Anglo-Texans applied immediately for admission to the Union, but because slavery was legal in Texas, the northern states kept Texas out until 1845. As a result, for ten years Texas was an insecure and bankrupt republic, periodically raided by Mexican armies.†

The practice of using filibusters as agents of American territorial expansion broke down with the Mexican War, which occurred when the Mexican government, refusing to accept the annexation of Texas, declared war on the United States. Mexico, like the Confederacy later, gambled that the British and perhaps the French would join in an effort to halt U.S. expansion; diplomatically isolated, Mexico was conquered and forced to cede New Mexico, the Southwest, and California. Even if the United States had not gone to war with Mexico, it seems likely that

---

*More Hispanic and Anglo-American Texans died in the suppression of the 1813 republic than in all the battles of the successful Texas revolution of 1835–36.

†John C. Fremont, taking Houston as his model, tried a filibustering expedition to Mexican California. Later still, white planters in Hawaii overthrew the native monarchy and established a republic, petitioning for admission to the United States (President Grover Cleveland refused to cooperate, but his successor McKinley backed the admission of Hawaii as a territory). Had William Walker's filibustering in Nicaragua succeeded, and had Nicaragua been annexed to the U.S., Walker would today be considered a regional founding father, like Houston, Travis, Bowie, and Crockett in Texas and John C. Fremont in California. Indeed, the State of Nicaragua, and the State of Cuba, another target of annexationists, would have made more predictable additions to the United States than the States of Hawaii or Alaska.

filibusters would sooner or later have detached California and the Southwest from Mexico and attached them to the United States.

Racial factors were critical in the form that U.S. expansion took. Stephen F. Austin, the Texan leader, described the Texas conflict as a war of a "mongrel Spanish-Indian and negro race, against civilization and the Anglo-American race."[43] A writer for the *Richmond Whig* described the Mexican war as a battle "of the Caucasian and Anglo-Saxon, pure white blood, against a mixed and mongrel race, composed of Indians, negroes, and Spaniards, all three degenerated by the admixture of blood and colors."[44] The Mexican War was opposed by champions of the older Anglo-American regions—by the Upper South's John C. Calhoun and by Daniel Webster of Massachusetts. They feared—correctly—that territorial expansion would transform America, not least in racial terms. Indeed, fear of the amalgamation of white Americans with Mexican mestizos was one reason the All-Mexico movement failed, and why the United States annexed only territories like Texas, California, and the Mountain West with little or no Mexican population.

Antebellum Americans, then, might have been more imperialist had they been less racist. The familiar shape of the United States on TV weather maps is a lasting monument to the Anglo-American ideal of racial homogeneity.

It is worth pausing for a moment to reflect that if the Civil War had not occurred, the history of the nineteenth-century United States would present an entirely different aspect. Because the war over Southern secession turned into a war to end slavery, all too often American history in the nineteenth century is presented as a series of philosophical debates about the true meaning of the American creed, inquiries into first principles that have their model in the Lincoln-Douglas debates. In fact, disputes over philosophical first principles were results, not causes, of primal struggles over national territory and the racial and ethnic composition of the American nation. The great struggles of the Anglo-American republic, up to its demise in the Civil War—struggles over Indian removal, the conquest of Mexico and annexation of the Mexican Northwest, the organization of white-only territories, and nativism—were "tribal" struggles. If there had been no Civil War, the Mexican War would loom in the American memory as the greatest event of the century, and James Knox Polk as the most important president, with the result that Americans might have a different, and more realistic, conception of their country as a "normal" nation-state, established by the territorial expansion of a dominant cultural group.

"By enlarging the empire of liberty," Jefferson wrote in 1805, "we multiply its auxiliaries, and provide new sources of renovation, should its principles, at any time, degenerate, in those portions of our country which gave them birth."[45] Jefferson hoped that the formation of a stratified class society on the Atlantic seaboard would be delayed by the migration of landless white citizens to the ever-expanding western frontier. Needless to say, the Jeffersonian plan for the westward migration of white yeoman farmers required the assimilation or removal of the Indians. Jefferson's harsh view of black Americans, whom he considered inherently inferior to whites, did not extend to American Indians, of whom he wrote, "we shall probably find that they are formed in mind as well as in body, on the same module with the 'Homo sapiens Europaeus.'" In 1803, he suggested: "In truth, the ultimate point of rest and happiness for them is to let our settlements and theirs meet and blend together, to intermix, and become one people." This would "finally consolidate our whole country to one nation only." He regretted in 1813 that white-Indian war had prevented this: "They would have mixed their blood with ours, and been amalgamated and identified with us within no distant period of time."[46]

To encourage the conversion of Indians into farmers, Jefferson instituted the land-allotment program, by which federal territory was divided into tracts for individual Indian farmers. Jefferson was not only aware that many Indians would fall into debt and be forced to sell their land to whites, but quietly sought to encourage this outcome. In an "unofficial and private" letter to William Henry Harrison, governor of Indiana, in 1803, Jefferson, who alternated between dreamy idealism and cynical politicking, wrote: "To promote this disposition to exchange lands, which they have to spare and we want, we shall push our trading houses, and be glad to see the good and influential individuals among them run into debt, because we observe that when these debts get beyond what the individuals can pay, they become willing to lop them off by a cession of lands."[47] (Jefferson paid off his own enormous personal debts by periodically selling slaves.)

In the area of Indian removal, as in others, Andrew Jackson was Jefferson's heir. As early as February 16, 1803, President Jefferson wrote the young Jackson, then a rising Tennessee politician, a letter urging that the Indians be confronted with the choice of becoming farmers or being removed to the west.[48] Though Jefferson was willing to contemplate white-Indian racial amalgamation, most of his fellow southerners—including Jackson, an Indian-fighting general—were not. The fact that the Choctaws and the Cherokees had become farmers and adopted many white ways did not prevent the Jackson administration, colluding with state governments in Mississippi and Georgia, from dispossessing them of their lands and relocating them on reservations. The removal of Indians from the Southern states peaked in 1838–39, when 15 thousand Cherokees were forced to march to the new "Indian territory"; one in four died on the Trail of Tears. The removal of the "civilized" nations of the Southeast was less like the later wars with the Plains Indians than like the despoliation and internment of the Japanese-American Nisei and Issei during World War II; the parallel extends to the cooperation of federal and state authorities and the battening of whites upon land and property the exiled nonwhites had owned.

Jacksonian Democracy, which is often presented as a radical innovation, in reality was little more than a later and somewhat cruder version of Jeffersonian Republicanism. The aged Jefferson himself in 1826 backed Andrew Jackson for president against John Quincy Adams. The ideal of universal white male suffrage, more or less achieved in all of the states by the mid-nineteenth century, was Jefferson's before it was associated with Jackson. The states' rights ideology of the Jacksonians descended from Jefferson and Madison, authors of the Kentucky Resolutions. The spoils system associated with Andrew Jackson was simply a further development of Jefferson's precedent, on assuming office in 1800, of purging Federalist officers and replacing them with Republican patronage appointments. Finally, the battle of President Jackson against Nicholas Biddle, president of the Second Bank of the United States, echoed the struggles of Jefferson and Hamilton in the 1790s (as those struggles, in turn, had re-created the conflict in Britain between opponents and defenders of Prime Minister Horace Walpole and his court party). Jackson's veto of the federal charter of the Bank in 1833, and his transfer of federal deposits to state banks that he favored, symbolized the triumph of Jeffersonian federalism over Hamiltonian nationalism. It also led to speculation and the Panic of 1837.

The Jeffersonian strategy for America thus prevailed over the Hamiltonian alternative during the generations of Southern political predominance between the Washington and Lincoln administrations. The political success of the Jeffersonians and Jacksonians rested on an electoral alliance between Southern slave owners, white yeoman farmers in the upper South and the West, and urban artisans and workers in the Northeast. The slave owners and the western farmers shared a common interest in territorial expansion. At the same time, the slave owners appealed to Northern workers by denouncing Northern manufacturers for degrading white men into "wage slaves." And a common racism, reinforced and disseminated by popular minstrel show entertainment, was shared by white labor and white farmers. Not egalitarianism in the abstract, but *white* egalitarianism, was central to Jacksonian democracy; and it served the planters well. To eliminate restrictions on white male suffrage, one antebellum Louisiana reformer argued, would "raise a wall of fire kindled from the united souls of freemen, around our state and its institutions, against the diabolical machinations of abolitionism."[49] All white men were equal, slave owner and slave hater alike.

The solicitude of the planters for their poor white allies was more symbolic than real. Although Jefferson and Madison might have been sincere in their hopes for the colonization of emancipated slaves, it became clear by the 1830s that American territorial expansion meant the expansion of slavery. Into the lands conquered from Indians and Mexicans in the South and Texas came the planters and their slave gangs, taking the richest lands and forcing poor white farmers into the Southern upcountry, where many of their descendants remain as part of the rural poor to this day.

EUROPEAN IMMIGRATION AND THE END OF ANGLO-AMERICA

The First American Republic, then, was a nation-state, based upon an Anglo-American Protestant nationalism that was as much racial and religious as it was political. Most Americans before the Civil War did not think of theirs as a melting-pot nation. The plot of the national story

was the expansion across North America of a nation of virtuous, republican, Protestant Anglo-Saxons, a master race possessed of the true principles of government and religion. The Anglo-American nation had a
great future ahead of it; but that future did not include cultural hybridization or genetic transformation through amalgamation with other,
lesser stocks. This conception of American identity and destiny would
be changed, by massive European immigration.

European immigration to the United States played a part in American politics from the beginning. As early as the 1790s, Irish-Americans
in eastern cities like Philadelphia and New York were active in the anti-
Federalist Democratic-Republican clubs, prompting Harrison Gray Otis,
a leading Massachusetts Federalist, to write: "If some means are not
adopted to prevent the indiscriminate admission of wild Irishmen and
others to the right of suffrage there will soon be an end to liberty and
property."[50] Irish and French immigrants, turning against the Federalists
as a result of the Alien and Sedition Act of 1798, may have tilted New
York City—and thus the election—to Jefferson in 1800.[51] By 1820, the
Irish controlled New York City politics through Tammany Hall, forming
an alliance with white Southern Democrats that would last a century
and a half.

Jefferson himself, though willing to court the votes of immigrants already in the United States, was opposed to the introduction of a "heterogeneous, incoherent, distracted mass" of European immigrants. In
1782, Jefferson calculated that the settled areas of the United States
(that is, the east coast) would approach the population density of Britain
in less than a century. "May not our government be more homogeneous,
more peaceable, more durable," he wondered, if the American nation
was replenished by natural increase, rather than by immigration?[52] In a
scientific treatise that would influence Malthus, *Observations Concerning
the Increase of Mankind,* Benjamin Franklin expressed similar views:
"Why increase the sons of Africa by planting them in America, where
we have so fair an opportunity, by excluding all blacks and tawnys, of increasing the lovely red and white?"—(a reference to the "peaches and
cream" complexion of northern Europeans). Franklin's notion of
"tawnys" included most Caucasians: "In Europe the Spaniards, Italians,
French, Russians, and Swedes are generally of what we call a swarthy

complexion; as are the Germans also, the Saxons only excepted, who with the English make up the principal body of white people on the face of the earth." In the light of later theories of Nordic racial superiority, Franklin's belief in the less-than-white status of most Germans (and Swedes!) seems ironic; this had been a bugbear for him since 1755, when he published a polemic denouncing the immigration of Germans—as "ignorant a set of people as the Indians"—to the then-British colonies: "Why should *Pennsylvania*, founded by the *English*, become a Colony of *Aliens*, who will shortly be so numerous as to Germanize us instead of our Anglifying them, and will never adopt our Language or Customs, any more than they can acquire our Complexion."[53]

Like Franklin, many of the great Patriots were opposed even to western European immigration. George Washington wrote a correspondent in England: "I have no intention to invite immigrants, even if there are no restrictive acts against it. I am opposed to it altogether." As he told Patrick Henry, "I want an *American* character, that the powers of Europe may be convinced we act for *ourselves* and not for others. This, in my judgment, is the only way to be respected abroad and happy at home."[54]

Alexander Hamilton agreed: "to render the people of this country as homogeneous as possible, must lead as much as any other circumstance to the permanency of their union and prosperity."[55] This suspicion of immigrants was reflected in the Constitution, which provided that a congressman had to have been resident in the United States for seven years, a senator for nine, and that the president had to be a native-born citizen.

Most of the Founding Fathers would have been astonished, and probably dismayed, by the volume of European immigration that was to follow. Between 1815 and 1860 five million Europeans—more than the entire population of the United States in 1790—moved to America. With each decade, the numbers expanded—151,000 in the 1820s, 599,000 in the 1830s, 1,713,000 in the 1840s, and 2,314,000 in the 1850s. The highest proportion of immigrants to native-born Americans—3 million of 20 million—was reached in the decade 1845–54.[56] Almost all of these old immigrants came from Ireland and other parts of Britain and Germany. Some Germans hoped to create a German state, in Pennsylvania, Wisconsin, or Texas.[57] In part as a result of this massive immigration, the U.S. population grew from 3,929,214 at the time of the first census in 1790 to 31,443,321 in 1860.*

Seven-eighths of the European immigrants to the United States went to the North. The census of 1860 showed that only 13.4 percent of the 4 million foreign-born Americans (in a population of 31.5 million) lived in the slaveholding states.[58] In 1856, Senator Stephen Adams of Mississippi was alarmed by the Europeanization of the northern population—and its political consequences for the South. Without immigration, he observed, the South would have gained more representatives than the North in the 1840s; instead, as a result of the European influx, the North gained twelve new congressional seats. Adams predicted that "by the next apportionment the North will gain upon the South twenty-four additional members from immigration alone." Soon "the North will have a majority of more than two to one in the other branch of Congress; and . . . a similar majority in this body."[59] Had there been no European immigrants in the antebellum period, the demographic and political history of the United States might have been quite different.

The North the immigrants went to was a modernizing region that was diverging rapidly from the South, which retained many features of an older North's Anglo-American order. In 1800, all regions had been primarily agricultural; by 1860 only 40 percent of the northern population consisted of farm workers, compared to 84 percent of the South. Anglo-America had been highly stratified by class, in the Hudson River valley as in the Chesapeake; by 1860 the South, with a third of the white population, had two-thirds of the country's wealthiest men, while the North was becoming a less aristocratic and more middle-class society.

One response to this massive European immigration was the rapid growth in the north of the anti-immigrant, anti-Catholic American Party (better known as the Know-Nothings, not because nativists were ignorant—in fact, many were prominent citizens—but because of the quasi-secret nature of nativist organizations). The nativists, in their opposition to immigration, were the true heirs of most of the Founding

---

*Antebellum immigration to the United States was only part of a broader phenomenon of European migration. Most European emigrants moved from farm to city within their own countries, or from one to another European country. Almost as many Irish moved to Great Britain as to the United States, and before 1830 more Irish went to Canada than to the U.S. Between 1818 and 1828, *twenty-five times* as many Germans moved to southern Russia as to the United States, and in the 1820s Brazil attracted more German emigrants than the republic to the north. (Maldwyn Allen Jones, *American Immigration*, 2nd ed., Chicago: University of Chicago Press, 1992, p. 85.)

Fathers.* The American party had its greatest electoral successes in 1854, when it elected eight governors, more than one hundred congressmen, and thousands of local officials, including mayors of Boston, Philadelphia, and Chicago. That same year immigration to the United States reached an all-time high. The proportion of foreign-born to native-born Americans peaked at 14.5 percent of the total, a percentage that has never been surpassed, even at the turn of the twentieth century. Alarm over immigration, however, may have been less responsible for the sudden success of the Know-Nothings than the party's stand against slavery. The nativists might have remained a fringe movement, scoring occasional successes in cities with large immigrant minorities, if the Whig party had not collapsed over the slavery question. In the summer of 1854, Whigs and free-soil Democrats, disgusted with both major parties for supporting the Kansas-Nebraska Act that opened the western territories to slavery, streamed into the American party. Its membership soared from 50,000 to more than 1 million in a matter of months.

The Jefferson-Jackson Democrats had become the victims of their own success. Against the wishes of those in the Federalist-Whig tradition, they had favored the territorial enlargement of the United States through the Louisiana Purchase, the annexation of Texas, and the Mexican War. In doing so, however, they inadvertently created conflict between the Jacksonian Democrats of the Midwest and North and the southern planters. The insistence of the planters on their right to bring black labor into the western territories broke up both the coalition of western farmers and southern planters in the Democratic party. It also divided and destroyed the Whigs, and led to the establishment of the first purely sectional party, the Republicans.

The Know-Nothings, inflated by the antislavery vote, collapsed just as quickly when a new and better vehicle for antislavery sentiment, the Republican party, coalesced. The party, named for Jefferson's faction, was founded in Ripon, Wisconsin on the night of March 20, 1854. One

---

*As I showed above, suspicion of European immigrants was present from the very beginning of the American republic. The fact that extreme and violent manifestations of Anglo-American nativism did not appear until large-scale European immigration began proves nothing. Had mass European immigration occurred earlier, radical nativism would have appeared earlier.

mitted the Republicans to benefit from antiblack sentiment among foreign-born as well as native-born whites. The colonization of blacks in Liberia or Latin America was favored by Lincoln, among others; he believed that whites and blacks could not live together as equals. Like Lincoln, Harriet Beecher Stowe was a colonizationist; in her preface to *Uncle Tom's Cabin,* she hoped that blacks in the future, living in freedom, would look back on their American captivity—from their new homes in Africa. In addition to removing the stain of slavery from the white American conscience, colonization, it was often suggested, would open up large regions of the postslave South, as well as the West, to settlement by white yeomen farmers. Strange as this idea seems today, the repopulation and "civilization," by northern white immigrants, of a South emptied of blacks by out-migration, was seriously considered by Republicans—and when it finally took place, in the 1970s and 1980s, after the great black migration to northern cities, the South not only boomed economically, but became increasingly Republican in its partisan politics.

The defeat of the Know-Nothings by the Republicans, then, did not represent a defeat of racism by a supposed American tradition of universalist citizenship; rather, it represented merely the defeat of a less inclusive white racism by a more inclusive white racism—the defeat of the Anglo-American definition of American ethnicity by a broader, Euro-American conception that could appeal to European immigrants. Irish immigrants, in particular, had an enormous stake in the idea that all whites—whether of English descent or otherwise—were superior to all nonwhites. In the Anglo-American United States, no one ever proposed expressly restricting Irish Catholic immigration—though in 1716 a South Carolina statute had forbade immigration into the colony of "what is commonly called native Irish, or persons of known scandalous character or Roman Catholics."[65] Even so, in the 1860 census, the white population was divided into "native," "foreign," and "Irish"—suggesting that the Irish were a distinct "race."[66]

In a sense the Know-Nothings were the last champions of Anglo-America. There was a certain patriotic logic in the attempt of "the American Party" to overcome the growing sectional divisions by uniting Anglo-Americans of all regions against a traditional ethnocultural foe:

the European Catholic. The Anglo-American nativists can be condemned for various things, but not for abandoning the Ellis Island conception of America as a "nation of immigrants," or a Euro-American melting pot, because no such conceptions existed in their time. For better or worse, they were the true conservatives, heirs to the definition of Americans as Protestants of British descent.

The redefinition of true whiteness by the Republicans helped them. The Civil War, which destroyed Anglo-America, was not simply a war between Anglo-Americans; rather, it can be described without much exaggeration as a conflict between the Anglo-American South and a new Euro-American society emerging in the North. The northern armies were ethnically different from the southern, because of the substantial German and Irish contingents. The decision by Republicans like Seward and Lincoln to repudiate Anglo-American nativism in order to bring European immigrants into their political coalition reflected sound strategy. One third of the Union army had been born abroad.[67]

CHAPTER TWO

The Second Republic

Euro-America

By the mid-twentieth century, the national story of the United States had been substantially rewritten. In 1850, the story of America was the tale of the manifest destiny of Anglo-Saxon Protestants, fulfilling a mission from God to create a citadel for true Christianity and republican government stretching from the Atlantic to the Pacific. By 1950, the conception of the United States as a Germanic Protestant nation had given way to a new mainstream vision of the country as a melting-pot nation-state blending old-stock white Americans with new European immigrants—a conception symbolized by Ellis Island and the Statue of Liberty. George Washington had been replaced by Abraham Lincoln as the greatest American of all time, and the leading figures among the Founding Fathers were now Thomas Jefferson and James Madison. The common ethic was no longer Protestant Christianity, but something called the Judeo-Christian tradition, promulgated by a tri-faith establishment that sent a delegation made up of a pastor, a priest, and a rabbi to pray at every high school commencement.

The *real* national religion, it sometimes appeared, was democracy itself, which since the 1850s had become an evangelical rather than a tribal faith. In 1850, most white Americans had assumed that the only way by which Americans could spread democracy through the world was

to actually conquer and settle large sections of it; it was taken for granted that nonwhites, and probably non-Saxon whites as well, were incapable of mastering the rudiments of republican government. By 1950,
however, the idea had become commonplace that the democratization
and Americanization of the entire human race was possible, and that
this was to be done through the United Nations, led by the United
States. After all, if Anglo-Americans and Italian-Americans, Christians
and Jews, could live in peace in the United States—by now often described as "a nation of immigrants united by an ideal"—why couldn't
freedom-loving Americans, Russians, Chinese, Japanese, and Germans
confederate as well in a planetary union?

In the writings of New Deal liberal "consensus" historians, Euro-
America found its national story.* The mainstream of American history,
according to the New Deal intellectuals, ran from Washington and Jefferson through Jackson and Lincoln to Wilson and FDR. That mainstream was Democratic, nationalist, secular, and egalitarian (at least
with regard to white class relations). The people were generally good,
the elites generally bad. Narrow-minded localists and elitists, at different
times, played their role as villains in the historical drama—Federalists,
nativists, Confederates, turn-of-the-century WASP immigration restric-
tionists. American society was not just an offshoot of England/Germa-
nia, but a true melting pot, at least among whites. In the popular mind,
American history was reduced to a few episodes—the Pilgrim settlement; the American Revolution; the Civil War (treated as a tragedy
with a good outcome, the reconciliation of white Americans); and the
settlement of the West.

This idealistic, vaguely egalitarian white melting-pot nationalism was
the consensus in the Second Republic of the United States, at the

---

*Among the chief consensus-school historians have been Marcus Hansen, Louis Hartz, Oscar
Handlin, Bernard Bailyn, and Daniel Boorstin. Some (like Louis Hartz) have stressed the continuity
of American liberal ideology, others (like Handlin) the importance of immigration in U.S. history
(Handlin has been criticized for neglecting the contributions of Anglo-Americans to American society.) A central role must be assigned to Arthur Schlesinger, Sr., and Arthur Schlesinger, Jr. The
two Schlesingers, father and son, did as much to reshape American self-understanding as the two
Roosevelt cousins did to remake the country's institutions.

height of its prestige and influence in the world in the years after World War II. Euro-America was a country transformed by European immigration—of the 50 million Europeans who emigrated from Europe in this period, 30 million settled in the U.S, making Anglo-Americans an ethnic minority by the late twentieth century. In 1950, even though, out of a population of 150 million, there were still nearly 11 million Americans born in a foreign country, and 24 million with at least one foreign-born parent, the distinctive European ethnic subcultures were on the verge of dramatic decline.[1] The "new man" that the eighteenth-century French-American writer Crèvecoeur had predicted would emerge from the amalgamation of European ethnic groups in the New World *has* emerged. The "melting pot" has worked—for white Americans. (We should note that Israel Zangwill's 1909 play *The Melting Pot* was about the amalgamation of *European* ethnic groups in the United States.)

Long before, in *Common Sense*, Thomas Paine had claimed: "Europe, and not England, is the parent country of America. This new world hath been the asylum for the persecuted lovers of civil and religious liberty from *every part* of Europe." Paine was fudging the facts, in the service of revolutionary Anglophobia; although in Pennsylvania, where he then resided, "Not one third of the inhabitants . . . are of English descent," the Anglo-American character of the majority was much more pronounced in the other colonies. As late as 1900, 60 percent of Americans were primarily of British descent. By 1920 that was down to 40 percent. By 1980, only 20 percent of the American population identified itself as being of British descent; the largest group was German-Americans. Paine thus foreshadowed the (white only) melting-pot ideal of Euro-America, an ideal that was not finally approximated until the middle of the twentieth century: "We claim brotherhood with every European Christian, and triumph in the generosity of the sentiment."[2]

THE NORTHEASTERN ESTABLISHMENT

"What costly stuff whereof to make a nation!" James Russell Lowell wrote after the Civil War.[3] The costs were indeed staggering. In five years, 623,026 soldiers died—a small number by the standards of twentieth-century Germany and Russia, but more than the number of Americans killed in every other U.S. war.* The financial costs and damage amounted to $21 billion, or eight times the amount necessary to have purchased the freedom of every slave.[4] But the South, of course, paid the greatest cost. One quarter of the white southern male population of military age was killed. The South's economy was devastated for generations, and it was turned into a low-wage internal resource colony for northern capital. Unlike defeated Nazi Germany or Imperial Japan, the defeated South received no significant federal aid from the United States. Nor was there compensation for the emancipation of slaves, even though the United States government had insisted on and received such compensation from Britain after the American Revolution and the War of 1812.† There were resources that could have been used to rebuild the South—but they went into western development instead. The failure of plans of moderates like Lincoln to restore a Whig-like coalition of northern and southern elites as the basis for a national Republican party meant that the South would be mutually exploited by the North (which, through the tariff, taxed southern agriculture to benefit northern industry) and the West (federal military pensions to midwesterners were partly paid for by defeated southern rebels). By 1880, the relative difference in per capita wealth between the North and the South was equivalent to the difference between Germany and Russia.[5]

Economically ruined, the South was politically marginalized as well. The southern ascendancy in the federal government, so pronounced from 1789–1860, when southerners provided a majority of the Supreme Court Justices, House speakers and Senate majority leaders, and presi-

---

*In the Civil War, there were 5 million people out of 31 million in the states of the Confederacy, or 16 percent of the country's population. 600,000 Americans, or 2 percent of the population, lost their lives. In today's America of 260 million people, the equivalent figures would be a secessionist population of 41.5 million—and 5.2 million dead.

†Lincoln's liberation of the southern slaves, it should be remembered, was the *third* wartime emancipation in the United States. The British had emancipated American slaves during the War of Independence (an act Jefferson denounces as an atrocity in the Declaration) and in the War of 1812. John Quincy Adams, one of the U.S. commissioners negotiating an end to the War of 1812 at Ghent, insisted that the emancipation of slaves was an uncivilized atrocity: "[P]utting to death all prisoners . . . might as well be pretended as a right of war; or the right to use poisoned arrows. . . ." The Tsar of Russia, called in to arbitrate, ordered the British to pay a lump sum to the aggrieved American slaveholders.

dents, was replaced by northern domination. There was no southern speaker or Senate majority leader for half a century, and in the same period only five of twenty-six Supreme Court Justices were southerners. And Lyndon Johnson, though best described as a westerner in his origins and attitudes, would be the first politician from a southern state elected president since the Civil War.[6] The first southern president in a century, by presiding over a revolution in race relations less violent but more radical than the Civil War, would help destroy the Euro-American republic created by Lincoln's Republicans—and would do so in the name of Lincoln's ideals.

From its origins to its violent collapse, the First Republic of the United States, Anglo-America, was shaped by the disproportionate influence in national politics of the southern planter class. The second republic of the United States was dominated by the northeastern elite that coalesced in the North during and after the Civil War—an elite which, in its origins, was often indistinguishable from the elite of the Republican party. The connections between Republican party officials and the northern business and professional elite could be illustrated by many examples. The leading Wall Street law firm of Cravath, Swaine and Moore, which has shaped the practice of American corporate law and legal education perhaps more than any other, grew from the pre–Civil War partnership of William Seward and Richard M. Blatchford, a major railroad lawyer.[7] The foundations of many of the great northeastern fortunes were laid during the war, as well. J. Pierpont Morgan, as a young man, financed arms manufacturers. John D. Rockefeller underwrote the consolidation of the nascent oil industry with the help of profits from government contracts. Philip Armour used the money he made from supplying beef to Union troops to make Chicago the center of the meat-packing industry. The federal government, through subsidies and land grants to railroads, contributed to the founding of great fortunes like those of the Vanderbilts and Harrimans; Leland Stanford, for example, grew rich from federal and state subsidies to the Central Pacific Railroad.

In politics, too, many Gilded Age careers had Civil War roots. The Republicans dominated the presidency from Grant to McKinley in part by nominating veterans of the Grand Army of the Republic. And many of those who participated in the restoration of the Union were leaders in the extension of American power at the turn of the twentieth century.

John Hay, Lincoln's secretary, became Secretary of State under McKinley and Roosevelt; he is best known today for "the Open Door doctrine," which attempted to protect American interests in China by preventing its division into European spheres of influence.

It was during the Civil War that the railroad industry became the major industry in the United States, a status it would hold until late in the century. The Hamiltonian tradition of which Lincoln was the heir emphasized the consolidation of the country and the promotion of commercial enterprise by means of government-backed infrastructure projects like turnpikes, canals, and railroads. Under the Lincoln administration, the federal government awarded more public land to railroads—more than 74 million acres—than was awarded under any other three administrations combined (during the Grant presidency from 1869–1877, only around 19 million acres were given to the railroads, which sold large tracts to settlers for a profit).[8] Some have speculated that Lincoln, an obscure railroad lawyer, may have owed his nomination to the influence of western railroad interests at the 1860 Republican National Convention. His assistant secretary of war, Thomas Scott, was also the vice-president of the Pennsylvania Railroad, and played an important part in the rationalization of the industry.

The railroad industry was the laboratory for what became the American version of modern managerial capitalism. Railroad corporations pioneered the adoption of modern large-scale business management and the separation of ownership from control. It was during the era of the railroads that close relationships developed between investment banking firms and the large corporate law firms that eclipsed the earlier small, general-practice law partnerships. This big business-finance-corporate law firm nexus flourished as railroad corporations were joined by mammoth corporations in other industries—for example, the Rockefeller-dominated Standard Oil, and U.S. Steel, America's first billion-dollar corporation, formed in 1901 from the amalgamation of numerous smaller companies under the guidance of the investment banking firm of J. P. Morgan & Co. (the House of Morgan first became important in railroad finance).*

---

*The House of Morgan, according to one estimate, directly or indirectly controlled up to 40 percent of all American financial, industrial, and commercial capital in 1914. (J. Bradford De Long, "What Morgan Wrought," *The Wilson Quarterly*, Autumn 1992, p. 17).

From the Gilded Age to the Great Depression, American capitalism, dominated by a few major banking and corporate groups, was much more like modern Japanese or German capitalism than like post–New Deal American capitalism. Powerful investment bankers, sitting on the boards of major corporations, used their influence to consolidate and rationalize American industry. They also dominated the Republican party. Indeed, Wall Street lawyers, bankers, and corporate executives were so influential in the U.S. government during the late nineteenth and twentieth centuries that Manhattan could almost be described as the political capital of the United States as well. The history of the federal administrative elite, especially in the period of maximum Republican hegemony in national politics between 1896 and 1932, is the story of a small number of northeastern families linked by marriage, education, social clubs, law firms, corporate directorships, and civic associations. Hamilton and Washington had dreamed of a National University, training a meritocratic elite; the Whigs had denounced the Jacksonian spoils system, countering with the ideal of a tenured, qualified civil service; but their heirs the Republicans, on coming to power, discovered the advantages of patronage, and made the federal government the instrument of a caste. The government of the United States, more than that of any other democracy in the late nineteenth or early twentieth centuries, resembled Marx's description of capitalist government as the executive committee of the bourgeoisie.

In a country that was rapidly becoming less Anglo-Saxon, the Northeastern elite was almost wholly Anglo-American and Protestant (in particular, Episcopalian). There were no powerful counter-elites that could challenge this regionally based northern oligarchy, as the planters had before the Civil War. Instead, the other regional elites tended to be the Northeastern elite's surrogates and subcontractors. The planter elite, reconstituted as the Southern Bourbon class, acted as the agent for northeastern business interests in the South; after the end of Reconstruction, the Bourbons were given a free hand to exploit poor blacks and whites. Protestant gentries in the Midwest, the Southwest, and the Pacific coast were similarly linked to the New York–centered Northeastern patriciate. While proud of their local identity and traditions, these regional elites looked to the northeastern establishment for a model, as the northeastern elite, in turn, looked to the British aristocracy. The prosperous businessmen and attorneys and college presidents of the South and West sent their sons East for expensive educations when they could, and sought to bring the symbols of eastern refinement—great universities, public libraries, symphony orchestras, country clubs—to their own communities, emulating the similar importation of British and Continental European refinement by the northeastern oligarchs.

In his essay on Hawthorne, Henry James listed the "items of high culture" that had been missing from antebellum America:

> No State, in the European sense of the word, and indeed barely a specific national name. No sovereign, no court, no personal loyalty, no aristocracy, no church, no clergy, no army, no diplomatic service, no country gentlemen, no palaces, no castles, nor manors, nor old country houses, nor parsonages, nor thatched cottages, nor ivied ruins; no cathedrals, nor abbeys, nor little Norman churches; no great universities nor public schools—no Oxford, nor Eton, nor Harrow; no literature, no novels, no museums, no pictures, no political society, no sporting class—no Epsom nor Ascot![9]

If this complaint had been valid in Andrew Jackson's America, it was becoming obsolete in McKinley's America, as the great cities of the Northeast—New York, Boston, Philadelphia—came to rival Old World metropolitan centers in wealth and sophistication. The Europeanization of America was marked in intellectual life at the turn of the twentieth century. Just as the latest British fashion in government, parliamentary centralism, was preferred by Progressives to an older British import, the Whig ideology of the eighteenth-century Framers, so Victorian Oxbridge and the German research university replaced the earlier model of the genteel Christian gentleman's college. (The two came into conflict when Woodrow Wilson—a product of the "Germanic" Johns Hopkins—tried to abolish the dining clubs of the "English" Princeton when he was president of that university.) Before the Civil War, elite Americans had studied Latin and rhetoric; the Anglophile Northeastern elite of Euro-America replaced the classics with the new-fangled discipline of "English." In 1865, Harvard added a requirement in reading English; in 1873, an English composition requirement, based on a work of standard authors, was instituted.[10] The chief author on the Harvard curriculum was

Shakespeare, whom the populist Walt Whitman disparaged as the "artist and singer of Feudalism."[11]*

The new national ruling class set itself up as an aristocracy on the British model, complete with a *de facto* established church, the Episcopalian; an Oxbridge in the form of the Ivy League (with pseudo-Gothic campuses); an aristocratic Foreign Service; the cults of football, polo, and yachting; the European Grand Tour; the country house; even the grouse shoot (a favorite pastime of the Anglophile Henry Stimson). The United States, Henry Cabot Lodge observed with satisfaction, was finally becoming "an aristocratic republic."

Upper-class Anglo-American nativists fantasized about the fusion of the dominant populations of the American and British empires (a fantasy that has been passed down to us in the anachronistic institution of the Rhodes Scholarship). Before World War I Colonel Edward House, Wilson's *eminence grise*, wrote a science-fiction novel, *Philip Dru*, in which the United States, reformed by a progressive, benevolent dictator, links up with the British to police the world. Henry James remarked, "I can't look at the English-American world . . . save as a big Anglo-Saxon total, destined to such an amount of melting together that an insistence upon their differences becomes more and more idle and pedantic."[12] James practiced what he preached; he not only moved to London, but became a British citizen at the outbreak of World War I. Radicals as well as reactionaries like James left for London, Paris, or Venice; those who stayed behind were equally Europhile (Mark Twain's sneers at Europe seemed provincial by World War I). This turn-of-the-century Anglicization and Europeanization of America preceded the post–World War II Americanization of Europe, and perhaps made it possible. Western Europe was the second home of the American ruling class, long before it became America's Cold War protectorate.

The attempt of the Northeastern establishment to turn itself from a

---

*Whitman's suspicions about the political implications of English literature were later vindicated by Walter Hines Page, Wilson's Anglophile ambassador to Britain, when he exclaimed that "we Americans have got to hang our Irish agitators and shoot our hyphenates and bring up our children with reverence for English history and in the awe of English literature." Quoted in Alexander DeConde, *Race, Ethnicity, and American Foreign Policy* (Boston: Northeastern University Press, 1992), p. 86.

class into a hereditary ruling caste, like the British aristocracy, entailed the institutionalization of antisemitic and anti-Catholic prejudice. As a result of the institution of geographical quotas in the 1920s, which had the purpose of diluting non-WASP elements in the student body by bringing in Anglo-Americans from the hinterland, Jewish enrollment at Columbia declined from 40 to 22 percent in two years.[13] Higher education was stratified along ethnic lines, with WASPS in the Ivy League and most colleges, Catholics at Notre Dame and Fordham, Jews at City College and New York University, and blacks at Fisk or Howard. At a time when the professions were being institutionalized, the gates to the professions—elite schools—had to be guarded against the wrong sort. The proliferation of professional requirements and of professional associations, whatever the intent, had a similar effect in making the professions near monopolies of well-born Anglo-Americans.

WHITE SUPREMACY AND THE SECOND GREAT COMPROMISE

In 1992, the 500-year anniversary of Columbus's arrival in the Western Hemisphere was greeted by considerable protest; American Indians sailed to Spain and claimed possession, and the Spanish were denounced as mass murderers because of the Eurasian diseases they inadvertently introduced to the Americas. A century earlier, however, the Columbian Exposition of 1893 in Chicago emphasized America's coming of age, as a great western power and a legatee of European civilization. On the fairgrounds of Chicago rose a model metropolis in Beaux-Arts style, a "White City" where facades evoking the Hellenic and Roman roots of western civilization gleamed on buildings devoted to an innovative industrial civilization—Railroads, Manufactures, Agriculture, Mining, Electricity. The Hamiltonian ideal of an imperial, aristocratic, and metropolitan America, the successor to the British and Roman empires, was given shape. Significantly, Chicago's blacks had been excluded from employment on the fairground staff in favor of working-class whites, making the fair a "White City" indeed.[14]

White working-class racism was critical for the structure of white supremacy, which in turn was a central element of the second republic of the United States. The first grand compromise, an extraconstitutional bargain between northern elites and the southern planter class, had been based on the inviolability of slavery in the South. White supremacy provided the basis for the second grand compromise, between the white upper classes and the white masses. By voting, and also by violence, the white majority advanced its status and material interests in white supremacist institutions.

In this respect, Euro-America differed little from other lands of European settlement. The nineteenth century saw the emergence of a family of white settler states, organized as *Herrenvolk* (master-race) democracies.* The Anglo-Canada of Sir John MacDonald and his successors was really a new country of recent immigrants, with little connection to the earlier Canada of trappers and Loyalists who fled the American War of Independence. In Australia, too, layers of white immigration transformed a settler society that had begun as a penal colony. The Anglicization of the inland Afrikaaner domain and the creation of Rhodesia provide other examples of the building of a nineteenth-century *Herrenvolk* regime on the remnants of an earlier European coastal settlement.

The immigration of white settlers also created what were in effect new nations in the frameworks of some of the Spanish-American creole republics. Although the numbers of new immigrants were smaller, the ethnic Europeanization of other Western Hemisphere countries was much more striking than that of the United States. In Brazil, whites were only one quarter of the population in 1821; as a result of the European influx, the country soon had a white majority.[15] Canada's proportion of European immigrants was higher than that of the United States, that of Argentina higher still. Whereas European immigrants never accounted for more than one in seven Americans, in Australia new immigrants (almost all from Britain) were three out of five in 1861, and one in five in 1901.[16]

In the United States, as in Australia, Canada, and South Africa, white farmers and the white working classes—enlarged by European immigration—were haunted by fears of social debasement and economic

---

*The comparative study of white-settler nations was pioneered by Walter Prescott Webb in his 1952 *The Great Frontier* (New York, 1952). The common history of European migration was given a further boost in 1960 by Frank Thistlethwaite. ("Migration from Europe Overseas in the Nineteenth and Twentieth Century," reprinted in Rudolph J. Vecoli and Suzanne M. Sinke, eds., *A Century of European Migrations: 1830–1930*, Urbana and Chicago: University of Illinois Press, 1991, pp. 17–57.) Thanks to the labors of these and other scholars, it is increasingly possible to view the Euro-American United States between the Civil War and the Vietnam War in its proper context.

displacement. The social and political equality of the races, they worried, might lead to amalgamation, and the total loss of status that implied in the caste system common to all countries of European settlement. They also feared that they would be displaced by wealthy white capitalists using gangs of nonwhite labor—whether antebellum Southern planters taking all the good land of the West from white farmers to be used as slave plantations, or Gilded Age railroad and mining magnates using Asian coolie gangs to undercut the wages and break the unions of white workers.

These fears were not unjustified. The same improvements in transportation that made the great migration from Europe possible also enabled employers in the white-settler states to bring inexpensive nonwhite labor.* In California and Hawaii, rich planters *did* engage in a deliberate strategy of keeping wage demands down by playing not only whites against nonwhites, but Chinese, Koreans, Japanese, and Filipinos against each other. In 1864, the Republicans passed the Contract Labor Law, permitting the importation of coolies. After the Civil War, some Southern planters experimented with using Chinese coolies, to frighten blacks into subservience out of fear of replacement; the restoration of elite white political power after Reconstruction eliminated an incentive for further such experiments. In the twentieth-century South the white populist nightmare came true—poor white sharecroppers had to struggle on an equal basis with poor blacks in areas controlled by wealthy Southern landlords, and as a result of progressive voting reforms as much as half the white population of the South was effectively excluded from voting. Even in New England, when the Secret Order of the Knights of St. Crispin, the largest American labor union, struck at Sampson's shoe factory in North Adams, Massachusetts, the owners brought in Chinese workers, forcing the white laborers to capitulate. "If for no other purpose than the breaking up of the incipient steps toward labor combinations and 'Trade Unions,'" wrote one author in *Scribner's Monthly*, "the advent of Chinese labor should be hailed with warm welcome."

---

*Between 1835 and 1920, 27.7 million Indians left India, mostly in coolie gangs; of these, 24 million returned home. There were far fewer Chinese coolies; these worked in the United States, Canada, Peru, and Australia, with their number concentrated in San Francisco and Vancouver. (William H. McNeill, *The Great Frontier: Freedom and Hierarchy in Modern Times*, Princeton: Princeton University Press, 1983, pp. 50–51.)

Multiracial labor unionism was not, in practice, a viable response, for psychological rather than material reasons. Working-class whites, not only in the United States but in Canada, Latin America, the Caribbean, Australia, New Zealand, and South Africa, had a relatively greater stake in their "whiteness" than upper-class whites, precisely because they had no other sources of pride—no personal wealth, no glorious family history, no first-rate education, no reassuring network of elite associations and connections. To cooperate with blacks and other nonwhites as equals, even if this had made sense economically, would have meant that they were, indeed, no better than "niggers" and "Chinamen"— something they suspected upper-class whites believed anyway.*

For these reasons, in every region of the country where whites faced large numbers of nonwhites—particularly in the South and on the West Coast—the leaders of working-class whites tended to be the most radical racists, and wealthy whites the most moderate. Samuel Gompers, the English-born Jewish leader of the American Federation of Labor, and Dennis Kearney, the Irish-American leader of white racist labor in California, both agreed in seeing a conspiracy on the part of white elites to lower the wages of the white working man by introducing nonwhite labor, either coerced or poorly paid, to the fields and factories.

The white-settler countries borrowed racist devices freely from one another. The Chinese Exclusion Act of 1882 in the United States inspired imitation in other lands of recent European settlement. Canada adopted a Chinese Immigration Restriction Act in 1885; in 1882 the Canadian Prime Minister, Sir John A. MacDonald, had argued for restrictions on "Mongoloid" immigration like those that the United States and Australia had adopted, on the grounds that Asians "would not and could not be expected to assimilate with our Aryan population."[17] The Australian colonies followed suit. Australia's anti-Chinese statutes did not affect Japanese, Hindu, and other Asian immigrants, as the *Sydney*

---

*It is significant that the term *miscegenation* for the ultimate form of social equality between white and nonwhite Americans is an American coinage. D. G. Croly, an immigrant Irish-American, and George Wakeman replaced the term "amalgamation" with a new word formed from the Latin terms to mix (*miscere*) and race (*genus*) in a famous 1863 pamphlet, *Miscegenation: The Theory of the Blending of the Races, Applied to the American White Man and Negro.* Both were partisan Democrats; the pamphlet purported to be a Republican tract in favor of racial intermarriage. (David R. Roediger, *The Wages of Whiteness,* New York: Verso, 1991, pp. 155–56.)

Daily Telegraph warned in 1896: "It is not much use . . . to shut out Chinese, and leave the door open to millions of Hindoos, Arabs, Burmese, Angolese, and other colored races which swarm British Asia."

The answer was the "Natal formula" adopted in South Africa in 1897—legislation which empowered immigration officials to turn back any immigrant who was not literate in a European language. Modeled on the literacy tests by which black voters were disfranchised in the United States, the Natal formula was quickly adopted by the white-settler countries. The Australian colonies joined in a federal commonwealth in 1901, partly to ensure that common immigration laws would promote a White Australia. A white Canada was the goal of laws passed by the Canadian government between 1900 and 1910. Even Latin American countries like Paraguay and Costa Rica passed legislation barring Asian or black immigration.[18]

Though it is seldom acknowledged, white supremacy *literally* shaped the Euro-American United States, as it had earlier shaped the borders after the Mexican War. Throughout this era much of the Republican foreign-policy elite was in favor of creating a Caribbean and Pacific empire by annexing Cuba, Hawaii, the Virgin Islands, and other outposts. In 1869, President Grant, reviving Lincoln's colonization project, argued that Santo Domingo, if acquired as a U.S. colony, could support "the entire colored population of the United States, should it choose to emigrate."[19] The Republican Senate opposed this project, along with others for annexing Cuba and Hawaii. Senate Foreign Relations Committee Chairman Charles Sumner of Massachusetts, despite his abolitionist past, believed that the United States should not annex "colored communities."[20] In 1898, the Teller amendment barred annexation of Cuba, chiefly because of the large black population. The Senate also opposed the annexation of the Philippines for racial reasons.

Just as whites in the West feared Asian competition, so working-class whites in the South resented black competition and the prospect of black social equality. The defeated southern white elite, attempting to thwart the federal attempt at a thoroughgoing social revolution in the South and seeking to restore their prewar predominance, had no trouble finding allies among ordinary whites. A determined campaign of terror against the federal occupying authorities and their local collaborators succeeded in making the northeastern elite abandon both black and white Republicans in the South. The northeastern capitalists made their peace with the southern planter class, reconstituted as a merchant-landlord oligarchy in what became, in effect, an internal Third World resource colony for the industrial North.

The fear on the part of elites that blacks would hold the balance of power in a color-blind, two-party electoral system led swiftly to black disfranchisement—first by terror, then by law—and to the one-party Democratic South. The political goal of the southern elite, political dominance, could have been achieved by simply disfranchising blacks, without an elaborate system of formal apartheid. The establishment of Jim Crow, after the Supreme Court gave a green light to official segregation in its 1896 *Plessy v. Ferguson* decision, was a cause less of elite southerners than of middle-class and working-class whites. Members of the southern establishment, indeed, were sometimes opposed to the extreme racism of populist demagogues. To compound the irony, some of the most viciously racist populists, like Tom Watson, had begun as proponents of cross-racial political alliances. The defeat of the populist movement both nationwide and in the South in 1896 convinced many populist politicians that they could never compete with the Bourbons unless they "out-niggered" them—which, being for the most part opportunists, they proceeded to do with few scruples.*

Outside of the South, the only area in which economic competition between whites and nonwhites existed on a large scale was on the West Coast. Midwestern and Pacific Coast farmers and workers had sided with the Union to keep planters and their black labor force out of the western territories won from Mexico and the native Indians; they were not about to tolerate competition for land and jobs with immigrants from China, Korea, Japan, Hawaii, and the Philippines. The link was made explicit by Hinton Helper, a white populist opponent of slavery from North Carolina who wrote of California in *The Land of Gold* (1855): "I should not wonder at all, if the copper of the Pacific yet becomes so great a subject of discord and discussion as the ebony of the Atlantic."

---

*Not only working-class anxieties, but urbanization, fed the racist radicalism that culminated in Jim Crow. In the rural South, blacks and whites, when they commingled, did so within a clear caste system; this was not the case in a city in which whites found themselves shoulder to shoulder not only with white strangers but with blacks. Jim Crow served to reinforce the confidence in their own superiority of nonelite white southerners in an age of baffling and rapid change.

White natives and white immigrants united in violence directed at Asian immigrants and their white employers. In California, where one-quarter of the wage workers were Chinese until the 1880s, two thirds of the white workers were European immigrants, primarily Irish and German. These immigrants joined with native-born whites in anti-Asian pogroms. The agitation of Californian whites for restrictions on immigration led Congress to pass the Chinese Exclusion Act in 1882, which historian George M. Fredrickson calls "perhaps the most successful labor-based political movement in American history."[21] Later rounds of legislation extended the ban to all of Asia, creating severe diplomatic conflicts with Japan in the early twentieth century. The Republican platform of 1896 sought to restrict immigration to "the English-speaking peoples of North America"—that is, Canada—and to bar the entry of "mixed races from Mexico and Central America."[22]

Under the 1790 naturalization law bequeathed by the Founding Fathers, which limited naturalization to "free white persons," Asians, as nonwhites, could not become U.S. citizens. (The fact that their children could, under the Fourteenth Amendment, created many legal anomalies.) When, in 1868, Senator Charles Sumner tried to remove all racial restrictions from the naturalization laws of the United States, arguing that Chinese immigrants would not be a problem as long as they were committed to American institutions, his amendment to remove "white" was defeated by more than two to one.[23] White supremacists in the West, working through state legislatures, created a system of anti-Asian apartheid, complete with segregated schools, occupational restrictions, and bans on jury service and testimony against whites. The shameful crescendo was reached during World War II, when Japanese immigrants and their citizen children and grandchildren were herded into concentration camps as enemy aliens.

White supremacy in the North was less overt than in the South or West, but just as real. It took the form of informal but systematic segregation in housing and the labor market.

By the turn of the century in northern cities like Philadelphia, Chicago, and New York, relatively well-to-do blacks who had previously lived in mostly white neighborhoods increasingly could find housing only in black neighborhoods. The color line in housing hardened during the

Great Migration of the early twentieth century as many blacks poured into the north from the rural South. The northern ghettos that formed in the late nineteenth and early twentieth century eventually engendered the isolated black underclass of the late twentieth century.

The antebellum mulatto elite, which had served upper-class white customers as barbers and caterers, lost its clients—by the early twentieth century, the stereotypical Italian barber would replace the black barber in cities like Philadelphia. The declining mulatto elite was succeeded by a new "black bourgeoisie" specializing in services like undertaking and barbering for the growing all-black populations of the new ghettos. Cut off from social intercourse with white clients, this insecure black elite preserved the white upper-class usages of an earlier era, with courtly and quaint manners. As E. Franklin Frazier pointed out in the mid-twentieth century, the black bourgeoisie was not a real bourgeoisie, that is, it did not have a significant independent position in the national economy. Rather, it was a middleman elite, a make-believe patriciate with its own separate-but-equal versions of such white elite institutions as fraternal clubs and cotillions, obsessed with hierarchies of social status—and skin color—within the isolated black community.

The pattern of white immigrants taking jobs from native-born blacks first appeared during the great Irish and German migrations of the early nineteenth century. An 1838 article in the *Colored American* complained that "these impoverished and destitute beings—transported from the trans-Atlantic shores are crowding themselves into every place of business and of labor, and driving the poor colored Americans out. Along the wharves, where the colored man once commanded . . . in stores where his services were once rendered, and in families where the chief places were filled by him, in all these situations there are substituted foreigners or white Americans." Frederick Douglass wrote in 1853, "White men are becoming house-servants, cooks, and stewards on vessels—at hotels—They are becoming porters, stevedores, wood-sawyers, hod-carriers, brick-makers, white-washers and barbers, so that the (free) blacks can scarcely find the means of subsistence."[24] Even in the antebellum North, European immigrants institutionalized their displacement of black labor by refusing to admit blacks to apprenticeship programs and trade unions they controlled.

By the turn of the century, the trade union was well established as one of the pillars of de facto white supremacy in the Euro-American republic. Samuel Gompers, the president of the American Federation of Labor, after initially supporting color-blind unionism, summed up the views of the majority of working-class whites when he told a St. Paul audience in 1905 that "the Caucasians are not going to let their standard of living be destroyed by Negroes, Chinamen, Japs, or any others."[25] Gompers proved himself an heir to Jefferson, Madison, Lincoln, Seward, and other champions of a homogeneous white workingman's America, when, as late as 1898, he proposed expatriating black Americans to Cuba or Liberia.[26]

The absence of widespread antiblack violence in the North was chiefly a function of the absence of blacks; when great numbers of blacks moved into northern industrial centers, northern whites showed that they were quite as willing as southern whites to attack and murder blacks who represented a threat to their status and wages. This fact is often overlooked in conventional histories of the United States, which portray nineteenth- and early-twentieth-century race riots (more accurately described as pogroms) as melodramatic two-sided conflicts between whites and blacks, rather than as tragic three-sided conflicts between white workers and what they perceived as an alliance of black workers with white business elites. For example, the Irish draft riots in New York in 1863 were inspired largely by the use of black strikebreakers against striking Irish longshoremen. Between the 1880s and the 1890s, the number of strikes protesting the use of black workers rose from eight to twenty-two.[27] Both the East St. Louis riot of 1917 (which left thirty-nine blacks and nine whites dead) and the Chicago riot of 1919 were prompted by the use of blacks by businesses to undermine white unionization. Northern employers also used black strikebreakers in New York (1895, 1916), Cleveland (1896), Chicago (1904, 1905), Detroit (1919), and Milwaukee (1922).[28]

White race rioters were thus sending a message, not only to black economic competitors, but to the white economic elite. Like the earlier grand compromise between the northern and southern elites, which repeatedly threatened to break down into violent disunion between 1789 and 1860, the grand compromise between the white upper classes and the white masses in Euro-America was maintained by violence or the threat of violence. Since the sixties, when one thinks of riots one thinks of urban blacks or Hispanics. The characteristic participant in urban violence in Euro-America, however, was the working-class white race rioter.

The nature of the Euro-American grand compromise is clearest from the comments of highly self-conscious American leaders like Theodore Roosevelt who believed that protections for working-class whites would promote harmony among the classes of the white majority, avoiding the extremes of populist revolution and reactionary plutocracy. In a telling criticism of *The Law of Civilization and Decay* by his friend Brooks Adams, Roosevelt maintained that Adams was mistaken in blaming the decline of Rome on financial conditions. Instead, Roosevelt argued, Rome had been done in by the ruination of the Italian peasantry by competition with cheap Egyptian labor and African and Middle Eastern slaves. The United States faced no such social debacle, because "the free workingman" was protected from ruinous competition by the transformation of the slaves into wage laborers, the restriction of Asian immigration, and convict labor laws.[29] For Roosevelt, as for the American labor movement, the primary examples of progressive labor laws were those that shielded white workers from nonwhite competition. Alarmed by the importation of Japanese and Chinese coolies to work the plantations of Hawaii, Roosevelt agitated for their replacement by "tens of thousands of Spaniards, Portuguese, or Italians, or any of the other races," so that "the islands may be filled with a white population of our general civilization and culture."[30] Roosevelt saw the American conquest of North America as part of a global process of the foundation of new white-settler nations: "American and Indian, Boer and Zulu, Cossack and Tartar, New Zealander and Maori—in each case the victor, horrible though many of his deeds are, has laid deep the foundations for the future greatness of a mighty people."[31] Imperialism, restriction of nonwhite immigration, and progressive reform could all be reconciled as elements of a forward-looking Euro-American nationalism.

A patrician Republican reformer like Roosevelt thus could agree with the attitude expressed earlier by Walt Whitman, a Jacksonian Democrat. Whitman applauded the Saxonization of Mexico: "What has miserable, inefficient Mexico to do with the mission of peopling the New World with a noble race?"[32] In 1858 Whitman exulted that Oregon's new state constitution excluded blacks:

We shouldn't wonder if this sort of total prohibition of colored persons became quite a common thing in new Western, Northwestern, and even Southwestern States. . . . (There) will be a conflict between the totality of White Labor, on the one side, and on the other, the interference and competition of black labor, or of bringing in colored persons on *any* terms. Who believes that Whites and Blacks can ever amalgamate in America? . . . Besides, is not America for the Whites? And is it not better so?[33]

The Second Republic of the United States, then, was dominated by the northeastern establishment, and rested on an extraconstitutional compromise between the white elite and the white majority—a compromise embodied in racial segregation and racist immigration restrictions. Like the earlier Anglo-American republic, Euro-America was legitimated by a mainstream consensus defining the elements of American national identity. Anglo-America had been a Saxon Protestant federal republic. Euro-America, at its height in the mid-twentieth century, was defined in somewhat more inclusive terms as a white Christian federal democracy. In the sections that follow I trace the development of Euro-American conceptions of the national community (pan-European), the common ethic (pan-Christian), and the political creed (federal democracy).

FROM ANGLO-AMERICAN TO EURO-AMERICAN: THE NATIONAL COMMUNITY

Between the Civil War and the Civil Rights Revolution, the unofficial definition of the American nationality was gradually enlarged from Anglo-American to Euro-American. The replacement of the "Saxon" by the "generic European" or "white" became the prevalent view, however, only after generations of strife between old-stock Anglo-Americans and immigrant Europeans.

The importance of European immigration for American population growth after the Civil War can hardly be exaggerated. If immigration had ceased after the American revolution, and if the rate of natural increase of the population had remained the same, the population of the United States in 1920 would have been only one-half of what it actually was.[34] The massive European immigration also significantly increased the ratio of whites to blacks.* The importance of the German and Irish migrations for the present-day population can be seen in the fact that in 1990, Americans who identified themselves by ancestry were predominantly of German descent (23 percent) and Irish descent (16 percent), with self-described English-Americans coming in third (13 percent).[35]

Five million Europeans emigrated to the United States between 1815 and 1860; they were followed by 10 million more, in the period 1860–90. The majority of these were from the British Isles, Germany, Scandinavia, Switzerland and Holland. This northwestern European immigrant flow dried up for various reasons. German industrialization created jobs and raised the standard of living (actually creating a shortage of agricultural labor in Germany, made up by foreign labor), while land reform in Sweden ended desperate rural poverty. British emigrants, by the turn of the century, preferred Canada, Australia, and South Africa to the United States as a destination. As a result, most of the fifteen million Europeans who emigrated to the United States between 1890 and 1914 came from southern and eastern Europe: Austria-Hungary (Czechs, Galician Poles, Jews, Slovaks, Magyars, Croats, Serbs, Slovenes), Italy, Russia, Greece.†

The immigrants created their own cultural enclaves in the United States. In 1920, there were 276 newspapers in German, 118 in Spanish or Portuguese, 111 in Scandinavian languages, 98 in Italian, 76 in Polish, 51 in Bohemian (Czech and Slovakian), 46 in French, 42 in Slovenian, and 39 in Yiddish.[36] As late as 1940, New York had 237 foreign-language publications, and Chicago 96.[37] In addition, there were numerous foreign-language radio shows, and, in the 1920s, a Yiddish film industry.

---

*In 1920 the black population was only 9.9 percent of the American population; in 1820 it had been 18.4 percent (a decline from 19.3 percent, the historic peak, in the first U.S. census in 1790). Figures from Lerone Bennett, Jr., *Before the Mayflower: A History of Black America*, 5th revised edition (New York: Penguin, 1984), pp. 448, 453, 521.

†The proportion of immigrants to native-born in 1910 (14.5 percent) was hardly higher than it had been in 1860 (13.2 percent). But the composition was significantly different. Southern and eastern Europeans, who had made up only 13 percent of the immigrants in 1882, were 80.7 percent in 1907. (Maldwyn Allen Jones, *American Immigration*, 2nd. ed., Chicago: University of Chicago Press, 1992, pp. 153–154.) European immigration grew until, in the early years of the twentieth century, more than ten out of every thousand Americans were european immigrants (compared to 0.3 per thousand in the 1970s).

In addition to churches, secular associations flourished in this era of immigrant neighborhoods, many of them ethnic mutual aid societies——the Ancient Order of Hibernians, the German-American Alliance, the Order of Sons of Italy, the Polish National Alliance, the Pan Hellenic Union, the Viking Council of the Mystic Brotherhood. The Knights of Columbus, founded by Irish-Americans in New England in 1882 as a fraternal insurance society, soon spread nationwide and eventually became the largest Catholic layman's group in the world.[38] National athletic clubs were also divided along ethnic lines; there were German *Turnverein,* Bohemian *Sokols,* Polish *Falcons.*

The neighborhood saloon, and its German equivalent, the beer garden, was another major institution in immigrant neighborhoods, from the Civil War to Prohibition. In turn-of-the-century Chicago, saloons outnumbered the combined total of groceries, meat markets, and dry goods stores. Saloons sold groceries, cashed checks, acted as restaurants. They were often working-class political clubs. The saloonkeeper-politician was a common figure in the big cities. "Mr. Dooley," created by the Chicago newspaperman Finley Peter Dunne (1867–1936), was an Irish saloonkeeper, whose shrewd comments on American politics, in dialect, were addressed to his regular customer, Mr. Hennessey. As Lincoln Steffens remarked, in *The Shame of the Cities* (1904), the fastest way to empty a city council chamber was to shout, "Your saloon's on fire."[39]

The urban political machine, run by bosses, was a familiar element of the immigrant milieu. Immigrant-based machines replaced Jacksonian Democratic party organizations in New York, Chicago, Detroit, Boston, and New Haven. New York's Tammany Democratic machine was a model for others. Before the Civil War, the Irish-Americans Mike Walsh and John Morrisey were important Tammany politicians. The infamous Tweed Ring engaged in mere old-fashioned vote-buying; after Tweed and his associates were packed off to jail in 1871, "Honest John" Kelly assumed control and built a disciplined organization. Each city machine was an alliance of city districts, or wards. The ward bosses looked after immigrants, providing a variety of services—assistance with citizenship papers, patronage jobs as policemen, firemen, clerks, coal, food, rent payments, help in fires and emergencies, bail, funeral expenses, permits and licenses, help with the law—in return for votes ("Vote early and often," the saying went).

Just as both parties engage in affirmative action today, so both national parties competed for the immigrant vote in big cities. Both built similar machines. Catholic immigrants—Irish, Italians, Poles—were usually Democrats; so were Germans alienated by Republican support for prohibition. On the other hand, the dominance of Irish Catholics in corrupt machine politics drove many Germans, Scandinavians, and Jews to the GOP. During the Roaring Twenties, the Republican machine of Chicago Mayor William Hale "Big Bill" Thompson protected Al Capone's bootlegging empire; Thompson won the affections of Anglophobic German- and Irish-Americans by threatening to punch King George V in the nose if he ever dared to visit Chicago. In 1931, Anton Cermak was elected Mayor, and built up the Democratic machine, before he was assassinated while riding in a parade in Florida in a car with president-elect Franklin D. Roosevelt. (The assassination, blamed on the anarchist sentiments of an Italian immigrant, is thought by some to have been the work of the Capone mob, which was after Cermak, not FDR.) Under Cermak's successors, Mayor Edward Kelly and Cook County Democratic Chairman Patrick Nash, the Democratic machine became firmly identified with municipal government. Forty-three of 50 Democratic ward leaders held jobs in the government; of 3,000 precinct committeemen, three quarters had government jobs. In addition, there were 30,000 patronage jobs to be distributed.[40]

"The Irish was born to rule," observed George Washington Plunkitt of Tammany Hall. Irish Catholics dominated urban machines from the Jacksonian era to the twentieth century. In the late nineteenth century, New York's Tammany Hall was controlled by "Honest John" Kelly, Richard Croker, and Charles F. Murphy, while Chicago was run by equally colorful characters—"Hinky Dink" Kenna and "Bathhouse" John Coughlin.[41] In New Haven in the 1930s, to name a typical example, Irish-Americans, although they were only 13 percent of the inhabitants, held 49 percent of the government jobs.[42]

The immigrant political machines overlapped considerably with the urban underworld. Among the 732 delegates to the 1896 Cook County (Chicago) Democratic convention were 48 who had served time in prison for homicide or other crimes, 17 who had been tried for homicide, 15 former policemen—and eleven former boxers. More than a third of the Democratic delegates ran saloons; several ran gambling casinos and bordellos.[43]

The history of organized crime in the United States depicts, in minia-ture, the assimilation of successive waves of European immigrants to the Second American Republic. In the decades preceding the Civil War, Irish-American gangsters ousted Anglo-American criminals in the cities of the Northeast (often preying on other Irish immigrants). In New York, Irish gangs like the Dead Rabbits, the Bowery Boys, the O'Connell Guards, and the Five Pointers allied themselves with the Irish-dominat-ed Democratic machine. The "new immigrants" of the turn of the cen-tury brought their own criminals; during Prohibition, Jewish and Italian gangsters replaced the Irish mob. Meyer Lansky, a Polish Jew, and Charles "Lucky" Luciano organized the first national crime "syndicate." The era of Jewish prominence in organized crime, with gangsters like Dutch Schultz, Bugsy Siegel, and Louis "Lepke" Buchalter, was brief, with Italians extending their domination of organized crime after World War II.[44]

As in the 1850s, mass immigration produced a backlash by old-stock Americans. Henry James was shocked by the fellow citizens he encoun-tered while strolling one Sunday afternoon on Boston Common: "No sound of English, in a single instance escaped their lips; the greater num-ber spoke a rude form of Italian, the others some outland dialect unknown to me. . . . The types and faces bore them out; the people before me were gross aliens to a man, and they were in serene and triumphant possession." Other patricians shared his alarm. "The agitation over slavery," Madison Grant wrote in his 1916 bestseller *The Passing of the Great Race,* "was inim-ical to the Nordic race, because it thrust aside all national opposition to the intrusion of hordes of immigrants of inferior racial value, and prevent-ed the fixing of a definite American type. . . . The native American by the middle of the nineteenth century was rapidly becoming a distinct type."[45] Woodrow Wilson, in his *History of the American People,* described the new immigrants as "men out of the ranks where there was neither skill nor en-ergy nor any initiative of quick intelligence" and "sordid and hapless ele-ments" (southern and eastern European immigrants, once acquainted with Wilson's views, voted for Taft and Roosevelt).[46]

Thomas Bailey Aldrich, at one time editor of *The Atlantic Monthly,* turned to verse to express his concern about immigration:

Wide open and unguarded stand our gates,
And through them presses a wild motley throng—
Men from the Volga and the Tartar steppes,
Featureless figures from the Hoang-Ho,
Malayan, Scythian, Teuton, Kelt, and Slav,
Flying the Old World's poverty and scorn;
These bring with them unknown gods and rites,
Those, tiger passions, here to stretch their claws . . .
O Liberty, white Goddess! Is it well
To leave the gates unguarded?

The 1924 National Origins Act completed a series of laws that had the effect of ending the flow of southern and eastern European immigrants, by ensuring that 60% of annual immigrants originated in northwestern Europe. The post-WWI national origins quota system did not reflect a mere revival of antebellum Anglo-American nativism, however. Rather, it reflected the enlargement of the definition of "whiteness" from Anglo-Saxon to Germano-Celtic. This was a triumph for the Irish, previously the targets of exclusion and prejudice, and for German-Americans, whose patriotism was suspect during World War I. While Americans today tend to lump all European immigrants together as victims of prejudice by what would later be called WASPs, the truth is that the older western European immigrant groups, chiefly the Irish and the Germans, did not identify with southern and eastern Europeans at the turn of the century. What is more, the older immigrants dominated the skilled trades, and feared that the unskilled new immigrants would be used as strikebreakers.*

Cutting off high levels of European immigration did not resolve the question of how the new immigrants were to relate to other American

---

*Old immigrants dominated the trade unions. In 1886, for example, Illinois trade unions were only 21 percent native, and 5 percent "new immigrant" (Polish, Bohemian, Italian). Seventy-four percent of their members were products of the old immigration—German, Irish, British, and Scandinavian. The new immigrants, few of whom were unionized, were often used by employers as strikebreakers (Maldwyn Allen Jones, supra, p. 189). AFL president Samuel Gompers, himself an immigrant English Jew, argued that the new immigrants were unassimilable. Under his influence, after 1906, the AFL backed literacy tests to reduce competition from unskilled labor; at the same time, the National Association of Manufacturers lobbied *against* restriction of immigration from Europe.

groups. In the early twentieth century, the scholar Milton M. Gordon has argued, there were three conceptions of American identity: Anglo-conformist, melting-pot, and cultural pluralist. The Anglo-conformists were heirs to the older Anglo-American conception of the American nation as an offshoot of the Anglo-Saxons, related to the other Teutonic peoples like the Germans and Scandinavians. Melting-pot nationalists, like Anglo-conformists, assumed that there was, and should be, a common American national culture that immigrants should join; melting-pot theorists, however, saw American culture as something that changed over time, as elements of various immigrant cultures were detached from their original matrices and incorporated into the whole. Melting-pot theorists also believed that the white ethnic groups of the United States would and should merge, through intermarriage, into a single population. The ideal of cultural fusion and ethnic amalgamation was popularized by Israel Zangwill, an English Jew, in his 1909 play, *The Melting Pot.**

The two patron saints of American cultural pluralism rejected both Anglo-conformity and the melting-pot ideal. In his February 1915 essay in the *Nation,* "Democracy vs. The Melting Pot," Horace Kallen was concerned (as the essay's title suggests) with rebutting the melting-pot conception, as well as the nativism displayed in Edward A. Ross's polemic *The Old World and the New* (1915), the immediate occasion of Kallen's essay. Randolph Bourne, in his July 1916 essay "Trans-National

---

*Israel Zangwill dedicated *The Melting Pot* to Theodore Roosevelt. When Zangwill wrote years later to ask him if he still supported the concept, Roosevelt replied: "But, my dear Sir, the idea that I have forgotten the 'Melting Pot,' and its dedication to me! Now as a matter of fact that particular play I shall always count among the very strong and real influences upon my thought and my life. It has been in my mind continually, and on my lips often during the last three years. It not merely dealt with 'the melting pot,' with the fusing of all foreign nationalities into an American nationality, but it also dealt with the great ideals which it is just as essential for the native born as for the foreign to realize and uphold if the new nationality is to represent a real addition to the sum total of human achievement." (TR to Israel Zangwill, November 27, 1912, in Roosevelt Collection, Library of Congress, quoted in Thomas G. Dyer, *Theodore Roosevelt and the Idea of Race,* Baton Rouge: Louisiana State University Press, 1980, p. 131.) The influence of Teutonophile Anglo-conformity is clear, however, in Roosevelt's belief that "Huguenots and Puritans and the German 'Forty-eighters' were on the whole the three best stocks that came here," and thought that "German immigration is a little better than any other." Dyer, p. 129.

America," concentrated on contesting the claims of Anglo-conformists for the superiority of Anglo-American culture.* Rejecting assimilation, in its Anglo-conformist and melting-pot forms, both of which, in their different ways, envision the United States as a conventional nation-state with a single predominant culture, cultural pluralists counterposed the ideal of the United States as a nonnational confederation of minorities, a country without a majority nation.

The idea of the United States as a "nation of nations" was rejected vehemently by progressives like Theodore Roosevelt and Woodrow Wilson. By World War II, however, it had passed from being a left-wing idea into a middle-brow cliché. In the forties Frank Sinatra could express the pluralist ideal in a motion picture, *The House We Live In*: "All races and religions/ That's America to me." During and after World War II, the pan-white platoon became a cliché of war movies and war fiction. In the introduction to his 1944 *A Bell for Adano*, novelist John Hersey explained, "America is the international country. Our Army has Yugoslavs and Frenchmen and Austrians and Czechs and Norwegians in it. . . ."[47]

Ironically, while a watered-down version of cultural pluralism became part of public discourse, European immigrants and Anglo-Americans were slowly amalgamating, in true melting-pot fashion. The melting pot worked first in popular culture. Between the late nineteenth and mid-twentieth centuries, a distinctive vernacular national culture evolved, different from the older Anglo-American culture, and far more than the sum of various European-immigrant subcultures.

Because most of today's American customs were standardized between the Civil War and the New Deal, they reflect the predominant cultural influence of the two dominant regions of the era, New England and the Middle Atlantic–Midwest. Thanksgiving and the characteristic

---

*Kallen and Bourne arguably were influenced by their ethnic backgrounds. Kallen was a Harvard-educated German Jew who had immigrated to the United States with his family at the age of five; a Zionist and a proponent of secular (but not religious) Jewishness, Kallen was concerned about the effect on a distinct Jewish-American identity of the melting-pot ideal that Zangwill (an English Jew) promoted. Randolph Bourne, the other founding father of American cultural pluralism, was a Columbia-educated patrician WASP rebelling against the genteel Anglo-American elite to which he belonged.

imagery of the American Christmas have Northeastern roots. Both were initially codified, as it were, in the midst of the Civil War, in 1863. President Lincoln formally set aside the fourth Thursday of November "as a day of thanksgiving and praise to our beneficent Father who dwelleth in the heavens." (Thanksgiving had been a New England regional custom since Governor William Bradford of the Massachusetts Bay Colony, in 1621, ordered a celebration with roast turkeys after a good harvest.) Also in 1863, in *Harper's Illustrated Weekly*, the German immigrant artist Thomas Nast gave the trademark red, fur-trimmed costume to Santa Claus in his illustrations of "A Visit from St. Nicholas." The poem introducing Santa Claus by Clement Moore of the Episcopal General Theological seminary, originally published in 1823, was based on the St. Nicholas tradition of Dutch settlers in New York.

Baseball and football, both New England sports unknown in the antebellum South and other regions, became national pastimes in Euro-America. Modern football was born at late-nineteenth-century Ivy League colleges. Much more violent then than now, college football in the Ivy League was intended to toughen the soft young men of the Northeastern aristocracy for their role as leaders in a British-type military empire. It often happens that customs once popular in a metropolitan center persist in the provinces long after they have been superseded at their point of origin. Thus it is that football today is something of a religion in the small-town South and West, its patrician New England origins long forgotten.

If Ellis Island was the symbol of entry to White America, its idealized heartland was the Midwest, where the pastoralism of Mark Twain met industry, where the Slavic workers of Chicago and Pittsburgh mingled with the Germanic intellectual community of St. Louis. Thanks to the migration of midwesterners to California and the propagation of their mythology by Hollywood, an idealized Midwest has became the "old country" to millions of Americans who have preferred to forget their European ethnic origins. In addition, the flat, nasal, "r"-pronouncing dialect of the Midwest has now become the Received Pronunciation of the national elite, many of whom in living memory still spoke New England and Southern variants of British English. This was appropriate, perhaps, insofar as it had been a midwesterner, Lincoln, who had destroyed the plantation South and the old America and established a European-style nation-state.

Hollywood also shaped the Euro-American conception of national history. Speculations by de Tocqueville and Whitman that the United States would produce the first literature in which the hero was the common man was fulfilled, in the forms of the western and the detective thriller. John Wayne and Humphrey Bogart played nonhyphenated Americans of indeterminate class status, sharing a distinctive ethical code: stoicism and sardonic wit disguising a deep humanity and idealism. They were descendants of Huck Finn, just as Bugs Bunny, another archetypical midcentury American, was the descendant of Br'er Rabbit.*

What nowadays would be called the culture wars between Protestant censors and the big-city and Hollywood entertainment industry grew muted in the 1940s and 1950s with the evolution of a bland middle-American culture developed by the largely immigrant entertainment industry: urban forms like black jazz, which Protestant republicans found offensive, were watered down in forms like "swing" and presented by assimilated new white-immigrant performers (Benny Goodman, Frank Sinatra). The uproar over Elvis's pelvis and rock 'n' roll would inaugurate a new and somewhat different culture war.

The process of cultural amalgamation of the diverse white groups, given a boost by immigration restriction, was accelerated by movement to the suburbs, where immigrant subcultures for the most part failed to be transplanted. The provision of entertainment by the mass media and social services by the new, bureaucratic welfare state created in the New Deal, along with civil rights reform and the professionalization of politics, led to the decline of the once-powerful urban European-immigrant political machines. Around the time Dwight Eisenhower and John F. Kennedy, representatives of the two major Old Immigrant groups, were

---

*Richard Grenier has pointed out that twentieth-century film versions of Cooper's *The Last of the Mohicans* change the story. In the original, the Daniel Boone character, Hawkeye, is the sidekick of the upper-class hero, Major Heywood, an English officer; Hawkeye, as a member of the white lower class, however heroic, could not wed the heroine, who is assigned to Heywood. "I am but a poor hunter," Hawkeye says, "and Mabel, I see, is fit to be an officer's lady." In the 1936 and 1992 versions, Hawkeye gets the girl. (Richard Grenier, "Hawkeye as a Moral Hermaphrodite," *The National Interest*, Winter 1992/93, pp. 70–72.)

elected president, Abraham Ribicoff became the first Jewish governor (of Connecticut), and Rhode Island's John Pastore the first Italian-American senator.

The integration of first- and second-generation European-Americans was accompanied by rising rates of intermarriage among white Americans. German immigrants, though they might be suspect politically (as socialists or agents of the Kaiser) had always been accepted as fellow Teutons, and amalgamated easily with the Anglo-American population. Finley Peter Dunne's Mr. Dooley explained, "An Anglo-Saxon . . . is a German that's forgot who was his parents."[48]

It took longer for the other major group of Old Immigrants, Irish Catholics, to be accepted. In time, however, the working definition of the white American race-nation was enlarged from Anglo-Saxon or Teutonic to Anglo-Celtic or Germano-Celtic. During the 1860 census, the Irish had been listed as a distinct group, along with "native" and "foreign" whites. Such invidious distinctions were quick casualties of the need for a Unionist coalition (and federal recruiting in Ireland). As early as 1862, a committee of the House of Representatives expressed a more liberal definition of genuine whiteness when it asserted that the natural population of the United States was "the white race, whether Anglo-Saxon, Celtic, or Scandinavian."[49] By the late 1880s, Anglo-Saxon nationalists were treating the Irish as honorary Saxons.[50] "The Irish will, before many years are past, be lost in the American (people). . . ." predicted a writer in *The Atlantic Monthly* in 1896.[51] In the early twentieth century, President Abbott Lawrence Lowell of Harvard thought that the Irish, as white Christians, could be "so merged in the American people" that they could not be "distinguished as a class," unlike nonwhites such as blacks, Chinese and Indians, or non-Christians such as Jews.[52]

The enlargement of the charmed circle to include not only German- and Irish-Americans but new immigrants—Jews, Slavs, Italians, Greeks—was slower. Even so, since World War II, intermarriage has done much to dissolve ethnic divisions among white Americans. According to one recent study, "intermarriage is extremely common—the rule, rather than the exception, among Americans with European ancestries." As a result, "a new ethnic group is emerging among whites" that can be described as "European Americans."[53] The descendants of Anglo-American settlers, Old Immigrants, and New Immigrants are gradually fusing into a single intermarrying population.* Roosevelt was prescient when he told the American Historical Association in his 1912 presidential address that future historians would write about the "formation of a new ethnic type in this melting-pot of the nations."[54]

The evidence suggests that the restriction of immigration in the 1920s increased the rate of assimilation among European-American groups.[55] "By drastically limiting the volume of European immigration," one scholar has noted, "the restrictive policy adopted in the 1920s accelerated the Americanization of those groups which had come earlier."[56] By 1960, when John F. Kennedy was elected the first Irish-American Catholic president of the United States, Ellis Island was a ruin. Only when it was effectively shut down did Ellis Island, along with the Statue of Liberty, become an idealized symbol of a (Euro-American) "melting pot."

THE PAN-CHRISTIAN ETHIC

A generalized Protestantism continued to be the informally established religion long after the Civil War. The "common schools" (public schools) promoted nonsectarian Protestantism, using the King James Bible (instead of the Catholic Douay Bible) and Protestant hymns and prayers. When Bishop Francis Kenrick of Philadelphia and Bishop John Hughes of New York lobbied to gain public aid for parochial schools, they provoked a backlash from mainline Protestants. In 1869 the National Teachers' Association (today the National Educational Association) denounced public funding of parochial schools as "a violation of the fundamental principles of our American system of education."[57] The Republican party, which since Nixon has courted Catholics by support-

---

*Four-fifths of Italian-Americans born since 1950 have married other Americans of non-Italian descent, compared to only one-third of those born before 1920. Roughly 75 percent of English-, Irish-, and Polish-Americans now marry outside of their groups. As many as half of all Jewish-Americans marry non-Jews today, compared to less than 10 percent before 1960. (Ben J. Wattenberg, *The First Universal Nation: Leading Indicators and Ideas about the Surge of America in the 1990s,* New York: The Free Press, 1991, p. 52.) Seventy-seven percent of Italian-American and 83 percent of Polish-Americans born since 1955 have married outside of their ancestral group. Since the 1960s, Jewish intermarriage has gone from 6 percent to 50 percent. (Ben Wattenberg, "Beneath the Foam on Top, Visible Signs of Melting," *The Washington Times,* June 17, 1993.)

ing federal aid to parochial schools, was the champion of nonsectarian public education in the nineteenth century.*

A central institution in the lives of many European immigrants was the church or synagogue. Many immigrant religious communities treasured their Old World traditions and resisted Americanization. The churches of immigrants of the same religion tended to be divided along national-cultural lines; instead of American Catholicism, there was Irish-American Catholicism, German-American Catholicism, Polish-American and Italian-American Catholicism. The tension between Old World values and New World identities were present in many immigrant communities, in none more so than in American Catholicism. The Catholic hierarchy in the United States often sought to keep members from becoming assimilated and leaving the subculture. One of the themes of popular Catholic literature was the resourceful priest who foils potential marriage outside the faith.†

---

*In 1876, Congressman James G. Blaine (in 1882 the Republican candidate for president) introduced a constitutional amendment that would have ensured that no money raised by any state "shall ever be under the control of any religious sect" or "be divided between religious sects or denominations." After passing the House, the amendment was narrowly defeated in the Senate. Later, Theodore Roosevelt called for "absolutely nonsectarian public schools" and declared it was "not our business to have the Protestant Bible or the Catholic Vulgate or the Talmud read in these schools." (Robert T. Handy, *Undermined Establishment: Church-State Relations in America, 1880–1920,* Princeton: Princeton University Press, 1991, pp. 40–41; 160.)

†Throughout the nineteenth century, the Vatican remained opposed to the separation of church and state. A group of American Catholic leaders sought to persuade the Catholic hierarchy that the American separation of church and state was compatible with Catholic doctrine. These Americanists, opposed by more conservative Catholics in the United States, were repudiated by Pope Leo XIII in his 1895 encyclical *Longinqua oceani,* in which he praised the United States for granting religious freedom to Catholics but warned that "it would be very erroneous to draw the conclusion that . . . it would be universally lawful or expedient for State and Church to be, as in America, dissevered and divorced." Americanists like Denis O'Connell, rector of the American College in Rome, and Bishop John J. Keane, the rector of Catholic University in Washington, D.C. (founded in 1887), were purged from their posts. Worse followed; in an 1899 encyclical, *Testem benevolentiae,* Leo XIII repudiated Americanism as a heresy. This Americanist controversy was followed by the modernist crisis, when Pius X succeeded Leo XIII in 1903. Pius X issued two encyclicals in 1907, *Lamentabilit sane exitu* and *Pascendi dominici gregis,* condemning attempts by Catholic intellectuals to reconcile their faith with new developments in science, history, and philosophy, and instructing the Catholic hierarchy to suppress dissidence. Not until the Second Vatican Council in the 1960s did the Catholic church commit itself to the separation of church and state and religious liberty.

The origins of today's evangelical Protestantism are found in the mid-nineteenth century. The Civil War, the Darwinian revolution in natural science, and the squalor that accompanied industrialization and mass immigration shattered the confident optimism of many Protestants. An alternative to the optimistic postmillennialism of the antebellum years was provided by the British theologian John Nelson Darby, who toured the northern United States in 1862. In the 1830s, Darby had come up with a scheme of seven periods of human history, corresponding to the seven vials poured out by an angel in the Book of Revelation. According to Darby, the present was the sixth and final "dispensation" before the Apocalypse. At any moment, Christ would return and "rapture" (claim) true believers. A seven-year tribulation of mankind would follow the rapture, and then Christ would set up his theocratic kingdom.

While postmillennialism continued to have influence, inspiring the Social Gospel movement of the turn of the century, and Christian liberalism today, premillennial dispensationalism diverted Protestant evangelicals from faith in ameliorative social reform to pessimism in the face of escalating wickedness and decadence. "I find that the earth is to grow worse and worse," the evangelist Dwight L. Moody declared in 1877, "and that at length there is going to be a separation" between the godly few and the condemned majority. Moody was one of the most important evangelical preachers who spread Darby's dispensational millennialism through preaching, prophecy conferences, and teaching in schools like the Moody Bible College. The most influential proselytizer was a Dallas minister, Cyrus Ingerson Scofield, who established Bible institutes around the country, founded a biblical correspondence course, and created the Scofield Reference Bible, first published in 1909 by Oxford University Press. The Scofield Reference Bible, along with the Ryrie Study Bible, continues to guide premillennialists in puzzling out the clues about the last days that God has hidden in scripture. In the 1920s, Scofield's protégé, Lewis Sperry Chafer, established the Dallas Theological Seminary, which continues to be one of the most important centers of evangelical thought and study.[58]

The Protestant evangelicals saw their country under attack by sinister forces within and without. In *Our Country* (1884), Josiah Strong, a leading American Protestant theologian, warned of the "seven perils" facing

America: Romanism, Mormonism, intemperance, socialism, wealth, immigration, and the city—the beachhead for an alien "army twice as vast as the estimated numbers of Goths and Vandals that swept over Southern Europe and overwhelmed Rome." The Populist firebrand Tom Watson, who became a violent racist demagogue after the failure of his first attempts at a cross-racial political alliance, attacked not only blacks but Catholics and Jews. Watson told readers of *Watson's Jeffersonian Magazine:* "The Roman Catholic Hierarchy is the deadliest menace to our Liberties and our Civilization." He called for the lynching of Leo Frank, a Jewish factory manager accused of murdering a female employee; lynching was necessary according to Watson, because "Frank belonged to the Jewish aristocracy, and it was determined by the rich Jews that no aristocrat of their race should die for the death of a working-class Gentile." Frank was mobbed and murdered in public while the authorities watched.[59]

During the 1920s, fundamentalists tended to support the revived Ku Klux Klan, which was opposed to Catholics and Jews as well as blacks. Both movements shared a concern with the moral purity of young people; in some parts of the country, Klansmen would patrol lovers' lanes, shining flashlights into parked cars. H. L. Mencken complained: "The intimate relations between church and Klan, amounting almost to identity, must have been plain to every intelligent American" in the early twentieth century.[60] Twenty-six of 39 anti-Catholic lecturers who worked for the Klan between 1922 and 1928 were fundamentalist Protestant preachers, 16 of them Klan officers. Colonel William J. Simmons, the creator of the "second Klan," began as a camp meeting revivalist; the career of the other important Klan leader, Edward Y. Clarke, went in the opposite direction; he left the Klan to become a fundamentalist agitator.[61]

The nativism of the 1840s and 1850s was echoed in the 1880s and 1890s, with the formation of anti-Catholic societies like the American Protective Association and the National League for the Protection of American Institutions (NLPAI). One Protestant crusader, Justin D. Fulton, an ordained Baptist minister, wrote a series of books with titles like *Washington in the Lap of Rome, Woman in the Toils of Rome,* and *The Fight with Rome,* in which he tells how drunken, lecherous priests "pass from the brothel to the altar and celebrate the mass."[62]

The passage of time, and the mingling of Anglo-Americans and Euro-

Americans in the suburbs, gradually muted religious strife. By the mid-twentieth century, the fierce hostility of nativist American Protestants and immigrant Catholics was giving way to a rather superficial ecumenicism, symbolized by President Eisenhower's famous comment, "Every American should have a religion, and I don't care what it is." The "triple establishment" proclaimed by Will Herberg in *Protestant, Catholic, Jew,* was a public phenomenon of the Eisenhower and Kennedy eras. High school commencements began to feature a priest and a rabbi along with the requisite Protestant minister. The term Judeo-Christian was invented in the interests of ecumenical courtesy—or rather reinvented. (Nineteenth-century European antisemites had sought to discredit Christianity by calling it "Judeo-Christianity."

Catholics and Jews won full acceptance in the post–World War II golden age of Euro-America only by paying a heavy price. At least in public, Catholics had to give up the claim that theirs was the only true church, and Jews had to play down the idea that they were a chosen people defined in terms of ethnicity rather than belief. In short, American Catholicism and American Judaism have surrendered their ancient claims and accepted the Protestant definition of them as denominations. Though it was an improvement over the old Protestant semi-establishment, the postwar triple establishment of religion was doomed by increasing interfaith marriage and by growing numbers of secular and Muslim Americans.

Because there were so few Jews relative to the population as a whole outside of a few cities, it is more accurate to say that Euro-America was a Christian nation; that is, almost all Americans were at least nominally Christian (western Christian in particular; there were few Orthodox Christians in the United States). Justice David Brewer, writing for the majority in *Church of the Holy Trinity v. United States* (1892), said: "Our civilization and our institutions are emphatically Christian . . . this is a Christian nation."[63] Lord Bryce, the perceptive British observer of late-nineteenth-century America, wrote: "The whole matter may, I think, be summed up by saying that Christianity is in fact understood to be, though not the legally established religion, yet the national religion."[64] Efforts were made to legally establish Christianity. In 1864 Protestant evangelicals formed the National Reform Association (NRA), which promised in its constitution "To secure such an amendment to the Constitution of the United States as will declare the nation's allegiance to Jesus Christ and its acceptance of the moral laws of the Christian religion. . . ."[65] The amendment failed, but by the mid-twentieth century a generic Christianity, deeply influenced by Protestantism, had succeeded generic Protestantism as the informally established religion of the United States.

FEDERAL DEMOCRACY

The de-Saxonization of American identity by mid-twentieth-century intellectuals and publicists combined with the redefinition of America as a nation of European immigrants united by democratic ideals, represented a truce in the culture war between old-stock Protestants on one side and Catholic and Jewish European immigrants and their descendants on the other. This served the purposes of the dominant Democratic party, at that time a coalition between white southerners and European immigrants and their descendants in the Northeast. At the same time, however, the redefinition of the United States as a nation of immigrants and the rejection of Saxon or Nordic racial unity as the basis of American society presented liberal thinkers and historians with a problem: what would hold a nation of immigrants together? The unity of American society was sought by New Dealers in what Gunnar Myrdal called the American Creed, an overarching ideology of liberal democracy shared by diverse ethnic groups.

The American Creed could be divided into two components: democratic idealism and a reverence for the procedures of democracy, symbolized respectively by the Declaration of Independence and the Constitution. In the pantheon of the New Deal historians, Thomas Jefferson, the sainted author of the Declaration, and Abraham Lincoln, the martyred saint of the secular American Creed, became the greatest American philosopher-statesmen. The two became a trinity when they were joined by James Madison, who was given primary credit for articulating, in the *Federalist,* the complicated workings of the Constitution that embodied the Jefferson-Lincoln democratic faith. The *Federalist* was always known and esteemed, but between Madison's time and World War II it did not hold the exalted canonical status it has since achieved; in earlier generations, the Declaration of Independence and Washington's Farewell Address held pride of place, followed by the great speeches of Webster and then Lincoln. Charles Beard, arguing for his Progressive interpretation of American history in terms of factional and sectional conflict, first drew attention to Madison's Federalist Number 10 in 1913; New Deal liberals put Madison's discussion of faction to quite different use, stressing not the idea of conflict but the idea of harmony and equilibrium through pluralism. In this way Madison was enlisted as a precursor of FDR and interest-group liberalism.*

FDR himself had a hand in rearranging American iconography to support the claim that New Deal Democrats represented the culmination of all that was best in American history. During the early years of his administration, FDR was careful to identify himself with Jefferson—issuing the Jefferson postage stamp and nickel, taking a personal interest in the construction of the Jefferson Memorial, and speaking at its dedication. Conservative states'-rights Democrats, however, soon invoked Jefferson in denouncing what they considered FDR's radical statism. Turning against FDR, Al Smith in 1936 told the Liberty League, an anti-Roosevelt group: "It's all right with me if they want to disguise themselves as . . . Karl Marx, or Lenin, or any of the rest of that bunch, but what I won't stand for is allowing them to march under the banner of Jefferson, Jackson, or Cleveland!"[66] FDR began searching for another symbol. He wore Jackson's gold watch chain on Election Day in 1936 and ordered a replica of the Hermitage for the inaugural parade.[67] Not Andrew Jackson, but Lincoln, however, was to succeed Jefferson in FDR's iconography.

"I think it is time for us Democrats to claim Lincoln as one of our own," Roosevelt wrote in 1929.[68] In recycling Lincoln as a Democrat, FDR had the help of able popular historians like Stephen Vincent Benét and Carl Sandburg, whose hagiographic multivolume biography of the

---

*The adoption of Madison by consensus liberals is ironic. In 1829, Madison, the "Father of the Constitution," predicted that by 1929 the United States, with a population of 192 million (within the 1829 boundaries, of course) would have the population density of the Britain of his day. At that point, he predicted, propertyless masses might use their power in an American democratic government to transfer resources from the rich to the poor. Institutional barriers to such projects were necessary. For Madison, among others, the federal constitution was intended to prevent anything like the New Deal from occurring. (James Madison, "Notes on suffrage," 1829, in *Letters and Other Writings of James Madison*, vol. 4, New York: R. Worthington, 1884, pp. 21–30.)

Great Commoner became a bestseller. In New Deal propaganda, the very identities of Lincoln and FDR became blurred. "How much of Lincoln does Roosevelt have in him?" Max Lerner asked, to answer, rather absurdly, "More, I am convinced, than any President since Lincoln or before."[69]

FDR took a personal interest in the process, making a pilgrimage to Lincoln's birthplace in 1936 and weaving quotes from Lincoln into his speeches (with the help of playwright Robert Sherwood, author of *Abe Lincoln in Illinois*). The Lincoln of FDR and his court poets and historians was not the Great Emancipator, but the hero of the white working man. To solidify his Southern base, FDR even managed to condemn Reconstruction in the name of Lincoln: "Lincoln, too, fought for the morals of democracy," he declared in 1938, "and had he lived the South would have been allowed to rehabilitate itself on the basis of those morals instead of being 'reconstructed' by martial law and carpetbaggers."[70] Black Americans, indeed, played almost no role in the mid-twentieth-century Lincoln cult. New Dealers argued that the equivalent of slavery in the twentieth century was not racial segregation—something they typically passed over in silence—but wage slavery practiced by the wealthy and big business (the equivalent of the clients of Whig railroad lawyer Lincoln). So it was that Lincoln, as a symbol of the white common man, whether native-born or immigrant, came to play the role in the iconography of the Second American Republic that George Washington, the Anglo-Saxon Cincinnatus, had played in the First.

To make room for the new trinity of Jefferson, Lincoln, and Madison, American statesmen who had been venerated earlier were demoted. Hamilton, considered a precursor of the Wall Street Republicans who hated the New Deal, became an "Un-Person." With him vanished those other great nationalists, Clay and Webster, whose chief offense was to have opposed an earlier incarnation of the party FDR now led. Washington remained important, but he was respected rather than venerated (the invocation by isolationists of his warning against foreign entanglements in his Farewell Address did not endear him to Wilsonian internationalists).

The tension between democratic idealism (Jefferson and Lincoln) and constitutional conservatism (Madison), in the revised American political creed was reflected in the check imposed by states'-rights federalism upon the nationalization and democratization of American politics during the Second Republic. The political ideal of the United States, during the Euro-American century, gradually changed from federal republicanism to federal democracy—from a decentralized system that permitted local variations in suffrage to one which, though still decentralized, favored universal manhood (and later, adult) suffrage, at least as an ideal. This shift began well before the Civil War, as one state after another eliminated restrictions on universal white male suffrage. The Civil War amendments enfranchised black Americans, at least nominally, while women's suffrage, pioneered in the western states, was written into the Constitution after World War I. The Seventeenth Amendment, mandating direct popular election of U.S. senators, eliminated one of the major vestiges of nondemocratic "republicanism" in the constitution (while converting the Senate into little more than a mechanism for overrepresentation of white westerners in the national government).

The powers of the federal government grew dramatically during the century between the Civil War and the 1960s. There were several waves of centralization: one in the late nineteenth century, which produced the Pendleton Civil Service reforms and the Interstate Commerce Act; and the later Progressive Era reforms, embodied in new bureaucracies like the Federal Reserve and the Food and Drug Administration. Most important of all was the New Deal, which radically expanded the role of the federal government in American life by providing direct social security benefits and numerous other subsidies to citizens out of federal taxes. Despite the expansion of government authority during Franklin Roosevelt's four terms in the White House, the most ambitious plans of early-twentieth-century Progressives for a rationalized, centralized state failed in the 1930s. Progressive state-building threatened the power over federal agencies of southern congressmen, who entered into a coalition with Republicans after 1936 to defeat comprehensive executive reorganization. The successful efforts by mid-century conservatives to associate a strong state with fascism and communism, instead of preventing the growth of the state, merely ensured the evolution of incoherent big government, dominated by the "iron triangles" of interest-group liberalism: special interests, their congressional representatives, and weak, co-opted agencies. John Chamberlain, a former radical who would end up as an extreme conservative, called the New Deal state the "broker state" (a term he used approvingly). The more nationalistic Progressives wanted big coherent government; the New Deal's legacy was big incoherent government.

World War II strengthened the federal government further, as did the Cold War and the shock of Sputnik, which stimulated a Hamiltonian program of internal improvements (the federal highway system, public education) and a genuine if informal national industrial policy led by Pentagon and NASA procurement. For all this, the American political system at the height of the Euro-American republic between the late forties and the early sixties cannot be described as a national democracy. The United States remained a highly decentralized federal democracy until the 1960s. Despite the increased involvement of the federal government in economic life during the New Deal, and tentative efforts to chip away at racial segregation, the states remained dominant in the areas of race relations and sexual and family rights. The political system of the 1940s was largely the same as it had been at the end of Reconstruction, with the same two parties, the Democrats and Republicans, each organized as a loose confederation of state parties controlled by state and local bosses, a pattern dating back to the invention of the party system by Martin van Buren in the 1830s. In the 1960s the states would be stripped of many of their major powers, and the parties would be transformed into more national (and weaker) organizations, but no one in, say, 1955 imagined the sweeping changes that lay just ahead.*

---

*One important feature of the working constitution of Euro-America was a little-known compromise that artificially magnified the votes of rural Protestants at the expense of European immigrants and their descendants in the big cities. Old-stock Protestants, with their idealization of small-town life in a Jeffersonian Arcadia, were horrified when the 1920 census revealed that for the first time a majority of Americans lived in urban areas. The conservative Republicans who dominated Congress refused to reapportion congressional districts throughout the 1920s—the first time this had happened in American history. The compromise that was finally worked out had two parts—congressional seats would be periodically reapportioned among the states, but the malapportionment of districts within the states (with rural overrepresentation and urban underrepresentation) would not be challenged. This rural overrepresentation, lasting until the Supreme Court's "one-man, one-vote" decisions in the 1960s, greatly exaggerated the power of conservative rural and small-town white Protestants in American politics and culture throughout much of the twentieth century. The permissiveness in American culture since the sixties in part reflects the shift of political power from the small towns to the big cities that followed the demise of the 1920s compromise.

Of the three republics of the United States to date, the Second Republic was arguably the most successful in its context. The First Republic, Anglo-America, was a rickety federation that collapsed, as a result of stresses induced by successful expansion, into the horror of civil war. Today's Multicultural American Republic, originating in the sixties, has been associated with declining living standards, polarized politics, and foreign policy failures (the one success, the victory in the Cold War, depended on simply carrying out the grand strategy of Truman, Acheson, and other mid-century liberal internationalists). The Second Republic, rising above the ashes of the Civil War, achieved first economic and then geopolitical primacy in the world in only a few generations. In recent centuries only post-Meiji Japan can match that meteoric rise.

For all its virtues, Euro-America, like Anglo-America, was built on white supremacy, though the Euro-American version was less harsh—segregation was an improvement, however slight, over slavery. The structure of race relations in Euro-America, as we have seen, was built on the interlocking framework of disfranchisement of blacks and Asians, social segregation, a segregated labor market, and restrictions on the immigration and naturalization of nonwhites. As late as World War II, 30 of the then 48 states had laws against black-white marriage.[71] White supremacy was so interwoven with American public and private institutions that it could not be removed without unraveling the entire fabric. For this reason, the effort to fully bring nonwhite Americans into the mainstream of American life shattered the settled constitutional arrangements of the Second American Republic. The Civil Rights Revolution of the 1960s, marked by the greatest domestic violence since the Civil War, proved to be even more radical in its lasting effects than the Civil War and Reconstruction. The third American revolution of 1957–1972 created the Third Republic of the United States, the republic we live in today: Multicultural America.

CHAPTER THREE

The Third Republic

The Making of Multicultural America

Two mistakes are commonly made in discussions of multiculturalism in the United States. The first is to suppose that multiculturalism is purely a matter of educational philosophy, a theory about which books or authors to allow in the canon of higher education. In fact, multiculturalism is a worldview, which cannot be understood in isolation from the proliferation in the United States of affirmative action, more accurately referred to as racial preference. The second mistake is the assumption that multiculturalism is a proposal, an option, a possibility, when in reality it is the de facto orthodoxy of the present American regime: Multicultural America.*

Multicultural America is the Third Republic of the United States. Its legal and political underpinnings were assembled in the late 1960s and early 1970s; in the intervening generation, there have been disputes over detail, but the framework has remained unchanged. To date, however, the Third Republic has failed to gain legitimacy in the eyes of most Americans. This is a serious problem, inasmuch as the Third Republic is already more than thirty years old.

---

*I will note, only to dismiss, the misleading usage of "multicultural" as a synonym of "multiracial" or "multiethnic"—encountered in clichés such as "America has always been a multicultural society" and "Immigration is making America more multicultural." A multiracial society is not necessarily multicultural.

Each of the American republics that preceded Multicultural America, I have argued, had its own national story, its own widely—though not universally accepted—conception of the American nation's identity and destiny. The Anglo-American national story told of the providential expansion of an Anglo-American Protestant nation in its destined North American homeland; the Euro-American story, of the formation of a new white Christian nation from the amalgamation of Anglo-Americans and European immigrants in the metaphorical melting pot, a nation that would use its power, not merely its example, to lead the world to a democratic millenium. To date, however, more than a generation after the origins of Multicultural America, there is no generally agreed-upon account of what the American community is, or how its place in the world or history should be conceived. Indeed, there are radically conflicting accounts of the significance of the first thirty years of the Third Republic.

The multicultural left's version of post-sixties American history goes something like this: The Civil Rights Revolution was not an emancipation of individuals seeking to be integrated into a more inclusive American nation but rather a liberation of groups, of minority nationalities. Multiculturalists believe that the melting-pot conception of American identity has been, or should be, repudiated in favor of a new understanding of American society as a "mosaic" of five races or racelike communities—whites, blacks or African-Americans, Hispanics or Latinos, Asian and Pacific Islanders, and native Americans. These races are not mere ingredients to be blended in a future unity, but permanently distinct communities, like the Francophone and Anglophone populations in Canada, or the German, French, Italian, and Romansch nationalities in Switzerland. Each of the five American races has its own distinct culture, to which immigrants belonging to that race are expected to assimilate (Mexicans and Cubans join Hispanic America; Chinese, Indians and Filipinos join Asian-and-Pacific-Islander America, and so on). Moreover, each race, in addition to preserving its cultural unity and distinctness, should act as a monolithic political bloc (particularly since white Americans, according to the multicultural left, are guilty of racial bloc voting). Those who criticize the fivefold race-culture-political bloc scheme are, by definition, racists who wish to turn back the clock to the era of white supremacy.

That is the myth of the multicultural left. The right's myth is quite different: In the 1960s, the United States was taken over by a sinister new class of liberal intellectuals and bureaucrats. This tiny but powerful minority is waging war against the virtuous American majority on two fronts. One campaign is the culture war, an attempt by the liberal new class to undermine patriotism and destroy Christian (or Judeo-Christian) morality and family values. The other campaign is statism; having learned nothing from the failure of Soviet-bloc socialism, the liberal technocrats wish to enslave the American people to an ever-expanding leviathan state. Unless it is checked, liberalism will result inevitably in the extinction of morality and high culture in the United States and the destruction of the American economy.

As different as they are, the left-liberal and conservative myths are both examples of what Charles Beard called the devil theory of politics. The devil theory holds that the social order is basically sound; all problems are the result of conspiracies by evil individuals or factions (white racists or godless new-class liberals, as the case may be). The devil theory, it should be noted, is rather optimistic. Replace devils with angels, and everything will be fine. Establish enough multicultural studies programs, set-asides for nonwhites, and majority-minority congressional districts—or, alternately, restore prayer in the public schools, slash taxes on the rich, and elect a sufficient number of "profamily," antistatist conservatives—and the United States will be harmonious and prosperous.

The opposite of the devil theory of politics is class analysis. Today, class analysis tends to be associated with Marxist pseudoscience and discredited by that association. This is unfortunate, because class analysis is much older than Marxism, and is not, in itself, linked to socialist or even liberal politics. Ideas about class interests and class conflict are integral elements of the political theories of Montesquieu and Aristotle, to name only two examples. In the United States, the authors of the Federalist Papers based their defense of the Constitution of 1787 on an analysis of class that presumed a permanent conflict of interest between the propertied and the propertyless. Later, Progressive historians and social philosophers such as Charles Beard, Frederick Jackson Turner, and Thorstein Veblen incorporated class conflict, as well as the conflict of sections and economic interests, into their understanding of American society and American history. The picture of modern American society I present in what follows draws on these non-Marxist, American Federalist, and American Progressive traditions.

Here is a summary of what might be called the overclass theory of post-sixties America:

The contemporary United States is dominated by the white overclass—a small group consisting of affluent white executives, professionals, and rentiers, most of them with advanced degrees, who with their dependents amount to no more than a fifth or so of the American population. The white overclass is the first truly national oligarchy in American history, having originated in the middle of the twentieth century in the merger of the Northeastern elite with other Anglo-American sectional elites and the assimilated, upwardly mobile descendants of nineteenth- and twentieth-century European immigrants. Almost all of the individuals in positions of responsibility in the major institutions of government, business, philanthropy, the media, and education are members of this strikingly homogeneous oligarchy by birth or—in a relatively small number of cases—by achievement. By means of their near-monopoly of campaign finance, members of the white overclass tend to control both the Democratic and Republican parties; they also provide the overwhelming majority of political candidates and political and judicial appointees from within their own ranks.

The "vertical" divisions between the officially designated races (stressed by the left) and between partisan subcultures (stressed by the right) are less important than the "horizontal" division between the top fifth of the population and the four-fifths majority. The gap is one not merely between income groups but between worldviews; the white overclass tends to be more consistently libertarian, in morals and economics, than the masses below. In effect, America is divided, if only metaphorically, into something like Disraeli's "two nations," with a small, almost exclusively white nation of affluent, highly educated, secular libertarians ruling a vast nation, predominantly white—but with substantial black and Hispanic elements—whose members tend to be religious and socially conservative and to hold populist views on economic questions. The views of the four-fifths majority seldom find expression in national political debates; "left," "right" and "center" are, for the most part, simply factions within the white overclass, whose members tend to limit debate to matters of detail in implementing the consensus they share.

The two most important trends in American society since the 1960s—the proliferation of racial preferences, and the decline in average wages and benefits—both serve the collective interests of the white overclass. By means of college-to-Congress racial preference policies, the white overclass, over the past thirty years, has attempted to create and maintain small, artificial black and Hispanic overclasses. It has done so, not out of charity, but in order to co-opt the potential leaders of black and Hispanic dissent. Inducting talented black and Hispanic Americans into separate-but-equal oligarchies, financed and protected by the white overclass, is much less expensive than would be a serious effort to upgrade the living standards and enhance the wages, benefits, and education of the majority of black and Hispanic Americans (to say nothing of raising the living standards of all Americans).

At the same time that it has been fostering harmless and dependent nonwhite overclasses, the white overclass has engaged in a low-key, bipartisan class war against the transracial middle class (defined as working Americans with a high school education or less). The oligarchy has used its predominance in both the Democratic and Republican parties to weaken labor and shift the burden of taxation from rentiers and professionals to wage earners (for example, through regressive Social Security taxes, sales taxes, and user fees). The overclass war on the wage-earning middle class has also included forcing American workers to compete with exploited workers in Third World sweatshops, low-wage legal and illegal immigrants, and a rapidly growing pool of temp labor whose members lack job tenure, benefits, or union representation.

The results of these campaigns should have come as no surprise—stagnant or falling incomes for the majority, and rising incomes for members of the white overclass. Nor is it surprising that the hired intellectuals of the white overclass, both liberals and conservatives, try to persuade the American public that these trends are not the predictable consequence of public policy, but rather the "inevitable" result of "irreversible" trends toward a "global economy," forces of nature which, purely by accident, happen to favor the rich and well-connected.

Multicultural America, then, is neither conventionally liberal nor conventionally conservative. The Third American Republic is a grotesque synthesis of New Left and New Right, of rhetorical radicalism and real plutocracy, of divide-and-rule multiculturalism and cheap-labor economic globalism. The basic arrangements of Multicultural America are stable, because they serve the political and economic interests of the dominant social class. We can be certain that, if racial preferences threatened the jobs or incomes of overclass Americans, those preferences would be abolished tomorrow. Similarly, if members of the white overclass themselves began to pay a price for mass immigration or foreign mercantilism, the borders would be closed to people and goods very quickly indeed. As long as they can shift the social costs of racial preference and economic globalism onto the transracial middle class, however, the members of the white overclass have no incentive to alter these policies. Thanks to their financial control of the two duopolistic political parties, moreover, overclass whites can ensure that populist rebellions against overclass policies will be neutralized before they can be translated into victories at the ballot box. Failing that, populist insurgencies can always be thwarted by federal courts and federal agencies, which protect overclass interests when all else fails.

That, in a nutshell, is the overclass theory of Multicultural America, which I elaborate in greater detail in this and the succeeding two chapters. The skeptic might ask how this class theory of American society differs from the devil theories of the left and right. Does it not simply substitute a new devil, the white overclass, for the white racist bloc (the demon of the left) or the liberal new class (the demon of the right)?

The answer is no. There is a profound difference between the overclass theory and its rivals. The overclass theory does not posit the existence of a shadowy, behind-the-scenes elite—covert racists, or new-class liberals—that is manipulating political and business and cultural authorities like puppets on a string. On the contrary, according to the overclass theory, the people who *appear* to be in charge in the United States really *are* in charge. The country really is run by affluent, mild-mannered white executives and professionals with advanced degrees, together with their allies (and, in some cases, employers), the heirs to family fortunes.

In this chapter and the two chapters that follow, I attempt to shine some light upon the workings of the Third American Republic, workings that the Haves in the United States would prefer to leave in obscurity. This chapter explains how, when and why, and in whose interest, the original goal of the Civil Rights Revolution, a color-blind legal and political system, was abandoned in favor of the opposite goal, a society organized around racial labeling and racial preference. In Chapter 4, I describe the white overclass and its most important client elite, the black overclass, in detail. Finally, in Chapter 5 I show how the white overclass, through its domination of our money-soaked political system, has waged its low-key but effective class war against the middle and working classes of all races in the United States for a generation.

THE THIRD AMERICAN REVOLUTION

Multicultural America is a repellent and failed regime, from the point of view of members of the wage-earning American majority. That should not be surprising, because it was not designed with their interests in mind.

The Civil Rights Revolution ended with the establishment of a system of racial preferences that grows more elaborate every year. The "classical" example of racial preference was race-based busing in the sixties. In the 1970s and 1980s, racial preference entered a "baroque" phase, as it was extended to college admissions, employment, and government contracting. In the early 1990s, the "rococo" era of racial preference began, as one congressional district after another was redrawn to encourage if not guarantee the election of candidates of particular officially designated races. This was the result of a civil rights revolution that had started out quite differently, as a movement to replace white supremacy in the United States with color-blind law and politics.

Each previous American republic was assembled by the victors of a domestic revolution that followed a great transformation of America's geopolitical environment. The British success in the Seven Years' War with France in North America upset a decades-long understanding between London and the colonies about the proper allocation of authority; the indirect result was the American Revolution. The territorial expansion following the U.S. victory in the Mexican War, by raising the question of slavery in the new territories, contributed to the breakdown of the Anglo-American sectional compromise and the outbreak of the Civil War. The origins of the Third American Republic, too, must be sought in a domestic revolution caused indirectly by the outcome of a foreign war—in this case, the Second World War and its aftermath, the Cold War.

The grand compromise underlying Euro-America, I argued in the last chapter, was an implicit agreement between white American elites and white workers and farmers that nonwhites would not be permitted to engage in economic or political competition with whites. By means of this compromise, ordinary whites gained a degree of economic security and status, and white capitalists and politicians, with the low-income white race rioter ever in mind, purchased social peace. The domestic grand compromise thus embodied in white supremacy first came into conflict with the great-power grand strategy of the United States in the early twentieth century, when the restriction of Asian immigration was taken as an affront by the leaders of Imperial Japan. Although American leaders like Theodore Roosevelt (whose own thinking was deeply influenced by racist ideas) worried about the diplomatic costs of American white supremacy, this was not a serious concern as long as the United States was only one great power in a world in which the other major powers, with the exception of Japan, were equally racist European empires. Thus Woodrow Wilson, with the support of the British, rejected a Japanese proposal at the Versailles Conference for the inclusion of an amendment supporting racial equality in the Covenant of the League of Nations. By contrast, after World War II, the principle of racial equality was endorsed by the United Nations at the San Francisco Conference in 1946.

One reason for the change in American elite attitudes was German National Socialism. By taking racism to its ultimate conclusion in genocide, Hitler had discredited ideas about supposed inherent Teutonic and Caucasian superiority and nonwhite inferiority that Europeans and members of their worldwide diaspora had taken for granted for generations. The resemblance of American to Nazi racism was particularly troubling after revelations of the Holocaust. The Supreme Court made the connection between American white supremacy and Nazi racism explicit in 1948 when, in striking down the anti-Asian alien land laws of California, it called them incompatible with the United Nations Charter and described the law as "an unhappy facsimile, a disheartening reminder, of the racial policy pursued by those forces of evil whose destruction recently necessitated a devastating war."

During the war against Hitler, the American establishment tried to distance itself from Nazi racism by promulgating a sanitized, middle-brow version of the left-wing cultural pluralism of Horace Kallen and Randolph Bourne as an element of U.S. propaganda. "Because America alone among the nations of the earth was founded on ideas which transcend class and caste and racial and occupational differences," Henry Luce wrote in *Life* in 1942, "America alone can provide the pattern for the future."[1] Wendell Willkie made a similar argument in his 1943 bestseller *One World*:

> Our nation is composed of no one race, faith, or cultural heritage. It is a grouping of some thirty peoples possessing varying religious concepts, philosophies, and historical backgrounds. They are linked together by their confidence in our democratic institutions as expressed in the Declaration of Independence and guaranteed by the Constitution . . . Our success thus far as a nation is not because we have built great cities and big factories and cultivated vast areas, but because we have . . . learned to use our diversities.[2]

All of this, down to the term "diversities," sounds familiar, even banal, now that it has become the American orthodoxy, in a much more radical form than Willkie could have imagined. At the time, however, this represented a departure from the earlier mainstream traditions of melting-pot white nationalism and Anglo-American nativism.

Another reason for the softening of white American racism during World War II was the need for black domestic support for the war effort. In 1941, threatened by A. Philip Randolph and the NAACP with an all-black march on Washington that could threaten war preparedness, FDR reluctantly signed Executive Order 8802, which created a temporary Committee on Fair Employment Practice (FEPC). (It reflects poorly on white Americans that from the Revolutionary War through the Emancipation Proclamation and the Cold War they have been reluctant to extend civil equality to nonwhite Americans except under the pressure of military necessity.) Civil rights reform might not have survived the war against Hitler; southern conservatives in Congress killed the FEPC in Congress in 1946 (it was later reincarnated in 1964 in the Equal Employment Opportunities Commission). The rapid dismantling of white supremacy might not have taken place when it did if American leaders had not come to believe that American racism crippled American world leadership in the war that followed—the Cold War. Between 1945 and 1990, the imperial rule of whites over nonwhite peoples collapsed around the globe. Within majority-white settler states like the United States, Australia, and New Zealand, systems of apartheid that were decades or centuries old collapsed as well (for example, the 1964 Civil Rights Act and 1965 Voting Rights Act were paralleled by the British Race Relations Acts in 1965 and 1968). The collapse of the formerly white-ruled European empires meant that the loyalties of the leaders of the new, postcolonial states (which collectively came to be known as the Third World) were now important objects of geopolitical competition between the United States and the Soviet Union. In 1947, for example, Secretary of State George C. Marshall warned, "The moral influence of the United States is weakened to the extent that the civil rights proclaimed by our Constitution are not fully confirmed in actual practice."[3] "We have assumed a role of world leadership," President Truman observed when he vetoed a bill seeking to extend segregation in 1951. "We should not impair our moral position by enacting a law that requires a discrimination based on race."[4] The proliferation of nonwhite states gave added urgency to this argument—between 1945 and 1965, as a result of decolonization, UN membership increased from 51 to 117.[5] In October 1947, W. E. B. DuBois (who had earlier lobbied at Versailles for the League Amendment) presented the United Nations with "An Appeal to the World: A Statement on the Denial of Human Rights to Minorities in the Case of Citizens of Negro Descent in the United States of America and An Appeal to the United Nations for Redress."[6] In the same year, the President's Committee on Civil Rights issued its report, *To Secure These Rights.*

In April 1947 the Congress of Racial Equality (CORE) and its allies sent black and white Freedom Riders into the South to test compliance with federal court decisions. A year later President Truman ordered the desegregation of the U.S. armed forces. In December 1946, President Truman created a Committee on Civil Rights by executive order. The NAACP was winning court victories against segregation as well, most of these in higher education, such as *Sweatt v. Painter*, *McLaurin v. Oklahoma State Regents* and *Henderson v. United States*. In 1953, the U.S. Supreme Court banned segregation in restaurants in Washington, D.C. Finally, in the landmark school-desegregation decision of *Brown v. Board* of *Education of Topeka* (1954), and its companion case, *Bolling v. Sharpe*, the Supreme Court made clear its determination to prohibit all government-sanctioned forms of racial discrimination.[7] In 1957, reform turned into revolution from above when President Eisenhower enforced the desegregation of public schools in Little Rock, Arkansas by sending federal troops into the South for the first time since the end of Reconstruction.

The culmination of the Civil Rights Revolution proper, following heroic struggles by black and white integrationists, came with the Civil Rights Act of 1964 and the Voting Rights Act of 1965, along with the 1965 reform of immigration law and the 1968 Fair Housing Act. The most offensive apartheid measures of all, antimiscegenation laws, were struck down by the Supreme Court (as late as World War II, 30 of 48 states outlawed black-white marriage).[8] Formal legal and political discrimination against nonwhites in the United States, always a gross injustice and now a diplomatic embarrassment, had come to an end.

The solution of one problem presented reformers with another. The dismantling of formal segregation did not begin to address many of the severe problems of the black community, particularly ghetto residents in metropolitan areas outside of the South. These problems included not only continuing de facto barriers to black integration in white-dominated professions, political machines, and neighborhoods, but a social breakdown within ghetto communities manifested in high degrees of illegitimacy, welfare dependency, drug addiction, and violent crime.

What was the next step, after desegregation? On the right, there were advocates of formal equal opportunity and nothing else, a Social Darwinist "root hog or die" policy in which blacks, now that *de jure* discrimination was abolished, were left to fend for themselves. In this view, the larger American community had no responsibility for addressing such black problems as poor educational attainment and poverty, even though those problems were the result of centuries of cultural deformation and economic deprivation under racist laws.

Liberal integrationists rejected laissez-faire in favor of color-blind social programs that would be available either universally or on the basis of need. In 1965 Bayard Rustin argued that the antisegregation movement had attacked Jim Crow structures "which are relatively peripheral both to the American socioeconomic order and to the fundamental conditions of life of the Negro people." The next step, he wrote, was to address "not *civil rights,* strictly speaking, but social and economic conditions." In 1966 Bayard Rustin and A. Philip Randolph devised the Freedom Budget, a ten-year plan for spending $180 billion on domestic reform, particularly job creation. Rustin had written, "What is the value of winning access to public accommodations for those who lack money to use them?"[9] Two years later, when he was assassinated, Martin Luther King, Jr., the champion of color-blind civil rights, was preparing a march on Washington on behalf of poor Americans of all races.

This philosophy of color-blind, social-democratic liberalism informed President Johnson's commencement speech at Howard University of June 4, 1965: "Freedom is not enough . . . You do not take a person who for years has been hobbled by chains and liberate him, bring him to the starting line and then say, 'You are free to compete with all the others,' and still justly believe that you have been completely fair." Johnson declared, "We seek not just freedom but opportunity, not just equality as a right and a theory but equality as a fact and as a result."[10]

How was "equality as a fact and as a result" to be achieved? Contrary to later misconceptions, Johnson did not have racial quotas in mind. Like other proponents of a gradualist approach, he favored universal social welfare, educational, and jobs programs that would help poor blacks disproportionately while being open to the needy of all races. Daniel Patrick Moynihan, then assistant secretary of labor, spelled out the goal in what became known as the Moynihan Report: "It is not enough that all individuals start out on even terms, if the members of one group almost invariably end up well to the fore, and those of another far to the rear." Integration would be a success in America only when the dispersal of blacks through economic classes and professions was similar to the slowly achieved dispersal of other American groups such as European immigrants. This dispersal was to result from genuine, gradual socioeconomic improvement, not from tokenism.

Integrationist liberals, then, sought to expand the civil rights revolution into a color-blind program of social-democratic reform, along the lines of the New Deal and the Great Society—a universal program benefiting black Americans disproportionately, but helping out wage-earning and poor white Americans as well. A minority of civil-rights reformers in the early sixties, however, favored a more radical approach. James

Farmer, the leader of the Congress of Racial Equality (CORE) in the early 1960s, arguably has had far more influence on modern race relations in the United States than Martin Luther King, Jr., or Lyndon Johnson. The real origins of today's racial preference system must be sought not in the Birmingham bus boycott or the March on Washington, but in the Philadelphia boycotts organized by CORE in 1960–62. If today's establishment were honest, Martin Luther King Day would be James Farmer Day.

The racial preference system was first devised as an alternative, not to southern Jim Crow laws, but to institutionalized occupational discrimination in the North. CORE was founded to protest northern bigotry in 1942 at the University of Chicago. Under the influence of the Christian pacifist Fellowship of Reconciliation and the Gandhian radical A. J. Muste, Farmer and the other founders of CORE sponsored Freedom Rides to protest segregated bus transportation in the South as early as 1947. Fading in the 1950s, CORE revived when Farmer returned as national director in 1961. While CORE fought southern segregation with Freedom Rides and other tactics, in the North it increasingly relied on the boycott as a weapon to force racial quotas on particular targeted corporations. In the 1960–62 boycotts in Philadelphia, as a result of boycotts coordinated by almost four hundred black religious leaders, twenty-four corporations, including Pepsi-Cola, Esso, Gulf Oil, and Sun Oil, agreed to hire blacks in specific numbers. Completely committed to racial quotas by 1962, CORE disseminated the strategy of boycotts for quotas in New York, Boston, and Detroit. CORE itself was outflanked to the left by new groups drawing on inner-city black support, like a Harlem group led by a Baptist minister, Reverend Nelson Dukes, who in 1963 threatened New York City Mayor Robert Wagner that "the dikes will break" unless blacks got 25 percent of all jobs on city contracts.[11] The new executive director of the National Urban League, Whitney Young, Jr., proselytized for this philosophy; he called for "a decade of discrimination" in favor of blacks, through means including racial preferences in employment.[12]

Most mainstream civil rights leaders like Bayard Rustin and Martin Luther King, Jr. publicly opposed racial preferences. President Kennedy rejected the idea of racial quotas in employment: "We are too mixed, this society of ours, to begin to divide on the basis of race and color . . . I don't think quotas are a good idea. I think it is a mistake to begin to assign quotas on the basis of religion, or race, or color, or nationality. I think we'd get into a good deal of trouble."[13] Vice-President Lyndon Johnson agreed, explaining the subtle conservative effects of tokenism to Mexican-Americans in Los Angeles: "We are not going to solve this problem by promoting minorities. That philosophy is merely another way of freezing the minority group status system in perpetuity."[14]

Even as Kennedy and Johnson spoke, however, the executive branch was moving toward the modern racial preference system. Kennnedy's Executive Order 10925, which created the President's Commission on Equal Employment Opportunity (PCEEO), the predecessor to the EEOC, introduced the phrase "affirmative action," a vague term which could be (and eventually was) taken to mean hiring by the numbers to prove compliance. Even worse, racial labeling of citizens and employees—initially disfavored by civil rights reformers—had been revived by 1963 among federal agencies. Ominously, by June 1962 the PCEEO had devised census forms identifying government employees as Spanish-speaking Mexicans and Puerto Ricans, Oriental origin, and American Indian (only two years earlier these groups had been listed as "Other" in addition to white and Negro in compliance forms for federal contractors).[15]

Thus all of the elements of the modern racial preference system— government racial labeling and requirements for compliance in hiring nonwhites; radical black pressure groups, like CORE, threatening boycotts and picketing of companies that did not hire blacks in specified numbers; mainstream black leaders like Whitney Young, Jr., adopting the racial-preference agenda—were in place *before* the climax of the color-blind Civil Rights Revolution with the March on Washington in August 1963 and the passage of the 1964 Act.*

The change from color-blind civil rights to color-conscious racial preferences took place very quickly. In his Howard University commencement speech of June 4, 1965, President Johnson expressed the

---

*The drafters of the 1964 Act were well aware of the racial preference alternative that was being discussed in 1960–63, which explains why Section 703(j) of Title VII of the Civil Rights Act of 1964 expressly forbids racial quotas (under any name). Racial preference, in its familiar contemporary form, was considered by Congress and the mainstream civil rights leadership in the early 1960s—and rejected.

color-blind liberal vision by calling for "not just legal equity but human ability" to be promoted by jobs, housing, and "welfare and social programs better designed to hold families together." On August 5, he signed the Voting Rights Act. On August 11, the Watts riot broke out.

Watts was not the first of the new round of black riots, but it was the largest. By the time the National Guard restored order, 34 had died, 1,072 had been injured, there had been 4000 arrests, and almost a thousand buildings had been harmed or destroyed. The Watts riot was only one of many. Between 1964 and 1968, at least 257 cities suffered from 329 violent upheavals. In 1967 alone, there were 164 riots, several lasting for several days until the National Guard imposed peace.[16] The riots represented the greatest domestic violence in the United States since the Civil War and Reconstruction.

The Civil Rights Revolution, far from assuaging black discontent, seemed to have triggered its violent expression. Black nationalists like Stokely Carmichael of the Student Nonviolent Coordinating Committee (SNCC) and Floyd McKissick of CORE emerged and repudiated the older generation of integrationists, like Martin Luther King, Jr. The shift from individual to group rights—which in practice was already taking place, with CORE's boycotts-for-job quotas in the North—was rationalized by Stokely Carmichael and Charles Hamilton in their 1967 book *Black Power: The Politics of Liberation in America*.[17] "Black people have not suffered as individuals but as members of a group; therefore, their liberation lies in group action."[18] The conclusion, it should be noted, does not follow from the premise; eliminating antisemitic practices means treating Jews no differently from other citizens, not subsidizing Jewish organizations or instituting favorable quotas for Jews. Nevertheless, unconvincing though its logic might have been, the group-rights theory gave the left wing of the civil rights movement a new rationale for goals such as black control of institutions in black areas and race-based categorical representation: "where Negroes lack a majority, Black Power means proper representation and sharing of control."[19]

Though Martin Luther King denounced the phrase "black power" as "racism in reverse,"[20] white radicals and liberals soon followed Carmichael and other black power advocates in deserting the color-blind ideal. Many attacked gradualists like Moynihan as crypto-racists, singling out the theory (which few today dispute) that the behavioral characteristics of the black underclass, the "culture of poverty," constituted at least part of the problem. At the same time, the massive resistance of southern segregationists, rallying around figures like George Wallace, was causing federal judges to rethink the gradualist approach of *Brown;* desegregation "with all deliberate speed" was to be replaced by integration, *now.* Integrationist liberals found themselves under assault from black power separatists and white radicals on the left even as they were attacked from the right. There was an even greater problem with a gradualist approach to integration based on expanded universal social programs—the white majority was in no mood to support its costs. The war in Vietnam siphoned off money that might have gone into social programs, and white voters were unwilling to submit to taxes that would be spent on the black rioters, looters, and protesters they watched on TV (their discontent would be tapped briefly by George Wallace during his presidential campaign and for decades by Republican presidential candidates). In the view of many white liberals, something had to be done, to break white racist resistance and to assure black Americans that real steps to further their interests were being taken, and it had to be done immediately.

In these circumstances, the racial preference approach associated with CORE, considered and rejected a few years earlier, quickly became *the* mainstream liberal answer to the problems of blacks and other disadvantaged racial minorities. In 1970 an Equal Employment Opportunity Commission administrator, Alfred Blumrosen—who despite his relative obscurity is one of the major architects and theorists of today's racial preference system—expressed this repudiation of color-blind liberalism with surprising candor:

> If discrimination is narrowly defined, for example, by requiring an evil intent to injure minorities, then it will be difficult to find that it exists. If it does not exist, then the plight of racial and ethnic minorities must be attributable to some more generalized failures in society, in the fields of basic education, housing, family relations, and the like. The search for efforts to improve the condition of minorities must then focus in these general and difficult areas, and the answers can come only gradually as basic institutions, attitudes, customs, and practices are changed.[21]

The solution, for Blumrosen and other left-liberal bureaucrats and judges, was to redefine discrimination to mean disparity, to permit the government, "by intelligent, effective, and aggressive legal action," to assign positions in schools, factories, offices, and government on the basis of racial proportions in the population at large. In this way, the federal government assumed the task of pressuring businesses from the activists of CORE and similar groups. The new federal policy of promoting categorical representation by race showed quick results in the private sector.* Public-sector employers and colleges, threatened by government action, also rapidly increased the statistical representation of blacks and Hispanics in their ranks.

Constant pressure for the extension of affirmative action came from the institutionalized civil rights lobby, which now formed one leg of an iron triangle, with the other two being the federal courts and certain federal agencies.† The EEOC, the major promoter of the new nonwhite racial preference system, itself became a leading patronage employer of nonwhites in the government.‡ The racial preference revolution was

---

*Under threat of federal litigation, the American Telephone and Telegraph Company increased the number of minority managers from 4.6 percent to 13.1 percent between 1973 and 1982. Black employees at IBM, only 750 in 1960, increased to 16,546 in 1980 (Stephen Steinberg, *The Ethnic Myth: Race, Ethnicity, and Class in America*, Boston: Beacon Press, 1989, p. 294).

†These included the Civil Rights Commission; the Equal Opportunity Employment Commission (EEOC); The Labor Department's Office of Federal Contract Compliance Programs (OFFC); Office of Minority Business Enterprise (OMBE); and civil rights offices within federal agencies like Justice, HEW, HUD, and Defense. According to Hugh Davis Graham, the civil rights lobby has created a new kind of "iron triangle." Instead of an iron triangle of interest group-federal agency-Congressional committee, they fashioned one of interest group-federal agency-courts, for a very simple reason: "minority groups seeking to displace non-minorities from jobs according to a controversial model of proportional representation, and doing so through a network of bureaucratic intrusion backed by federal coercion, could count on stiff opposition from congressional conservatives . . ." (Hugh Davis Graham, *The Civil Rights Era*, New York: Oxford University Press, 1990, p. 365.)

‡Between 1966 and 1980 its budget grew from $2.3 million to $125 million, and its staff increased from 314 to 3,746. In 1971, blacks, who represented only 12 percent of the U.S. workforce and only 15 percent of the federal civilian workforce, made up 49 percent of the EEOC staff (in 1978 the proportion was 49.1 percent), while white males, at 20.6 percent, were present in proportions far below their proportion of the workforce. The EEOC rationalized this evident "disparity" by explaining in 1975 that it was exempt from the rules it applied to other government agencies and the private sector; its situation was "rather unique in that women and most minority groups hold a larger share of the jobs than labor force figures might deem appropriate." (Hugh Davis Graham, supra, pp. 459–60.)

Ironically, in part as a result of the segregation of the private sector, by the 1960s blacks were al-

carried further by the federal judiciary. The Supreme Court, in its decision in *Green v. County School Board* (1968), transformed the imperative
of desegregation into one of integration; in *Swann v. Charlotte-Mecklenburg Board of Education* (1971), the first busing case, the Supreme Court
held that the assignment of students by race—though clearly proscribed
by the Civil Rights Act of 1964—was a legitimate "remedy" for past discrimination.[22] In a series of cases in the 1970s and 1980s, the Supreme
Court upheld racial discrimination against whites as long as nonwhites
could be shown to benefit, invoking the "remedy" rationale.*

Black proponents of quotas found their most effective allies in affluent
white judges and legal scholars. In 1968 Archibald Cox, then a professor
at Harvard Law School, published *Constitutional Decision as an Instrument
of Reform*, an elaborate justification of liberal judicial activism arguing
that "to escape the dead hand of the past," the Court needed "a new and
grander conception of its place in the constitutional scheme."[23] Yale Law
scholar Alexander Bickel argued against this idea in *The Supreme Court
and the Idea of Progress* (1970), but Cox's view prevailed. Richard Neely,
Chief Justice of the West Virginia Supreme Court, has been astonishingly
frank in expressing the view that elite judges should be allowed to impose
their views of racial justice on the unenlightened majority, on the
grounds that upper-class whites know better than lower-class whites:

> Certainly a majority of the educated elite, as reflected by the attitudes of
> the faculties, trustees, and student bodies at major universities, consider

---

ready overrepresented in the federal workforce. In the spring of 1962, blacks, who made up only
10.5 percent of the U.S. population in 1960, accounted for 13 percent of the federal civilian workforce, though usually at lower levels. In particular agencies their overrepresentation was even
greater: the Post Office (17 percent), Labor (18 percent), HEW (20 percent), the Veterans Administration (23 percent) and a striking 34 percent in the General Services Administration (GSA). By
the logic of categorical representation, their numbers should have been limited in favor of whites.
(Hugh Davis Graham, ibid., p. 61.)

Griggs v. Duke Power Co., 401 U.S. 424 (1971) (ordinary employment criteria can be struck down,
if they disproportionately disqualify blacks); *Regents of the University of California v. Bakke*, 438 U.S.
265 (1978) (The Civil Rights Act's Title VI prohibition of racial discrimination by federally funded
institutions does not apply to discrimination against whites); *United Steelworkers v. Weber*, 446 U.S.
193 (1979) (the prohibition of discrimination against "any individual" in Title VII of the Civil
Rights Act does not include whites); *United States v. Paradise*, 480 U.S. 149 (1987) (state institutions do not violate the Constitution if they discriminate against white citizens in employment).

affirmative action, although predatory, morally justifiable. It is just as certain, however, that a majority of Americans disapprove. There is no theoretical justification for continued support of affirmative action other than the elitist one that the courts know from their superior education that affirmative action is necessary in the short run to achieve the generally applauded moral end of equal opportunity in the long run. That is probably not illegitimate, since judges are social science specialists and have available to them more information and have pursued the issue with more thought and diligence than the man in the street. Courts should probably be accorded as much deference in their decisions over means as medical doctors, professional architects, or plumbers.[24]

Guided by theories like these, federal courts, in the name of combating discrimination and under the color of constitutional imperatives or federal statutes, quickly assumed entire areas of government from the states. Federal judges imposed busing plans, redrew political districts, assumed control of prisons. The Second Radical Reconstruction, with federal judges and federal bureaucrats taking the place of federal military governors, had begun. It has not ended yet.

In a prophetic speech to the graduating class of the New School for Social Research in 1968, Daniel Patrick Moynihan warned against the adoption of racial and ethnic quotas: "Once this process gets legitimated there is no stopping it."[25]

Moynihan was right. As with other government entitlements, racial preference has been rapidly expanded by entrepreneurial politicians eager to win electoral rewards by making new groups eligible for benefits. The extension of the racial preference system, originally designed for black Americans, to American Indians and Asian-Americans was not surprising—these two groups had suffered from regimes of legal discrimination identical in many respects to Jim Crow. A turning point in the evolution of racial preference, however, came with the inclusion of so-called Hispanics.

In every national census (except 1930) before the 1970s, Americans of Latin American descent were defined as white (even if they were mestizos or more or less full-blooded Latin American Indians) and many if not most Mexican-Americans thought of themselves as a white ethnic group.[26] There had never been *de jure* segregation and disfranchisement of Mexican-Americans, as there had been of Indians, blacks, and Asians or "Orientals." The social and economic discrimination suffered by Hispanics in the Southwest, while serious, was more like the experience of the Irish than that of blacks or Asians. Unlike those minorities, Mexican-Americans were never formally segregated in education and public accommodations, denied the right to vote or serve on juries or become naturalized citizens; even in racially segregated Texas, Hispanics of almost completely Mexican Indian descent were treated under the law as white.

In order to participate in the racial preference spoils system, however, Mexican-Americans, Puerto Ricans, and other immigrant communities had to be redefined as members of a race comparable to blacks. To this end, the Hispanic category was promulgated by the Mexican-American Legal Defense and Education Fund (MALDEF) and its allies in the Democratic party and civil rights establishment in the 1960s and 1970s. The pseudo-race of Hispanics now includes people of predominantly European, Latin mestizo, black, and American Indian descent; people who speak Spanish, and people whose families have not spoken it for generations; recent immigrants from Spanish-speaking countries and descendants of long-assimilated *Californios* and *Tejanos;* Catholics, Protestants, Jews, atheists, and practitioners of the Caribbean religion of Santeria.

The next step, some argued in the late sixties and early seventies, was to extend the rapidly growing racial preference entitlement program to include so-called white ethnics, the descendants of the eastern and southern European new immigrants of the turn of the century: Italian-Americans, Polish-Americans, Greek-Americans, Jewish-Americans with Central European antecedents. Racial preference for white ethnics (subdivided into Celtics, Slavics and Mediterraneans) is no more preposterous an idea than racial preference for Hispanics. After all, in the old days the Naturalization Service had classified Mexicans and Poles, Filipinos and Hungarians alike as "races."[27]

The white ethnics lost their battle to be included in the growing racial preference system—but white women *were* included. Gender quotas have, in effect, and with absurd results, extended the racial preference system to women, a numerical majority of the U.S. population, and of every social class. For purposes of affirmative action, women are treat-ed as the fifth minority race after blacks, Hispanics, Asians, and Ameri-can Indians. That black Americans, when they got a chance, created their own spoils system, is not surprising; most ethnic and racial groups in the United States have tried to do that. What *is* surprising is the lack of black protest at the enlargement of affirmative action to benefit the women of the white overclass. The old Irish- and Italian-American boss-es, one is inclined to think, would have put up a fight, if Mrs. Astor had demanded a plum position in Tammany Hall on the grounds that she was oppressed by the likes of Mr. Astor.

The repudiation of working-class and middle-class white ethnics in favor of white overclass feminists by the civil rights leadership symbolized the death of the New Deal coalition between blacks and white ethnics, and the cementing of the New Politics coalition between a preference-based black overclass and the white overclass. Since then, the black overclass has tended to be allied with (and dependent upon) upper-in-come white liberals, largely mainline Protestant and Jewish, against mid-dle-income white Catholics and white evangelical Protestants.

It is worth pausing for a moment, to consider whether an alternative civil rights strategy was possible—namely, a re-creation of the New Deal coalition, in the form of a coalition of the black and white middle classes *against* the white overclass, instead of the coalition between the affluent white overclass and the new black overclass—"women and minorities"—that actually emerged. Could such a transracial coalition have emerged? Could it have supported the color-blind program of social democratic re-form that King and Rustin and Humphrey and Johnson saw as the suc-cessor to the Civil Rights Revolution? In this scenario, black leaders would have been accommodated in politics and business informally, as Irish- and Italian- and Jewish-Americans had been previously, without any formalized racial preference policies.

Perhaps the entrenched racism of working-class and middle-class whites and their leaders would have doomed such a strategy. From the South, however, comes interesting evidence to the contrary. After he re-pudiated white supremacy, George Wallace built a biracial white-black coalition that defeated white conservative Republicanism. Black voters saw Wallace as the lesser of two evils, particularly because of the governor's populist economic views (Wallace, considerably to the left of main-stream Democrats in this area, wanted to tax the churches to pay for programs for working-class Americans).

Of the many ironies of race relations in the United States, not the least is that the last major practitioner of biracial liberal populism may have been George Wallace.

THE FIVE NATIONS OF MULTICULTURAL AMERICA

Like its predecessors Euro-America and Anglo-America, the Multicul-tural American Republic has its own threefold definition of American-ness, consisting of a conception of national community, a common ethic, and a political creed. Instead of a single national community, there are five, corresponding to the five official races: white, black, His-panic, Asian, and American Indian. The common ethic—a generalized Protestantism in Anglo-America, a generalized Christianity in Euro-America—has been replaced, in Multicultural America, with an ethic of authenticity, a secular ethic endorsing conformity to one's official race-culture. The Euro-American political creed of federal democracy has been replaced by a new political creed of multicultural democracy, a new sort of federalism in which race rights take the place of states' rights.

THE FIVE OFFICIAL RACES. The redefinition of American identity begins with the idea of the five official races or American "nationalities" recog-nized by the federal government and major private institutions like col-leges and foundations. David A. Hollinger has called this "the new American ethno-racial pentagon."[28]

Why five? Why not twelve? Or twenty? Liberal Democrats, busily adding new groups to the spoils system in the late sixties and early sev-enties—Pacific Islanders here, women there—gave little thought to the exact number of "victim groups" that would ultimately be included. It was left to federal bureaucrats to try to impose some kind of conceptual order on the proliferating categories of minorities eligible for quotas and subsidies.

Very few Americans have heard of O.M.B. Statistical Directive 15, but it is just as important in modern American life as the Constitution and the Bill of Rights—perhaps more important, now that the latter have been reduced to mere occasions for unprincipled judicial lawmaking. Statistical Directive 15 is part of the secret history of the racial preference revolution, a history that runs not from Birmingham to the Supreme Court, but from CORE in the Northeast to the Office of Management and Budget; a history in which little-known individuals like James Farmer and Alfred Blumrosen are more important figures than Martin Luther King and Lyndon Johnson. The story begins in 1973, when Secretary of Health, Education, and Welfare Caspar Weinberger asked the Federal Interagency Committee on Education (FICE) to develop consistent rules for classifying Americans by ethnicity and race (liberals, having earlier favored the abolition of racial labeling, now promoted it in order to facilitate the imposition of quotas). The FICE came up with five races: American Indian or Alaskan Native; Asian or Pacific Islander; Black; White; and Hispanic. The O.M.B. moved the category of people from the Indian subcontinent from the White category, where they had been assigned by the FICE, to the Asian and Pacific Islander (thus permitting high-caste Hindus to qualify for racial preference).* Then they adopted the FICE five-race schema as its own, in Statistical Directive 15.[29]

The formal division of Americans into five races, then, resulted from the collision of the desire of liberal Democrats to indefinitely expand the racial preference patronage system with the desire of federal bureaucrats for a few relatively broad categories. Since the racial categories reflect political and bureaucratic imperatives, not cultural realities, there might just as well be three official races in America—Eurasian-American, African-American, American Indian/Mestizo—or eight: American Indian, Mestizo, Black, Indo-European, Turko-Arabic, Malay, Mongoloid, Mulatto. It is really that arbitrary.

Today officially designated nonwhites (a category that in practice includes English-speaking white Americans with a Spanish surname who know no Spanish) benefit from a variety of formal legal privileges, including the right to be admitted to public and private schools with dra-

---

*Asian Indians exulted in 1910 and 1913, when the Supreme Court declared that they were white citizens eligible for U.S. citizenship under the 1790 naturalization act—and despaired when the Court changed its mind in 1923 and decided that, because the Founding Fathers would not have considered the Indians white, they were ineligible for naturalization. (*U.S. v. Balshara*, 1910; *Ajkoy Kumar Mazumdar*, 1913; *U.S. v. Bhagat Singh Thind*, 1923).

matically lower scores than people labeled as whites, the right to a congressman of their group from a racially gerrymandered district, and the right to certain government contracts. The rationale is that four of the five official races have allegedly been comparably and uniformly oppressed by the fifth, the non-Hispanic white. In the words of the report on a "Curriculum of Inclusion" by the New York State Board of Regents, "African Americans, Asian Americans, Puerto Ricans/Latinos and Native Americans have all been victims of an intellectual and educational oppression that has characterized the culture and institutions of the United States and the European American world for centuries."[30] Non-Hispanic whites are, for purposes of law, second-class citizens in the contemporary United States. Not only do non-Hispanic whites have no special legal privileges as a group, but overt discrimination against them, by government agencies and private institutions, is permitted by the federal government—indeed, it is required under many circumstances by numerous laws, regulations, and judicial rulings. As Justice Brennan observed in his concurrence in *United Jewish Organizations v. Carey*, federal law recognizes "the permissibility of affording preferential treatment to disadvantaged nonwhites generally"—the fiction being that entire races are economically disadvantaged, and not merely low-income individuals.

As this suggests, racial identification in Multicultural America is not a mere anthropological quiddity, because how one is classified has important legal and material consequences. Whereas in the past nonwhites hoped to pass as whites to receive a privileged position in American society, today many whites try to take advantage of racial preferences by claiming a black or American Indian or Hispanic ancestor. In San Francisco, where a federal court has imposed quotas limiting the number of whites who may enroll in the best public schools, white children have begun describing themselves as black, Hispanic or Asian on their enrollment forms.[31] In 1988, twin brothers Philip J. Malone and Paul J. Malone were fired by the Boston fire department. They were charged with having lied, by stating on their job applications that they were black. The Malones, both blond and blue-eyed, claimed that their great-grandmother had been black.[32] The Malones might well have qualified as black, under the Jim Crow laws that defined Adolph Plessy—who was seven-eighths white—as legally "black."

This case speaks volumes about the present American regime. Any system of official racial classification inevitably requires complex and crude rules of decision—is the child of a black father and a white mother white or black, for affirmative action purposes? Should old-time southern state constitutions be ransacked, for official definitions of negritude and whiteness? Should we adopt the "one drop" theory, or the "one-quarter" theory? Rules for race classification are very old; in 1662, Virginia passed a statute defining that the child of a white man and a black woman would be legally considered black. But all rules must be interpreted by some authority. In colonial Brazil, it was possible for blacks and mulattoes to purchase "certificates of whiteness" from the imperial government. In the South before the civil rights revolution, all-white juries sometimes decided whether someone who claimed to be white really was. In contemporary Los Angeles, in some cases, "ethnic committees" decide. When, as a result of a new race-based school assignment policy, teachers in Los Angeles began to claim they were of different races to avoid reassignment, the Los Angeles board of education established five-member ethnic review committees to hear claims. Two members of the committee had to be from the ethnic background that the teacher claimed as his or her own. Whether one was white, or black, or Hispanic, or Asian, for purposes of school district policy, was decided by a vote.[33] (This ceding of racial-classification authority to ethnic groups also has historical precedents. In 1885, Croatan Indians in Robeson County, North Carolina, seeking to expel people of mixed Indian and black ancestry from their ranks, succeeded in winning the legal right to determine who was and was not a Croatan.)[34]

In the 1980s, white policemen in New York, being passed over for promotion as a result of affirmative action, sought to be reclassified as blacks or Hispanics. Why not? In the Old South, people sometimes sued to establish that they had been misclassified as black instead of white—and some won, with all that meant in terms of legal privileges. Why not try to "pass" for black, if that makes promotion easier? According to George Sanchez, the police commissioner for equal opportunity, "the cops can qualify by proving that either one parent, two grandparents or four great-grandparents were black or born in a Spanish-speaking country. . . ."[35]

What about orphans whose parentage is unknown? Until the mid-seventies, the New York Foundling Hospital, as part of its policy of plac-ing orphans with families of their race, often sent abandoned children of indeterminate background to the Museum of Natural History where an-thropologists—in a chilling echo of Nazi racial pseudoscience—would try to determine their racial origins by examining their skin color, facial characteristics, and skull dimensions.[36]

Today black activists have replaced white supremacists as the advo-cates of same-race adoption. For the purposes of the Minnesota Minori-ty Heritage Protection Act, a statute passed in the 1980s that mandates same-race adoption, a child who is 90 percent white and 10 percent black is *legally* "black."[37] This same-race adoption policy can be inhu-mane in its application: in Texas recently, a black 3-year-old was forcibly removed from the home of his white foster parents when they filed a re-quest to adopt him: "A black social worker carried him off while he screamed "Mommy, Mommy" at his tearful foster mother."[38]

Where there is a conflict between subjective self-identification and government race-labeling, the latter prevails. Even people who want to identify themselves as members of the majority are sometimes labeled as minority-group members by the government. New York City was forced in the early 1980s to redraw its city council districts in order to create Hispanic districts. Forty percent of New York's Hispanic (mostly Puerto Rican) population described itself as white in answering the census. Whether the "65 percent" rule mandating majority-minority reappor-tionment was triggered or not depended on whether the self-classifica-tion of many Puerto Ricans as whites or the government's classification of all Puerto Ricans as Hispanics prevailed. The government's definition of Puerto Ricans as members of a Hispanic race or quasi-race prevailed over the subjective self-definition of many Puerto Ricans as a white im-migrant group, like Italians or Poles.[39]

THE IDEAL OF AUTHENTICITY. The redefinition of America as a multicul-tural democracy rather than a democratic nation-state has been accom-panied by a change in the common ethic from a generalized, Prot-estant-inspired Christianity to a secular ideal of authenticity. It might be thought that an ideal of authenticity might lead to an individualism sub-versive of the bureaucratic categories of Multicultural America, but this is not the case. To be authentic, in Multicultural America, means to conform to the standards of one of the five official races of Statistical Directive 15.

Most people have various identities—national, ethnic, religious, partisan—many of which conflict: think of conservative Catholics disapproving of their church's stand on nuclear weapons, or black liberals opposed to affirmative action. The ideal of authenticity seeks to eliminate such conflicts, by positing the identity of your true self and your official subculture. To find yourself, you need only find your ghetto, and adopt its politics, its style of dress, and its approved beliefs about the world and humanity. Having done so, you can then demand that society at large recognize your individuality—that is to say, your abject conformity.

In older western ethics, if a person was virtuous, the community was obliged to respond with manifestations of honor. In Multicultural America, personal authenticity is supposed to evoke public recognition of dignity. Instead of striving toward virtue through self-denial, the authentic American strives toward self-esteem through self-acceptance; and the moral community, instead of encouraging self-denial and self-transformation, should encourage that easy self-acceptance. In an honor-society, failure of others to honor one's status or virtue might lead to a duel or a feud; in the esteem-society of Multicultural America, failure to treat a person of a particular status with dignity might lead to a lawsuit.

What is this self that must be accepted? It is not the achieved self, the constructed self, of classical ethics (Greek, biblical, Confucian); rather, it is the raw self *before* improvement (or disfigurement), before education, the basic biological self, constituted by genetic ancestry, sex, temperament. These are treated, not as accidental impediments to participation in a transracial, transgender, transhistorical community, but as the defining characteristics of the self.

The ideal of authenticity, then, is profoundly reductionist—to be oneself is to be determined by biology. Even this is ambiguous—if one already *is* black, female, gay, how does one act to express self-acceptance? The answer is, through conformity to this or that subculture. Those who reject the norms of the subculture—though they are just as black, female, or gay—are not authentic.

Those conservatives who see an upwelling of radical individualism in today's identity politics are therefore mistaken. Identity politics is meekest conformity, masquerading as anarchic rebellion. It is subculture collectivism, rather than society-wide collectivism, but just as anti-individualist. Far from being radically postmodern, identity politics is reminiscent of premodern feudal orders of status. Instead of a hierarchical ranking of races and genders, there is a horizontal distribution of separate-but-equal "cultures"; with that difference, the ideal of authenticity is a society as rigidly defined by race and gender as in the caste societies of the past.

The conformist pressures arising from the ideal of authenticity are hinted at in remarks by black legal theorist Lani Guinier. According to Guinier, it is not enough for a black American politician to have African ancestors:

> Authenticity refers to community-based and culturally rooted leadership. . . . Authentic black leadership is electorally supported by a majority of black voters and is, at its best, culturally similar to its constituency base. Thus, authenticity subsumes two separate concepts, the political and the cultural. Black representatives are authentic because they are elected by blacks and because they are descriptively similar to their constituents. In other words, they are politically, psychologically, and culturally black.[40]

To be a good, that is, authentic, person in Multicultural America, then, is to conform "politically, psychologically, and culturally" to the official culture of one's official race, that is, one of the five races defined by Statistical Directive 15. Once a race has been invented by bureaucratic fiat, inventing a culture to correspond to it is relatively easy. Joane Nagel has argued that governments not only recognize but sometimes actually create "new ethnic groups out of extant . . . unorganized ethnocultural categories."[41] The federal government, as I have shown, created the Hispanic and Asian and Pacific Islander groups, which do not correspond to any self-conscious ethnic or racial populations in the real world. Or at least did not until recently. One study of Hispanic activism in Chicago revealed that affirmative action for Hispanics actually encouraged the growth of Latino identities and Latino political organization.[42]

At the University of California at Berkeley, students are required to take a comparative course focusing on three of five American groups: African-Americans, Latinos, Asian-Americans, Native Americans, and

European Americans. These groups, needless to say, are those first officially defined by Statistical Directive 15. In manufacturing traditions and histories to correspond to these categories, would-be radical intellectuals are acting, in effect, as collaborators with federal bureaucrats.[43]

Even the official or authentic black American culture is as much the product of invention and marketing as of genuine folk tradition. Jesse Jackson's feat in persuading the press to substitute "African-American" for "black American" represents the best-known such attempt to ethnicize what remain bureaucratic racial categories. Jesse Jackson has explained his reasons for wanting to substitute the term "African-American" for "black" (itself a term adopted at the insistence of black militants in the sixties):

> To be called African-Americans has cultural integrity. It puts us in our proper historical context. Every ethnic group in this country has a reference to some land base, some historical cultural base. . . . There are Armenian-Americans and Jewish-Americans and Arab-Americans and Italian-Americans; and with a degree of accepted and reasonable pride, they connect their heritage to their mother country and where they are now.[44]

Michael Novak, who championed white ethnicity in the sixties, approves: "Positively one must applaud the shift represented by the usage 'African-American' instead of 'black American'—a shift from race to ethnicity; in effect, from genetic appearance to cultural difference."[45] The term "African-American" suggests "Italian-American" or "Polish-American"—but the suggestion is misleading. To begin with, black Americans are *not* "African-Americans"—what "cultural difference" divides them from the white American majority has very little to do with Africa. Almost all of the West African culture of American blacks was lost centuries ago; enslavement was accompanied by deculturation. What survives—certain intonations and kinds of body language, music, a few words like "cat" for "man" (from a West African root)—is a minor ingredient in a unique black American culture that exists only in the United States.

Given the absence of a surviving African culture in the United States, some black American intellectuals have simply made one up. The African-American holiday Kwanzaa (from a Swahili word for "first fruits of the harvest") is a seven-day celebration from December 26 to January 1. Each day is dedicated to a different principle supposedly derived from traditional African communal life—unity, self-determination, responsibility, cooperative economics, purpose, creativity, and faith. This purportedly African holiday, which has been taken up by ever more black Americans in recent years, was created in 1965 by Maulana Karenga, the chairman of the black studies department at California State University, Long Beach, and head of Us, a black nationalist group. Karenga's holiday was obscure, until the New York Urban Coalition persuaded the New York Museum of Natural History in 1979 to begin an annual celebration.[46]

The problem with redefining black Americans as an immigrant ethnic group, like Italian-Americans, is that there is no African nationality to which the prefix in African-American can correspond. The very idea of an African identity is something constructed by people outside of Africa. Molefi Kete Asante, one of the leading theorists of Afrocentrism, concedes this: "By 'African' I mean clearly a 'composite African' not a specific discrete African orientation which would rather mean ethnic identification, i.e., Yoruba, Zulu, Nuba, etc."[47] Composite Africans nowhere exist, any more than composite Europeans or Hispanics. Real Europeans are Greek, or German, or Czech; real Hispanics think of themselves not as generic Hispanics, but as Mexicans or Puerto Ricans or Cubans or Chileans; and real West Africans do not think that they, the ancient Egyptians, and English-speaking, Protestant western hemisphere mulattoes are one and the same people.

Suppose that the federal government created a category of citizens of eastern European descent called Slavics, and made them eligible for affirmative action benefits. Soon, one can confidently predict, many Americans of partial Polish, Russian, Czech or Romanian descent would discover their common Slavic identity, and apply for favorable treatment in college admissions, minority set-asides, and so on. Before long, no doubt, there would be "Slavic Studies Departments" at major colleges and universities, where intellectuals would debate the exact elements of the "Slavic" culture common to Catholic Poles, Orthodox Russians and Protestant Hungarians. There might even be a Slavic Caucus in the House of Representatives, many of whose members were chiefly Irish or German and only slightly Slavic in descent. As night follows day, so would a renaissance of Slavic ethnicity follow the disbursal of government favors to Slavs.*

MULTICULTURAL DEMOCRACY. Like the previous American republics, the Third Republic of the United States has its own political ideal. The third element of the Multinational American synthesis, after the definition of the American community as a collection of racial nations, and the redefinition of the common ethic as the ethic of authenticity, is a new political creed: multicultural democracy.

The political ideal of Anglo-America was federal republicanism; of Euro-America, federal democracy. In Multicultural America, the political ideal is multicultural democracy. The divisions that count are not sectional divisions, but racial divisions—white and black neighbors, anywhere in the country, are thought to have more in common with other members of their races elsewhere than with each other. In theory, such a conception should lead to the scrapping of federalism altogether, in favor of nationwide elections to a single house, in which each race is separately represented, according either to relative numbers or the concurrent-majority principle of equal voting for numerically unequal races.† In practice, the architects of Multicultural America have had to be content with promoting their design within the basic limits imposed by the 1787 federal Constitution.

The major way that multicultural liberals have promoted this new conception of the United States as a multicultural democracy has been by reviving the old curse of racial gerrymandering in a new form. Section 5 of the Voting Rights Act of 1965, intended to guarantee black access to the polls, has been interpreted by the Supreme Court and successive Justice Departments as mandating the reconstruction of state and local

---

*"Because the government uses these artificial categories as units in allocating political and economic resources," Rita Jalali and Seymour Martin Lipset have observed, "over time such diverse groups begin to act collectively as they see themselves sharing common interests and experiences of oppression and also benefits." See Rita Jalali and Seymour Martin Lipset, "Racial and Ethnic Conflicts: A Global Perspective," *Political Science Quarterly*, vol. 107, no. 4 (Winter 1992–93), p. 599. See also William Petersen, "Politics and the Measurement of Ethnicity" in William Alonso and Paul Starr, eds., *The Politics of Numbers* (New York: Russell Sage Foundation, 1986), pp. 187–234.

†Lani Guinier has advocated something like the latter, in the process, ironically, reinventing the theories of John C. Calhoun, the philosopher of the southern planter class.

districts and electoral mechanisms to ensure that racial minorities will elect candidates of their races. The 1975 amendments to the Act have extended gerrymandering in the interests of ethnic categorical representation to linguistic minorities such as Mexican-Americans and Asian-Americans.

After the 1990 census, legislative redistricting along racial lines resulted in an increase of black-majority districts from seventeen to thirty-two. The number of Hispanic-majority congressional districts also more than doubled, from nine to twenty. In one new district in Houston gerrymandered to encourage the election of a Hispanic member of Congress, Hispanics represented 55.4 percent of the voters, compared to 10 percent blacks. In a court-ordered second runoff in the Democratic primary in July, however, a white Democrat, State Senator Gene Green, again defeated Houston's first elected Hispanic city council member, Ben Reyes. In his concession speech, Reyes warned, "You've not heard the last from us . . . This seat belongs to our community."[48]

In 1987 Mikhail Gorbachev suggested to visiting U.S. Congressmen that the United States, to be truly pluralistic, should establish autonomous regions for its racial and religious minorities. Representative Les Aspin (D-Wisconsin) rejoined that the concept of group rights was alien to the United States.[49] Around the time of this exchange, an organization of black professionals was trying to turn the largely black Boston neighborhood of Roxbury into an autonomous city named Mandela after the black South African leader.[50] The effort failed, but three years after Gorbachev's suggestion, congressional district lines were radically redrawn across the country to create artificial "majority-minority" districts and ensure the election of blacks and Hispanics. In 1992, Congressman Aspin would be appointed Secretary of Defense by president-elect Bill Clinton, whose cabinet reflected a careful balancing of rich people from various racial and gender groups. By that time, the Soviet Union was gone; but Soviet-style minority regions and group rights were flourishing in the United States.

Radical as the differences are between the old discrimination and the new, the centrality of one's race, for official purposes, remains the same. The primacy that is accorded to race over culture—that is, over *real* ethnicity—in the politics of Multicultural America was made clear in a

1977 Supreme Court case, *United Jewish Organizations v. Carey.*[51] In 1970, Brooklyn and Manhattan were brought under the coverage of the Voting Rights Act because a judge decided that New York's failure to provide Spanish-language ballots constituted a prohibited literacy test. As a result, New York had to submit its 1970 reapportionment plan to the Justice Department for approval. The Nixon Justice Department pressured New York officials to create Brooklyn state senate and assembly districts with nonwhite majorities of at least 65 percent (Hispanics being defined as nonwhites). Part of the concentrated, 30,000-member Hasidic Jewish community of the Williamsburgh neighborhood, already in a 61 percent nonwhite district, was transferred to a neighboring district in order to increase the nonwhite majorities in both districts.

The Hasidim sued, claiming that their rights had been violated. The Supreme Court dismissed the argument that cultural differences among whites should be respected: "nothing (in the Voting Rights Act as amended) . . . indicates that Hasidic Jews or persons of Irish, Polish, or Italian descent are within the scope of the special protections defined by the Congress in the Voting Rights Act." At any rate, the Court observed, whites elsewhere in Brooklyn were in the majority; presumably the abstract interests of Hasidim as whites (if such interests exist) were more fundamental than their interests as Hasidic Jews. After all, Hasidim and Italian-American Catholics are part of the same racial community, according to Statistical Directive 15.

MASS IMMIGRATION AND DIVERSITY

By the 1990s, a new rationale for reverse discrimination was desperately needed. Racial preferences showed every sign of becoming permanent. Many members of several generations of blacks and Hispanics now owed their educations and jobs wholly or in part to affirmative action. A number of members of Congress and elected officials in state legislatures and city councils owed their seats to court-ordered racial gerrymandering. The civil rights establishment, which had drifted after the achievement of its earlier goal of desegregation, had reorganized itself into a permanent lobby for black and Hispanic privileges. If racial preference were to be permanent in the United States, as the new black and Hispanic overclasses wanted it to be, then the system needed to be presented, not as a temporary, necessary evil, but as a good in itself, even in the absence of past or present discrimination.

Responding to this crisis, a number of left-liberal legal theorists have attempted to read racial and gender preferences into the Constitution or traditional Lockean liberal political theory. In his influential 1976 article, "Groups and the Equal Protection Clause," Owen Fiss, a professor at Yale Law School, reinterpreted the Fourteenth Amendment's equal protection clause not only to permit, but to *mandate*, the promulgation of group rights at the expense of individual rights in America. In somewhat mystical language, Fiss, with women as well as black Americans in mind, explains that "the group has a distinct existence apart from its members."[52] Ronald Dworkin has argued that discrimination against members of a generally favored majority is permissible, as discrimination against members of a generally favored minority never is (ignoring the question entirely of whether the majority-group individual discriminated against is in fact favored as an *individual* vis-a-vis others in society).[53] In *The Constitutional Logic of Affirmative Action*, published posthumously in 1992, the late Ronald J. Fiscus, a professor of political science at Skidmore, attempted to root racial preferences in something like the Lockean-liberal social-contract or state-of-nature theory. If we assume all people to be equal at birth, and assume that in an egalitarian society opportunity would be equal to all people, then in a society free from discrimination opportunities would be distributed precisely in proportion to racial and sexual proportions in the population. The application of this reasoning, according to Fiscus, "means that white males who are disadvantaged by affirmative action programs, and who are ostensibly being discriminated against because of their race and/or gender, are in most cases not being treated unfairly at all—not, that is, being discriminated against at all."[54] None of these liberal theories has prevailed.

Instead, the dominant new rationale is multiculturalism, or the ideal of *diversity*—the assumption that the coexistence of different nationalities in a single American state is an inherent good, even in the absence of historic racial discrimination. The United States, formerly a white tribal state, will now be a multitribal state. The more tribes, the better.

From praising cultural diversity, that is, *racial* diversity (since culture equals race in Multicultural America's corrupted vocabulary) as a good in itself, it is only a small step to rationalizing the present racial preference system as a *means* of *promoting* diversity. This new diversitarian basis for the older racial quota system has recently been given a blessing by the Supreme Court. In its 1990 opinion in the case of *Metro Broadcasting, Inc., v. Federal Communications Commission*, Justice Brennan, writing for the majority, upheld race preferences by Congress that were adopted solely to promote diversity, in the absence of any showing of past discrimination. The Court's approval of government discrimination against whites in the name of diversity frees the ideologues of Multicultural America from the increasingly burdensome necessity to rationalize the multicultural program as a remedy for discrimination. The existing set of nonwhite preferences can now be forthrightly defended by appeal to their tendency to promote racial and cultural diversity, as something desirable on its own.

The diversity rationale, then, permits black Americans to argue for racial preference as a permanent system, not a temporary measure used in the immediate aftermath of segregation. "Diversity" has another benefit: it justifies the permanent extension of racial preference privileges to Latin American, Asian, and African immigrants, whether or not their own ancestors actually suffered any harm from segregation in the United States in the past.

As a proportion of the U.S. population, the groups eligible for racial preference benefits are rapidly growing, thanks to mass immigration from Latin America and Asia. As a result of large-scale immigration, Hispanics will probably surpass black Americans in the next generation as the nation's largest officially designated minority—and the largest beneficiary of racial preference patronage.

Like the racial preference system, today's policy of legal mass immigration emerged from the Civil Rights Revolution as an unintended consequence of what was intended to be a modest reform. The Cold War motivation behind the original reform in each case was the same. The national-origins system established in the 1920s had been crumbling for some time. By the mid-sixties, two thirds of the immigrants to America were already exempted from national-quota exemptions, as reunited family members, refugees, or beneficiaries of special legislation.[55] Nevertheless, the national-origins system still seemed offensively racist—more than 70 percent of the visas were allocated to England, Ireland, and Germany, with less than 2 percent going to Asia and 1 percent to Africa.[56] Secretary of State Dean Rusk argued for abolishing the racist immigration law because it undermined America's policy of offering nonwhite Third World nations an alternative to communism: "The biggest single burden that we carry on our backs in our foreign relations in the 1960s is the problem of racial discrimination."[57] The connection between immigration reform, domestic civil rights reform and the Cold War was made clear by President Johnson in his first State of the Union address: "Americans of all races stand side by side in Berlin and Vietnam. They died side by side in Korea. Surely they can work and eat and travel side by side in their own country. . . ."[58]

The immigration reform legislation proposed first by Kennedy and then Johnson sought to replace the national-origins system with a skills-based system. The color-blind liberals of the mid-sixties did not seek to bring millions of unskilled Third World immigrants into American cities and border states. In President Johnson's view, "A nation that was built by immigrants . . . can ask those who now seek admission: 'What can you do for our country?' But we should not be asking: 'In what country were you born?'" Congress, however, modified the Immigration and Naturalization Act of 1965 to replace the emphasis of Kennedy and Johnson on skills and training with an emphasis on family reunification, which was expected to benefit European immigrants (more Italians were arriving each year than the Italian quota could accommodate). Attorney General Robert Kennedy claimed that, though five thousand Asian immigrants would arrive in the United States the first year, "we do not expect that there would be a great influx after that."[59] His brother, Senator Edward Kennedy, asserted, "The bill will not fill our cities with immigrants. It will not upset the ethnic mix of our society."[60]

The Kennedys proved to be quite wrong. The 1965 Act produced the greatest flood of legal immigration since the turn of the century, most of it unskilled and nonwhite. The share of total U.S. population growth accounted for by immigrants rose from 11 percent between 1960 and 1970 to 33 percent between 1970 and 1980 and 39 percent between 1980 and 1990—well above one third of all growth. In the 1950s, 68 percent of the legal immigrants originated in Europe or Canada. By contrast, between 1971 and 1991, the overwhelming majority of immigrants came from Mexico, Latin America, and the Caribbean (47.9 percent, with Mexico accounting for 23.7 percent) and Asia (35.2 percent); Europe and Canada contributed only 13.8 percent. This does not count the millions of illegal aliens, mostly Mexican.[61] By the mid-1980s, as a place of origin for immigrants, Britain ranked twelfth, after Mexico, the Philippines, Korea, Cuba, India, China, the Dominican Republic, Vietnam, Jamaica, Haiti, and Iran.[62] Most of the immigration has been concentrated in a few major metropolitan areas in six states: California, Texas, Florida, New York, New Jersey, and Illinois. As a result of mass immigration, the Hispanic population of California, the biggest state, grew from 19.2 percent to 25.8 percent of the total population between 1980 and 1990.[63]

This new immigration is dramatically changing the demography of the United States. In the middle of the twentieth century, blacks were by far the largest minority, at around 12 percent; Americans were overwhelmingly European in ethnic origin. Between 1990 and 2030, according to a 1989 Census Bureau estimate, the black population will grow by 68 percent, the Asian-American, Pacific Islander and American Indian populations by 79 percent, and the Hispanic population by 187 percent; in the same time, the white population will grow by only 25 percent. By 2080, the Population Reference Bureau predicts, more than half of the U.S. population will be nonwhite, as conventionally defined—12 percent Asian-American, 15 percent black, and 24 percent Hispanic (these figures do not take intermarriage into account). By 2100, thanks to high levels of immigration, the U.S. population, now 250 million, may increase to 400 million.

In Chapter 5 I discuss the controversy over the economic consequences of the influx of more than a million immigrants a year in an economy in which jobs for unskilled Americans are scarce and wages declining. Here it is sufficient to note that the new immigrants are arriving in a country in which racial preference entitlements and multicultural ideology encourage them to retain their distinct racial and ethnic identities. Earlier European immigrants faced subtle and not-so-subtle sanctions for failing to assimilate quickly; by contrast, today's Hispanic and Asian immigrants are tempted by a variety of rewards for retaining their distinctive identities, even their different languages. The moment a Mexican or Chinese immigrant becomes a naturalized citizen of the United States, he can qualify for special consideration in admission to colleges and universities, at the expense of better-qualified white Americans; expect and receive special treatment in employment; apply for minority business subsidies denied to his neighbors; and even demand to have congressional district lines redrawn to maximize the likelihood of electing someone of his race or ethnic group—even though neither he nor any of his ancestors, living or buried far away, have ever suffered from discrimination in the United States.

In Multicultural America, the melting pot as a metaphor for the emergence of a new American type from the fusion of immigrant groups has been replaced by different symbols. One is the mosaic—"A gorgeous mosaic," former Mayor David Dinkins said of New York City, that sizzling cauldron of ethnocultural conflict. Sometimes a salad bowl metaphor, rather than the metaphor of a mosaic, is used as an alternative to the allegedly discredited melting-pot ideal (ironically, the salad bowl image has been part of American imagery all along: the motto *E pluribus unum* comes from a poem by Vergil describing the preparation of a rustic Italian salad).[64] "America used to be called a melting pot," Takashi Oka writes in *The Christian Science Monitor.* "Today some people call it a salad bowl. Different ethnic and racial groups retain their own distinct identities when tossed together, but if the salad dressing works its magic as it should, the taste of the whole is better than the sum of its parts."[65]

This mosaic or salad-bowl conception, based on a rejection of melting-pot amalgamation, was made explicit by New York State Education Commissioner Thomas Sobol at Columbia University in 1989:

> The old idea was that it didn't matter where you came from, that what mattered was being an American. . . . The assimilationist idea worked for ethnic peoples who were white but is not working nearly as well for ethnic peoples of color. . . . Replacing the old, assimilationist view is a competing ethnic-cultural pluralism. . . .[66]

The pluralism of which Sobol speaks is, in practice, a plurality of five racial nativisms. Assimilation is fine, in Multicultural America, as long as it takes place within the confines of one of the five official races established by Statistical Directive 15. It is unacceptable for Hondurans to be expected to assimilate to a generic American identity; but they are expected and encouraged to submerge their Honduran national identity in a new Hispanic American identity unique to the United States. Similarly, Czech and Norwegian immigrants will assimilate to White America, Ibo and Jamaican and Zulu immigrants to Black America, Indian and Chinese and Filipino immigrants to Asian America. Historian David A. Hollinger calls this the theory of the quintuple melting pot.[67]

Of the five official races of Multicultural America, the Hispanic "nation" is growing the most rapidly. Between 1980 and 1988 the Hispanic population grew by 34.4 percent, more than five times more rapidly than any other group.[68] At some point early in the twenty-first century people defined by the government as Hispanics will become the most numerous officially designated racial minority in the nation; in many major cities and states they may outnumber blacks *and* whites. Many, perhaps most, of the Hispanics will be immigrants or children of immigrants who came *after* 1965. They will inherit the affirmative action system designed to help black Americans. One by one, Hispanic mayors will replace black mayors; Hispanic contractors will edge out black contractors; Hispanic quotas in education and hiring will price; Hispanics will demand their own congressional districts, at the price, if necessary, of the destruction of black-majority districts. In New York City and Texas, Hispanic activists have already claimed that Hispanic votes have been diluted by efforts to create black-majority districts.[69]

One wonders what James Farmer, the patron saint of quotas, would have said, if he had been told, in 1960, that by boycotting Northern corporations until they hired fixed numbers of black Americans, he was inspiring a system whose major beneficiaries would ultimately be, not only well-to-do white women, but immigrants and the descendants of immigrants who, at the time of his struggles, were living in Mexico, Cuba, Salvador, Honduras, and Guatemala.

The Third Republic of the United States is the first American republic to be formally organized as a nonnational state. The United States today is—or so we are supposed to believe—a multicultural democracy, a federation of five races or cultures. The elaborate, ritualized, legally enforced segregation of nonwhite Americans has been replaced in the Third Republic by elaborate, ritualized, legally mandated co-opting of nonwhite Americans. The official classification and differential treatment of American citizens by race continues.

The failure of the Third Republic of the United States to obtain popular legitimacy is clear from the fact that, thirty years after the revolution that replaced Euro-America with Multicultural America, a new, widely accepted American iconography has yet to be devised. Not that the revolutionaries of the sixties—now the establishment of the nineties—have not tried to promulgate a new set of symbols for their new American regime. They have tried, for example, to make Martin Luther King, Jr., the patron saint of Multicultural America, as Abraham Lincoln was the patron saint of Euro-America, and George Washington the icon of the Anglo-American Republic. Only King, of all American figures, is today honored by federal observance of his birthday (Lincoln's and Washington's birthdays are celebrated along with the birthdays of William Henry Harrison and Gerald Ford on a generic Presidents' Day). Streets in every major city have been renamed in King's honor (a sure sign that a revolution has taken place). For all that, King remains, regrettably, a "black hero"—and not even the major black hero, to judge from popular black American veneration of his rival, Malcolm X.

When one turns from the figure of King to the other symbols of Multicultural America one finds—nothing. No agreed-upon national history, shared by elite and public, like the Euro-American story of the white immigrant melting pot, or the Anglo-American myth of westering Anglo-Saxons; no new popular holidays, joining those inherited from earlier American republics, like the Fourth of July (Anglo-America) and Thanksgiving (Euro-America); no new monuments or works of art joining Mount Rushmore or the Golden Gate Bridge or the Lincoln Memorial in the landscape of the American imagination; no new commonplace, no place in common.

The differences between Multicultural America and the older Euro-American republic it replaced are brought out by a contrast between that great symbol of post–Civil War American nation-building, the St. Gaudens memorial to Colonel Shaw in front of the Boston statehouse, with the Vietnam memorial. The Shaw memorial is European and classical in inspiration and design; although Shaw's Union regiment was black, the monument's hero is Shaw himself, a model young Brahmin leading deferential blacks in a crusade against Southern slavery, a relic of barbarism. It is the coherent monument of a people secure in their identity.

By contrast, the Vietnam memorial reflects today's class and racial tensions in its very design. The original design by a Yale art student, an avant-garde black wall in a ditch, completely inverts, even subverts, the western tradition of heroic monuments, which tend to be luminous, elevated, and celebratory. Its greatest defenders were among the cosmopolitan, modernist American art establishment; opposition was strong among veterans' groups and populists like Ross Perot, who had helped to fund the monument in the first place. Perot and the veterans hated the black wall so much that they managed to get an American flag and a realistic sculpture of soldiers by Frederick Hart added. Three soldiers—one white, one Hispanic, and one black—had to be portrayed, because a white American could no longer stand in for nonwhite soldiers. The symbolism is disturbingly apt—the white elite is separated from the masses in taste and value, and the masses are divided among themselves along racial lines.[70]

CHAPTER FOUR

The White Overclass and the Racial Spoils System

For a generation, the multicultural left has claimed to be leading a radical assault on "the white power structure." The white power structure has responded by granting the multicultural left practically every one of its demands, consistently expanding racial preference policies and adopting the language of diversity and multiculturalism from classrooms to newsrooms to congressional and judicial chambers. The white power structure, a naive observer would be inclined to conclude, is surely the most feeble and cowardly oligarchy in recent history. One might even conclude that the white power structure is a myth.

That would be a mistake. There *is* a white power structure in the United States, and it is anything but feeble. The hypocrisy and cunning of its members should not be mistaken for weakness. Machiavelli observed that one must rule either by *sforza* or *frodo*, by force or fraud. The white overclass in the United States since the sixties has specialized in ruling by fraud. Racial preference and multiculturalism are two of the biggest frauds. They provide the illusion of integration, while imposing minimal costs on the white overclass. Today's imitation radicalism is subsidized and applauded by the white elite, which continues to exercise a predominant influence in the economy and national politics. The new American mosaic is an avant-garde sculpture in the lobby of a bank.*

In this chapter I describe the white overclass as what it is—not a conspiracy, not an institutional elite, but as a genuine social class, the successor to the former Northeastern establishment. Surprisingly little has been written about the white overclass as such. Perhaps this silence should not be surprising. No ruling class wants the scandalous details of its maintenance and recruitment policies discussed in public. No secrets are more preciously guarded in any society than the truth about how power and wealth are actually handed on. The British establishment does not appear on TV with charts and graphs, detailing old school ties. The Soviet Academy of Sciences did not publish studies of nepotism in the *nomenklatura*. Knowledge of the inner workings of the Mexican oligarchy is limited to rumor, mixed with fantasy. The dominant class in every country would prefer to pass in silence over its own workings, and focus on the shortcomings of other classes. This explains, I think, why American public discourse is full of detailed discussions of the black underclass, while the subject of the white overclass hardly ever comes up—even though, in any objective account of America's troubles, the powerful and rich white overclass, not a small number of poor and violent ghetto residents, must be seen as playing the central role.

To the predictable reticence of a ruling class is added, in the United States, the myth of the classless society. There are rich and poor, Americans are taught, but there are no social classes, with distinct folkways, accents, lifestyles, values. Conservatives and liberals collaborate in maintaining this illusion. Conservatives exaggerate the extent to which Americans rise and fall into and out of wealth. They want the public to believe that the average rich American is just a middle-class American who worked his way to the top, when in fact the average rich American inherited his or her wealth from Dad or Granddad and has very limited experience of the world in which most Americans live.† Left-liberals, for their part, attack the notion that there is a hereditary underclass, with

---

*David Rieff has drawn attention to the fit between multiculturalism and the corporate marketing strategies. David Rieff, "Multiculturalism's Silent Partner," *Harper's Magazine* (August 1993), p. 62.

†President Bush's amazement on going through an automated checkout line in a supermarket gave the public a glimpse into how insulated from everyday life the wealthy can be.

its own distinctive culture and mores, as a racist notion, an attempt to blame the victim.

The multicultural left (not, it should be noted, the Marxist or Old Left) takes the strategy of denying the existence of social classes one step further, by denying, or ignoring, the class divisions among blacks, Hispanics, and white women. In this regard, the use of the cant word "community" in Multicultural America is very revealing. America is not a society of classes, stacked one on top of the other like pancakes; rather, it is frequently described as a society of communities, united by common race or gender or sexual orientation. Each community is a classless society, in which the black businessman and the black beggar, the gay movie mogul and the gay truck driver, experience a mystical fraternity.

The irony is that the major beneficiary of this kind of thinking is the white overclass, the white power structure itself. Class consciousness, weak enough in the United States to begin with, has been almost obliterated by the multiplication of particularistic communal mysticisms subsidized by the very government and white overclass that they purportedly threaten. Far from being revolutionary, identity politics is merely America's version of the oldest oligarchic trick in the book: divide and rule.

In this chapter I present the most detailed description of the contemporary American white overclass that has appeared in print. I then argue that the most important beneficiaries of the racial preference policies of Multicultural America are not middle-class black and Hispanic Americans, but members of the white overclass, who by supporting tokenism buy social peace and an untroubled conscience.

PORTRAIT OF AN OLIGARCHY

Understanding the white American overclass requires revising the most common misconceptions about class. The discussion of social class has been confused for generations by Marxist thinkers, who made the mistake of completely identifying class with economic function. Like the Marxists, old-fashioned American liberal pluralists tend to misunderstand class. What they refer to as class is typically not a social class at all, but a mere occupational or income category, such as service-sector workers or millionaires. Meanwhile, the New Left which came to prominence in the sixties has tended to drop the idea of class altogether, in favor of race and gender. Members of the New Left assume that the vertical divisions between biological identities, as whites or blacks, males or females, are far more important than class differences. Women on Park Avenue are thought to be suffering the same oppression as women in trailer parks—dressed in fur or polyester, they are sisters. In recent years, conservative ideologues have added further confusion by defining political factions and lifestyle subcultures as classes. The country, they claim, is run by a new class consisting of bureaucrats, academics, and intellectuals (with the exception, of course, of conservative bureaucrats, academics, and intellectuals).

In order to think about class in twenty-first century America, we must first clear our minds of these Marxist, liberal, New Left, and conservative definitions of class, and return to the older notion of class found in classical and European political thought from Aristotle to Montesquieu.

A social class is a group of families, united by intermarriage and a common subculture, whose members tend to predominate in certain professions and political offices, generation after generation. Note that the class—the group of similar families—has an identity and existence independent of the offices which its members tend to hold. Indeed, we cannot talk intelligently about class unless we make a distinction between a social class and a mere institutional elite. Those who talk about "the political class" or, with C. Wright Mills, about "the power elite," are confusing two different things. Every modern society, even the most perfectly egalitarian, will have an institutional elite—top civilian politicians, military officers, judges, diplomats, financial and industrial executives, publishers, editors and leading intellectuals, clerical leaders, and so on. The subject of class is raised only when you examine the social origins of the particular individuals who hold office in the institutional elite or elites. Learning the organization of judicial offices in a country tells you nothing about class. However, if you find out that most of the judges tend to come from old-money families in a particular region of that country, and that most attended one of half a dozen schools, then you have learned something important about that country's class system.

The United States at the end of the twentieth century has both an institutional elite and a dominant social class. The institutional elite is composed of upper-level officials in the federal and state governments, plus executives and professionals in the concentrated private sector and foundation and university executives (low-level government officials and small business owners are not part of the institutional elite). Almost all of the members of the American institutional elite also happen to be members of a single social class: the white overclass. To put it another way, the labor pool from which most elite positions are filled is the white overclass. The overlap is not complete. Though most members of the institutional elite belong to the white overclass, most members of the white overclass are not part of the institutional elite (since the overclass greatly outnumbers the elite); and—though this is uncommon—a person can become a high-ranking politician, military officer, judge, CEO, foundation president, or university president in the United States without having been born into the white overclass. It is possible to imagine a United States in which most members of the institutional elite did not have similar class origins. But that is not the country in which we live.

What precisely *is* this white overclass that supplies most of the positions in the American institutional elite from its own ranks? The white overclass is the child of the former Northeastern Protestant establishment, produced by marriage (not only figurative but literal) with the upwardly mobile descendants of turn-of-the-century European immigrants and white Southerners and Westerners. Unlike the Northeastern establishment of Euro-America, this relatively new and still evolving political and social oligarchy is not identified with any particular region of the country (though it is concentrated in East and West Coast metropolitan regions). Nor does the white overclass dominate other sections through local, surrogate establishments, as the Northeastern establishment once did. Rather, overclass Americans are found in the higher suburbs of every major metropolitan area, North and South, coastal and inland. Unlike the sectional elites of the past, members of the white overclass are often not even identified with the regions in which they happen (temporarily) to live. The white overclass, homogeneous and nomadic, is the first truly *national* upper class in American history.

The white overclass is the product, not merely of the amalgamation of elite Anglo- and Euro-Americans, but of the fusion of the rentier and managerial-professional classes. This blurring of the upper and upper-middle strata is a relatively new development in the United States. In earlier generations, there were distinct regional landowning and rentier classes, with their own lifestyles and institutions—cotillions, seasons spent in the country, and the like. The elaborate rituals that governed upper-class life, such as changing for dinner, were designed to conspicuously display wealth, including a wealth of leisure time. That was a long time ago. There is a class, or rather category, of the celebrity rich, and there are still pockets of old-fashioned rentiers in the U.S.—in Virginia, there are still planters who do not work and who hunt foxes with hounds—but these subcultures are detached from the summits of power. Members of the upper class who want to make a mark in the world tend to adopt the style of life and dress and speech of the managerial-professional elite. Even though they do not have to, most members of the small hereditary upper class go to college and get executive or professional jobs, and work, or at least pretend to. Instead of serving as a model for well-to-do executives and lawyers and investment bankers, the hereditary segment of the American overclass conforms to the segment immediately below it, the credentialed upper middle class.

Now, to describe the white overclass in more detail. The composition of the student bodies at Ivy League schools is a good surrogate for the composition of the white overclass. If you factor out black and Hispanic students admitted under affirmative action programs, you are left with a student body that is disproportionately of British or Germanic-Scandinavian Protestant and European Jewish descent. There are relatively few evangelical Protestants and Catholics in the overclass, despite their significant numbers in the general population. If you are Episcopalian or Jewish, have a graduate or professional degree from an expensive university, work in a large downtown office building in an East or West Coast metropolis, watch MacNeil/Lehrer on PBS, and are saving for a vacation in London or Paris, you are a card-carrying member of the white overclass, even if your salary is not very impressive. If you are Methodist, Baptist or Catholic, have a B.A. from a state university, work in or for a small business or for a career government service, watch the Nashville Network on cable, and are saving for a vacation in Las Vegas, Atlantic City, Branson, Missouri, or Orlando, Florida (Disneyworld), you are probably not a member of the white overclass—no matter how much money you make.

Although there are residual religious and ethnic differences among members of the white overclass, these are minor compared to what they have in common. There is, for example, a common white overclass accent, which is more or less identical in corporate boardrooms from one end of the continent to another—the "NBC standard," which is the equivalent of BBC English or Britain's Received Pronunciation (RP). As formerly distinct local elites have fused into a single national ruling class equally at home in New York and Texas and California, this accent has become the badge of elite status. In order to advance in overclass circles in America, a white American has to suppress any regional or ethnic dialect, whether it be a Southern drawl or a Boston honk or Brooklynese, and learn to speak this flat, clipped, rather nasal version of American English. There are distinctive sublanguages within this mandarin dialect: in recent years, for example, the "Valley Girl" dialect has spread from California to become the standard subdialect of young overclass women at expensive private campuses and ski resorts across America.

Besides dialect, fashions and folkways separate members of the white overclass from the American majority (white and nonwhite alike). These are hard to categorize, because they are constantly changing (otherwise the middle class, by emulating overclass ways, might be able to blur class distinctions). The overclass eats paté and imported cheeses; the middle class eats peanut butter and Velveeta. The overclass sips wine; the middle class drinks beer. The overclass plays squash and tennis; the middle class plays pool and bowls (both play golf, but the middle class does so at second-tier country clubs and public courses). The overclass jogs; the middle class does not. . . . These are clichés, but they are a better guide to the real class structure in the United States than income categories in the census or pseudoscientific sociological measures like the SES (socioeconomic survey).

Anglophilia has long been characteristic of American upper classes— the Southern planters, the Northeastern establishment. In the United States, as in Argentina, the regnant elites have always looked to London as the capital of culture and fashion (Paris rather than London has been the metropole for most other elites in the Americas). Pseudo-British style simultaneously presents a standard to which the ruling class of the day can conform, while helpfully excluding the majority of Americans. Every rising American elite has gone through a phase of Anglicization: the Patriots in the 1760s and 1770s (the most vigorous nationalists were well-traveled Anglo-Americans like Franklin, long resident in London); the Southern nationalist planters in the 1840s and 1850s (fans of Sir Walter Scott); and the Northeastern patricians of the 1890s (who married their daughters—like Winston Churchill's American mother—to impoverished English aristocrats, rebuilt the Ivy League colleges in Gothic style, and even founded, in 1897, the Baronial Order of Runnymede).

After the New Deal and World War II, which churned and blurred the social classes in the United States to a considerable degree, the futuristic, technological look associated with industrial America shaped everything from suburban shopping malls to TV sets—clean, angular, modernist, new. Since the white overclass coalesced in the sixties, however, tastes have drifted toward the pseudo-British and the pseudo-antique: TV sets in polished mahogany cases, upscale suburban shopping malls decorated with pseudo-Victorian grillwork where lawyers and corporate executives can shop for Polo clothes and buy little prints of fox- and pheasant-hunting for the office wall. The rage for things British and upper-class is one of many clues that the new white overclass—most of whose members are a generation or two away from middle-class roots in the ethnic neighborhood or the small town—is evolving into the latest American aristocracy. The Rhodes scholarship to Oxford serves as a ticket of admission to the white overclass that the European Grand Tour did for the rich sons and daughters of the robber barons. In being a Rhodes Scholar, as well as having a wife working in the same profession whom he met at Yale Law School, Bill Clinton is an archetypal member (by adoption, rather than birth) of the latest American oligarchy.

Throughout history, aristocracies and oligarchies have developed their own peculiar arrangements for marriage and family life, which have been structured to preserve the assets that were central to their status as a class. In Britain, for example, primogeniture and entail—the inheritance of an estate by the eldest son—was a device by which great estates were passed on intact, generation after generation. This mechanism for preserving the concentration of landed wealth had a variety of social side effects—for example, the presence of younger sons of aristocratic families in great numbers in the church, the military, and in imperial colonies. In Venice at its height, the small oligarchy that dominated the commerce and politics of that republic devised a method of preserving family estates involving the partnership of brothers. In today's Third American Republic, the major form of property for the managerial-professional elite is the credential—an expensive degree, often coupled with a professional license. The sex lives and family patterns of the white overclass are therefore organized to facilitate the acquisition of educational and professional credentials.

Delayed marriage is one manifestation of this phenomenon. As a rule in the United States, the lower one's class, the earlier one gets married. This corresponds more or less to the educational hierarchy. Blue-collar workers are more likely to marry their high school sweethearts; lower middle class white-collar workers to marry their college sweethearts; upper middle class professionals to marry the girl or guy they met in first-year law or business school.

Since the upper middle class professional, as a rule, does not complete his education until his mid- or late twenties, and then goes through a probationary period of several years (as a law-firm associate, or a medical intern), the experience of having a regular job and setting up a family and household can be delayed well past the age of thirty. Deferred marriage among upper-status Americans does not mean celibacy. The tension between deferring marriage until the completion of what may be a decade of higher education and the natural drives for sex and companionship has been resolved in the institution of living together—in practice, an informal first marriage that spans the years of professional education and accreditation. This institution of the contemporary professional elite is quite different from what used to be known as common law marriage or "shacking up." For one thing, it has no lower-class connotations; since the sixties, it has become widely accepted among all generations of the suburban upper middle class. Young would-be professionals who live together while going to school or engaging in the apprentice phases of their careers are engaging, in effect, in an informal, childless first marriage. Cohabitation among college-educated white Americans is an aristocratic institution, inasmuch as the financial and status incentives for deferring marriage to 26 or 32 do not exist for the great majority of Americans who complete their educations and begin their adult careers at 22, or 19.

The family ideal of the white overclass, it might be suggested, is the three-parent family—a husband and wife, each with a lucrative professional job, plus a maid. The child-care problems of Zoe Baird and Kimba Wood gave the public a rare glimpse into the private lives of the white overclass: only 1 percent of the American population employs live-in nannies.[1]

One of the most fashionable overclass diseases is co-dependency, a disorder defined as excessive emotional dependence on one's mate (in the old days, this was known as love). The very idea of co-dependency is inextricably bound up with the upper-middle-class ideal of marriage as a sort of business alliance between two emotionally independent professionals, each with a prestigious career and (perhaps) a personal banking account—not Ozzie and Harriet, but Oberon and Titania. In the older bourgeois elite (and to a degree among the lower middle and working classes today), there were separate masculine and feminine social spheres, so that same-sex company provided some relief to husbands and wives. The idea that there should be separate masculine and feminine spheres (the saloon or pub, the ladies' club or church group) is frowned upon by overclass feminism, however. Since couples are expected to do everything together, socializing with other couples also joined like Siamese twins, it is no wonder that overclass men and women feel mutually enslaved.

The new American elite has other high-status diseases. Anorexia, bulimia, and diet-pill addiction are prestige diseases of upper-status women. These eating-related disorders all are closely connected with the ideal of the androgynous, sylphlike body as the pattern for both sexes. The ambition to undertake the strict dieting and exercise regimens necessary to produce such unnatural physiques cannot be explained except in terms of submerged class anxieties. For the new American overclass, conspicuous consumption has been replaced by conspicuous abstention. Fear of fat is fear of lower-middle-class vulgarity, of the animal grossness, the unselfconscious corporeality associated with "rednecks" and "hardhats" and "Bubbas" and "ethnics" and "white trash."

The androgynous ideal of the white overclass causes problems for its men, as well as for its women. The weakening of sex-role distinctions between overclass men and their girlfriends and wives brings their masculinity into question, not only in their own minds (consider the poet Robert Bly's "men's movement") but—more ominously—in the minds of lower-status men. Bill Clinton is typical of men of his generation who, by birth or achievement, are part of today's overclass in his manipulation of the draft process to avoid draft duty during the Vietnam era. Such perfectly legal draft evasion, or combat evasion, is not a phenomenon of the left alone; conservative Republicans like former Defense Secretary Dick Cheney (student deferment) and former Vice-President Dan Quayle (Indiana National Guard) manipulated the system in exactly the same way.*

This kind of thing is not unknown among America's elites; during the Civil War, for example, many wealthy fathers purchased exemptions from draft duty for their sons (thus the James brothers, Henry and William, escaped serving in the Union uniform). What is new is the prospect of not just one but several generations of civilian leadership, most of whose members have never been associated with the military in any way, even as members of the militia. Over time, this lack of participation in the military by the white overclass could lead to an increasing divergence between the norms of the civilian and the military elites in the United States, and a declining respect for civilian authority by a heavily middle-class and working-class military. The incidents of insubordination that greeted President Clinton's attempt to end the ban on homosexual men and women in the military showed the existence of both the cultural gap and the possible consequences.

The white overclass, in addition to having its own recognizable accents and folkways, also has its own distinctive ethical and political worldview. Its members tend to be liberal on social issues and conservative on economic issues, in contrast to the majority of Americans, who are populist in economics but relatively conservative in sexual and aesthetic matters.† If

---

*Between 1962 and 1972, 29,701 men graduated from Harvard, MIT, and Princeton; only twenty died in Vietnam. Of the 58,000 Americans killed in the Vietnam war, twelve were graduates of Harvard College. As James Fallows observes, the American Army in Vietnam "was principally made up of men from working-class and lower-middle-class backgrounds, and the American elite was conspicuously absent." (James Fallows, "Low-Class Conclusions," *The Atlantic Monthly*, April 1993, pp. 43–44.)

†A survey of students at Ivy League universities—a good cross section of the next generation of the American elite—demonstrated this overclass mixture of social liberalism and fiscal conservatism. Eighty-four percent favored abortion rights, and 73 percent were in favor of repealing the ban on gay citizens in the military; at the same time, 75 percent supported the fiscal conservative idea of a balanced-budget amendment. ("Ivy Students March Left, Right," *Washington Times*, Associated Press, Tuesday, April 6, 1993, p. A4.)

the U.S. population were divided into two parties on the basis of class, the parties would be Libertarians and Populists, not liberals and conservatives.

The white overclass is much more secular in its outlook than the rest of the population. Whether completely agnostic or nominally Christian or Jewish, overclass Americans tend to subscribe to a common ethic of secular self-improvement, a sort of suburban eudaimonism. This secular ethic is perfectly captured in in-flight magazines, with their ads for consumer goods targeted at the suburban professional, intermingled with pages and pages of instructional tapes ("How to Organize Your Time"), motivational seminars ("How to Succeed in Life"), and Anglophile country-gentleman delights ("Authentic Scottish Walking Stick"). The ethic of the white overclass is of a recognizably aristocratic kind—sexual morals are negotiable, but institutional manners must be upheld (the term *the appearance of impropriety*—today's replacement for *dishonor*—strikes terror into the hearts of elite nominees for public posts, and campus speech codes evoke the gentility of yesteryear).

The motto of the white overclass might be, "Live right, think left." Members of the new American oligarchy, in genuine aristocratic fashion, manage to combine their liberal social views with snobbery and social condescension. Incorrect attitudes play the role in America's class system that nonstandard pronunciations do in the British class hierarchy. For example, to be opposed to affirmative action is thought to be an admission of the prejudices of a lower-class white. This explains an outburst by J. Stanley Pottinger, former head of affirmative action at the Department of Health, Education, and Welfare (HEW), on being told that affirmative action discriminates against whites: "That is the biggest crock I have ever heard. It is the kind of argument one expects to hear from a backwoods cracker farmer."[2] According to historian David Hackett Fischer, writing of eighteenth-century American slang, "A third word for this rural proletariat which also came from Britain—along with *hoosier* and *redneck*—was *cracker*, which derived from an English pejorative for a low and vulgar braggart."[3] An insistence that even white Americans should be protected from legal discrimination on the basis of race is considered not so much immoral as simply *vulgar*.

The white overclass, then, is a real social class—a new American oligarchy with its own characteristic dialect, folkways, sex roles, and a worldview that is essentially secular, individualist and libertarian. This class would simply be one of many American subcultures, but for its near-monopoly of the private-sector and political branches of the American institutional elite. The white overclass ensures that its offspring staff the private-sector elite by means of institutionalized nepotism in college admissions and by artificial barriers to entry in the professions. The predominance of the white overclass in the political parties and the government, in turn, is assured by the abject dependence of American elected officials on a small number of major individual and institutional political donors.

Let us first consider the private-sector institutional elite. The economic elite in the United States is not a capitalist elite, that is, most of its members are not investors or entrepreneurs. Though it dominates a capitalist country, the major group in the white overclass consists of managers and professionals—lawyers, bankers, corporate executives—who live by salaries plus stock options, fees, or commissions, and who owe their status to their educational attainments and their achieved positions in private-sector bureaucracies. The American business class is not a bourgeoisie, but a sort of guild oligarchy, like the ones that ran early modern Italian and Dutch city-states. To be sure, the American institutional elite as a whole is not composed exclusively of members of the professions and their rentier imitators. There are other important elites in the United States—entrepreneurs, rentiers, military officers, entertainers, athletes, celebrity clerics. Even so, it is the managerial-professional group (rather than, say, the hereditary upper class, or the officer corps, or self-made businessmen) that sets the tone and style of elite life in the United States. Within the professions, the most prestigious and lucrative careers are those in the concentrated, bureaucratic part of the private-sector economy. Real prestige in American society comes from being the CEO of a Fortune 500 company, or a partner at a blue-chip law firm, not from running a small business or a small law practice, even if the latter generate incomes equivalent to the former.

American capitalism and society, then, are post-bourgeois; the key figures are institutional officers and professionals of one kind or another, not investors and individual owners of property, however important those individuals may be in some cases. Indeed, in a managerial capitalist society like ours, the essential distinction, it can be argued, is not between the "bourgeoisie" and the "proletariat" but between the professional class (a category which includes professional corporate managers and professors with doctorates) and the wage-earning salaried class. Most Americans belong to the salaried class—that is, they are nonunionized, at-will employees, lacking a four-year college education, paid by the hour, who can be fired at any time, and have few or no managerial responsibilities. Between the "new collar" proletariat of secretaries, office workers, salesmen, and store managers who have partly replaced blue-collar assembly line workers, and lower-middle-class white-collar salaried employees, there is little social distinction. The real middle class should be defined, not as the two-car suburban elite, but as the high school educated, economically insecure salaried class, whose members make up more than two thirds of the U.S. population.

The great social gap, then, is between the professionals and the wage-earners. Entry to the professional class—and hence to the commanding heights of the economy, politics, and even civil society—depends on two institutions: prestigious universities and state systems of professional accreditation. These represent the primogeniture and entail of the white overclass.

Access to elite education in the United States is based not on intellectual merit alone, but on merit in conjunction with family income and family connections. The class bias of American education is consistent from the lowest to the highest levels. Many affluent children, of course, are educated in expensive private schools. But even public education is not as public as it might seem. Suburban schools in practice are quasi-private institutions; the role of affluent parents in PTAs accounts for the gross disparities in the same school system between suburban schools with clean buildings, modern sports and science facilities, and well-stocked libraries, and inner-city schools with broken windows, deteriorating buildings, and empty bookshelves. The practice of financing local schools out of regressive property taxes, instead of general state and local tax revenues—a practice that has encouraged tax revolts by affluent property owners who do not have children in the public schools—is another custom that gives our system of public education a feudal flavor.

The post–secondary school system is organized in a hierarchy, with universities at the top, above four-year colleges and two-year colleges. Only a few dozen of the top private institutions and selective state universities can be considered first-rate; most of the rest are best described

as diploma mills. Those admitted to selective universities would like to
believe that they have achieved their status on the basis of merit alone.
Many, though, have benefited from the quasi-aristocratic arrangements
that govern elite college admissions. Access to the most selective private
universities depends not only to a large degree on family income but—to
an extent that is seldom realized—on alumni connections (I discuss
legacy preference in detail later in this chapter).

After legacy preference as a means of entrance to the prestigious universities, the second barrier guarding the gates of the managerial elite
against members of classes other than the white overclass is the professional licensing system—or, rather, the separate professional licensing systems of the fifty states. The laws regulating professional accreditation
further protect the class interests of the managerial-professional oligarchy.
Law, for example, which in European civil-law countries is an undergraduate degree, requires three years of strenuous and expensive graduate education in the United States, following at least four years of undergraduate
instruction—a truly massive investment of money and time. Most fast-
track business careers also require graduate training, an MBA, perhaps, or
a Ph.D. in economics. Since very little of what is learned in law, business,
or graduate school is ever used in practice, these educational requirements look a lot like arbitrary guild rules designed to keep professional
salaries high by keeping the number of practitioners artificially low.

The job of protecting guild privileges is assigned to professional associations like the American Bar Association (ABA) and the American
Medical Association (AMA). Of all the lobbies in what Theodore J.
Lowi has called our system of interest-group liberalism, these are among
the most powerful. The ABA has won extraordinary privileges—for example, the customary right of rating presidential nominees for the
Supreme Court. One can hardly imagine such a prerogative being granted to the auto workers' or electricians' union.

The class bias of professional associations is manifest in a number of
different ways. In policing the bar, bar associations tend to concentrate
on low-status attorneys who have committed improprieties, turning a
blind eye to the abuses of name partners at prestigious firms. At the same
time, the political positions taken by professional associations like the
ABA and the AMA usually reflect the liberalism on social issues of the
suburban oligarchy.

Once you have passed the hurdles of an elite college education and an expensive professional degree—with a little help, perhaps, from Dad's or Mom's alumni connections and bank account—and joined a profession, you enter the comfortable world of the American elite. However much devotees of capitalism may glamorize the self-made billionaire entrepreneur, the Sam Walton or Ross Perot who sees an opportunity and builds a business empire, the typical member of the American business establishment is a quite different type—a professional employed by a large, bureaucratic corporation which he did not found and does not own (except, perhaps, as a shareholder). The separation of management from ownership is what distinguishes modern managerial capitalism from proprietary capitalism around the world. The distinctive American version of managerial capitalism is characterized by the extreme privileges of the professional management.

In 80 percent of American corporations, the CEO is also the chairman of the board. By contrast, this is the case in only 30 percent of companies in Britain and 11 percent of firms in Japan. The practice is unknown in Germany.[4] Since the board of directors sets the CEO's salary, friendship with the CEO may lead directors to violate their duty to shareholders by granting excessively generous salaries and compensation packages. Insofar as two thirds of directors in the U.S. are also top executives in other companies, it can be argued that they have an interest in keeping average executive salaries high.

These factors might explain why, in the United States, the average CEO makes four times as much as the average German CEO—and eight to ten times as much as the average Japanese CEO. International comparisons of worker-management pay disparities are even more striking. In Britain, CEOs make 35 times as much as the average worker; in Japan, only 17 times as much. The average American CEO makes 109 times as much as the average American worker. In the 1980s, while worker pay in the United States increased only 53 percent, the pay of CEOs increased 212 percent.[5]

This might not matter, if the past several decades had seen tremendous growth in American prosperity. Instead, the decline in American productivity growth and economic competitiveness has been accompanied by the most dramatic rises in corporate compensation in history. In

1960, when the American economy was supreme, CEOs were paid only 41 times as much as the average factory worker; by 1993, after two decades of unimpressive American economic performance, American CEOs were making 157 times as much as factory workers.[6] That upper-level corporate compensation has increased far out of proportion to the performance of companies or the growth of the economy suggests that something other than the laws of the free market are at work. Indeed, Japanese CEOs, paid much less relatively than American CEOs even when fringe benefits are taken into account, have presided over decades of economic growth far more impressive than that of the U.S.* It is far from clear, indeed, that the textbook model of the free market can explain organizational and salary practices within large American corporations. In classical economic theory, the government is a neutral umpire, and CEOs and directors share the best interests of the shareholders whom they serve. In reality, in many large U.S. corporations the executives are an entrenched, self-perpetuating oligarchy, willing to use their influence in the state and federal governments to rewrite laws in order to protect the interests of corporate managers as a group.

This rewriting of the rules to protect managers from the harsh verdict of the market is made easier by the legal fragmentation produced by American federalism. U.S. corporations operate under the legal systems of fifty different states. In a number of states, corporate managers have won changes in corporate governance laws that protect them not only from hostile takeovers but from the company's own shareholders. A typical U.S. company spends $1.3 million a year on insurance protecting its directors and officers from lawsuits by shareholders themselves.[7] The laws that regulate corporate governance in the United States are not inevitable responses to the imperatives of the free market in a managerial-capitalist society; they can best be explained in terms of the interests of middle- and upper-level corporate managers as a specialized class within the broader managerial-professional class. Recognizing this, *Business Week* has denounced the coalescence of American corporate managers

---

*Claims by defenders of America's corporate compensation system that Japanese CEOs really make roughly as much as their American counterparts when hidden perks are counted have not been borne out. See "What Do Japanese CEOs *Really* Make?" *Business Week*, April 26, 1993, pp. 60–61.

into a class with prerogatives independent of performance: "The (wage) disparity tears at the social fabric. It is unacceptable to the large polity as CEOs configure themselves into a new monied elite."[8]

Even more than the proliferation of lawyers, the rise of the MBA degree symbolizes the rise of the new American oligarchy. During the 1950s, advanced engineering degrees outnumbered MBAs—4700 to 3800. During the 1970s, however, there were 36,600 MBAs each year, compared to 16,100 advanced engineering degree graduates. By the 1980s, only 20,000 advanced engineering degrees were awarded annually, compared to 64,200 MBAs. Since many of the engineers were foreign students who took their skills back home with them, the situation was even worse than it appears.[9]

The globalization of the world economy could not explain why there were twelve times as many engineers as MBAs in Japan by the end of the eighties—and more than three times as many MBAs as engineers in the U.S. The glut of MBAs and law degrees in the U.S. was the result of class-driven status politics by Americans desperate to join the new social oligarchy. To be a lawyer or a corporate executive or a banker promises to certify an American as a prestigious member of the white overclass. By contrast, engineering as a profession is too close to actually making and manipulating things to be truly refined.

From its fortified command post in the large organizations of the private sector, protected by the concentric moats of alumni preference, college tuition, professional licensing and pro-managerial state laws, the white overclass dominates U.S. politics through its predominant role in campaign financing and the staffing of key federal offices—particularly offices in the high-toned executive and judicial branches.

Campaign financing is by far the most important mechanism for overclass influence in government. The real two-party system in the United States consists of the party of voters and the tiny but influential party of donors. The donor party in the United States is made up of an extraordinarily small number of citizens. In 1988, according to one study, only 10.2 percent of the American public made a contribution to a candidate, party, or partisan group.[10] Most of the members of this minority made only minimal contributions. If regular contributors of more than $25 to the national Democratic party alone are counted, there are about

100,000 national Democrats—compared to 10 million dues-paying members of the National Committee to Preserve Social Security and Medicare, 14 million dues-paying members of the AFL-CIO, 6 million members of the National Parent-Teacher Association, and 2.5 million dues-paying members of the National Rifle Association (NRA).[11] The group of large political donors is a still more exclusive club. According to a study by Citizen Action, in the 1989–90 election cycle only 179,677 individual donors gave contributions greater than $200 to a federal candidate, political action committee (PAC), or party: "Thirty-four percent of the money spent by federal candidates was directly contributed by no more than one-tenth of one percent of the voting age population."[12] One may reasonably doubt that this one tenth of one percent is representative of the electorate or the population at large.

While individual corruption on the part of American legislators is probably lower than it has ever been in U.S. history, "honest graft" on the part of interest groups, rather than individuals, has been industrialized. In 1961, 365 congressional lobbyists were registered; by 1987, the number had grown to 23,011. At the same time, the number of lawyers registered with the D.C. Bar Association rose from 12,564 to 46,000. Between 1968 and 1986, the number of corporations with Washington offices grew from 100 to 1300.

Special interests buy favors from congressmen and presidents through political action committees (PACs), devices by which groups like corporations, professional associations, trade unions, investment banking groups—can pool their money and give up to $10,000 per election to each House and Senate candidate. Today there are more than 4,000 Political Action Committees (PACs) of various kinds registered with the Federal Election Commission; in 1974, when they were sanctioned by law, there were only 500.[13] PAC money is driving campaign costs to new heights. In 1992, the average Senate incumbent spent more than $3.6 million for re-election; that is the equivalent of raising $12,000 a week in a single six-year term. Members of Congress, by comparison, spend only an average of $557,403 to be re-elected—a "mere" $5,000 a week for a two-year term.[14] The average cost of a House campaign has risen to this level from $140,000 in 1980—and $52,000 in 1974.[15]

The chief beneficiaries of rising campaign costs and PAC contributions have been incumbents. In 1972, 52 cents of the average PAC dollar went to incumbents, compared to 25 cents to challengers (the rest went to candidates for open seats); in the 1988 House elections, incumbents received 84.4 cents of each PAC dollar and challengers only 8.6 cents. It makes more sense for lobbies to buy access to established members of Congress and senators—particularly those with important leadership positions—than to fund challengers, who, if elected, would have no seniority and little influence. The disproportion between what incumbents and challengers can raise is sometimes breathtaking; by the date of the Texas Senate election in 1990, Texas senator Phil Gramm had accumulated more than *three hundred times* as much money as his challenger—$6.2 million to $20,000.[16] Would-be public servants who are not adept at fund-raising on this scale are squeezed out of politics. Former Senator Barry Goldwater has lamented, "The Founding Fathers would frown in their graves if they saw us rationing candidacies sheerly on the basis of money: who has—or can raise—the millions necessary to run for office."[17]

Democrats, when they were members of the majority party, received more PAC money than Republicans, though both parties are saturated with it. Contrary to conservative claims that liberal lobby groups dominate Congress, PAC funds come overwhelmingly from business: in 1990, 65 percent of PAC contributions came from business PACs, compared to 24 percent from labor and only 11 percent from ideological groups (including conservative as well as liberal pressure groups).[18] "At one point," John Judis has pointed out, "the American Petroleum Institute employed more lobbyists in Washington than the entire labor movement."[19]

One of the effects of the postpartisan PAC system is to weaken the link between members of Congress and senators and the districts and states they are supposed to represent. Out-of-state money from special interests often flows into House and Senate elections.* This means that

---

*In one three-year period, for example, Representative Edward J. Markey (D-Mass.) collected $333,675 in donations of more than $200 from contributors living outside of Massachusetts—compared to only $146,950 from Massachusetts residents. Most of the out-of-state contributors were connected with telecommunications and finance (Markey was chairman of the House Telecommunications and Finance Subcommittee). In 1988, a quarter of all donations in Senate races came from out of state; in 1990, half of the senators took most of their large individual donations from states other than their own. (Richard Morin and Charles R. Babcock, "Out-of-State Donations to Candidates Are on the Rise," *Washington Post,* July 31, 1990.)

many senators are, in effect, at-large representatives of free-spending national business constituencies.

Some argue that special-interest expenditures have no significant influence on public policy. If all of this money is *not* buying special favors from congressmen and senators, a great many groups and individuals who are otherwise careful with their resources are acting in a highly irrational manner, year after year.

The disproportionate influence of overclass whites in American government is reinforced by two other peculiarities of American politics: low voter turnout and the malapportionment of the U.S. Senate.

Since the sixties, voter participation by lower-middle-class and working-class Americans has steadily declined. Between 1960 and 1980, the spread between white-collar and blue-collar voting rates increased from 16.4 percent to 22.9 percent.[20]* In many elections, voters themselves are a minority of the eligible electorate.

The major beneficiaries of low voter turnout are the Republicans, because in terms of party affiliation, the members of the white overclass are disproportionately Republican.† The political power of the predomi-

---

*In the 1992 presidential election in California, whites, who made up only 55 percent of the population, provided 82 percent of the voters; Latinos, who make up 25 percent of the population, provided only 7 percent of the votes; Asians, nearing 10 percent of the state, accounted for merely 3 percent of the vote. Blacks are 7 percent of the California population and 6 percent of the presidential vote. While 62.8 percent of adults of voting age voted for president in 1960, only 50.2 percent voted in the 1988 presidential election. A minority of eligible voters regularly elects the members of Congress; for example, in 1986 only 33.4 percent of voting-age citizens voted in the mid-term congressional elections. (Richard M. Valelly, "Vanishing Voters," *The American Prospect*, Spring 1990, p. 140.)

†White Americans with college educations, high-status occupations, and high incomes tend to be Republican rather than Democrats; one 1988 exit poll showed that almost twice as many Americans with incomes of over $40,000 were Republican (62 percent) than Democrat (37 percent), while college graduates were more likely to be Republican (59 percent) than Democrat (39 percent) (CNN-Los Angeles Times exit poll, November 8, 1988, cited in John J. Harrigan, *Empty Dreams, Empty Pockets: Class and Bias in American Politics*, New York: Macmillan, 1993, p. 158). Though elite executive and judicial officials of both parties tend to be quite affluent, Republican political appointees tend to be significantly wealthier than their Democratic counterparts; for example, 22.3 percent of the federal district judges Reagan appointed in his first term had a net worth of more than a million dollars, compared to only 4.0 percent of Carter's district-judge appointments. (David M. O'Brien, "The Reagan Judges: His Most Enduring Legacy?" in Charles O. Jones, *The Reagan Legacy: Promise and Performance*, Chatham, New Jersey: Chatham House Publishers, 1988, Table 3.6, p. 77.)

nantly Republican national economic elite is further magnified by a de facto alliance between affluent conservatives in the populous states and conservative whites in the sparsely populated Rocky Mountain and New England states. Today, thanks to the constitutional provision that assigns two senators to every state regardless of population, a small minority of the population can elect a majority of U.S. senators. Indeed, the Republicans won the Senate in 1980 for six years only because of their strong showing in the least populated states (which tend to be conservative and white); the territorial basis of the Senate, a form of built-in rural overrepresentation, permitted them to win a majority of seats with a minority of the nationwide popular vote. Thanks to malapportionment, a California voter, merely by moving to Nevada, can increase his influence in the U.S. Senate thirtyfold.

As it happens, nonwhite Americans are concentrated in the populous states whose influence suffers the greatest dilution in the Senate. Senators representing whites in the smaller states tend to vote against federal programs favored by the House and the president that chiefly benefit the disproportionately nonwhite lower classes in the populous states.*

The ideal of "one person, one vote," is not realized, or even remotely approached, in the contemporary United States. The dependence of politicians on a small number of large donors skews national politics in favor of affluent whites; low voter turnout skews it further, and Senate malapportionment skews it further still. The decline of the parties has resulted in a media-driven, plebiscitary presidency and a Congress filled with members dependent upon campaign funds provided by wealthy lobbies, both American and foreign. The French political scientist Maurice Duverger suggested that a government with weak parties "is of necessity a conservative regime. To suppress parties would be an admirable way for the right to paralyze the left."[21] Referring to the diffuse, one-party system of the New South between the Civil War and the Civil Rights Revolution, V. O. Key concluded that "over the long run the have-nots lose in a disorganized politics. They have no mechanism

---

*President Clinton's budget package passed only after the gasoline tax was lowered to appease Western senators. Clinton's domestic stimulus program, which was aimed at helping alleviate unemployment in the major metropolitan areas, was effectively killed by conservative Democrats from the small Western states, led by Senator David Boren of Oklahoma.

through which to act and their wishes find expression in fitful rebellions led by transient demagogues who gain their confidence but often have neither the technical competence nor the necessary stable base of political power to effectuate a program."[22]

THE THIRD GRAND COMPROMISE

A single sentence from Marx explains the strategy of co-opting black and Hispanic leaders that continues to shape Multicultural America: "The more a ruling class is able to assimilate the most prominent men of the dominated classes, the more stable and *dangerous* its rule."[23]

Since the 1960s, the white overclass has sought to co-opt potential black leaders of dissent (and, to a lesser extent, Hispanic leaders) by means of racial preference machinery that has grown more elaborate with each passing decade. In doing so, the white overclass has indirectly encouraged the formation of the third major black elite in U.S. history after the antebellum mulatto elite and the post–Civil War black bourgeoisie: the black overclass.

The black overclass is not a wealthy elite, by the standards of the white overclass. The black elite, though well-off compared to poor urban blacks, controls very little private-sector business, compared to affluent whites. Using 1983 data, sociologist Bart Landry points out that "The top 163 companies on the *Fortune* 500 list had gross sales exceeding the top 100 black businesses *combined*."[24] Even among whites and blacks with similar incomes, whites had far more in assets: "In the upper middle class, white wealth exceeded that of blacks by *more* than two and one-half times."[25] Government employment is extremely important for the black middle class. Half of all black managers and professionals in the United States, according to one estimate, work for government at some level.[26] In 1980, 53.5 percent of blacks with managerial-professional jobs were employed by government at all levels, compared to only 27.5 percent of whites.[27] The data suggest a picture, not of a healthy black business and professional class, but of an economically insecure elite, heavily dependent on government work and government favors.

The new black overclass is not so much a middle-class as an imitation oligarchy, like its historic predecessors, the black bourgeoisie of Euro-America and the mulatto elite of Anglo-America. Of the two, the affirmative action elite resembles the antebellum mulatto elite of free urban blacks the most closely, in its dependence on white elite patronage. Unlike the black bourgeoisie, which was driven out of the white market and forced to serve ghetto clienteles, the pre–Civil War mulatto elite of barbers, caterers, and the like depended directly on the patronage of affluent white clients; the dependence of the affirmative action elite on the white oligarchy which instituted and preserves racial preference policies is less direct, but just as real. There is a striking contradiction between the radical talk of many members of the black overclass and their actual dependence on the white oligarchy that promotes and subsidizes them for reasons of its own.

Racial preference embodies the third grand compromise in American history. Each grand compromise, as I have argued, has been an extraconstitutional bargain, nowhere written down, but understood by political and social leaders. The Grand Compromise of Anglo-America was the extraconstitutional bargain between the northern elite and the southern planters, by which the planters agreed that the South would stay in the Union as long as the federal government did not interfere with southern slavery. In Euro-America, the Grand Compromise was an informal understanding between white leaders and white wage earners that nonwhites would not be used to undermine the economic and social status of the latter. The Grand Compromise of Multicultural America is the tacit understanding between the white overclass and the new nonwhite overclasses that, in return for being granted benefits in the form of racial preference programs, black and Hispanic leaders will not engage in disruptive mass agitation like that of the sixties.

In 1964, following demonstrations and pressure-group tactics by the Congress of Racial Equality (CORE), the A&P chain of food stores capitulated and made an agreement with CORE that 90 percent of its new employees in 1965 would be nonwhite.[28] The Dodge Revolutionary Union Movement (DRUM), a violence-prone organization of black auto workers in Detroit, demanded in 1968 that more black foremen be hired by the auto companies—or else.[29] "What most militants want," presidential candidate Richard Nixon explained in 1968, using the language of gangsterism, "is not separation, but to be included in . . . to have a share of the wealth, and a piece of the action."[30] Giving black leaders "a piece of the action" apparently succeeded. The cities stopped burning, though there were still occasional explosions, like the Los Angeles riots. The interests of the black poor and the black middle class—always arguably distinct—were further separated. The energies of middle-class black and Hispanic politicians and social activists were diverted from agitation on behalf of the poor into self-interested efforts to defend categorical entitlements for members of their own race *and* class. The opponents of the system became its clients, by being given "a share of the wealth, and a piece of the action."

The major beneficiaries of racial preference, it can be argued, are overclass whites, who by this policy of ethnic division and co-opting buy social peace. They also, incidentally, undermine any potential mass-based populism in the country. I do not mean to suggest actual conspiracy by members of the white overclass. There was never some secret meeting in the 1960s or 1970s, in a boardroom or penthouse or government office, where middle-aged white executives drafted a long-term plan for ruling-class domination. That is not how such social bargains are established. Rather, they are the result of incremental decisions, by many individuals and many groups, without central direction and often with conflicting purposes.

Nevertheless, while the origins of any particular grand compromise are obscure, there comes a moment where its nature is manifest. It is hard to pinpoint the exact origins of the North-South covenant at the heart of Anglo-America—the appointment of George Washington to command the rebels? the three-fifths clause in the 1787 Constitution? Still, by the time of the Compromise of 1820, if not earlier, the shape of the North-South deal was reasonably clear. Similarly, white labor won status and material concessions from white elites at different times in different parts of the United States; by the time the last black Reconstruction congressman left Congress and the door slammed shut on Asian immigration, the nature of the Euro-American compromise between white labor and white capital was apparent.

By 1977, the year in which the Office of Management and Budget, with Statistical Directive 15, formalized the new five-race division of the American population, the outlines of the Third Grand Compromise were clear. In November of that year, the *Atlantic Monthly* published an essay entitled "Who Gets Ahead in America?" by one of the paladins of the post–World War II American ascendancy, McGeorge Bundy, former

Special Assistant to the President for National Security Affairs, Deputy Secretary of State and then head of the Ford Foundation. Bundy—a leading example of who gets ahead in America—argued against racially neutral standards in college admissions: "To get past racism, we must here take account of race."*

Curiously, in his defense of racial preferences Bundy did not mention legacy preference policies at elite universities, the largest affirmative action program in the United States, which chiefly benefited—and continues to benefit—whites of his class. It was not that he was unaware of the effects on nonelite whites and nonwhites of legacy preferences, nor of the fact that legacies are significantly less qualified on average than students admitted on the basis of merit. After all, in addition to all his other honors, Bundy was former Dean of Harvard College.[31] Bundy, it appears, was in favor of making room for less-qualified nonwhite students at select universities—but by narrowing the number of pure merit admissions, so as not to affect the large quota for the mediocre children of the white oligarchy to which he belongs.

Members of the white overclass, insulated to a large degree from competition with middle-class Americans, can live with cultural separatism and categorical entitlements for nonwhites, as an earlier white elite learned to live with minor economic and social privileges for white labor. At the turn of the century it was much cheaper to ban Asian immigration and segregate trains than it was to pay for social programs for working-class Americans. Similarly, today it is much easier to co-opt the black and Hispanic middle classes through tokenism and symbolic concessions like ethnic-studies programs and a few more congressmen, elected from racially gerrymandered "majority-minority" districts, than

---

*The author of this endorsement of reverse discrimination against ordinary white Americans was born to a rich Boston Brahmin family. On his mother's side, he was kin to the influential Lowells. His father, Harvey H. Bundy, a partner in the elite Boston law firm of Choate, Hall & Stewart, succeeded John Foster Dulles as board chairman of the Carnegie Endowment for International Peace. Young McGeorge Bundy attended Groton and then Yale. His older brother William married Dean Acheson's daughter, while his sister Katherine was related by marriage to Jacqueline Onassis and Louis Auchincloss, the lawyer-novelist and chronicler of the American upper class. Bundy's career would hardly have been possible, but for his family connections. Members of the Bundy clan could well afford not to be bothered by racial quotas which reduced the upward mobility of white Americans without such connections.

it would be to undertake the dramatic reforms of American government and business that are necessary to integrate working-class and poor blacks and Hispanics, along with the absolute majority of the poor who are white, into the larger society.

In practice, racial preference means categorical representation *within* each class: upper-middle-class blacks in upper-middle-class professions, and working-class blacks in working-class occupations. The ritual that symbolizes Multicultural America is the "integration" of an all-white country club; invariably integration means admitting one of the wealthiest black citizens who can be found in the local community. Similarly, when it comes to presidential Cabinet appointments, race and gender are counted for diversity purposes, even if the Cabinet is uniform in socioeconomic terms—in terms of elite professions, high incomes, and elite educational backgrounds. Diversity means having rich professionals educated in the Ivy League who happen to belong to different races and sexes.

In every area where racial preference has been established, the tacit cooperation of the white overclass and the dependent black overclass is clear:

HIGHER EDUCATION. Nothing better illustrates the Third Grand Compromise than the existence of affirmative action in higher education for affluent black and Hispanic Americans—*and* for affluent white Americans.

In the late 1960s and early 1970s, the desire to impose categorical representation in a hurry led the federal judiciary in much of the country to take over local school systems and order busing for racial integration—defined as numerical parity of whites and nonwhites in classrooms. Although court-ordered busing continues, the enterprise has backfired, by provoking whites to leave urban areas for "white-flight" suburbs so their children will not be bused to inner-city schools. The result has been the collapse of urban tax systems and the further deterioration of inner-city schools, many of which now have black or Hispanic majorities.

Racial preference policies in higher education are enforced not only by federal agencies and courts, but by educational and professional accrediting associations, such as the regional college accrediting associations and the American Bar Association (ABA).* Legislation was introduced in California in 1989 to force the state's universities to "strive to approximate by the year 2000 a diverse student body which mirrors the composition of recent high school graduates . . . for individuals from historically and currently underrepresented or economically disadvantaged groups."[32]

In order not to lose accreditation, most colleges and universities try to have approximately as many black students as there are black Americans in the general population, around 12 percent. These goals and timetables can only be met by drastically lowering admissions standards for black students, who for obvious historical reasons are far less academically prepared than many of their white competitors. A black high school graduate in California with the minimum high school GPA has a 70 percent chance of being accepted to Berkeley, while a white high school student with the same score has only a 9 percent chance of admission.[33] At the University of Virginia, two thirds of black applicants were accepted, compared to fewer than half of the Asian-American applicants—even though the black students had SAT scores averaging 180 points lower than those of the Asian students.[34] Between 1985 and 1990, the average LSAT score for white students admitted to the University of Texas Law School was the 92nd percentile—and only the 55th percentile for black students. This enormous gap gives the lie to the argument that affirmative action affects only marginally qualified whites— the "margin" in this case is 37 percentile points. In order to accommodate a few less-qualified black students, the University of Texas Law School, like other leading law schools, must turn down hundreds or thousands of academically superior white students every year.[35]

Academic authorities frequently attempt to suppress discussion of preferential policies. In Spring 1991, for example, Timothy Maguire, a law student at Georgetown University Law Center, published an article entitled "Admissions Apartheid" in a school newspaper. The article de-

---

*The ABA requires accredited law schools to manifest "by concrete action, a commitment to providing full opportunities for the study of law and entry into the professions by qualified members of groups (notably racial and ethnic minorities) which have been victims of discrimination in various forms." *American Bar Association Standards for Approval of Law Schools* (1979), Standard 212, quoted in Lino Graglia, "Racial Preferences in Admission to Institutions of Higher Education," in Howard Dickman, ed., *The Imperiled Academy* (New Brunswick: Transaction, 1993), footnote 44, p. 150.

tailed the disparity between the test scores of successful black applicants to the law school and successful white applicants. In 1989, for example, the median LSAT score for entering white Georgetown Law students was 42; for blacks, it was 33 (the national average figures for white and black entrants to all law schools are 36 and 28). That black applicants are routinely preferred in college and professional-school admissions over whites with higher scores is common knowledge. Nevertheless, the Georgetown administration ordered the confiscation of every available copy of the newspaper with Maguire's article, tried to expel Maguire, and ordered two faculty members not to defend him (they refused, and Maguire successfully resisted expulsion).[36] Ordeals like Maguire's no doubt have had their intended effect—frightening potential white critics of affirmative action into silence.*

Few university officials have been as frank as one at the University of Wisconsin at Madison: "Millard Storey, director of undergraduate admissions, said that all minority students who are capable of success at Madison are admitted. White applicants then compete for the remaining places. . . . Many white applicants who could succeed at Madison are rejected, he added." Or James A. Blackburn, dean of admissions at the University of Virginia in 1988: "We are committed to a program of affirmative action, and we want to make the university representative of the population of the state as a whole. . . . We take more in the groups with weaker credentials and make it harder for those with stronger credentials."[37] Among those with "stronger credentials" are Asian-Americans, a diverse group chiefly made up of immigrants from East Asia and India, who along with whites are victims of government-sanctioned discrimination in Multicultural America. "Diversity" serves to keep their numbers artificially low in elite universities. According to the U.S. Commission of Civil Rights, "At such prestigious colleges as Harvard, Brown, Princeton, Yale, Stanford, and the University of California at Berkeley and Los Angeles, Asian American applicants were admitted at a lower rate than

---

*The Georgetown administration, like other university administrations, while denying that race was a compelling consideration, claimed that scores were not the only factor taken into account; essays were also important. If this is taken seriously, then one must conclude that black applicants to colleges and universities consistently write essays that are far superior to the essays of their higher-scoring white and Asian competitors.

white applicants at one point or another in the 1980s, although Asian American applicants had academic qualifications comparable to those of white applicants"—to say nothing of blacks or Hispanics.[38] In the 1980s, the Labor Department's U.S. Employment Service, which favored the use by state employment agencies of applicant screening by means of the General Aptitude Test Battery (GATB), recognizing that Asian-Americans as well as whites did well on tests, reduced the categories used in race-norming (percentile ranking of test takers only within their race) to three groups: blacks, Hispanics, and "Others." "The resulting percentile scores reflect an applicant's standing with reference to his or her own racial or ethnic group, thus effectively erasing average group differences in test scores."[39] Educational race-norming (which has since been outlawed) thus, for a time, created an entirely new "racial or ethnic group" through the combination of white and Asian-Americans: Other-Americans.

Racial preference in college admissions disproportionately benefits well-off black and Hispanic Americans. At Harvard, for example, 70 percent of black undergraduates are the children of parents in managerial or professional fields, while at Cornell twice as many minority students, in some years, come from the suburbs as from the cities.[40] At Berkeley in 1989, 17 percent of the Mexican-American students admitted under affirmative action came from families earning more than $75,000 a year; the median family income of Mexican-Americans enrolled at Berkeley, $32,500, was higher than the national median for all Americans, $32,191.[41] In 1978 Joseph Adelson described his experience on a graduate admissions committee at the University of Michigan:

> Of the five minority 'finalists,' three were attending elite private colleges, and two were at selective state universities. Only one had received scholarship help. Three of the five came from affluent—not merely comfortable—families, and one of these gave every evidence of being rich. The committee member who interviewed most of them reported back to our faculty, somewhat ruefully, that their average family income was considerably higher than that enjoyed by the faculty itself.[42]

Members of the white overclass in the United States tend to avoid criticism of racial preference in higher education, and with good reason: their own sons and daughters often benefit from an even more extensive program of favoritism based on ancestry. "I do not mean to overlook the resentments that can arise on the part of whites who feel unjustly excluded from the school of their choice," Derek Bok, then-president of Harvard University, wrote in 1985, defending racial preferences by reference to alumni legacies and athletic scholarships. "These disappointments are real, although I wonder why there are not similar resentments against other groups of favored applicants, such as athletes and alumni offspring."[43] There *would* be similar resentments, if the public were aware of just how many incompetent alumni offspring and athletes there really are. The extent of affirmative action in higher education for alumni relatives, and their academic mediocrity, compared to the nonlegacy students who are admitted, is one of the best-kept secrets of the American oligarchy. Neither overclass liberals nor overclass conservatives want the public to know about it, since in many cases their own children depend on legacy preference to get into selective schools.

Legacy preference is affirmative action for the white overclass. For almost half a century, one fifth of Harvard's students have been legacies, or children of alumni. Forty percent of alumni children are accepted to Harvard—compared to only 14 percent of ordinary applicants.[44] They are three times more likely to be accepted to Harvard than other high school graduates with the same (sometimes better) scores (at Harvard, the dean of admissions reads legacy applications—but not those of nonlegacies). Children of Yale graduates are two-and-a-half times more likely than nonalumni kin to be admitted to Yale. Stanford is somewhat more meritocratic—children of alumni are only *twice* as likely as equally qualified members of the general public to be admitted.

These alumni children are significantly less qualified than other students; according to the Office of Civil Rights (OCR) of the U.S. Department of Education, "with the exception of the athletic rating, nonlegacies scored better than legacies in *all* areas of comparison." The gap between legacies and nonlegacies, though not as striking as that between whites and minorities other than Asians, is still significant: according to a former Princeton dean of admissions, legacies at "one Ivy League university" had average SAT scores of 1,280—compared to the average of 1,350 out of a possible 1600 for the total freshman class. In order to accommodate such lower-scoring students from the upper classes, Harvard reserves 20 percent of its admissions, turning down much more talented young Americans from more modest social backgrounds. For every legacy who is admitted to an Ivy League university, dozens, perhaps hundreds, of applicants with better academic records and higher scores are turned away.

The best-kept secret in the United States is this: *legacy preference in college admissions is by far the biggest affirmative action program.* While blacks and Hispanics are more likely than middle-class whites to be admitted to Harvard, "a legacy is about twice as likely to be admitted as a black or Hispanic student." As one author notes:

> If alumni children were admitted to Harvard at the same rate as other applicants, their numbers in the class of 1992 would have been reduced by about 200. Instead, those 200 marginally qualified legacies outnumbered all black, Mexican-American, native American, and Puerto Rican enrollees put together. If a few marginally qualified minorities are undermining Harvard's academic standards as much as conservatives charge, think about the damage all those legacies must be doing.[45]

The legacy system was devised seventy years ago to keep Jews out of prestigious universities. Alarmed by Jewish academic success, Harvard, Yale, and Princeton—which previously had admitted students on the basis of entrance exams—began to use lineage as a qualification in the 1920s. In 1925, Yale announced that it would admit "Yale sons of good character and reasonably good record . . . *regardless of the number of applicants and the superiority of outside competitors* [italics added for emphasis]." The system persists, universities claim, because alumni would not contribute money to the university if they could not buy special consideration for their relatively untalented children. Whatever the excuses offered to the public, the effect of legacy preference is to retard social mobility and to turn the new American oligarchy into a semihereditary aristocracy.

To the seventy-year-old system of upper-status affirmative action embodied in legacy preference has been added a new one: quotas for women. If there is a quota for women in a freshman class in an elite university, that quota is likely to be filled by better-educated women from the families belonging to the white overclass, not by lower-middle-class, working-class and poor women. (Many affluent women, of course, can get in under two quotas—as women and as legacies). Coeducation, combined with quotas for women, hardens class distinctions by increasing the chances that elite whites of both sexes will marry within their own class (literally, in some cases—Digby Baltzell has joked that the dean of admissions is the new marriage broker).

RACIAL PREFERENCE IN THE PRIVATE SECTOR. Title VII, Section (703)(j) of the 1964 Civil Rights Act states that nothing in the Act "shall be interpreted to require any employer . . . to grant preferential treatment to any individual or to any group . . . on account of an imbalance which may exist with respect to the total number or percentage of persons of any race, color, religion, sex, or national origin employed by an employer. . . ." Senator Hubert Humphrey explained, "Title VII does not require an employer to achieve any sort of racial balance in his work force by giving preferential treatment to any individual or group."[46] As the law has been interpreted by bureaucrats and judges, of course, it *does* mandate quotas, in effect if not strictly according to the letter. The intent of Congress to outlaw both segregation and reverse racism was quickly subverted by the executive branch and the judiciary. While the Civil Rights Act was debated in public, the present racial regime in the United States was created in secrecy, by executive fiat. In May 1968, the Department of Labor issued regulations defining "affirmative action." The phrase had been used in President Kennedy's Executive Order No. 10925 and President Johnson's Executive Order No. 11246 to mean advertising for nontraditional applicants. In the hands of Labor Department bureaucrats, affirmative action was reinterpreted to mandate "specific goals and time-tables" for the employment of certain groups—"Negroes," "Orientals," "American Indians," and "Spanish Americans" (of "Latin American, Mexican, Puerto Rican, or Spanish origin.")[47] The ever-present threat of federal litigation and public scandal already has made tokenism standard operating procedure for most large businesses and law firms. Forty-eight of 500 CEOs surveyed by *Fortune* complained that competitors try to lure away their best minorities.[48]

Quotas in employment, as in education, chiefly benefit the affluent black and Hispanic Americans who need them least. It is true that many black professionals in the private sector encounter a "glass ceiling" when they try to rise in corporate management. Many are shunted into marginal posts in which they deal chiefly with other blacks, like vice-president for minority liaison. These experiences are often taken as proof that American society is incorrigibly racist. In fact they merely reveal racial preference for what it is—tokenism by the white overclass.

By 1989, nearly two hundred local governments and thirty-six states had minority set-aside programs for minorities and women (including white women).[49] Washington, D.C. set aside 35 percent of its contracts for nonwhites or women.[50] In what may be the crudest example of this form of patronage to date, the city of San Francisco decided that 80 percent of its legal services work should be equally divided among Asians, Latinos, blacks, and women.[51] Often these were mere fronts for organizations run by white men. A *Washington Post* survey of the Maryland Department of Transportation found that the top recipient of minority set-aside contracts was a man who had always been identified as white but claims to be five-eighths Indian.[52]

Section 8(a) of the Small Business Act defines an economically disadvantaged member of a minority group as someone with a personal net worth of less than $750,000. The average net worth of those who benefited from this provision was $160,000—more than twice the national average net worth of American families, white and black ($78,000) and *eight times as much* as the net worth of the average black family ($20,000). The $3.2 billion that went to "economically disadvantaged" minority-group members in 1988 alone clearly was not reaching many poor blacks or Hispanics.[53]

Urban development projects show the collusion between the white overclass and affluent blacks at its most blatant. In the 1970s, while cities like New York, Chicago, Cleveland, Detroit, Minneapolis, Philadelphia and other large cities were laying off disproportionately nonwhite public employees—not just bureaucrats, but police officers, firefighters, nurses, teachers—they were granting enormous tax abatements to private developers and funded programs intended to stimulate downtown development. New York, originally intending to subsidize apartments for the poor and middle class in lower Manhattan's Battery Park City, a complex of apartment buildings and office towers, instead granted tax abatements to luxury apartments. The city subsidized the opulent Trump Tower on Fifth Avenue, containing million-dollar condominiums, with $100 million in tax abatements.[54] Thanks in large part to such sweetheart deals, urban business districts have boomed even as the livability of the cities has declined. According to Joel Garreau, "From Boston to Philadelphia to Washington to Los Angeles to San Francisco to Seattle to Houston to Dallas to Atlanta, the business districts of the downtowns thrived" in the 1980s.[55]

If subsidies to developers are one side of the urban-development bargain, favoritism for nonwhites is the other. Minorities got 1,100 of the 1,900 new jobs in Boston's Copley Place. In Baltimore, black leaders pressured the developer James Rouse to promise 10 percent of contracts, 25 percent of construction jobs, and 50 percent in Rouse Company–controlled jobs in return for their support of a bond issue to finance the Harborplace project. In Detroit, Mayor Coleman Young followed a similar strategy—cutting city services and granting tax abatements to white businesses in return for favoritism to blacks: "He and his business allies worked openly to develop a black professional and managerial class and to encourage black entrepreneurs."[56] In Los Angeles, Mayor Tom Bradley sought to solve the city's financial problems by empowering the Community Redevelopment Agency (CRA), which in the words of one critic "bought up large parcels of land and sold the most expensive real estate in California to private developers at fire-sale prices." Although Bradley "did quite a bit to advance a small stratum of black elected officials, business people, and professionals," he failed to arrest the deterioration that contributed to the 1992 riots in L.A.[57] Conventional liberals, though, are unable to admit that well-to-do black and Hispanic machine politicians as well as overclass whites may share responsibility for disastrous municipal policies.

Just as white overclass women benefit from affirmative action under gender quotas, so they can share the spoils of "minority" business programs. In 1983 Vernon Jordan applied for the licenses of two radio stations in the Washington area as a partner of Vernell Broadcasting, a minority-owned firm. The partnership that won the licenses paid Vernell $765,000 in order not to litigate the FCC's decision; another $2.05 million went to another minority-owner group in which Jordan's stepdaughter Antoinette Cook held a 26.5 percent equity interest. Later Jordan wrote an amicus brief defending the kind of racial preference policies in broadcasting from which he and his family had thus personally profited (the Supreme Court upheld such preferences in its 1990 *Metro Broadcasting vs. FCC* decision).[58] Jordan became Bill Clinton's transition chairman.

The "minorities" who owned Vernell Broadcasting included black men like Jordan, a Hispanic woman, and members of that other oppressed minority, white women. In the previous chapter I noted the political calculus that led to the exclusion of white "ethnic" men from the affirmative action spoils system, no matter how disadvantaged, and the inclusion of white women, no matter how rich. It should come as no surprise that the top-ranking "minority" brokerage firm in the United States, in terms of the total value of long-term municipal new issues in 1993, was Artemis Capital Group, a "women-owned" brokerage house.

Firms like Artemis take advantage of requirements that federal agencies sell fixed proportions of their bonds (quotas) through minority-owned brokerage firms. To channel this largesse, around 300 minority firms have been founded—half of them, according to one scholar, being mere "storefront" firms that exist only to channel bonds from government agencies to big Wall Street houses in return for a share of the profits. Often Wall Street firms themselves help found minority firms—and then buy stakes in them.[59]

RACIAL PREFERENCE IN POLITICS. Section 5 of the Voting Rights Act of 1965, intended to guarantee black access to the polls, has been interpreted by the Supreme Court and successive Justice Departments as mandating the reconstruction of state and local districts and electoral mechanisms to ensure that racial minorities will elect candidates of their race. The 1975 amendments to the Act have extended gerrymandering in the interests of ethnic proportional representation to "linguistic minorities" such as Mexican-Americans and Asian-Americans.

After the 1990 census, legislative redistricting along racial lines resulted in an increase of black-majority congressional districts from 17 to 32. The number of Hispanic-majority districts more than doubled, from 9 to 20. Rigging electoral rules has resulted in dramatic increases in black representation without any corresponding increase in the size of the black electorate. In the elections of 1992, members of the Congressional Black Caucus (CBC) increased from 26 to 39. The significant leap in the number of black representatives was purely the result of racial gerrymandering. Meanwhile, the Democrats in Congress who are the chief defenders of racial preferences continued to exempt themselves from the civil-rights laws they impose on everyone else. Only 3.7 percent of the 8,200 influential jobs in Congress are held by black Americans—and almost half of those work for minority members of Congress.[60] Affirmative action, it appears, is good for every public and private institution in the United States—except the Congress.

It may very well be that conservative whites are the greatest beneficiaries of racial gerrymandering. The corralling of black voters in bizarrely shaped districts like the infamous twelfth Congressional District in North Carolina strips them from adjacent districts. One black-majority or Hispanic-majority district may be a small price to pay, from the point of view of conservatives, for two or three new lily-white districts. This explains why Republican appointees to the Justice Department in the Reagan and Bush administrations collaborated with black state legislators across the country to promote racial gerrymandering.

Why should conservative Republican support for racial gerrymandering come as a surprise? Racial gerrymandering is only a liberal idea if one accepts the equation between "black American" and "liberal." The conventional black agenda, far from being a liberal agenda, tends to be the agenda of a self-interested black establishment (whose members are no worse, but no better, than the white establishment). The domination of American politics in general by the wealthy and highly educated is paralleled by the predominance, in black political organizations such as the National Association for the Advancement of Colored People (NAACP) and the National Urban League, of affluent and educated black Americans. According to one authority, "The existing Black political organizations, therefore, currently enhance, rather than diminish, the political participation gap within the Black community based on social class."[61]

CLASS CONFLICT AND RACIAL MYSTICISM

The Multicultural American system of racial-preference policies, with special educational, business, and political privileges for blacks, has been in place for three decades. During that time, the ratio of poor blacks to the total black population, about a third, has remained constant.[62] Indeed, while racial preference continues to be extended to new areas (the

1992 congressional elections marked a new, much more radical phase of racial gerrymandering), the situation in the black ghetto has grown far worse than it was in the sixties.

In the ghetto, Bayard Rustin noted in 1967, to "segregation by race, was now added segregation by class, and all the problems created by segregation and poverty—inadequate schooling, substandard and overcrowded housing, lack of access to jobs and job training, narcotics and crime—were greatly exaggerated."[63] Since then, illegitimacy rates have risen to alarming levels. In 1989 the illegitimacy rate among black Americans was 65.7 percent (it would have been higher, but for the 37 percent of black pregnancies that are terminated by abortion). By 1990 63 percent of black children lived in single-parent families. Only the most obstinate radicals could now deny that there was some link between family breakdown, cultural deviance, and social disorder. The link between fatherless families and poverty is well established: in 1990 a single-parent black family had a median income of only 36 percent of that of a two-parent black family (the figure was 42 percent for whites).[64] In the northeastern cities, the black poor continue to be concentrated in nearly all-black neighborhoods, isolated from the rest of society. In 1980, an average black resident was likely to live in a neighborhood that was at least 80 percent black in Atlanta, Baltimore, Chicago, Cleveland, Detroit, Gary, Newark, Philadelphia, St. Louis, and Washington, D.C.[66] No other minority group, including Hispanics, is separated to this degree. As Douglas S. Massey and Nancy A. Denton note, "People growing up in such an environment have little direct experience with the culture, norms, and behaviors of the rest of American society and few social contacts with members of other racial groups."[66] Although a majority of black Americans have improved their educational and professional status, the ghetto underclass has been diverging from the rest of the nation not only in behavior—with an unprecedented rate of births out of wedlock, drug addiction, and violence—but in language. Since the 1960s, the Black English vernaculars of New York, Boston, Chicago, and other large cities have become increasingly similar, even while these dialects diverge from standard English. Increasingly, poor black Americans speak a separate language, with its own distinct grammar, pronunciation, and vocabulary.[67]

Today's policies of preferential treatment on the basis of race, William

Julius Wilson has argued, "improve the opportunities of the advantaged without necessarily addressing the problems of the truly disadvantaged such as the ghetto underclass."[68] According to Wilson, "If you were to wave a magic wand, and there was no more racism, the situation of the ghetto underclass would not change significantly unless you did something about the economy and the communities they live in."[69] In the 1960s, Bayard Rustin had made a similar argument about the irrelevance of affirmative action to the desperately poor: "I fail to see how the (civil rights) movement can be victorious in the absence of radical programs for full employment, abolition of slums, the reconstruction of our educational system. . . ." Calling for "a refashioning of our political economy," Rustin argued that federal action was necessary to integrate unskilled and semiskilled black workers into the job market: "'Preferential treatment' cannot help them."[70] His criticism had been anticipated by Ralph Bunche, who as early as 1940 criticized the NAACP for concentrating on the concerns of middle-class blacks and ignoring the threats posed by "deprivation" and "destitution" to poor blacks: "They cry for bread and are offered political cake."[71]

The irrelevance of the concerns of the black middle and upper-middle class to those of inner-city blacks was symbolized by a telling incident that occurred during the Los Angeles riots in 1991. During his announcement of a citywide curfew during the Los Angeles riots, Mayor Tom Bradley, a representative figure of the new black political establishment, called on everyone to "stay home and watch the Cosby show"—referring to the final episode of an anodyne sitcom about a wealthy, all-American black family in the suburbs whose lives were unimaginably remote from the experiences of the black poor in the burning ghetto.

In order to justify the fiction that privileges for well-to-do blacks benefit the black American population as a whole, including the urban poor, members of the black overclass often stress racial unity and downplay class differences among black Americans. Surveys show that consciousness of race rather than class is much stronger among affluent black Americans. According to one study, more than 60 percent of black Americans who identified themselves as middle-class said they felt closer to their race than to their class, compared to only 5 percent of self-described poor and working-class blacks.[72] Other studies have confirmed that race-consciousness is highest among upper-status, not lower-status, black Americans.[73]

Racial mysticism—the idea of a homogeneous black community that transcends class and partisan and regional differences among black Americans—reinforces the idea that whatever benefits upper-income black Americans is a victory for all black Americans. It reinforces the idea that the way to help the black ghetto poor is to do favors for the black overclass.

In this connection, it is interesting to note that the black American population is divided along class lines with respect to attitudes toward government programs. College-educated blacks are just as likely to support affirmative action and minority aid, programs that benefit affluent as well as poor blacks. However, college-educated blacks are more likely to be opposed to increased spending on jobs, food stamps, and Medicare—programs that disproportionately benefit low-income blacks.[74]

Residential integration, the most promising method of eliminating the ghettos forever, is in the interest of disadvantaged black Americans—but not necessarily in the interest of the black political class. Douglas S. Massey and Nancy A. Denton, students of the politics of residential segregation, observe: "It has been many years since civil rights leaders have organized marches in support of residential integration, demanded desegregation in the real estate industry, or supported efforts to disperse black housing outside the ghetto—most likely because it has not been in their interest to do so."[75] Black congressmen attacked a 1978 General Accounting Office report critical of the slow progress of HUD in "deconcentration"—the dispersal of poor blacks in public housing in nonblack majority communities.[76] The dilution of black ghettos would undermine the power of black politicians from ghetto districts.

One aspect of racial mysticism is the blurring of the distinction between anarchic ghetto violence and legitimate civil rights protests—both are supposed to be manifestations of the rage of a classless, national, homogeneous black community. A version of this gambit is evident in *Black Looks,* a collection of essays by bell hooks (the *nom de plume* of Gloria Watkins, a professor of English and women's studies at Oberlin). In her essay "Why L.A. Happened," hooks strives to exonerate black rioters, criminals, and looters from any personal responsibility for their crimes. Blacks who steal from burned-out businesses, according to hooks, provide a "tragic expression of powerlessness." To the contrary, looting would seem to be the ultimate exercise of illegitimate power, that is, force, unchecked by law, at the expense of those with legitimate property rights but lacking in power to defend them, either their own power or that of the state. According to hooks, those who condemned the riots sought "to justify and reinforce white supremacy."[77] In fact, no one used the L.A. riots as an occasion to call for the restoration of white-supremacist institutions such as the banning of nonwhites from juries, police forces, elective offices and schools, or separate white and black drinking fountains and doorways.

But white supremacy when used by ideologues such as bell hooks does not really mean white supremacy—it is merely part of the ritualized rhetoric of cross-class black racial unity, like the metaphor of lynching. During the Anita Hill controversy, Clarence Thomas accused the Senate Jurisprudence Committee of staging a "high-tech lynching," although the accusations against him were lodged by a black woman, and had nothing to do with race. This was a demagogic appeal to black Americans to rally behind him, not as liberals or conservatives, or men or women, but *as blacks.* Similarly, Lani Guinier, before her nomination (later withdrawn) by President Clinton to head the Justice Department's Civil Rights Division, compared the Supreme Court decision in *Pressley v. Etowah County,* a decision under the Voting Rights Act, to a lynching, and accused the justices of resurrecting "the rhetoric and logic of white supremacy." The lynching motif is not so much partisan language as class language—the language of the new black overclass, regardless of political affiliation.

Despite its origins on the left wing of the civil rights movement in CORE and SNCC (and their successor, Jesse Jackson's PUSH), racial preference is in reality a conservative policy, a form of elaborate but ultimately superficial tokenism that is much less costly, to affluent whites in general and the business class in particular, than expensive universal programs designed to improve the educations and standard of living of the bottom half of the population, of all races. Compared to color-blind liberalism, racial preference is *cheap.*

Far from being an assault on the white male power structure, racial preference is a means by which the black and Hispanic affirmative action elites are turned into dependent clients of the white overclass. Thanks to legacy preference at elite schools, the lower-scoring children of the white overclass benefit from the same kind of affirmative action in college admissions that has been extended to affluent black and Hispanic students. Quotas for women, imposed without means tests, permit wealthy white women to join well-to-do blacks and Hispanics in obtaining special treatment in hiring and taxpayer-subsidized set-asides. Racial gerrymandering concentrates black and Hispanic voters in a few districts, increasing the number and racial homogeneity of white-majority districts, to the benefit of Republicans and conservative Democrats.

In 1963, on the eve of the racial preference revolution that destroyed color-blind liberalism and created Multicultural America, Lyndon Johnson warned: "We are not going to solve this problem by promoting minorities. That philosophy is merely another way of freezing the minority group status system in perpetuity."[78] His words were prophetic.

CHAPTER FIVE

The Revolution of the Rich

Since the 1960s, two apparently contradictory trends have been trans-forming American society. On the one hand, racial preference policies, associated with the political left, have been extended into one area of American life after another: primary education, college admissions, em-ployment, congressional redistricting. At the same time, since the six-ties, government policies favorable to business and unfavorable to labor, of the kind one thinks of as conservative, have been pursued under both Republican and Democratic administrations. As a result, the income gains and economic security achieved by middle-class Americans in the middle of the twentieth century, under New Deal presidents like FDR, Truman, and Johnson, have been steadily rolled back. Between 1973 and 1992, while the richest 10 percent of American families experienced an 18 percent increase in real income, the real income of the poorest 10 percent sank by 11 percent. Income inequality in the United States today is greater than it has been since the 1930s.[1]

In reality, there is no contradiction between the left-wing civil rights policy and right-wing economics of the contemporary United States. Both racial preference and free-market economic conservatism serve the interests of the new American oligarchy, the white overclass.

The Civil Rights Revolution was perverted into a racial preference revolution by white leaders in the public and private sectors who sought to end disruptive black agitation by quickly appeasing and co-opting black leaders. One of the unintended side effects of this shift in civil rights strategy was to shatter the New Deal coalition that had supported progressive reform in the United States since the 1930s. Conservatives were quick to take advantage of this; remember how Richard Nixon and George Shultz pushed racial quotas in unions, in order to stoke resentment on the part of white workers against black Americans and the Democratic party. As Nixon realized, the greatest beneficiary of the demise of transracial class politics has been the white overclass. Since the 1960s, the effect—and, in the minds of at least some cynical conservative politicians, the purpose—of racial preference and the multicultural ideology that justifies it has been to divert attention from the class divisions in American society and focus it on racial/cultural squabbles.

The divisions between white, black, and Hispanic wage earners, the natural constituents of a broad liberal coalition, have made it easier for members of the white overclass—an extraordinarily homogeneous, powerful, and well-organized group—to pursue their own narrow economic agenda at the expense of most other Americans. The disproportionate influence in government of the white overclass, provided by a near-monopoly on campaign finance and the staffing of elite offices in both national parties, helps explain why, since the sixties, the bipartisan political elite has made the American tax system more regressive, undermined the New Deal social market contract through free-market globalism and mass immigration, and promoted a new feudalism, through the privatization of formerly public amenities.*

While colleges and congressional classes have been rearranged according to the logic of racial tokenism, the white overclass has steadily carried out its generation-long class war against wage-earning Americans of all races. As racially gerrymandered congressional districts proliferate, union membership falls, the victim of a government-sanctioned onslaught against organized labor by corporate America. As the number of black and Hispanic heroes and heroines in school textbooks increas-

---

*In personifying the overclass and describing its strategy, I do not mean to imply the existence of a literal conspiracy. When members of a disproportionately powerful class pursue similar class-based interests, the result will be similar to that of a conscious program even if there has been no concerted action.

es, the average wages of black and Hispanic workers, along with those of white workers, continue to stagnate or decline.

Meanwhile, behind the Potemkin-village façade of Multicultural America, with its five separate-but-equal official races and its decorative racially authentic folk art, the Amerian oligarchy is quietly cannibalizing the remnants of mid-century New Deal America to construct its own enclave society, an America-within-America, linked to the global economy and detached from the destiny of the American middle class. Members of the white overclass withdraw their children from the public schools, then finance and lead taxpayer revolts that cause local school systems to collapse in bankruptcy (to add insult to injury, some of them then support school voucher plans, which would force working-class parents to subsidize the expensive private education of rich children). Affluent suburbanites hire their own police forces—then agitate to cut back on the taxes that pay for the municipal police that protect the majority of their neighbors. When inadequate policing results in high crime rates, the politicians who serve the white overclass, as a rule, do not vote to pay for more police (that would cost their wealthy constituents money) but call for draconian punishments: more prisons, more executions, public floggings, three strikes and you're out. Finally, as part of an ominous trend, the wealthy residents of a growing number of overclass suburbs are trying to turn them into "gated communities," physically separated from the the vulgar majority of their countrymen.

In any other democracy, the majority would have coalesced by now in a populist rebellion. In Multicultural America, however, the majority is fragmented while the elite is unified. The bipartisan white overclass can pursue its goals with little opposition, as long as racial preference policies, the ideology of diversity, and culture-war politics encourage potential opponents to battle among themselves. The constitution of nineteenth-century Russia, it was said, was autocracy tempered by assassination. The constitution of the Third American Republic is plutocracy tempered by tokenism.

THE REDEFINITION OF LIBERALISM AND CONSERVATISM

The shifting of the center of political gravity in both parties toward the top 5 or 10 percent of the white population has transformed the definitions of liberalism and conservatism in American politics. Whereas in the mid-twentieth century liberals and conservatives tended to share a common moral and cultural consensus, disagreeing over economic issues, at the end of the twentieth century mainstream liberals and conservatives share a common economic consensus and focus on mostly symbolic cultural disputes. Liberals and conservatives today tend to agree on the fundamentals—free trade (or what is called free trade) and an activist, universalist, interventionist foreign policy—but agree to disagree on inflammatory but marginal issues like abortion, gay rights, and the question of public subsidies for the arts.

Despite appearances, Republicans have made their peace with the new racial order of Multicultural America. Republicans practice tokenism in appointments (for example, appointing Clarence Thomas to "the black seat" on the Supreme Court), and support race-based redistricting. Richard Riordan, the Republican Mayor of Los Angeles, made sure that exactly half of his appointments were women, with six Latinos, five black Americans, and four Asian-Americans. Lynn Martin, Labor Secretary under Bush, pressured businesses to promote minorities and women under her "Glass Ceiling Initiative."[2] Conservatives also follow the standard practice of getting only nonwhites to criticize the civil rights lobby and women to criticize feminism—a practice that reinforces the very conceptions that are attacked.

Many Republicans, however, follow the Machiavellian example of Richard Nixon, who promoted racial preference policies while tacitly stoking resentment against them on the part of white Americans. Today's Republican strategy also resembles that of the old Southern Bourbons, who for generations after the 1890s used racism and cultural populism to prevent the formation of a biracial alliance devoted to economic reform. Genuine populism is always a threat to overclass conservatism. Real Southern and western populism could be glimpsed in the presidential campaigns of George Wallace and Ross Perot, both of whom were economic as well as cultural populists. Perot, whom many believe denied the White House to the Republican Party, talked like a Republican but took up the cause of blue-collar workers and attacked the conservative dogma of free trade. This kind of consistent social and economic populism makes establishment conservatives in the 1990s shudder, just as it frightened Southern Bourbon Democrats in the 1890s.*

Like the Bourbons of yesteryear, today's conservatives play up "culture war" in order to play down "class war." To be sure, some conservatives claim that all social classes will benefit from the conservative program of lower taxes on the rich and fewer restraints on business. Rush Limbaugh makes the claim of a community of economic interest between the corporate elite and his middle-class listeners explicit: "Just keep this in mind: Today it's the pharmaceutical manufacturers, the cable TV industry, insurance companies, physicians, and chief executive officers of major corporations (Clinton is) targeting. Tomorrow it could be you."[3] The problem with this attempt to base a conservative alliance on cross-class economic interests was explained by Lee Atwater in a 1984 campaign memo:

> Populists have always been liberal on economics. So long as the crucial issues were generally confined to economics—as during the New Deal—the liberal candidate would expect to get most of the populist vote. But populists are conservatives on most social issues. . . . When social and cultural issues died down, the populists were left with no compelling reason to vote Republican. . . .[4]

Cultural populism, according to Republican pollster Fred Steeper, "gets us a lower-end vote that we wouldn't get on just economic issues."[5]

As part of this neo-Bourbon cultural populism, since the sixties the Republicans—who from Lincoln to Eisenhower saw themselves, if only intermittently, as defenders of black Americans—have subtly played on antiblack sentiments among lower-income white voters, especially white Southerners. The left, to be sure, exaggerates the extent to which the

---

*Both Perot and Wallace show the influence of an older Populist-Progressive alliance against Southern Bourbon conservatism in Texas politics. Wallace, who governed from behind the scenes when his wife Lurleen became governor, was inspired in part by the populist-progressive Texas Governors "Ma" (Miriam) and "Pa" (James E.) Ferguson, a husband-and-wife team who dominated early-twentieth-century Texas politics and, among other things, decimated the Ku Klux Klan. Lyndon Johnson, whose father was a major Ferguson supporter in the Texas legislature, told Wallace the story of the Fergusons at a White House luncheon for governors in 1966. See Stephan Lesher, *George Wallace: American Populist* (New York: Addison-Wesley, 1994), pp. 359–360.

right speaks in a racial code. The ideal of color-blind, equal-rights integration—adopted, belatedly, by conservatives who had earlier supported segregation—is a perfectly liberal idea, not racism in disguise. Nor is "law and order" a racist issue simply because a disproportionate number of criminals are black (so are a disproportionate number of the victims of violent crime).

No such excuse can be found for other conservative practices, such as deriding black women as "queens."* The term *queen* is an allusion to a standard element of minstrel-show humor, the black American who puts on royal or upper-class airs, like the self-important "Kingfish" in *Amos 'n' Andy*. The conservative press activates these lingering racist associations by appending the term queen to any black woman in public life whom it seeks to vilify (no white woman has ever been dubbed a queen by conservative publicists and politicians). The more that American conservatism becomes a lobby for lower taxes on the rich, the more important it is to establish its populist credentials, by covert appeals to white racism as well as theatrical patriotism and diatribes against intellectuals, bureaucrats, homosexuals, and the poor.

The neo-Bourbon strategy of the right since the sixties might have been thwarted by a strong, transracial economic populism. But a program of radical reform on behalf of middle-class and working-class Americans is not in the interest of a Democratic party which, like the Republican party, has been captured by the white overclass.

The Democratic party of today is not the Democratic party of FDR, Truman, and Johnson. The big change came in the sixties and seventies, when the old white labor–Southern white coalition was replaced by a

---

*Lani Guinier, the nominee for assistant attorney general whose nomination Clinton withdrew, was labeled a "quota queen" by conservative journalists and activists. The former Surgeon General of the United States, Dr. Joycelyn Elders, has been described as a "condom queen" because she favors the distribution of condoms by public high schools to sexually active teens. Where did this politically charged description of black women as queens come from? The answer is Ronald Reagan. In his first presidential campaign in 1976, Reagan, a millionaire, campaigned against welfare, repeatedly alluding to an apocryphal Chicago "welfare queen" whose "tax-free cash income (from the government) is over $150,000" as though she were typical of welfare recipients (*New York Times*, February 15, 1976, cited in Mark Green and Gail MacColl, *Reagan's Reign of Error*, New York: Pantheon, 1987, p. 85). The "welfare queen" was understood to be black. See Miles Harvey, "Queen for a Day," *In These Times*, October 4, 1993, p. 40.

suburban white liberal–black and Hispanic coalition. There *was* a re-alignment in national politics, but it took place *within* the dominant Democratic party, almost a generation ago. Although the Democratic party has more middle-class and working class voters, the power of organized labor has radically declined, as suburban activists, more interested in race and gender quotas and environmentalism than bread-and-butter populist issues, have replaced labor leaders in the inner circles of the party. Business interests are now more important than labor in the Democratic party; in 1984, corporate contributions to the Democratic party exceeded labor-movement donations for the first time.

The growing solicitude toward the class interests of the wealthy and the neglect of the economic interests of ordinary Americans displayed by the Democratic party in the past generation cannot be blamed on the old bipartisan coalition of Republicans and conservative Democrats that was once called the permanent congressional majority.[6] Since the liberal revolt against the Southern-dominated New Deal congressional elite in the 1960s and 1970s, the conservative coalition has declined in importance, while party-line votes have increased. In the 1980s, the conservative coalition materialized only in 10 percent of votes.[7] The shifting of the tax burden from wealthy rentiers, investors, corporate executives, and elite professionals to working Americans was not the work of back-room plotting by Southern Dixiecrats and Republicans; it was done in broad daylight by Congresses dominated by a largely northern, socially liberal party, grown addicted since the seventies to cash flows from business PACs and wealthy individual contributors.

White overclass liberals have redefined liberalism to mean support for multicultural pseudonationalism instead of old-fashioned economic egalitarianism. The real progenitor of modern overclass liberalism, it can be suggested, was Abbie Hoffman, when he proclaimed the existence of a harmless simulacrum of black nationalism, "Woodstock Nation." Black nationalism, for all the falsity of its claims, does have historic roots in America. By contrast, Woodstock Nation, Queer Nation, and all the other pseudonations—Hispanic, Asian, feminist—are about as real as the Pepsi Generation.

The yuppie populism of Lee Atwater and the yippie nationalism of Abbie Hoffman solve the same problem for white overclass leaders in both the Republican and Democratic parties: averting economic populism, by means of a symbolic politics of culture and race. Post-sixties liberals and post-sixties conservatives share a tacit agreement not to question the basic arrangements and outcomes of contemporary American capitalism, and to allow impassioned debate only on largely symbolic issues.

All of this represents a victory for the man who, more than any other, is responsible for Multicultural America—not Lyndon Johnson, not Martin Luther King, not even James Farmer, but Richard M. Nixon. The replacement of transracial class-war politics benefiting social-democratic liberal politicians by the kind of racially polarized culture-war politics at which conservatives excel was neither natural nor inevitable. It is the result, in part, of a conscious divide-and-rule strategy by upper-income Republicans in the early 1970s, a strategy that sought to pit white and black workers against one another.

The Philadelphia Plan, devised during the Johnson administration by the Labor Department, was derailed by critics who claimed it imposed racial quotas. In the Nixon administration, however, it was revived and pushed through by George Shultz. Why would Republicans push for racial quotas in unions? According to John Ehrlichman, "Nixon thought that Secretary of Labor George Shultz had shown great style in constructing a political dilemma for the labor union leaders and civil rights groups."[8]

REGRESSIVE TAXATION

While middle-class and working-class Americans have divided over racial preference and symbolic issues, the overclass-dominated political elite of both parties has waged a generation-long class war against the middle class. That class war has been waged on three fronts: regressive taxation, free-market globalism, and the new feudalism.

The first front in the overclass war on the middle class has been the shift from progressive to regressive taxation. The upward redistribution of political power, caused by the decline of the parties and the rising importance of campaign finance, has been accompanied by a downward redistribution of the tax burden, from the white overclass to the majority. This downward redistribution of taxes was the most important effect of the Reagan Revolution.

Ronald Reagan was the first Republican president in history to campaign and govern claiming that government tax revenues would go up after tax rates were drastically lowered. In 1980, in the face of a $74 billion deficit, candidate Reagan claimed that it would be possible to cut taxes by 30 percent, keep major social programs intact, double defense (the largest budget item)—and, at the same time, produce a $100 billion *surplus* within the first three years! This was fantasy, of course, as Reagan's Republican rivals argued (George Bush called supply-side theory "voodoo economics," and David Stockman has since confessed that Reaganomics was a hoax). Just as conventional economists predicted, the result of Reaganomics was not a $100 billion surplus but a deficit that hovered around $200 billion throughout Reagan's two terms—almost three times what the deficit had been under Carter. During the first six years of the Reagan administration, the federal deficit, which between 1950 and 1980 grew at an average of only $50 billion a year, grew by an average of $161 billion annually.[9]* Unlike any other democracy in the First World, the United States since Reagan has treated massive borrowing, rather than taxation, as a more or less permanent method of financing government expenditures in peacetime.

While the deficit has exploded, federal spending has continued to grow, not only in absolute terms but as a percentage of GDP, expanding from 20 to 22 percent to more than 24 percent in the 1980s. The greatest growth has been in nondefense spending, which rose from 10.1 percent in 1965 to 17.5 percent in 1985.[10] Most of this nondefense spending growth was in entitlements which benefit middle- and upper-

---

*According to one study, 90 percent of the deficit-swelling shortfall in revenues in the 1980s is the result of Reagan's Economic Recovery Tax Act (ERTA) of 1981 (Richard M. Valelly, "Divided They Govern," *The American Prospect*, Fall 1992, p. 130). David Stockman writes, "As of August, 1981, Uncle Sam had been left to finance a 1980s-sized domestic welfare state and defense buildup from a general revenue base that was smaller relative to GNP than at any time since 1940!" (David A. Stockman, "America Is Not Overspending," *New Perspectives Quarterly*, Spring 1993, p. 13.) According to one estimate, if the richest 1 percent of the population had continued to pay taxes at the 1977 rate, adjusted for inflation, the federal deficit in 1990 would have been $160 billion less in 1990, and interest payments on the debt would have been $73 billion lower. (Robert S. McIntyre, "The Reaganites and the Renegade," *The American Prospect*, Winter 1991, p. 13.) By 1992 the debt of the U.S. government was the largest of twenty-three capitalist democracies, both in absolute terms and as a share of GDP, while total American taxes (federal, state and local) were *lower* than in any of these countries, except for Turkey. (Walter Dean Burnham, "The Legacy of George Bush: Travails of an Understudy," in Gerald M. Pomper, F. Christopher Arterton, Ross K. Baker, Walter Dean Burnham, Kathleen A. Frankovic, Marjorie Randon Hersey, Wilson Carey McWilliams, *The Election of 1992: Reports and Interpretations*, Chatham, New Jersey: Chatham House, 1993, pp. 16–17.)

income Americans; federal spending declined in the 1980s for public goods like law enforcement and government (by 42 percent), for education and training (by 40 percent) and for the transportation infrastructure (by 32 percent).[11] The peacetime federal budgets under Reagan consumed more, as a proportion of GDP (about a quarter), than the Vietnam-era wartime budgets under Johnson and Nixon.

To whom did this civilian spending go? Conventional political journalists and think-tank experts bemoan the greed of "the middle class"; we cannot blame the economic elite, they solemnly say, we are all to blame for the deficit. Perhaps so, but the economic elite gets far more in benefits from the government than the middle class and the poor. The Social Security checks that go to households with incomes of $100,000 or above tend to be twice as large as those of households with income under $10,000. Tax expenditures (tax deductions) are even more skewed in favor of the affluent; in 1993, while taxpayers earning $20–30,000 received on average only $478 from the home-mortgage interest deduction, households with incomes over $100,000 received $3,453. Eighty percent of the value of the home-mortgage interest deduction ($46 billion) will go to households whose incomes exceed $50,000 in 1994.[12]

These entitlement programs with affluent recipients are far more expensive than those directed to the poor—and far more popular. To no one's surprise, they were left untouched by Reagan and Bush. By contrast, between 1977 and 1990, chiefly as a result of cutbacks in federal social programs, the income of the poorest fifth of the American people fell by 14 percent in constant dollars.[13] The median value of Aid to Families with Dependent Children (AFDC) payments in the states for a family of four declined from 1975 to 1990 from $669 to $451 per month (in constant 1991 dollars). Since AFDC is not indexed for inflation, the real value of AFDC payments declined by 35 percent between 1975 and 1990.[14] Though conservatives claim to want to encourage poor people to work, during the Reagan years the working poor were hurt by the policy of deliberately keeping the minimum wage at $3.35 an hour in spite of inflation. The result was a disguised reduction in pay for minimum-wage workers, and other low-income workers whose salaries were keyed to the minimum wages, while transfer payments for the affluent remained generous.

"In order to succeed, the poor need most of all the spur of their poverty," writes conservative ideologue George Gilder.[15] According to supply-side theory, giving relief to the poor would discourage them from working at all—while leaving more money with the rich would make *them* work much harder, making the rest of us much better off. The origins of this motivational difference between the poor and the rich are never explained by conservatives. There is no evidence, however, that the wealthy have worked more, or shown a greater propensity to invest in productive ventures, as a result of the Reagan tax cuts. In 1989, the richest 1 percent of the population, or 932,000 families, together owned more than 90 percent of the American population did; 49 percent of their income, it has been calculated, consisted of returns on passive investments (real estate, stocks, bonds, trusts, and bank accounts).[16] Between 1983 and 1989, according to one study, the richest 1 percent of families increased their share of the nation's total private wealth from 31.3 percent to 36.2 percent. These tax savings for the super-rich did not produce a renaissance of productive investment. In fact, the percentage of the income of the top 1 percent derived from work, as opposed to passive investments (interest, capital gains, dividends), was roughly the same after the tax cuts as before.[17] The rate of new investment in addition to replacement of worn-out capital equipment actually declined during the Reagan administration to the lowest levels since 1961.[18] Notwithstanding the Reagan tax cuts, real nonresidential private investment in the United States fell from 10.4 percent of GDP in 1965 to only 3.4 percent in 1991.[19]

Though conservatives continue to claim that the eighties were a period of general prosperity, the evidence indicates that under Reagan and Bush only the rich got significantly richer.* The distribution of tax burdens provides a better index of political clout in America—and here a

---

*Estimates of income distribution are notoriously unreliable. According to one, since 1977, in constant dollars, the bottom three fifths of American families have seen their pretax incomes decline, while the fourth quintile has had only a 2 percent increase in income since the seventies. Only the top fifth of American families—and especially the top one percent—have seen significant gains in income as a result of Carter- and Reagan-era tax cuts. For the top 1 percent, it has been estimated, pretax income has risen an astonishing 86 percent. (Robert S. McIntyre, "The Reaganites and the Renegade," *The American Prospect*, Winter 1991, pp. 12–13. McIntyre relies on the data of the Congressional Budget Office.)

pattern of shifting the overall tax burden from the rich to the middle and working classes is clear. If average Americans thought that they were getting permanent tax relief as a result of the Reagan revolution, they were soon disappointed. The 1981 tax cuts were offset by later tax increases, beginning in 1982. By 1989, the federal tax burden as a proportion of GNP was higher than it had been in 1979. In the last two decades, federal taxes, as a percentage of GNP, grew from 18.2 percent in the 1960s to 18.3 percent in the 1970s and 18.9 percent in the 1980s. The tax burden imposed by all levels of government—federal, state, and local—increased from 33.7 percent of GNP in 1970 to 34.9 percent in 1980 and 36.2 percent in 1986.[20] While government has slowly but steadily expanded, the burden of paying for it has been shifted from the wealthy and business to ordinary Americans. Under Reagan and Bush, much of the burden of paying for the continuing growth of government was transferred from the rich (and from much of the poor, who were removed from the tax rolls by the 1986 tax reform law) to middle Americans by three means: increased Social Security payroll taxes, rising state and local taxes, and deficit spending.

In 1983, even as Congress was dramatically lowering income taxes on the rich, it raised the Social Security payroll tax. The Social Security tax increase, which wiped out any savings to the middle class that resulted from the 1981 tax cuts, was one of the largest tax increases in U.S. history. As a result, the Social Security fund had a surplus of $50 billion at the beginning of the 1990s. The payroll tax, which had been the source of funds for only 11.5 percent of federal spending in the 1950s, grew to account for 29.2 percent in the 1980s.[21] The magnitude of the substitution of regressive Social Security taxation (which most affects ordinary Americans) for progressive income taxation (which most affects the rich) is brought out by the following figures. Had the 1970 income tax distribution remained unchanged, by 1989 the income tax burden would have been $11.8 billion greater—but the Social Security tax burden on middle-class and working-class Americans would have been $124.5 billion *less*: a more than tenfold difference.[22]

Between 1980 and 1989, the combined federal tax on middle-class and working-class Americans in the bottom three quintiles of income distribution rose, while taxes declined for affluent Americans in the top two quintiles. The disparity was most pronounced at the extremes—

while those in the top 1 percent of the income distribution received a 14.4 percent federal tax cut, the poorest families saw their federal tax total go up by 16.1 percent.[23] According to one study, after the Reagan-era tax reforms, 90 percent of the American people owed more taxes than they would have owed had the 1977 tax laws been left untouched; only the wealthiest 10 percent of the public received any significant benefit from the tax cuts.[24]

All of this, for federal taxes alone. Per capita state taxes, hitting middle-income and low-income Americans the hardest, doubled in the 1980s.[25] At the state level, the federal pattern was repeated—declining tax payments by corporations along with rising regressive taxes on individuals, such as fees. Income taxes on individuals have gone up slightly at the state level, however.[26]

Average Americans were not only taxed *instead* of the rich; they were taxed to *repay* the rich. Borrowing, which accounted for only 2.5 percent of federal spending in the 1950s, increased to 17.7 percent in the 1980s.[27] The net interest costs on the national debt tripled from 1980 to 1989, from 8.9 percent of the total federal budget to 14.3 percent.[28] Interest payments on the debt, furthermore, represent a transfer of wealth from ordinary American taxpayers to rich Americans and foreigners without precedent in history.

The American public caught a glimpse of the bipartisan consensus in the 1990 budget deal, agreed upon by President George Bush and the Democratic leaders of Congress. The deficit-reduction plan (derailed by a coalition of dissident Republicans and liberal Democrats) showed the priorities of America's political class—it would have raised taxes on people making more than $200,000 only 1.7 percent, while raising taxes 2.9 percent on people making $30–40,000. Thanks to regressive consumption taxes, poor families, trying to live on less than $10,000 a year, would have seen their overall federal taxes increase by 7.6 percent![29] In 1990 Senator Daniel Patrick Moynihan (D-NY) did the unthinkable and proposed tax relief for American wage earners by cutting back Social Security taxes to their early 1980s levels, a move that would have put a great deal of money in the pockets of lower-income taxpayers. His proposal was coldly ignored not only by President Bush (whose great cause was reducing capital gains taxes, a reform that would have had no significant benefits for 93 percent of the public) but also by the elite in the Democratic party. Dan Rostenkowski (D-Ill), who as chairman of the Ways and Means Committee dominated tax rule-writing in the House, scornfully suggested that Moynihan's proposal might be the "worst idea of the year."[30]*

In 1992 Bill Clinton ran for president promising a middle-class tax cut, then, after being elected, abandoned the idea. Clinton's tax increases, though a step in the right direction, affect chiefly the very rich; neither party dares asks sacrifices of overclass voters with family incomes between $60,000 and $200,000 a year. While these families are a small minority of the population, they are a majority of the white overclass that dominates American politics. Indeed, a strategy of reducing the deficit by means of regressive excise and consumption taxes like a federal sales tax, which would hit poor and working-class Americans the hardest while sparing the need for significant sacrifice by upper-middle-class suburbanites, is favored by many members of the American political and financial establishment as an alternative to higher progressive taxation on the incomes of managers, professionals, and rentiers. Having relieved the top by shifting tax burdens to the lower-middle and working classes in the 1980s by means of the payroll tax, the bipartisan establishment that represents the economic interests of the white overclass may try to balance the budget on the backs of the lower three-fourths in the 1990s by means of regressive consumption taxes.

FREE-MARKET GLOBALISM VERSUS THE NEW DEAL

The class war of the white overclass against the multiracial middle class is not limited to the downward redistribution of taxation. The American

---

*Since Rostenkowski played a major role in the Reagan-era shift of the tax burden from the affluent to the middle and working class, it is worth noting that between 1980 and 1990, he was the largest recipient of honoraria in the government. He was paid speaking fees by Blue Cross–Blue Shield ($42,500), the Chicago Board of Trade ($37,000), Public Securities Association ($22,500), Citicorp–Citibank ($20,000), the American Stock Exchange ($19,500), the American Bankers Association ($18,000), the Securities Industry Association ($15,500) and on and on. . . . Businesses and lobbies with an interest in tax legislation paid Rostenkowski $1.7 million in speaking fees during this period—more than twice his total salary. (Donald L. Bartlett and James B. Steele, *America: What Went Wrong?*, Kansas City: Andrews and McMeel, 1992, pp. 192–194.) Congress has since banned honoraria, but created a loophole in the form of personal congressional foundations. Rostenkowski has been indicted for corruption by a federal grand jury, and voted out of office.

business class—almost all of whose members are born into the white over-class—is now attempting to use global free trade to drive down American wages and roll back the New Deal/Great Society social safety net.

Between 1929 and 1969, economic inequality in the United States declined. Since 1969, inequality has dramatically risen. Is it merely coincidence that 1932–1969 was the age of the New Deal Democratic liberalism, of FDR, Truman, and Johnson, and that the period since 1969 has seen the most right-wing Republican presidents since Coolidge, and two Democratic presidents—Carter and Clinton—who, in economics, have been more conservative than Nixon and Eisenhower?

The evidence indicates that much of the rise in income inequality in the United States has been driven by two factors: the decline of unionization and free trade. This is denied, of course, by the leading intellectuals of modern liberalism and modern conservatism (that is to say, the right and the far right). Robert Reich, Clinton's Secretary of Labor, claims that the growing importance of skills is the main reason for rising inequality in America. Charles Murray, the most influential public policy thinker on the right, claims that rising inequality reflects genetic inequality, as a meritocratic society sorts out the well-paid smart from the poorly-paid dumb.

If either of these explanations were true, then the pattern of rising inequality should be the same in industrial democracies similar to the United States. The widening gap in earnings, whether based on a differential in skills or a differential in innate intelligence, should have grown as much in Germany, France, and Japan as in the United States. In fact, income inequality in Germany, Japan, and other industrial democracies has remained much lower than in the United States in the post–1969 period. The reason: more generous government policies combined, in most cases, with stronger labor movements.* Strong labor movements are particularly important. Wage inequality is highest in countries with weak labor movements. There is far less inequality in Germany, where roughly 40 percent of the population has remained unionized since the seventies, than in the United States, where union membership has fallen

---

*The exceptions are the other English-speaking democracies—Britain, Australia, New Zealand, Canada—where conservative political parties have carried out laissez-faire reforms with the same results as in the United States: rising inequality, falling wages, and growing underclasses.

(thanks to Reagan-era antilabor reforms) from 30 percent in 1970 to 12 percent today.[31]

If Democratic presidents and Congresses in the New Deal tradition had been elected from 1969 to the present, if 30 percent of the U.S. population were unionized today, if the AFL-CIO still had more clout than the Business Roundtable, it is safe to speculate that income inequality would have grown far less, and wages and benefits fallen far less, than they have under the past thirty years of Republicans and conservative Democrats in the White House. The main reason for growing inequality in the United States has been the success of the business and professional classes, aided by both parties, in decimating New Deal social protections and the American labor movement.

Even in a revitalized New Deal America, there might have been downward pressure on wages as a result of global free trade. The political and journalistic establishments of the contemporary United States are almost unanimous in their support for ever greater global economic integration under a laissez-faire model. There might be minor dislocations and losses, they concede, but in the long run all Americans will be enriched by global free trade. If the rich benefit disproportionately today, the wage-earning classes will be enriched by the world market tomorrow.

The truth is somewhat different from the official overclass line. The dirty secret of mid-century capitalism is that high First World living standards were not natural—they were achieved only by rigging the rules of the economic game in favor of middle-class workers. Each First World country has had its own "social market contract" between labor, capital, and the government, a contract that replaces free-market capitalism, to varying degrees, with "social market" capitalism. All industrial democracies today are social market states, in which the government has assumed a responsibility for the economic security and well-being of citizens of a kind that nineteenth-century social reformers only dreamed of. Among the advanced countries, models of social market capitalism vary. The American model goes back to the New Deal, as supplemented by Lyndon Johnson's Great Society; Clinton has tried and failed to fill the remaining gap in American social market capitalism left by the defeat of universal health care by the medical and insurance lobbies in the forties and sixties. The generous (perhaps overgenerous) German version of social market capitalism has been based on an elaborate, post–World War II system of tripartite negotiation among the government, business, and labor unions, resting atop the earlier welfare state of Bismarckian Germany. Japan's social market economy has been more informal, combining minimal government support with paternalist corporate practices like lifetime employment and make-work jobs for people who in the United States or Germany would simply be fired.

Social market capitalism in the industrial democracies was adopted in the middle of the twentieth century, not out of altruism on the part of the political and business classes, but as an expedient in order to secure social peace. In the United States, the New Deal may have saved liberal capitalism by averting more radical populist challenges like those of Huey Long and Father Coughlin. The German system of class collaboration was adopted by the founders of the Federal Republic, a truncated and occupied state that could not afford labor strife as it sought to rebuild a ruined economy. Japanese corporations only reluctantly adopted their paternalist practices, after a period of violent labor conflict immediately following World War II. The importance of social market capitalism in maintaining social peace for several generations means that its contemporary crack-up should be a cause for alarm. Beginning with the collapse of the "Swedish model," one European country after another has cut back on its generous social market institutions. The collapse of the Liberal Democratic Party's political monopoly in Japan has been accompanied by a greater willingness by Japanese corporations to fire workers and transfer production abroad. In the United States, the New Deal system—which was not all that generous to begin with—has been crumbling since the seventies under a business-led assault against unions, generous wages, and generous middle-class transfers.

While a number of trends are contributing to the strains on the mid-century versions of First World social market capitalism—automation, the graying of populations, low productivity growth—one of the major causes is increased economic competition from low-wage countries. This is taking on the characteristics of cross-country class war, as many American, German, and Japanese corporations shut down facilities in their home countries and open up, or buy from, factories abroad, in order to take advantage of relatively skilled workers with low wages, low or no benefits, and often no legal or political rights.

U.S. corporations lead the world in the race to low-wage countries; for example, Motorola's American employees declined from almost 100 percent of its workforce in 1960 to 44 percent in 1992.[32] German corporations are laying off workers in Germany and moving production facilities abroad. Some Japanese corporations are following U.S. multinationals to the Third World for export not merely to third countries but to the home market; for example, Nissan's automobile factory in Aguascalientes, Mexico, will make cars for Japan as well as Mexico and the rest of the Western Hemisphere.[33]

Much of this transnational investment is concentrated in "export-processing zones," economic enclaves in Third World countries, usually not integrated into the local economy, which bring together foreign capital and technology with inexpensive and docile labor to manufacture consumer electronics, shoes, luggage, or toys.* The special economic zones of China are the most important; most of the rest are scattered through Southeast Asia and the Caribbean and Latin America (where the Mexican *maquiladora* zone along the U.S. border is the most important). The export-processing zone is nothing new; it used to be called the plantation. In the nineteenth and early twentieth centuries, plantations owned by American, British, and European investors produced raw materials and agriculture for export; modern technology now permits

---

*Much of the labor supply for offshore manufacturing is young and female. In 1990, a private business group in El Salvador that received 94 percent of its budget from the U.S. Agency for International Development (AID) placed an ad featuring "Rosa Martinez" in the magazine of the U.S. spinning industry, *Bobbin*: "You can hire her for 57 cents an hour. Rosa is more than just colorful. She and her co-workers are known for their industriousness, reliability, and quick learning." Charles Kernaghan et al., *Paying to Lose Our Jobs* (New York: National Labor Committee Education Fund in Support of Worker and Human Rights in Central America, 1992), p. 11. One 20-year-old Honduran woman, fired for trying to organize a union, told Congress about working for Global Fashions, a contractor for American clothing manufacturers: "We are forced to work overtime, sometimes more than 12-hour shifts . . . There are many girls as young as 13 who work in Global Fashions . . . The doors are locked and you can't get out until they let you. It can get very hot, sometimes 100 degrees, and there is no clean drinking water." Instead of paying American workers $7.80 an hour, many American companies have chosen to pay workers like this Honduran woman 41 cents an hour during a 58-hour workweek. (Bob Herbert, "Leslie Fay's Logic," *The New York Times*, Op-Ed, June 19, 1994, p. E 17.)

factory work to be done in the same countries. The banana republic is being replaced by the sweatshop republic.

The products of American-owned plantation industry now account for a substantial proportion of American imports. According to the U.S. Bureau of Economic Statistics, more than 20 percent of all imports to the United States come from foreign subsidiaries or affiliates of U.S. multinational corporations. Since that number does not take into account foreign contractors of U.S. companies, the actual proportion of U.S. imports that results from offshore production is undoubtedly higher. This is why American business is so adamantly opposed to tariffs—not fear of foreign retaliation, but fear of tariffs on products from American-owned industrial plantations.

In part because of this shift to offshore plantation production, the United States was the only leading industrial country in which average real wages declined between 1979 and 1988 (during that time, the real wage of Japanese industrial workers rose by 6.92 percent a year).[34] Some studies purport to show that there have been no net job losses or declines in wages in the United States as a result of the shift of production to low-wage countries. Other studies claim to find links between unemployment and wage decline and low-wage foreign competition.* Even if the effect of Third World competition on First World wages has been exaggerated to date, this does not mean that it will not grow in the future.†

The libertarian conservative answer to the conflict between free trade and high wages is to let American wages fall toward Third World

---

*Jagdish Bhagwati and Vivek Dehejia ("Freer Trade and Wages of the Unskilled: Is Marx Striking Again?," American Enterprise Institute) and Robert Lawrence and Mark Slaughter ("International Trade and American Wages in the 1980s: Giant Sucking Sound or Small Hiccup?," Brookings Papers on Economic Activity, Microeconomics, 1993), claim that international trade has had little or no effect on the wages of unskilled American workers. However, the most thorough recent study, by a former senior economist at the World Bank, concludes that the effect of Third World competition on First World incomes has been greater than hitherto realized. See Adrian Wood, *North-South Trade, Employment and Inequality: Changing Fortunes in a Skill-Driven World* (Oxford: Clarendon Press, 1994).

†*The Economist*, despite its staunch free-trade editorial line, admits: "So even if international trade is not to blame for the fall in real wages over the past couple of decades, it is possible that it may have a bigger influence on the real wages of the unskilled in the future as more developing countries enter the world market." "First Among Unequals," *The Economist*, January 15, 1994.

levels. Competition from low-wage countries gives conservatives a new reason to favor lowering or abolishing the American minimum wage, along with welfare-state benefits that purportedly make the United States uncompetitive compared to nations like China or Honduras. Indeed, some libertarian conservatives would address the contradiction between the free flow of capital and wage differentials between countries by encouraging a free flow of labor. The *Wall Street Journal* has called for an amendment to the U.S. Constitution consisting of five words: "There shall be open borders." If the U.S. and Mexican labor markets, as well as the capital markets which have been integrated by NAFTA, were merged, then American investment would flow south to take advantage of cheap labor, and tens of millions of Mexican workers would migrate north to better-paying jobs, until wages stabilized somewhere above the contemporary Mexican level (one seventh of the American) but far below the current American average. (This assumes that competition with extrahemispheric workers does not drag wages below even present-day Mexican levels.)

At least the libertarian conservatives take the conflict between high wages and free trade seriously. That cannot be said for liberals who favor a laissez-faire trade policy. A number of liberal scholars and policymakers, including President Clinton, Labor Secretary Robert Reich, and New Jersey senator Bill Bradley, have tried to devise a synthesis of laissez-faire globalism and social-democratic liberalism. This school of thought might be called "free trade plus." The United States will benefit from global free trade, these liberals argue, as long as the skills and productivity of American workers are upgraded. Higher skills translate into higher productivity, which will in turn translate into higher wages.

Here a good theory falls victim to an evil fact: productivity *has* been going up in America, without resulting wage gains for American workers. The average productivity of American workers increased by more than 30 percent between 1977 and 1992, while the average real wage *fell* by 13 percent.[35] No mystery here: higher labor productivity means fewer workers are necessary to do the same job. What is more, productivity is increasing as a result of technological innovation, not worker education. The secretary with an office computer is not far more educated than the dozens of punch-card operators she has replaced. Today's supermarkets are more efficient than yesterday's, notwithstanding the fact that checkout lines are manned by innumerates who would be at a loss if, like previous generations of cashiers, they had to ring up items themselves instead of using a computer monitor.

No matter how much productivity increases, wages will fall if there is an abundance of workers competing for a scarcity of jobs—an abundance of the sort created by the globalization of industry as well as large-scale immigration. Beginning in the 1970s many U.S. companies in the consumer electronics field—a sunrise industry on anyone's list—moved their production to Southeast Asia to take advantage of low wages and minimally educated workers. No problem, replies the free-trade liberal; let low-value-added activities be relocated abroad, American workers will simply specialize in intellectual tasks, like software design. Even skilled production, however, can often be done more cheaply elsewhere. Metropolitan Life employs 150 insurance examiners in Ireland to examine claims from around the world, at 70 percent of the costs of American examiners.[36] Software research and design is now being done by local computer specialists in India by Texas Instruments; in Russia, by Sun Microsystems, Inc.; and in Poland by CrossComm Corp., a Massachusetts-based company. The 34 Polish software developers who have designed its most recent and advanced software for CrossComm from offices at the University of Gdansk make between $7,000 and $18,000 a year.[37]

If even software design can be done better elsewhere, what high-wage, high-skill jobs in the United States are safe from expatriation? One answer is professional jobs. Since 1979, the real wages of high school dropouts have declined by 20 percent, while the incomes of workers with more than four years of college have risen by 8 percent, according to the Economic Policy Institute.[38] Edward E. Leamer of the University of California at Los Angeles has tried to calculate the effect of the growth of international trade on U.S. wages from 1972 to 1985. According to his model, increasing trade raised the income of professionals by 9 percent ($33 billion) and reduced the income of nonprofessionals by 3 percent ($46 billion). Lest this seem like an even trade, it should be remembered that nonprofessionals enormously outnumber professionals in the United States (only 8.7 percent of the American male workforce has completed a graduate or professional education).[39]

There are two ways to interpret the better performance of professionals relative to other workers in the new, internationalized economy. The most common explanation is that the world economy, in some vague way, rewards skill, intelligence, initiative. A more plausible, if less dramatic, explanation is that professionals are the beneficiaries of a hidden protectionism based on credentialism and licensing. A corporation can hire an Indian computer programmer to do the work of an American computer programmer for a fraction of the wage; but it cannot hire an Indian lawyer to try a case in the United States. Thanks to licensing requirements, the jobs of lawyers, accountants and other financial professionals, doctors, realtors and tenured professors cannot be expatriated; not only are they not threatened by offshore moves, but their wages are kept artificially high by barriers to entry in the form of ever-increasing and expensive requirements for professional practice (which now include continuing legal education, in addition to a four-year undergraduate education and a three-year law school diploma). American professional accreditation is a nontariff barrier *par excellence.* Permit legal briefs to be written in India and submitted to American courts by fax from Indian lawyers, and legal fees in the U.S. will quickly plummet, the skill, education and productivity of American lawyers notwithstanding.

Even the hidden protectionism of professional licensing, however, can be defeated, if corporations replace full-time professional work with part-time professional work *in the United States.* During the 1980s, temp work grew ten times faster than overall employment; as a result, Manpower Inc., a temporary employment agency, has replaced General Motors as the largest private employer in the United States. In order to cut costs, the Bank of America is cutting its full-time employees; ultimately it hopes to have 80 percent of its staff made up of part-time workers working less than 20 hours a week—and ineligible for benefits.[40] Instead of hiring a full-time lawyer, why not hire two or three part-time lawyers through a temp agency? Even managers are not exempt; in 1991, unemployment among managers rose 55 percent, compared to only 15 percent among the population as a whole, as a result of corporate downsizing.[41]

To date the First World countries have been protected from the full force of Third World competition by relatively low Third World productivity levels. Even the most conservative projections of the growth of populations in the Third World, however, suggest that labor forces in

poor countries will grow faster than the supply of jobs. Within a generation or two, the burgeoning Third World population will contain not
only billions of unskilled workers, but hundreds of millions of scientists,
engineers, architects, and other professionals willing and able to do
world-class work for a fraction of the payment their American counterparts expect. The free-trade liberals hope that a high-wage, high-skill
America need fear nothing from a low-wage, low-skill Third World.
They have no answer, however, to the prospect—indeed, the probability—of ever-increasing *low-wage, high-skill* competition from abroad. In
these circumstances, neither better worker training nor investment in
U.S. infrastructure will suffice. Investment in domestic infrastructure,
for example, is desirable, but when relatively competent labor can be
found to work for a fraction of the American wage in Mexico or China
or Malaysia, better highways in the Midwest are not going to deter U.S.
corporations from expatriating jobs.

It is difficult to avoid concluding that civilized social market capitalism and unrestricted global free trade are inherently incompatible.
While today's free-trade liberals deny this conclusion, it would have
been taken for granted by hardheaded nineteenth-century classical liberals. David Ricardo, the English stockbroker who developed the doctrine of comparative advantage which remains the conventional academic justification for free trade, also argued that government should
not interfere with the "iron law of wages," according to which the free
market will inevitably lower the wages of the majority to subsistence levels. Herbert Spencer, the Social Darwinist champion of the free market,
also denounced government regulation of working conditions in mines
and factories, and free public museums and free public libraries.[42] In
1919, the Austrian economist Joseph Schumpeter denounced not only
the protectionist tariff strategy of the British conservative leader Joseph
Chamberlain, but also his promotion of a welfare state to help the working classes, as the "exploitation of the consumer."[43] These callous mas-
terminds of laissez-faire economics condemned not only all government
regulation of international trade in the national interest but all government measures to ameliorate the lot of the poor and working classes as
incompatible with a free market. Their present-day intellectual descendants, however, claim that the results of social democratic welfare-state

policies and national industrial policies can be reconciled with the re-morseless operations of global market forces—a claim their predecessors were too intelligent, and too honest, to make.*

Nor would the incompatibility of modern social market capitalism and free trade have been any surprise to Karl Marx. In *The Communist Manifesto,* he and Engels celebrated unregulated global economic inter-dependence in terms almost identical to those of today's enthusiastic champions of the borderless global economy:

> All old-fashioned national industries have been destroyed or are daily being destroyed. . . . In place of the old wants, satisfied by the production of the country, we find new wants, requiring for their satisfaction the products of distant lands and climes. In place of the old local and nation-al seclusion and self-sufficiency, we have intercourse in every direction, universal interdependence of nations.

On the question of the improvement of the living standards of ordi-nary workers by means of free trade, Marx agreed with the laissez-faire school of Smith and Ricardo: it was impossible. Under conditions of free trade, wages would be depressed to subsistence levels. "You have to choose: Either you must disavow the whole of political economy as it ex-ists at present, or you must allow that under the freedom of trade the whole severity of the laws of political economy will be applied to the working classes," Marx wrote in 1847.[44] In an 1848 address, he observed:

> Generally speaking, the Protective system in these days is conservative, while the Free Trade system works destructively. It breaks up old nationali-ties and carries antagonism of proletariat and bourgeoisie to the uttermost point. In a word, the Free Trade system hastens the Social Revolution. In this revolutionary sense alone, gentlemen, I am in favor of Free Trade.[45]

It is beginning to look as though Marx, though he was wrong about so-cialism, was right about the destructive effects of free global trade on the

---

*Milton Friedman is an exception; he is in the habit of pointing out that many of the welfare-state policies that Republicans would not dream of repealing, like social security and minimum wage laws, were part of the platform of the early-twentieth-century American Socialist party—as though that discredits them.

working classes in advanced capitalist countries. The enrichment of the working classes of the West took place in the past only when they lacked effective foreign competitors (Britain in the early nineteenth century, the United States after World War II) or were protected by tariffs or other means from low-wage competition (the United States, Germany, and Japan between the mid-nineteenth century and the mid- twentieth). Only now is a genuine global labor market forming—and its effects in depressing wages and incomes are precisely those predicted by classical economics.

If Marx was right in one respect, he was probably wrong in another. Today "the Social Revolution" in the industrial democracies is less likely to take the form of bearded revolutionaries taking to the barricades than interethnic violence at the bottom of the social ladder (white skinheads versus Pakistani immigrants in Britain, neo-Nazis versus Turks in Germany, blacks and Hispanics versus Korean grocers in the United States). What is more, the neo-fascist right is more likely than the cosmopolitan left to benefit from erosion of living standards by free-market globalism. Laissez-faire globalism may breed its own nemesis, in the form of the most radical and destructive kinds of ethnic nationalism and economic statism.

These considerations have yet to darken the sunny optimism of the American overclass. The utopian economic theory shared by both the neoliberal and conservative wings of the white overclass is a kind of inverted Jeffersonian agrarian exceptionalism. Jefferson and Madison, it will be recalled, believed in a division of labor, in which the United States would preserve its virtue and national character by specializing in the export of foodstuffs to industrialized (and therefore corrupt) western Europe. Pseudo-Jeffersonian economic globalism replaces the idealization of agriculture with the idealization of services; the American people will specialize in office jobs, while ceding manufacturing to various newly industrialized (and therefore corrupt) developing countries. The yeoman farmer, in effect, is to be replaced by the yeoman banker and the yeoman software designer, the wholesome farm by the wholesome office; but the exceptionalist belief, or rather delusion, that the international division of labor can spare the United States the necessity of having its own extensive heavy manufacturing base remains the same.

This fantasy on the part of white American businessmen of turning themselves into a post-American global elite explains the enthusiasm in

U.S. business circles for the "virtual corporation," a dematerialized entity consisting solely of a small management team temporarily contracting out work to low-wage Mexicans here, South Koreans there, Czechs and Hungarians there. The virtual corporation at least may be chartered in the United States, with its headquarters here; not so, the truly global corporation. "The United States is the wrong country for an international bank to be based," John Reed, CEO of Citibank, recently argued, overlooking the fact that U.S. taxpayers must bail out Citibank if necessary. "The United States does not have an automatic call on our resources," says a vice-president of Colgate-Palmolive. "There is no mindset that puts this country first."[46] In 1972 the Chairman of Dow Chemical Company, Carl A. Gerstacker, daydreamed in public about buying "an island owned by no nation" that could serve as "truly neutral ground" and permit Dow to "operate in the United States as U.S. citizens, in Japan as Japanese citizens, and in Brazil as Brazilians rather than being governed in prime by the laws of the United States."[47]

Related to this vision are commercials for new computers and telecommunications equipment, showing a white middle-aged executive communicating with his office from a beach resort, or a professional woman tucking in her child via a videophone in a busy airport. Virtual capitalism thus meets the virtual family, in the utopia of the American overclass: Dad will bask in the Caribbean sun sketching out marketing designs on his laptop computer, while Mom keeps an eye on Baby, via satellite, as she flies from New York to Frankfurt to Tokyo. Off-camera, never seen, is the Latina maid who actually changes Baby's diapers, and, in this or that Third World shantytown, the employees, or rather contractors, of Dad's or Mom's virtual corporation, workers as likely as not without benefits, without insurance, without civil rights, without a voice in their government, laboring to make products they can never afford to buy.

Not all jobs can be expatriated to Mexico or Malaysia in the new virtual or global economy. A great many low-skilled services—from truck driving to nursing and sales and restaurant work—must still be performed on the spot in America. That is where immigration comes in. A generous immigration policy, resulting in a constant supply of unskilled, poor immigrants, competing with poor and less-educated Americans for a fixed supply of jobs, has the same effect as the enlargement of the labor pool through the expatriation of American-owned industry. It keeps wages low and unions weak—to the benefit of the white overclass.

Despite increasing popular concern about mass immigration, the establishment press remains solidly in favor of high levels of immigration. Conservative columnist George Will and liberal commentator Michael Kinsley have defended mass immigration. The *Journal* has run editorials denouncing "People Protectionism" and "In Praise of Huddled Masses."[48] The *Journal*'s editors have written that "if Washington still wants to 'do something' about immigration we propose a five-word constitutional amendment: There shall be open borders."[49] In 1985, the editors of *The New Republic* called for an open-borders policy, limited only by a willingness to avoid welfare and become proficient in English.[50]* The business magazine *Forbes*, less radical than *The Wall Street Journal* or *The New Republic*, merely wants up to 1.8 million legal immigrants—a threefold increase—to be admitted to the United States every year.[51] For obvious reasons, big business has consistently opposed any serious measures to reduce illegal immigration (its opposition to the Simpson-Mazzoli bill led Congressman Barney Frank (D-Mass.) to observe, "Today is apparently the day that the large agricultural owners joined the American Civil Liberties Union").[52] While passing in silence over the desire of big business for cheap and docile labor, the elite press has been quick to accuse proponents of immigration restriction of racism, the ultimate slur in contemporary America.†

During the years that the political class has been almost unanimously in favor of present or higher levels of legal immigration, an overwhelming majority of Americans of all races have favored restriction, a fact that speaks volumes about the alienation of the American ascendancy from the majority's interests and concerns. Indeed, like free-market globalism, immigration is an issue that pits the affluent top 20 percent

---

*In 1993, *The New Republic* conceded that concern for "the casualties of competition" in the United States "*may* eventually mean an immigration policy that limits competition for nonexportable service-sector jobs (in, say, restaurants). This final option is a last resort: it is a real sacrifice of liberal internationalist principle, and justified only as the lesser of evils if some such sacrifice is unavoidable." ("For NAFTA," editorial, *The New Republic*, October 11, 1993, p. 8.)

†In 1990 the *Wall Street Journal* accused Senator Alan K. Simpson of bias against Mexicans because of his support for stronger border-control measures. ("Democrats for Vitality," *Wall Street Journal*, October 1, 1990, p. A-14; "Immigration Victories," *Wall Street Journal*, October 29, 1990.)

against the wage-earning majority below. Every poll shows overwhelming majorities of Americans in favor of strict reductions of immigration levels. Nevertheless, every revision of immigration law has *raised* levels of legal immigration. While agitation by ethnic lobbies and agribusiness goes a long way toward explaining this phenomenon, that lobbying probably would not succeed if upper-income Americans did not support, or at least tolerate, high levels of legal and illegal immigration.

The chief way in which mass immigration helps the white overclass is its tendency to drive down wages for working-class and working-poor Americans. Though experts disagree, the best evidence indicates that the flood of unskilled workers has kept wages for low-income workers in major metropolitan areas in the United States from rising as they otherwise would have.* A number of economists argue that rapid, immigration-driven growth in the American labor supply (one tenth of which is now foreign-born) has driven down wages and discouraged companies from investing in technology as an alternative to relying on cheap labor.[53] Thanks in large part to the flood of low-wage Hispanic labor, wages have collapsed in southern California from 2 percent above the U.S. metropolitan average in 1969 to 12 percent below the average by 1980.[54] Inexpensive immigrant labor has displaced black urban workers in many regions, a factor that probably contributed to the Los Angeles riots. Most of these immigrants compete with unskilled Americans; according to one authority, as a result of the emphasis on unification of immigrant families (by now, Latin American and Asian), "the United States is losing the international competition for skilled workers to other host countries such as Australia and Canada."[55] Even the libertarian economist Julian Simon, an advocate of an open-border world, admits that "the illegals, and especially those from Mexico, tend to have less education and less skill relative to legal immigrants. This means that they have a disproportionate negative effect on natives with low skills and education."[56]

From the point of view of members of the white overclass, of course,

---

*According to a 1991 study for the National Bureau of Economic Research by economists George J. Borjas, Richard Freeman and Lawrence Katz, the immigration of unskilled labor, along with import competition, was responsible for as much as half of the 10 percent decline from 1980 to 1988 in the wages of Americans who never finished high school. See John Judis, "Can Labor Come Back?" *The New Republic* (May 23, 1994).

this is good news—if mass immigration ended tomorrow, they would probably have to pay higher wages, fees, and tips. Some immigration advocates have publicly argued for immigration on the grounds that it makes life more convenient for affluent Americans. Thomas Muller, in a recent study of immigration for the Twentieth Century Fund, concedes that the cut-off of immigration in the 1920s opened up employment and housing opportunities for black Americans; he concedes, in addition, that present-day immigrants often displace native-born workers, depend disproportionately on welfare and other public services, and add to the crime rate in many communities. Muller also admits that NAFTA will be an incentive to further illegal immigration, as the development of the *maquiladoras* already has been: "New job opportunities are an incentive for more aliens to cross into the United States." Nevertheless, Muller argues for keeping immigration levels high, in order not to inconvenience middle-class Americans who have grown dependent on low-wage workers as restaurant workers, service station attendants, maids, nannies, and gardeners. "As the number of working mothers increases," Muller writes, "such (household) help, once considered a luxury, is becoming more and more a necessity. Were it not for recent immigrants, nannies, maids, and gardeners would be a vanishing breed. . . ."[57]

The fact is that the vast majority of Americans still do not consider the employment of "nannies, maids, or gardeners" to be a necessity rather than a luxury. Small as it is as a proportion of the population, the white overclass is one of the major employers of recent Third World immigrants. In 1980, 23 percent of immigrants (who together represented 3 percent of the U.S. population) worked as housekeepers and 15 percent as servants.[58] Since only 1 percent of the American population employs live-in nannies,[59] this means that there is a striking dependence on immigrant menials by the families of the upper-middle and upper classes, whose lifestyle could not be sustained without a supporting cast of deferential helots. Many overclass Americans, like previous American elites, live in intimate daily contact with servants of different ethnic and racial backgrounds to an extent that most middle-class and working-class Americans cannot imagine. The nanny problems of Zoe Baird, Kimba Wood, and Arianna Huffington have given the public a glimpse into the private lives of the American ascendancy. Overclass Americans of today are as dependent on Latina maids as members of the Northeastern establishment were on Irish "Bridgets" and as Southern planters were on house slaves. In this connection, J. P. Morgan's definition of the leisure class, which he saw as the bulwark of civilization, is instructive: "All those who can afford to hire a maid."[60]

The white overclass also saves itself a considerable amount of money by importing foreign talent such as the East Asian graduate students who have become so important in American university science departments. Why spend tax dollars to educate poor native-born white, black, and brown Americans for various professions, when it is possible to import the products of superior educational systems abroad? Let Taiwan educate scientists; we will employ them. Indeed, if taxes were raised to improve the education of native Americans of all races, one of the chief attractions of the United States to immigrant European and Asian scholars and professionals and technicians—the low level of taxation, compared to other First World democracies—might be eliminated.

In addition to fulfilling their immediate functions—selling egg rolls, measuring blood sugar—Vietnamese vendors and Filipino lab technicians serve an additional function for the white overclass: they relieve it of guilt about the squalor of millions of native-born Americans, not only ghetto blacks and poor Hispanics but poor whites. The daily sight of hardworking immigrants in jobs that underclass blacks and poor whites spurn, and folkloric anecdotes about Vietnamese Westinghouse scholars and valedictorians, confirm the suspicion of members of the white overclass that the native-born poor, those Appalachian coal miners and ghetto residents, are really just lazy, compared to Juan the doorman or Mrs. Lin the laundry lady. It has even been suggested in public that immigrants are useful as a means of disciplining native-born workers, who are less likely to be inefficient or rude if they know that an immigrant can always be found to take his job for a low wage. In the 1980s, during the "Massachusetts Miracle," the state's unemployment rate fell to half the national average, 2.7 precent. As a result of a tight labor market, wages for workers at McDonald's rose to more than $7.00 an hour. Muller thinks that this local rise in wages for the poorest workers was an unfortunate development: "In many areas of the Northeast, a scarcity of clerks in the late 1980s caused a noticeable deterioration in service. . . . This is not an argument that long lines or *flip behavior by salespeople* will fundamentally affect America's well-being, but they do constitute an irritant that can diminish the quality of life (emphasis added)."[61] Ben Wattenberg has testified to Congress that immigration, by preserving a reserve army of cheap labor, improves customer service by making low-wage workers more afraid of being fired and therefore less likely to be rude.* In a seller's market for labor, it seems, there is a danger that the help will get uppity.

According to economist George J. Borjas in the *Journal of Economic Literature* (December 1994), the economic benefits of immigration to upper-income Americans are substantial; employers of immigrant labor reap annual gains of $140 billion a year. The gains come at the expense of native workers, who lose an estimated $133 billion a year as a result of competition with immigrants for jobs. The members of the American overclass, then, have profited from today's policy of large-scale legal immigration, even as that policy has contributed to the decline of living standards for the American majority.

THE NEW FEUDALISM

The third class-war campaign of the white overclass, after regressive taxation and a cheap-labor strategy based on free trade and mass immigration, involves what Lewis Lapham has called the new feudalism. The new feudalism reverses the trend of the past thousand years toward the assumption by the government of basic public amenities like policing, public roads and transport networks, and public schools. In the United States—to a degree unmatched in any other industrial democracy— these things are once again becoming private luxuries, accessible only to the affluent few.

The privatization of public services makes sense in some cases; for example, many municipal services like trash collection might be performed more efficiently by private corporations under contract with municipali-

---

*"In some areas, grave labor shortages have already surfaced, and not just at entry levels. A future of more jobs than workers may sound like a happy circumstance, but it reflects imbalances for which there can be penalties. One such penalty is deteriorating service, and an increase in underqualified, rude, and weakly committed employees. Another may be the advent of wage inflation. . . . Many of these dislocations can be avoided by immigration. . . ." (Ben Wattenberg, Statement before the House Judiciary Subcommittee on Immigration, Refugees and International Law and the House Labor Committee Immigration Task Force, March 1, 1990.)

ties and states. Proposals to privatize basic public functions like schools and public amenities like parks, however, are a different matter. Replacing the public school system with a private school system, without imposing standard tuition caps, would almost certainly lead to far more extreme social inequality, since schools would have the ability to reject students on the basis of their parents' ability to pay. Providing students with publicly financed vouchers would not alter this, because the more expensive private schools would simply raise their tuitions to compensate. (Jefferson, who is often invoked by conservatives seeking to destroy the public schools, proposed compulsory, publicly financed education for all white children in Virginia to promote republican virtue and a meritocratic social order.)[63]

In the case of public amenities like parks, it is simply disingenuous to say that poor and working-class people, already worried about paying the rent, would have the "right" to pool their resources to pay for their own private parks. In practice, they would spend any small amount of extra money on more immediate needs. This being the case, the elimination of, say, public golf courses would not lead to new private country clubs funded by working-class subscribers, but rather the disappearance of any golf courses other than those at the country clubs of the affluent. Whatever libertarians may argue, ambitious privatization efforts would dramatically diminish the amenities available to middle-class and working-class Americans, while leaving the affluent few unaffected.

Hyperfederalism—the radical decentralization of power to the state and local levels—would have similar destructive effects on republican society. Because far fewer people take part in state and local than national elections, wealthy donors and intense and well-organized ideologues (of all persuasions) can have much more impact at the state and local level than at the federal level. Although decentralization might result in empowering the political left in some areas, this is a price that right-wing libertarians are willing to pay for the increased political independence of enclave communities segregated by class.

Taken to its ultimate conclusion, the replacement of the American republic with a decentralized and privatized society would create something like a high-tech Holy Roman Empire on American soil. Conservatives, libertarians and left-anarchists like to imagine the harmonious coexistence of flourishing Jeffersonian hamlets. In the absence of a strong central government financed by adequate taxation, however, the more likely result would be a wasteland of crime-ravaged slums between the fortified private neighborhoods of the white overclass, compounds connected, no doubt, by private toll roads. Protected like medieval barons by their private police forces, the affluent classes could transact worldwide business or seek diversion at their computer workstations, while only a few miles away the poor lived and died in conditions of Third World squalor. Not a Jeffersonian utopia, but a high-tech feudal anarchy, featuring an archipelago of privileged whites in an ocean of white, black, and brown poverty, would be the likely outcome of the conservative antistatist program, if it were seriously pursued.

If this picture of a neo-feudal United States seems overdrawn, consider these "feudal" elements of modern America:

• The conservative plan to replace public schools with taxpayer subsidized vouchers to private schools would reinforce the growing segregation of America by class. If vouchers were not linked to government caps on tuition, expensive private schools would simply raise their tuitions by the amount of the voucher, to continue pricing out all but the wealthiest students. Even worse, middle-class American parents would find themselves being taxed to pay for the vouchers of rich children attending schools from which middle-class children could be legally turned away because their parents did not make enough money.

• Increasing numbers of affluent white Americans are withdrawing into gated enclave communities. Many of these are in effect private cities, whose community associations provide not only security but trash collection, street cleaning, and utilities. The inhabitants of these enclaves have sought permission from local governments to block off public streets with gates and other barriers to traffic (a California appeals court recently ruled that seven metal gates installed by the Los Angeles suburb of Whitley Heights represented an illegal "return to feudal times"—but only *after* their installation had been approved by the Los Angeles City Council). Some of the rich inhabitants of gated communities are seeking, not only permission to barricade themselves, but the right to be exempt from taxes—on the grounds that taxes for public municipal services, on top of the fees they pay their private community associations, constitute "double taxation."[64]

• The U.S. military—unlike the citizen-militaries of most modern democracies—is already a "volunteer," that is, a mercenary, force, disproportionately made up of lower-income Americans. From the reliance on private police to the use of private armies—pioneered by Ross Perot, who hired mercenaries to rescue his employees in revolutionary Iran—is not a tremendous leap.

• Because of the unwillingness of affluent Americans to pay reasonable taxes that benefit classes and races other than their own, the ratio of police officers to population in the United States is much lower than in other western democracies. In Los Angeles at the time of the 1992 riots, for example, there were 2.3 police officers per 1000 inhabitants, compared to a nationwide ratio of 4.2 per 1000 in Italy.[65] Indeed, because the affluent would rather hire mercenary forces than pay for police, the number of private security guards in the United States now exceeds the number of publicly employed policemen in the U.S.[66]

• The idea of replacing the national highway system with a quasi-medieval system of private toll roads is not a fantasy confined to dystopian science fiction. Rodney E. Slater, appointed by President Clinton to head the Federal Highway Administration, has suggested that one way of repairing interstate highways might be to let private businesses collect tolls on them.[67] More than ten states now have projects for *private* toll roads—something that has been unheard of in most of the civilized world for centuries. In every other industrial democracy in the world, the government somehow manages to pay for adequate public police and public highways out of taxes or user fees. Only in the United States have the rich, with the encouragement of libertarian and conservative ideologues, used their disproportionate political influence to starve government of the minimal funds necessary to maintain the basic amenities of a civilized society like police and roads. Even Adam Smith thought that building and maintaining public roads was a responsibility of the sovereign (he argued that if there were tolls then the wealthy owners of carriages should pay much higher tolls than the drivers of carts). The privatization of the American physical infrastructure might *literally* create a two-tier society; the affluent would whiz along in expensive cars on their state-of-the-art computer-enhanced highways, while ordinary

Americans fumed in traffic on crumbling public highways and streets below.

• In New Orleans, the feudalization of American life has been taken to a new extreme. The tax-starved city now performs basic public services only for a fee. Under the "Adopt-A-Pothole" program, residents of streets with potholes have to personally raise the money to pay city work crews to repair them.

The white overclass can afford to be indifferent to the decline of the wages and quality of life of the average American because its members have devised ways to insulate themselves from rotting cities, poor jobs, crumbling urban public schools, wandering maniacs, crime. The managerial and professional jobs of its members are not affected by the expatriation of entry-level manufacturing jobs to Latin America and Asia; their neighborhoods are patrolled by private security services; their day-care needs are provided by live-in maids from Salvador or Peru. The white overclass, gazing down on America from gated communities or the more exclusive suburbs, conceives of the public good as the aggregation of private goods—private schools, private neighborhoods, private security services. The ideal of the white overclass, the oligarchy that dominates the Third American Republic, is not the city on a hill, but the mansion behind a wall.

BRAZILIANIZATION

It is often said that multiculturalism and social preference are "Balkanizing" America. But it is a mistake to talk about the threat to national unity as Balkanization—the fragmentation of American society along ethnic lines. Today's Latin American and Asian immigrant communities will almost certainly follow the path of previous immigrants toward adoption of the English language and American vernacular national culture; that process of assimilation may be slowed by high levels of immigration and by disincentives in the form of affirmative action and bilingualism, but it will not be stopped. Nor is there any danger of communal violence escalating into real war of the Balkan kind; the greatest threat of violence in the United States comes from the urban black underclass, which is not a separate nationality, and at any rate cannot aspire to a national homeland.

The chief danger confronting the twenty-first century United States is not Balkanization but what might be called Brazilianization. By Brazilianization I mean not the separation of cultures by race, but the separation of races by class. As in Brazil, a common American culture could be indefinitely compatible with a blurry, informal caste system in which most of those at the top of the social hierarchy are white, and most brown and black Americans are on the bottom—*forever*. Behind all the boosterish talk about the wonders of the new American rainbow is the reality of enduring racial division by class, something that multicultural education initiatives and racial preference policies do not begin to address.

In the absence of sustained popular pressure from below or concern about America's international status, the white overclass has no incentive to combat Brazilianization in the United States. For one thing, any serious effort to reduce racial separation by class would inevitably mean higher taxes on the affluent—not just the rich, but the politically powerful upper-middle class. What is more, the dominance of the white oligarchy in American politics is strengthened by the emergent dynamics of a polarized society. In a more homogeneous society, the increasing concentration of wealth and power at the top might produce a populist reaction by the majority. But in a society like that of present-day America where a small, homogeneous oligarchy confronts a diverse population that shares a common national culture but remains divided along racial lines, the position of the outnumbered elite can be very secure. This is because the resentments caused by economic decline are likely to be expressed as hostility between the groups at the bottom, rather than as a rebellion against the top. In the Los Angeles riot, black, Hispanic, and white rioters turned on Korean middlemen, rather than march on Beverly Hills.

This suggests the test that alternatives to Multicultural America must meet. It is not enough that the formal legal structure and the public philosophy be transformed. The American class structure must be transformed, as well. Otherwise one Potemkin-village façade will merely be substituted for another, while the mansion remains secure behind its wall.

CHAPTER SIX

Alternative Americas

Democratic Universalism, Cultural Pluralism, and the New Nativism

Multiculturalism—the idea that all Americans can be assigned to one of five racial/cultural/political blocs—has been the organizing principle of the United States for some time. Government-mandated racial preference, the practice justified by the theory of multiculturalism, is now the rule in education, employment, and, increasingly, in politics. The white leaders of American government, business, foundations, and universities, with few exceptions, have made their peace with multiculturalism. Corporate America even tries to exploit diversity, by targeting this or that racially defined segment of the population. In light of these triumphs, the attempt of multicultural ideologues to present themselves as an embattled avant-garde is laughable. As a serious force in civil rights or politics, the old Euro-American nationalism is moribund. The multicultural left has won. Their political reforms have been imposed on the country, and so has their rhetoric. They are the quasi-official ideologists of the Third American Republic that has been constructed since the sixties.

The hypocrisy of contemporary American public debate about American identity is not limited to the pretense of multiculturalists to be opponents of the establishment, instead of a new establishment. The unreality of the debate is compounded by the illusory nature of most of the supposed alternatives to Multicultural America. In recent years, critics of the new orthodoxy of racial preference and multiculturalism have offered alternative conceptions of American identity. The most important of these are democratic universalism, cultural pluralism, and the new nativism.

Democratic universalism is the claim that the United States is not a nation-state at all, but a purely political association of individuals united only by common democratic ideals. Cultural pluralists also stress a common democratic faith as the cement of American society, but envision the United States less as a federation of deracinated individuals than of ethnic groups (real ethnic groups, not biological races masquerading as cultures). The new nativists reject both approaches, as well as multiculturalism, for a racial and religious, or purely religious, conception of American nationality: America as a white Christian, or, in another version, a multiracial pan-Christian community.

Of these three familiar alternatives to multiculturalism, the only one that has any roots in the values and beliefs of a substantial number of ordinary Americans is the new nativism (particularly in its nonracial, pan-Christian form). The theories of cultural pluralism and democratic universalism appeal to intellectuals and pundits, but they have no constituencies outside of the campus or the newsroom. Born on the Op-Ed page, these ideas live and die there. At the same time, the power of nativist conceptions of American identity could never be guessed, from the discussion allotted them in the prestige press and academic journals.

The power of nativism comes from its unapologetic appeal to American patriotism. Of the familiar accounts of American identity, the nativist is the only one that affirms belief in the value of American patriotism, defined not merely as political allegiance but as loyalty to an extrapolitical, extraconstitutional American nation. The rivals of nativists—multiculturalists, cultural pluralists, democratic universalists—cannot give straight answers to the questions "Is the United States a nation-state?" and "Is patriotism a virtue?" Their answers—sort of, maybe, kind of—may be defensible, from the point of view of academic philosophy. It may be that any nationalism, in the nature of things, must lead to war and dictatorship (though if this is true, one wonders why so many detractors of American nationalism find themselves denouncing it from podiums and editorial offices, rather than from prison cells). However persuasive the answers of democratic universalists and cultural pluralists may be to a small intelligentsia, they are not answers that can address the longing—in itself, morally neutral—of Americans to find some congruence between themselves, a larger cultural community, and their government. A nonnativist, liberal nationalism, I argue in the remainder of this book, can answer this need just as well as pan-white or pan-Christian nativism. Until now, however, liberal nationalism has not been part of the discussion.

The greatest long-term threat to multicultural ideology, it may be, is some form of the new nativism, driven underground but gradually gaining in strength among alienated Americans of various races. The triumph of the new nativist conception of American identity would most likely come, not in the form of a restoration of Euro-American white supremacy, but in the shape of a right-wing multiculturalism giving "separate but equal" a new meaning. Ironically, the twentieth-century multiculturalists of the American left may be building a house that the twenty-first century multiculturalists of the American right will inhabit.

DEMOCRATIC UNIVERSALISM

On Columbus Day, October 12, 1892, the day of the dedication of the Chicago Columbian Exposition, millions of children in schools across the United States recited a Pledge of Allegiance drafted by Francis J. Bellamy, editor of *Youth's Companion:* "I pledge allegiance to my flag and to the Republic for which it stands, one Nation indivisible, with liberty and justice for all." In the 1920s, under pressure from the American Legion, "my flag" would be changed to "the flag of the United States of America" (lest there be any doubt in the minds of immigrants) and in 1954 Congress enlisted divine help in the Cold War by appending the words "under God" (events in Europe since 1989 suggest that the Almighty was indeed pleased by the amendment).

Underlying the Bellamy pledge is a simple and powerful idea: the United States is a nation-state. Like France and Germany and Japan, America is *both* a legal and political structure and a community of people, whose members are bound together by a common culture and a national consciousness. In the Bellamy pledge, "republic" and "nation" are treated as synonyms. The American citizenry (republic) is at one with a unitary (indivisible) American people, or nation. The pledge of allegiance is, at one and the same time, a pledge of loyalty to a state and a nation.

One Alex Stella, an enterprising citizen of Susquehanna, Pennsylvania, has devised a new pledge purged of such regressive nationalism: "Before the flag of the United States of America, I freely pledge allegiance to that nation's Constitution and to the republic founded thereon, one democracy, under God, indivisible, with liberty and justice for all." Stella's American pledges allegiance—or rather, *freely* pledges allegiance—not to the American nation, but to that nation's constitutional democracy. It should come as no surprise that one of the hundreds of celebrities to whom Stella mailed his creation, the conservative columnist James Kilpatrick, thought it lacked "sis, boom, bah," while left-liberal folk singer Pete Seeger worried that any symbol, even this, could be misused.[1]

The Stella pledge accurately reflects the democratic universalist conception of American identity. In his 1991 Commencement Address at Duke University, George Will described that conception in these terms: "We are, as Lincoln said at Gettysburg, a nation 'dedicated to a proposition.' There is a high idea-content to American citizenship. It is a complicated business, being an American. We are all like Jay Gatsby—made up, by ourselves."[2] Will echoes Gatsby's creator, F. Scott Fitzgerald: "France was a land, England a people, but America, having about it still that quality of an idea, was harder to utter."[3] The late Theodore H. White wrote: "Americans are not a people like the French, Germans, or Japanese, whose genes have been mixing with kindred genes for thousands of years. Americans are held together only by ideas. . . ."[4] The conservative scholar George Weigel writes that "the continuity of America is not the continuity of race, tribe, or ethnic group—the continuity of blood, if you will. Rather it inheres in the continuous process of testing our society against those defining public norms whose acceptance *as* defining norms constitutes one as an American. In other words, American continuity is the continuity of *conviction*." Weigel refers to "the concept of America-as-experiment."[5]

Foreign observers have often echoed this American self-definition. The Austrian visitor Francis Grund wrote in 1837: "An American does not love his country as a Frenchman loves France, or an Englishman loves England: America is to him but the physical means of establishing a moral power . . . 'the local habitation' of his political doctrines."[6] Subsequent visitors have agreed. "Every American is . . . in his own estimation, the apostle of a particular political creed," wrote another nineteenth-century visitor, the British journalist Alexander Mackay.[7] "America is the only nation in the world that is founded on a creed," G. K. Chesterton wrote in 1922. "That creed is set forth with dogmatic and even theological lucidity in the Declaration of Independence; perhaps the only piece of practical politics that is also theoretical politics and also great literature."[8] Another Briton, former Prime Minister Margaret Thatcher, contrasted European nations, which "are the products of history and not of philosophy" with the United States: "No other nation has been built upon an idea—the idea of liberty." (In the same speech, Thatcher also claimed that "Americans and Europeans alike sometimes forget how unique the United States of America is"—something that it is hard to believe, given the constant invocation of American exceptionalism by Americans and foreigners alike.)[9]

To be American, according to these diverse observers, is to believe in a particular political ideology. In the words of Robert Penn Warren, "to be an American is not . . . a matter of blood; it is a matter of an idea— and history is the image of that idea."[10] The only kind of social unity conceivable in America is that produced by assent to a liberal political ideology (slightly more free-market or more egalitarian, depending on one's preference) that is thought to explain history, conceived as the unfolding of a providential plan. "The genius of this country—which cannot and does not wish to treat its citizens like plants rooted in its soil—has consisted in a citizenship that permits reflection on one's own interest and a calm recognition that it is satisfied by this regime," wrote the late Allan Bloom. "This is the peculiarly American form of patriotism."[11] Woodrow Wilson may have said it best, when he addressed a group of newly naturalized citizens in Philadelphia on May 10, 1915: "You have taken an oath of allegiance to a great ideal, to a great body of principles, to a great hope of the human race."[12]

And perhaps not only the *human* race. According to the editors of *The Economist*, the U.S., as a nonnational idea-state, has the potential to become *literally* a universal nation:

> America is an immigrants' land, open to anyone of any race or culture who accepts the ideas of the European Enlightenment on which it was founded. Provided the ideas remained intact, an America populated with Martians would still be America.[13]

The effect of purging American nationalism of its traditional racial and religious elements—and even its requirement for membership in the human species!—without at the same time emphasizing the common extrapolitical but nonracial heritage of language, culture, custom, and history, is to put enormous emphasis on the ideological element as the sole foundation of American identity. It practically requires the transformation of the American version of constitutional democratic liberalism into a secular religion. The "American Creed" is a *political* religion, which has a role for the supernatural (in the vague form of Providence) and draws heavily on Protestant imagery and symbolism. The debt of the American Creed to Protestantism is so great that it is possible to describe it in terms familiar from Christianity: the Creed has a theodicy or view of providential history, sacred scriptures, saints, even a sacrificed Savior and Redeemer in Abraham Lincoln.

The American Testament according to democratic universalism is something like this:

> In 1776 (or 1787), something utterly unprecedented in human history took place. A group of wise and virtuous Founding Fathers created the first nation in history based on natural rights and the consent of the governed. They created not merely a new government, but a radically new kind of society, indeed a new civilization. Unlike all other previous human societies, America was founded as an abstract experiment in political philosophy.
>
> The ideal expressed by the Declaration—all men are created equal— was not fully realized at first, because of America's original sin of human slavery. The destruction of slavery by Abraham Lincoln, the saintly martyr of freedom, and the eradication of legal racism in the 1960s, completed the American Revolution and made the United States the most perfect society the world has ever known. The shining example of America has

inspired a worldwide democratic revolution, soon to be consummated with the downfall of the last tyrannical regimes. Because democracies do not go to war with one another, once every state on earth is organized along American lines, millenia of peace, prosperity, and lawful order will result.

Even in a world of democracies, the United States will continue to stand out, not merely as the first but the best. All other democracies on the planet are based on sinister Old World notions of "blood-and-soil" nationalism and tribalism. America, by contrast, is a group of individuals who share nothing in common other than their common experience of rebirth through immigration and their dedication to a proposition. Not only does American identity consist exclusively of rational allegiance to the American Creed, but no other basis for American nationality is conceivable, inasmuch as the United States is a nation of immigrants more diverse than any other society in the world.

This lack of the traditional foundations for national identity—language, customs, religion, race—far from being a weakness, is America's greatest strength. It enhances American prestige, encourages the best and brightest from around the world to become American citizens, and permits America's democratic political institutions to remain stable even though a pluralistic society is constantly in flux as it is improved by a never-ceasing stream of immigrants. Because there is no basis for American identity apart from the ideals of liberal democracy, if those ideals were abandoned or substantially modified "America" would cease to exist, even if the same population, with the same language, customs, and social institutions continued to inhabit the same territory. Conversely, if English were replaced by Turkish as the national language and most Americans became Buddhists, this would not alter American identity in the slightest, as long as the citizens of the United States believed in the ideals of the Declaration of Independence and the Gettysburg Address (as translated into Turkish).

Lincoln said it best, in his 1838 address to the Young Men's Lyceum:

Let reverence for the laws, be breathed by every American mother, to the lisping babe that prattles on her lap—let it be taught in schools, in seminaries, and in colleges;—let it be written in Primers, spelling books, and Almanacs;—let it be preached from the pulpit, proclaimed in legislative halls, and enforced in courts of justice. And, in short, let it become *the political religion* of the nation.[14]

American democratic universalism, in the tradition of Lincoln, asserts as a fact what it endorses as a virtue: the alleged uniqueness of American society. Precisely *because* America is not a nation in the conventional sense—so the argument goes—its identity cannot be anchored in history, culture, tradition. This insistence that America is different in kind and not merely in degree or emphasis from other societies is necessary for the universalist argument. If America were not radically different in kind from all other countries in the world, then American nationality would be similar, if not to French or Swedish identity, then to the national identities of other postcolonial settler societies like Australian or Argentinian. Liberal political ideology, however important, would be at best only one element in American identity. Democratic universalism, then, stands or falls on the truth of American *exceptionalism*—the claim that the American nation is different not just in quality but in kind from all other nations in the world.

One of the most familiar arguments of American exceptionalism is the claim that America, compared to other societies in the world, is unique in being a "young" or "new" nation of immigrants lacking in a monolithic cultural tradition and characterized by extraordinary social mobility. In this view, America is as protean as Dryden's Duke of Buckingham—"A man so various, that he seem'd to be/ Not one, but all Mankinds Epitome"—though, one presumes, without the Duke's sort of variety—"Stiff in Opinions, always in the wrong;/ Was every thing by starts, and nothing long." The implicit comparison of fluid, multiform America is to sinister Old World societies, which, we are supposed to believe, have been unified for ages, do not accept immigrants, have a rigid and conformist culture and an aristocratic social order. The American nation is a green and burgeoning sapling in the midst of a petrified forest.

More than a century ago, Mark Twain observed: "The world and the books are so accustomed to use, and over use, the word 'new' in connection with our country, that we early get and permanently retain the impression that there is nothing old about it."[15] Similarly, George

Santayana wondered: "What sense is there in this feeling, which we all have, that the American is young? His country is blessed with as many elderly people as any other, and his descent from Adam, or from the Darwinian rival of Adam, cannot be shorter than that of his European cousins. Nor are his ideas always very fresh. . . ."[16] The United States, according to Henry Steele Commager, is "the oldest republic, the oldest democracy, the oldest federal system; it has the oldest written constitution and boasts the oldest of genuine political parties."[17] "In terms of continuous constitutional experience without revolutionary disruption," C. Vann Woodward reminds us, "the United States has the oldest, but one, of all existing governments—including those of the original parent nations" like Britain.[18] The London *Economist* recently pointed out that America is one of the *oldest* countries in the modern world, having "had the same form of government for the longest period of time."[19]

All right, the American exceptionalist might argue, America has an old *government* but a young *society*. There is a certain amount of truth in this; many features of American culture are much younger than American political institutions. If the American nation is defined in terms of language and culture, however, then the nation as well as the state appears to be one of the oldest in the world.

Consider the conservatism of American English, which preserves usages that vanished in Britain long ago. Modern English stabilized around the year 1500. The first permanent British settlement in North America was in 1607. For four-fifths of the time that there have been modern English speakers—almost half a millennium—there have been Anglo-Americans. American English, one of the major elements of American cultural nationality, is about as old as modern German, Italian, and other contemporary languages. And it is much older, as a living language, than tongues which have been revived or artificially upgraded from peasant dialects by nineteenth- and twentieth-century nationalists: the vernacular Hebrew of Israel, Lithuanian and Ukrainian, Tagalog, Hindi. Noah Webster published his *Dictionary of the American Language* several generations before anyone thought of reviving Hebrew as the language of a Jewish nation-state in Palestine.

When one turns from language to tradition, it soon becomes clear that most of the ancient traditions of European, Asian and African nations were recently invented. "Britain is an invented nation, not so much older than the United States," Peter Scott has written.[20] Historian Linda Colley argues that a distinctive "British" nationality, encompassing English and Scots, developed between the Act of Union of England and Scotland in 1707 and the accession of Queen Victoria in 1837.[21] In Britain, so often invoked as the foil to America's youth, most of the things that are thought of as *echt*-English do not antedate Queen Victoria: royal ceremony, Dickensian Christmas imagery, the imagery of the Empire.

Although we think of France, like Britain, as an old nation compared to young America, this, too, is an illusion. The universally recognized symbol of France, the Eiffel Tower, is little more than a century old. As late as 1870, Eugen Weber argues, France "was neither morally nor materially integrated; what unity it had was less cultural than administrative." He concludes that "The national ideology was still diffuse and amorphous around the middle of the nineteenth century. French culture became truly national only in the last years of the century."[22] Even in the early twentieth century, some French dialects were incomprehensible to others. There has never been a time when New England Yankees and the southernmost of Southrons could not make out what their compatriots were saying, with perfect ease, if not enjoyment.

Are Americans younger in their attitudes than others in the world? G. K. Chesterton dismissed "the fallacy of the young nation" as "a childish blunder, built upon a single false metaphor." According to Chesterton, "Of course we may use the metaphor of youth about America or the colonies, if we use it strictly as implying recent origin. But if we use it (as we do use it) as implying vigour or vivacity, or crudity, or inexperience, or hope, or a long life before them, or any of the romantic attributes of youth, then it is surely as clear as daylight that we are duped by a stale figure of speech."[23]

Is the typical American an example of abundant vitality, freshness, curiosity, *joie de vivre*? H. L. Mencken thought not:

It is absurd to say that there is anything properly describable as youthfulness in the American outlook. It is not that of young men, but of old men. All the characteristics of senescence are in it: a great distrust of ideas, an habitual timorousness, a harsh fidelity to a few fixed beliefs, a touch of mysticism. The average American is a prude and a Methodist under his skin. . . . His vices are not those of a healthy boy, but those of an ancient paralytic escaped from the *Greisenheim* (old folks' home).[24]

Perhaps it is appropriate that Uncle Sam—now more than two hundred—has always been depicted as an old geezer.

The assertion that the United States is a "universal nation" is another recurring claim of American exceptionalism. Emerson, like other American contemporaries, argued that a sort of generic humanity was coming into being in the United States: "A nation of men will for the first time exist, because each believes himself inspired by the Divine Soul which also inspires all men."[25] Most modern nationalisms have used similar messianic language. Compare Johann Gottlieb Fichte in his *Addresses to the German Nation* in 1806: "The German alone can therefore be a patriot; he alone can for the sake of his nation encompass the whole of mankind; contrasted with him from now on the patriotism of every other nation must be egoistic, narrow and hostile to the rest of mankind."[26] Ernst Moritz Arndt, writing in the early nineteenth century, declared that the German was "a universal man" and Germany "the greatest world-nation of the present earth."[27]

It is sometimes argued that the American people are a "universal nation" because we are a "nation of immigrants," unlike other nations, whose members presumably sprang up spontaneously from the soil. Even "monocultural" France, though, can be defined as a nation of immigrants. "We are French," President Mitterrand of France has observed. "Our ancestors are the Gauls, and we are also a little Roman, a little German, a little Jewish, a little Italian, a small bit Spanish, more and more Portuguese, who knows, maybe Polish, too. And I wonder whether we aren't already a bit Arab."[28]

Perhaps the term "nation of immigrants" should be limited to lands of recent European settlement. By that definition, the American nation is indeed a nation of immigrants—along with most other societies in the Western Hemisphere, Australia, New Zealand, and white South Africa. America has been the largest of the European settler states, but it has not been unique in forging a new identity among European immigrant groups. English, Scots, and Irish immigrants formed a common British and then a common "Anglo-Celtic" national identity in Australia, as in the American colonies; like the United States, Australia accepted increasingly diverse immigrants, first from Greece and Italy and now from Asia. Great numbers of Italians, British, Germans, and others have been absorbed into the white populations of Argentina, Brazil, and other Latin American countries. Significant numbers of Ukrainians, Scandinavians, and others have emigrated to Canada, so that the proportion of the Canadian population that is neither British nor French in descent is now almost a third. Indeed, Canada has a much greater claim to being a nation of immigrants than the United States—the chance that a U.S. citizen is an immigrant is one in fourteen; that a Canadian citizen is an immigrant, one in six.[29]

Far from being a unique blend of all the peoples of the world, the American population is much less diverse in its ethnic origins than other nations in the Western Hemisphere and the Caribbean, in which there are larger Indian populations and great numbers of mestizos and mulattos produced by intermarriage. In Surinam, for example, the population is divided among people of European, Hindu, Javanese and African descent. The majority of Americans have no black, Indian, mestizo, or Asian ancestors. Brazil and Mexico, too, can make much better claims for being universal nations than the American nation. Nor, as we have seen, has the United States always welcomed immigrants from all over the world. U.S. immigration policy, from 1792 until the 1960s, sought to limit immigration to whites. The argument that the American tradition is one of welcoming all ethnic and racial groups is simply false; that tradition is only a generation old.

By far the most important element of American exceptionalism is the claim that the United States is unique among nation-states in having a special "mission" in the world. In *White-Jacket* (1849), Herman Melville articulated the American sense of a democratic mission:

> We Americans are the peculiar, chosen people—the Israel of our time; we bear the ark of the liberties of the world. God has predestined, mankind expects, great things from our race; and great things we feel in our souls. The rest of the nations must soon be in our rear. We are pioneers of the world; the advance-guard, sent on through the wilderness of untried things, to break a new path in the New World that is ours.[30]

The idea of a universal American nation with a world mission, in both its religious and secular forms, has many parallels elsewhere. As Conor Cruise O'Brien has noted, many countries define themselves as "God Land."[31] Protestants in Ulster, Afrikaaners, and Zionists in Israel have all had "covenantal cultures," defining their nations in terms of a chosen people mythology derived from the Hebrew scriptures.[32] Long before Lincoln described the United States as "the last best hope of man on earth," and a nation "conceived in liberty," Milton described the world mission of Britain, "the mansion-house of liberty." The English were "ever famous, and foremost in the achievements of liberty." The rest of the world was following England's example to freedom: "we have the honour to precede other Nations who are now laboring to be our followers."[33] Lincoln called the American nation "an almost chosen people;" for Milton, England was "this Nation chos'n before any other."[34]

In tones scarcely distinguishable from those of American exceptionalists, J. A. Cramb, Professor of Modern History at Queen's College, London, described the destiny of nineteenth-century Britain: "Never since on Sinai God spoke in thunder has mandate more imperative been issued to any race, city, nation, than now to this nation and to this people."[35] As Lincoln mingled God and Freedom with American destiny in calling his countrymen to arms in the Civil War, so Cramb, during the Boer War (another attempt by a central government to bring white secessionists, enemies of minimal rights for blacks, back under central control), called on his fellow British for "our answer, that response which by this war we at last send ringing down the ages, 'God for Britain, Justice and Freedom to the world!'" Somewhat more succinctly, Mr. Podsnap, a self-satisfied London merchant in Dickens's *Our Mutual Friend*, explains to a Frenchman that Providence favors England: "This island was blest, sir, to the direct exclusion of such other countries as . . . there may happen to be."

Other parallels can be found in Russian messianism. The contrast of the moral East with the decadent West by nineteenth-century Russian Slavophiles was no different in kind from Jefferson's contrast of the virtuous New World with the corrupt Old. Not only was Russia a universal nation—a claim often made for the United States—but according to one Slavophile it represented a humane and pacific alternative to Europe: "In the foundation of the Western state: violence, slavery, and hostility. In the foundation of the Russian state: free will, liberty, and peace."[36] Another nineteenth-century Slavophile writer considered, and rejected, the claim that "the goal of humanity" had been reached in the United States in the 1830s: "America, on which our contemporaries have pinned their hopes for a time, has meanwhile clearly revealed the vices of her illegitimate birth. She is not a state, but rather a trading company. . . ." The genuine universal nation was Russia: "Oh Russia, oh my Fatherland!. . . . You, you are chosen to consummate, to crown the development of humanity, to embody all the various human achievements . . . in one great synthesis, to bring to harmony the ancient and modern civilisations, to reconcile heart with reason, to establish true justice and peace."[37] Russia, not America, was the true universal nation. "The Rus-sian people is not a people", the nineteenth-century Russian nationalist Konstantin Aksakov wrote, "it is a humanity; it is a people only because it is surrounded by peoples with exclusively national essences, and its humanity is therefore represented as nationality." All Slavs did not agree with the Russian messianic nationalists, of course. The Polish poet Adam Mickiewicz called Poland, oppressed by tsarist Russia, the "Christ among the peoples"; the resurrection of the "crucified nation" would signal the liberation of the entire human race from tyranny and war. As early as 1797, Polish nationalists had fought under the banner "For freedom ours and yours."[38]

The French notion of a democratic mission in the world is perhaps even stronger than the American. In France, as in the United States, republican idealism is older than many of the features that are associated with the modern national culture. E. J. Hobsbawm goes so far as to distinguish "the revolutionary-democratic" conception of a nation in French revolutionary thought from later racial or linguistic ideas of nationality. "The equation state = nation = people applied to both, but for the nationalists the creation of the political entities which would contain it derived from the prior existence of some community distinguishing itself from foreigners, while for the revolutionary-democratic point of view the central concept was the sovereign citizen-people = state which, in relation to the remainder of the human race, constitute a 'nation.'"[39] Abbe Sieyes defined the French nation in purely political, consensual terms: "What is a nation? A body of associates living under one common law and represented by the same legislature."[40] American exceptionalists tend to caricature Old World patriotism as meaningless "blood and soil" nativism, but French patriotism has had an equally high content of idealism. The phrase "the American experiment" was foreshadowed by a French journalist, who wrote in 1794: "The French Revolution might be described as the first experiment performed on the grand scale on a whole nation."[41] Charles Peguy wrote that France "is undeniably a sort of patron and witness (and often a martyr) to freedom in the world."[42] The French historian Michelet wrote that France is a "universal fatherland," "the moral ideal of the world," a nation "that has best merged its own interest and destiny with those of humanity." France's mission to "help every nation be born to liberty" is one that "makes the history of France that of humanity."[43]

Nor is the United States uniquely the "land of equality." True, the United States pioneered universal suffrage and other forms of equality—if only for whites. In the mid-nineteenth century, American society was indeed much more egalitarian and libertarian than those of Europe. By 1900, however, these "American" characteristics were more in evidence in Australia, which had a higher average standard of living, a more equitable income distribution and more progressive democratic institutions than the turn-of-the-century United States (U.S. reformers imported the Australian ballot and New Zealand's system of workmen's compensation, itself derived from Bismarck's Germany).

By now, in most of the industrial democracies, aristocracy has given way to a more egalitarian social order. Almost all European democracies are run by men and women of the middle classes. Thatcher was a grocer's daughter, Major a high-school dropout, Kinnock a coal miner's son. The House of Lords is full of self-made businessmen. Japan, ruled by princes and barons in the early twentieth century, has a system of meritocratic co-opting that promotes social mobility. Indeed, the weakness of parties in the United States makes it much easier for the rich to simply buy their way into office in America than in other democracies. America, which once led the world in democracy, now has perhaps the most grossly plutocratic political life of any major democratic nation, with the exceptions of Italy and Japan. The corrupt practice of awarding U.S. ambassadorial and other high offices to campaign contributors has no parallel in democratic Europe. The distribution of income in the United States is much greater than in those Old World societies, Britain, France, Germany and Japan. Indeed, the only societies that resemble American caricatures of the monarchical and aristocratic Old World today tend to be some in Latin America and our allies, the Arab monarchies. The emir of Kuwait was restored to power by an American president who as a child was driven to kindergarten in a limousine.

The argument that America is utterly unlike other modern nation-states, whether in its lack of a distinct nationality, its youth, its friendliness to immigrants, its egalitarianism, its idealistic self-conception, or its superior constitution, is chauvinist mythology. Not only is the multiracial American cultural majority a nation like other nations, but among the nations of the modern world it is one of the oldest and—until recently—one of the most homogeneous. Compared to most European countries, the United States, in spite of the Civil War, has an extraordinarily uninterrupted political and constitutional tradition and stable borders. Compared to most postcolonial Asian, African, and Middle Eastern regimes American culture, defined as language, customs, and holidays, is extraordinarily widely shared, well defined, stable, and venerable. And the racial, ethnic, and regional cleavages in America, although serious and increasing, are still less significant than those that afflict many other societies in the Western hemisphere, from Central America and Peru, where Indian-white conflicts underlie a number of civil wars, to Canada, threatened by a rift between its two founding peoples.

The exceptionalist myth depends on a caricature of the patriotism of the inhabitants of other democratic countries as being a matter of blind, racist jingoism, devoid of morality or political principle. This is nothing new, of course. In *Democracy in America*, de Tocqueville noted, "For the last fifty years no pains have been spared to convince the inhabitants of the United States that they are the only religious, enlightened, and free people . . . hence they conceive a high opinion of their superiority and are not very remote from believing themselves to be a distinct species of mankind."[44] A later visitor, Matthew Arnold, made a similar complaint, describing the lack of "commonsense criticism" of American exceptionalist rhetoric—"all this hollow stuff." America, he wrote, has "cultivated, judicious, delightful individuals" who "know perfectly well how false and hollow the boastful stuff talked is; but they let the storm of self-laudation rage, and say nothing."[45]

The United States *is* exceptional, among industrialized countries, in two respects, which have little or nothing to do with the liberal democratic ideal of American universalists. Thanks to the unwillingness of affluent white Americans to pay the taxes necessary for police patrols and asylums, the cities of the United States resemble those of the Third World, with their swarms of homeless vagrants, often insane or addicted to drugs. And thanks to its lack of effective gun control laws, the United States has by far the highest rates of homicide and imprisonment, not only among English-speaking democracies but among all democratic countries. America is not significantly freer or more democratic than other industrial democracies today. It does, however, lead Europe and Japan in beggars, murders and prisons per capita.

To refute the myth of American exceptionalism is to demolish democratic universalism, which claims that the United States is a unique idea-state. At any rate, the idea of a subcontinental population functioning as a kind of giant congregation of a political religion, a secular church, is inherently implausible. If Americans really believed they had nothing in common with each other apart from common government institutions or a common ideology, then in the absence of repression the country probably would have crumbled the way another would-be "idea-state," the Soviet Union, recently did.

Democratic universalism, then, is not a convincing alternative to the ideology of multiculturalism. In the past, in practice, democratic universalism as a political creed was attached to melting-pot Euro-American nationalism. Detached from the old melting-pot conception, and unattached to any notion of a transracial melting pot, the theory of democratic universalism can easily complement and reinforce multiculturalism. This is because the more that democratic universalists stress the absence of a common American ethnocultural nationality, the more Americans who wish to identify with a nation will value their own subnational identities—immigrant ethnicities, or the five officially designated races of Multicultural America. Democratic universalism, by weakening the idea of a common extrapolitical nationality, might inadvertently promote the crudest kinds of racial and subcultural parochialism. This is also the fatal flaw of another purported alternative to multiculturalism: cultural pluralism.

A NATION OF NATIONS

In 1974, a group of self-appointed urban ethnic and racial representatives organized themselves as the Bicentennial Ethnic Racial Coalition and sought a role in the American Revolution Bicentennial Administration (ARBA), the federal body in charge of coordinating the celebration of the two-hundredth anniversary of American independence. The Bicentennial Ethnic Racial Coalition organized an Ethnic/Racial Forum in 1976 in Boston, which issued a resolution in favor of rewording the pledge of allegiance: "I pledge allegiance to the flag of the United States of America, and to the republic for which it stands, one nation of many peoples, cultures, languages, and colors under God, indivisible, with respect, liberty, and justice for all."[46] A similar philosophy is expressed in a revision suggested by George P. Fletcher, of Columbia Law School: "I pledge allegiance to the flag of the United States of America and to the Republic for which it stands, one nation, united in our diversity, committed to liberty and justice for all." Fletcher argues for the deletion of the phrase "under God," "in order to maintain the Pledge as a ritual that unites all children, regardless of their religious background." Fletcher's Pledge promises "to capture ethnic, racial, and religious diversity as the bedrock of American culture."[47]

Unlike democratic universalism, cultural pluralism makes room for American nationalism—or, to be more precise, for American *nationalisms*. Cultural pluralism agrees with multiculturalism that the United States is a multinational democracy; it agrees with universalism that America needs to be held together by a strong commitment to the ideals of the Founding Fathers. It is, in short, a rather unstable compromise between hard-edged racial multiculturalism and rigorously abstract universalism; depending on how it is presented, cultural pluralism can look like universalism plus ethnic pride, or multiculturalism-and-water.

Cultural pluralism in the United States has been inspired by the philosophies and examples of two multinational federations, the Austro-Hungarian empire and Canada. As I noted in Chapter 2, cultural pluralism first entered the United States via New York from fin-de-siècle Vienna, where two of the leaders of Austrian Marxism, Otto Renner and Max Bauer, were devising plans for accommodating ethnic particularism within a unitary, supranational socialist state that would succeed the Hapsburg monarchy in Central Europe. In the socialist Central Europe of the future, political unity would advance economic and social progress, while cultural diversity would be respected by separate German, Czech, Polish, Hungarian, and Ukrainian ethnic authorities, school systems, and linguistic and historical associations. These Austro-Marxist ideas were in the air and well known to American intellectuals. The clearest link between Vienna and New York is Randolph Bourne, who wrote his 1916 essay "Trans-National America," one of the manifestos of American cultural pluralism, a few years after traveling as a member of the Columbia chapter of the Intercollegiate Socialist Society to the socialist Second International in Vienna. Cultural pluralism is, in large part, the Austro-Marxist multinational socialism of Bauer and Renner transmitted via Bourne and Kallen to several generations of American intellectuals.[48]

Though Kallen mentions Switzerland as a model for a multinational America, his version of cultural pluralism shows the influence of the Austro-Marxists. Of the ideal United States, Kallen writes, "Its form would be that of the federal republic; its substance a democracy of nationalities, cooperating voluntarily and autonomously through common institutions in the enterprise of self-realization through the perfection of men according to their kind." In a famous passage, Kallen, having earlier borrowed Aristotle's distinction between unison and harmony, uses the metaphor of an orchestra:

> As in an orchestra every type of instrument has its specific *timbre* and *tonality*, founded in its substance and form; as every type has its appropriate theme and melody in the whole symphony, so in society, each ethnic group may be the natural instrument, its temper and culture may be its theme and melody and the harmony and dissonances and discords of them all may make the symphony of civilization.[49]

Later, in the 1960s, American cultural pluralism was revitalized by a transfusion from Canada. Searching for a serviceable metaphor to dramatize their cultural pluralism-cum-multiculturalism, American liberals borrowed the somewhat self-satisfied description by Canadians of their country as a pluralistic mosaic rather than a repressive, conformist melting pot. Former Canadian Prime Minister Pierre Trudeau expressed the ethnic-federalist ideal recently: "Canada could become the envied seat of a form of federalism that could become a brilliant prototype for the molding of tomorrow's polyethnic civilization, a better model even than the American melting pot. Rather than forging a new alloy, the Canadian model would preserve the characteristics of each group in a mosaic of cultural coexistence."[50]*

This kind of thinking had a precursor in the English-speaking world in the writings of the nineteenth-century English liberal Lord Acton. According to Acton:

> A great democracy must either sacrifice self-government to unity or preserve it by federalism. The coexistence of several nations under the same State is a test, as well as the best security of its freedom . . .
>
> The combination of different nations in one State is as necessary a condition of civilized life as the combination of men in society. Where political and national boundaries coincide, society ceases to advance, and nations relapse into a condition corresponding to that of men who renounce intercourse with their fellow men . . . A state which is incompetent to satisfy different races condemns itself; a State which labors to neutralize, to absorb, or to expel them is destitute of the chief basis of self-government. The theory of nationality, then, is a retrograde step in history."

---

*Trudeau couples his encomium to cultural pluralism with an attack on nationalism, including liberal melting-pot nationalism: "Nationalists, whether of the left or right, are politically reactionary because they are led to define the common good as a function of an ethnic group or religious ideal rather than in terms of 'all the people' regardless of individual characteristics. This is why a nationalistic government is by nature intolerant, discriminatory and, when all is said and done, totalitarian." To make his meaning perfectly clear, he adds, "Democratic government stands for good citizenship, never nationalism." And, to be perfectly, *perfectly* clear: "In general, freedom has a firmer foundation under federalism than in any kind of unitary nation-state."

The Acton-Trudeau version of cultural pluralism joined the Bauer-Renner version, as it were, in the melting pot of American cultural pluralism, in the 1960s and 1970s. It was then, in the early years of the Third American Republic, that the mosaic metaphor—originally devised by Canadians as a way of contrasting their nonnational patriotism with American melting-pot nationalism—was adopted by the theorists of multiculturalism in the United States and put to somewhat different use as a way of justifying a system based on race rather than on linguistic nationality (like that of the Quebeckers and Anglo-Canadians). The metaphor quickly made its way into American public discourse, most notably in Mayor David Dinkins's reference to New York City as "this gorgeous mosaic."* Michael Walzer, a leading theorist of modern cultural pluralism, makes the Canadian inspiration explicit. Distinguishing liberal nationalism from nonnational liberalism, he writes that the latter "is the official doctrine of immigrant societies *like the United States (and federal Canada too),* and it also seems entirely appropriate to its time and place. For the United States isn't, after all, a nation-state, but a nation of nationalities, as Horace Kallen wrote in the second decade of our century, or a social union of social unions, in John Rawls's more recent formulation."[51]

Today cultural pluralists tend to be considered to be to the right of multiculturalists. It is important to recall, though, that the earliest version of American cultural pluralism, that of Horace Kallen and Randolph Bourne, constituted an attack by the far left, not on the right, but on the center-left. Kallen and Bourne hoped to discredit the then-new and progressive ideal of melting-pot nationalism, an ideal that was centrist or liberal in a time when the right was still strongly racist and nativist. Melting-pot assimilationists, like Anglo-Saxon nativists, assumed that

---

*After spreading rapidly in journalistic and political usage during the seventies and eighties, the mosaic metaphor is being edged out by the description of America as a salad bowl. The idea seems to be to contrast one culinary appliance with another; the term melting pot, of course, originally referred to a crucible, but many Americans with a limited knowledge of metallurgy seem to assume that it refers to a mixing bowl. Some supporters of integration and amalgamation have tried to replace the old melting-pot ideal with a new metaphor, also inspired by the kitchen, America-as-blender. The salad bowl and blender metaphors have the virtue of familiarity, but lack the dignity that attaches to crucibles and mosaics. It is hard to imagine a mayor referring to his city's diverse population as "this succulent salad."

there was and should be a common American national culture which immigrants joined; melting-pot theorists, however, saw American culture as something that changed over time, as elements of various immigrant cultures were detached from their original matrices and incorporated into the whole.

The two patron saints of American cultural pluralism rejected both Anglo-American nativism and the melting-pot ideal. In his February 1915 essay in the *Nation,* "Democracy vs. The Melting Pot," Horace Kallen was (as the essay's title suggests) concerned to rebut the melting-pot conception, as well as the nativism displayed in Edward A. Ross's polemic *The Old World and the New* (1915), the immediate occasion of Kallen's essay. Randolph Bourne, in his July 1916 essay "Trans-National America," concentrated on rebutting the claims of Anglo-conformists for the superiority of Anglo-American culture. Rejecting assimilation in its nativist and melting-pot forms, both of which in their different ways envision the United States as a conventional nation-state with a single predominant culture, cultural pluralists counterpose the ideal of the United States as a nonnational confederation of minorities, a country without a majority nation. In the words of Kallen, "the United States are in the process of becoming a federal state not merely as a union of geographical and administrative unities, but also as a cooperation of cultural diversities, as a federation or commonwealth of national cultures."[52] Instead of sharing a new American national culture formed from elements of many other cultures, immigrants would remain divided among permanent enclave communities that were linked only by a common government.

Bourne's ideal of a "trans-national America" is similar to Kallen's ideal of a federal republic of nationalities and Walzer's ideal of a community of distinct ethnic nations. Bourne uses the term *cosmopolitan* in a misleading way, to mean multiethnic, or multinational, not postethnic and postnational. "America is already the world-federation in miniature," he writes, "the continent where for the first time in history has been achieved that miracle of hope, the peaceful living side by side, with character substantially preserved, of the most heterogeneous peoples under the sun."[53] The operative phrase is "with character substantially preserved"—something that requires German-Americans to preserve German as their primary language, and Bohemian-Americans to continue, forever, speaking Czech at home. Far from thinking cosmopolitanism requires an attenuation of Old World—as well as Anglo-American—identities in favor of a new cosmopolitan identity, Bourne calls for a "dual citizenship" and tolerance for "that free and mobile passage of the immigrant between America and his native land."[54] Bourne favors, not a new American people, but a federation of existing European-American "peoples," in the plural—"The attempt to weave a wholly novel international nation out of our chaotic America will liberate and harmonize the creative power of *all these peoples* (emphasis added)."[55] (Kallen also used the plural in his 1924 book, *Culture and Democracy in the United States: Studies in the Group Psychology of the American Peoples*.)

What Bourne is offering is not a novel synthesis of new Old Worlders and old New Worlders, but the permanent, static survival in the New World of identities fixed in the Old. Kallen is similarly focused on Europe, hoping that "'American civilization' may come to mean the perfection of the cooperative harmonies of 'European civilization'—the waste, the squalor, and the distress of Europe being eliminated—a multiplicity in a unity, an orchestration of mankind."[56] Kallen went so far as to argue that assimilation and amalgamation among different European nationalities in America was *biologically* impossible. He dismisses the idea that the descendants of Anglo-Americans and German, Irish, Polish, and Italian immigrants will intermarry, creating a generic white American type:

> The notion that the program might be realized by radical and even forced miscegenation, by the creation of the melting-pot by law, and thus the development of the new "American race" is . . . as mystically optimistic as it is ignorant. In historic times so far as is known no new ethnic types have originated, and from what is known of breeding there comes no assurance that the old types will disappear in favor of the new . . . Biologically, life does not unify; biologically life diversifies; and it is sheer ignorance to apply social analogies to biological processes. In any event, we know what the qualities and capacities of existing types are; we know how by education to do something toward the conversion of what is evil in them and the conservation of what is good.[57]

The biological "types" to which Kallen refers are the German, the Scandinavian, the Pole, the Jew, each with its distinctive inherited

"qualities and capacities" that can be modified only slightly by education. Kallen, who is thought of as a great precursor of left-liberalism, is
ready to apply the term "miscegenation" to such unnatural unions as,
say, the marriage of a German-American and an Irish-American.

Kallen's identification of ethnicity with biological race cannot be dismissed as irrelevant. Indeed, he equated the Jews with another white
"nation," the Irish: "An Irishman is always an Irishman, a Jew always a
Jew. Irishman or Jew is born, citizen or lawyer, or church-member is
made. Irishman and Jew are facts of nature; citizen and church-member
are artifacts of civilization."[58] Kallen was a racial Zionist, defining Jews,
believing or not, as members of an immutable race: "Men . . . change
their religions . . . they cannot change their grandfathers."[59]

The rejection of the belief in the genetic transmission of ethnic characteristics like Irishness presents modern cultural pluralists with a
dilemma. If cultural pluralism presupposes the indefinite perpetuation
of a number of immigrant enclaves in the United States, how are those
distinct communities to be preserved against the erosive forces of assimilation and intermarriage? Recognizing the degree to which the European immigrants (contrary to the expectation of Horace Kallen) have
been absorbed into the general white population, Walzer calls for keeping the process of assimilation to the American majority culture at bay
by a constant stream of new immigrants: "Don't shut the gates. This is
not Europe; we are a society of immigrants, and the experience of leaving a homeland and coming to this new place is an almost universal
American experience. It should be celebrated." Walzer transfers responsibility for realizing the old cultural-pluralist fantasy from the all-
too-assimilated white ethnics to new ethnic groups from other parts of
the world. "Whatever regulation is necessary—we can argue about
that—the flow of people, the material base of multiculturalism, should
not be cut off."[60] Walzer hopes that separate ethnic communities in the
United States can be kept alive artificially, to *prevent* the development
of a common American cultural identity: "If that vitality cannot be sustained, pluralism will prove to be a temporary phenomenon, a way station on the road to American nationalism."[61] Assimilation, or
nationalism, is a misfortune: "A radical program of Americanization
would really be unAmerican. It isn't inconceivable that America will

one day become an American nation-state, the many giving way to the one, but that is not what it is now; nor is that its destiny."[62] The public schools, according to Walzer, must be structured to actively discourage the assimilation of immigrants to the majority heritage: "Strengthen the public schools, and focus them . . . on two things: first, the history and contemporary forms of democratic politics, and second, the immigrant experience."[63]

In Walzer's view, then, everyone in America should have an ethnic nationality—with the exception of "generic" Americans: "A certain sort of communitarianism is available to each of the hyphenate groups—except, it would seem, the American-Americans, whose community, if it existed, would deny the Americanism of all the others."[64] Thus Irish-Americans will celebrate Irishness, Greek-Americans will celebrate Greekness, African-Americans will celebrate African-Americanness, Asian-Americans will celebrate their Asian heritages—but the vast majority of assimilated Americans should not celebrate their own "generic American" identity.

What will hold this federation of immigrant communities together? For an answer, cultural pluralists tend to invoke the democratic universalist's panacea for national disunity—the American Creed. "In the United States," Diane Ravitch writes, "one may be a good citizen without relinquishing one's native culture, language, religion, food, dress, or folkways." For Ravitch, it is enough for Americans to be united by nothing more than political philosophy: "We are bound together as a people by a common commitment to the political ideas and values contained in the Constitution and the Bill of Rights and elaborated by those (like Thomas Jefferson, Abraham Lincoln, and Martin Luther King, Jr.) who have extended and articulated the definition of our civic culture in each generation."[65] Nathan Glazer writes:

> Our diversity has one major binding force in the Constitution. . . . It guarantees that the Amish need not attend schools after the age when they feel their children will be corrupted, and that the Mormons and the Black Muslims can teach their own variant of the truth, which is as fantastic to many of us as the furthest reaches of Afrocentrism. . . . This common political bond keeps us together: nationalists and antinational-

ists, Eurocentrists and Afrocentrists, and may continue to do so through the storms of multiculturalism."

Even Glazer has his doubts: "Perhaps I am giving too much credit to our common political procedures and understanding."[66] Indeed. The real reason that cultural diversity is not a serious threat has nothing to do with the Constitution; it is the continued existence of a numerically overwhelming cultural majority. Suppose that 30 percent of the population were German-speaking Amish, 20 percent separatist Mormons, and 20 percent Black Muslim, with only 30 percent being what we today think of as belonging to what Walzer calls "American-American" culture. Does anyone seriously believe that in such a society widespread commitment to the procedures of the Constitution and widespread belief in the ideals of the Founding Fathers and Abraham Lincoln and Martin Luther King, Jr., would by itself prevent civil unrest? Such a culturally heterogeneous population, lacking consensus on even minor matters of substance, could be held together only by a strict segregation of its "nationalities" to minimize conflict, or by a dictatorship imposing ethnic peace.

The idea that in the United States common procedures might by some miracle produce social unity has been expressed before. J. S. Mill wrote that de Tocqueville showed how the American was "made to feel that besides the interests which separate him from his fellow citizens, he has interests which connect him with them; that not only the common weal is his weal but that it partly depends upon his exertion."[67] In the first volume of *Democracy in America*, de Tocqueville writes: "I will never admit that men constitute a social body simply because they obey the same head and the same laws. Society can exist only when a great number of men consider a great number of things under the same aspect, when they hold the same opinions upon many subjects, and when the same occurrences suggest the same thoughts and impressions to their minds." Walzer and other cultural pluralists, however, think—or at least hope, in the face of all experience—that agreement on democratic procedures and ideals is sufficient to make a nation of an aggregate of culturally distinct populations. Walzer writes: "It is not implausible to imagine a heterogeneous but egalitarian society: the heterogeneity, cultural and private; the equality, economic and political."

On the contrary, such a society is highly implausible, here or anywhere else. The crack-up of multinational states is one of the major phenomena of our time. The fact is that cultural pluralists have misunderstood the relation between ethnicity and race in America. In the American environment, ethnicity vanishes in a generation or two. Racial categories, defined by objective physical characteristics, endure. To the extent that cultural pluralists wish to support enduring communal subdivisions in the American nation, those permanent subdivisions can only be racial. Multiculturalists show that they implicitly recognize this, by talking about culture and ethnicity but meaning biological race.

In his autobiography, an ex-gangster from South-Central Los Angeles describes *real* cultural pluralism in the United States:

Lines of race, of national unity that defied political logic and overstanding [sic], were clearly drawn in Youth Authority, which served as a junior college for the larger university of prison. The most blatant was that of the Allied Forces of Southern Chicanos—"southern" meaning any land south of Fresno—with all Americans [whites]. The Americans could have "White Pride," "White Power," swastikas, lightning bolts, "100% Honkey," and such tattooed all over them, clearly stating they were stone-cold racists, and the Chicanos would be more than comfortable in their presence. New Afrikans [blacks] allied themselves with the more cultured Northern Chicanos. The Northern and Southern Chicanos were, and still are, locked in a very serious war. . . . So, like the warring factions of New Afrikans, the Chicanos were split by geopolitical boundaries. What's striking is that the division of the two is signified in colors. The Northern Chicanos—Nuestra Familia, Northern Structure, and Fresno Bulldogs— wear red flags. The more numerous Southerners—Mexican Mafia, Southern United Raza, and South Side Government—wear blue.[68]

This, and not the cultural pluralist vision of cheerful hyphenated Americans going from the ethnic heritage festival to the democratic socialist debate, is the most likely consequence of pronounced cultural diversity within a democratic state.

Like democratic universalism, Austro-Canadian cultural pluralism seems at first glance to be an appealing alternative to the rigid race-based multiculturalism of Multicultural America. However, the celebration of immigrant subcultures by cultural pluralists defines Americans in terms of ancestry just as certainly, if not as crudely, as multiculturalism. Democratic universalism avoids this problem, only because it has no conception of a cultural identity distinct from political identity.

By making political idealism—and *only* political idealism—the only thing that connects diverse Americans, cultural pluralists and democratic universalists put a burden on the American political tradition it cannot bear. A constitution is not a country; an idea is not a nation. A purely "constitutional patriotism," whether welded to immigrant ethnicities or not, is too flimsy a bond to link Americans to one another. The failure of a nonnational patriotism can only encourage the illiberal nationalism of racists (including multicultural racists) and nativists—and justify the indifference of the white American overclass to the national interest.

It is worth pausing for a moment to ponder the significance of the fact that cultural pluralist ideas originated in two multinational, imperial structures: Austria-Hungary and British Canada. While those nostalgic for the Dual Monarchy or the empire on which the sun never set tend to idealize them as nonnational regimes, treating all subjects according to a single rule, in fact both empires, like multinational regimes throughout history, survived as long as they did by adroitly playing off one nationality against another. Upon the imperial concessions to the French minority is based the official doctrine that Canada is a binational society, with two founding nations. Similarly, the ethnic German aristocracy controlled the Hapsburg Empire by pitting the non-German nations against one another and extending privileges to the elites of favored nationalities, like Hungary's Magyar aristocracy. Both Canada and the Dual Monarchy whose territorial integrity Bauer and Renner sought to preserve, then, embodied divide-and-rule multinationalism in their very constitutions. Liberal and socialist reformers like Acton and Bauer and Renner who wanted to reform their respective empires, not break them up along lines of national self-determination, had to find some idealistic way of rationalizing the continued coexistence of various nationalities within a single government which only existed in the first place to promote the interests of a distant colonial power or a ruling family. The theory of cultural pluralism is that rationalization.

The motives of cultural pluralists may be perfectly sincere; but given the inequality of power and resources among American races, and the overwhelming dominance of the small white overclass within the white population, the inevitable consequence of cultural pluralism would be to reinforce a policy of *divide et impera*. In the United States, as in Austria-Hungary and Canada, an official doctrine of cultural pluralism might serve just as well as multiculturalism in disguising the same depressing social reality, a pattern of racial division that works to the benefit only of the Haves.

THE NEW NATIVISM

Democratic universalism and cultural pluralism are doctrines that appeal chiefly to a small intellectual and political elite. Of the two, universalism probably has the greatest resonance among the public, thanks to elementary-school recitations of the Gettysburg Address and the ritual employment of hackneyed universalist rhetoric by politicians. The alternate vision of American identity that has the most appeal to the American majority may well be one that is rejected by the guardians of public orthodoxy: nativism.

In order to understand contemporary American nativism, it is important to understand what it is not. Nativism is not opposition to immigration as such; even old-fashioned Anglo-American nativists favored immigration by certain groups (for example, Germans and Scandinavians). Concerns about the effects of large-scale immigration on the American economy or American culture are perfectly legitimate. Nor is nativism to be identified with protectionism or isolationism, as it frequently is by Wilsonian globalists, or with opposition to racial preferences. All of these policies may be supported, alone or in combination, by Americans whose view of American nationality cannot be described as nativist.

If nativism is not support for immigration restriction, protectionism, isolationism, or opposition to racial preference, then what is it? Nativism can be defined as a definition of the national community not simply in terms of language and culture, but in racial or religious terms (the two are usually related, but need not be). In the contemporary United States, nativism is in essence Euro-American Christian nationalism, surviving in the Third American Republic as a legacy from the Second. Though officially disfavored, a surreptitious and largely subconscious pan-white, pan-Christian nationalism exists in America today, influencing far more people than the relatively small number of unapologetic racists on the right.

The new nativism chiefly unites evangelical Protestants and conservative Catholics. Despite talk of a conservatism based on Judeo-Christian values, and the attraction of some reactionary Jews to nativist ideology, the new nativism is essentially trinitarian Christian. As Patrick Buchanan told a convention of the Christian Coalition, "Our culture is superior because our religion is Christianity and that is the truth that makes men free."[69] Conor Cruise O'Brien has identified the existence of a contemporary American pan-Christianity; "traditionalist" pan-Christianity might be even more precise, distinguishing right-wing Protestants and Catholics from moderate and liberal members of their own denominations. This pan-Christian synthesis on the far right was foreshadowed in the alliance between two notorious antisemites of the 1930s, Father Charles E. Coughlin and Gerald L. K. Smith, himself an evangelical preacher and the son of a minister, who in 1947 established the Christian Nationalist Crusade.[70] Right-wing Catholics and Protestants also rallied behind Senator Joseph McCarthy, who claimed, "Today we are engaged in a final, all-out battle between communistic atheism and Christianity."[71]

Instead of a secular state, the nativist ideal is of a pan-Christian (or nominally Judeo-Christian) state, which does not discriminate among denominations but *does* actively favor religion—identified with biblical religion as defined by fundamentalist Protestants—over irreligion or secular humanism. This state sponsorship of generalized religion, it is claimed (not entirely without justification), was the intent of the Founding Fathers. Just as the state should be pro-Christian, so should the larger society. The nativists look back with nostalgia to the first two-thirds of the twentieth century, when pressure from the Protestant and Catholic churches on schools, government at all levels, and the entertainment industry and publishers maintained a regime of censorship of objectionable content in books, movies, plays, and popular music.

The incorporation of conservative Catholics as well as Protestants into the new nativist identity represents a development of historic importance. For most of American history, the great demon in the nativist imagination was the Catholic Church. From Jamestown to Lexington, the Antichrist was identified with Catholicism; anti-Catholicism, although latent in American Protestantism, flared up in the early nineteenth century and the 1920s. Today's nativism has managed to unite fundamentalist Protestants and reactionary Catholics only by sublimating anti-Catholicism in attacks on allegedly non-Christian or anti-Christian conspiracies by evil forces opposed to all Christian denominations. That there is an audience for a kind of pan-Christian American nationalism is suggested by the fact that Dan Quayle in January 1994, at a conference of the religious right in Fort Lauderdale about "Reclaiming America," joined the crowd in reciting, "I pledge allegiance to the Christian flag, and to the Saviour, for whose Kingdom it stands, one Saviour, crucified, risen, and coming again, with life and liberty for all who believe."[72]

The new nativism has inherited a certain amount of black-baiting and Jew-baiting from the old nativism (though anti-Catholicism has been suppressed). Many of the leaders of the religious right, like Jerry Falwell and Billy Lee Hargis of Christian Crusade, are veterans of campaigns against racial integration; Falwell in 1958 cited Scripture to demonstrate that the Supreme Court's *Brown* decision integrating the public schools was part of a satanic conspiracy.[73] The argument of Richard Herrnstein and Charles Murray in their controversial book *The Bell Curve* that black and Hispanic Americans on average are inferior to white Americans by nature may serve to revive and reinforce the white-supremacist notions that undoubtedly continue to influence large numbers of white Americans.

Antisemitism also survives on the American right. In August 1980, at a Religious Roundtable gathering in Dallas at which Republican presidential nominee Ronald Reagan was in attendance, Bailey Smith, president of the Southern Baptist Convention, criticized political rallies for including prayers by Jews as well as Christians: "With all due respect to those dear people, my friends, God Almighty does not hear the prayer of a Jew." In 1987, Tim LaHaye, the fundamentalist minister whose wife Beverly founded the influential Concerned Women of America, was forced to resign as cochair of the Jack Kemp presidential campaign because of his written observation that Jews have "all too frequently been devoted to philosophies that proved harmful to mankind." Throughout his book *The New World Order*, Pat Robertson, founder of the Christian

Coalition, claims that Jewish bankers like the Rothschilds started the French and Russian revolutions, assassinated Abraham Lincoln, and plotted to found the Federal Reserve—all in the service of a satanic conspiracy to found a world government: "Until we understand the commonality of interest between left-wing Bolsheviks and right-wing monopolistic capitalists, we cannot fully comprehend the last seventy years of world history. . . ."[74] What is more, in a reprise of the old practice of listing "Christian" merchants, in recent years evangelical Christians have been encouraged to shop from merchants listed in the "Christian Yellow Pages" (CYP). Two Jewish businessmen in Los Angeles, told they could not advertise in the CYP, sued, but eventually the case was settled in favor of the directory's publisher.[75]

Allegations of antisemitism have also been made against Patrick Buchanan, on the basis of his writings and public remarks. Buchanan's defenders claim that he has made legitimate criticisms of American Jews and of Israeli foreign policy. Many of Buchanan's conservative colleagues disagree. William Bennett accused Buchanan of "flirting with fascism," while William F. Buckley, Jr., examining antisemitism on the right, concluded that there was reason to be disturbed by a long list of Buchanan outbursts.[76]

Many right-wing thinkers and activists, however, support what can, without contradiction, be described as a multiracial and somewhat ecumenical nativism. Richard John Neuhaus, the editor of the conservative journal *First Things*, in a long essay on immigration, has argued that the real threat to American social unity comes not from immigrants but from elements of the native-born American population: "A serious problem is posed by the aliens among us." These "aliens" are "the urban and mainly black underclass," "a civil rights overclass," "homosexuals" who "are the very definition of social marginality" and "journalists, writers, academics, and a significant portion of the religious leadership" of the United States. Ralph Reed, executive director of the Christian Coalition, agrees with this strategy of mobilizing nonwhite immigrants against unpopular but nonracial minorities like homosexuals and intellectuals: "Much of the new immigration from Latin America and the Pacific Basin tends to be conservative, pro-family and devoutly religious. They're our voters." This strategy has been put into practice by conservative operatives who try to appeal to antigay prejudice in the black population in order to destroy the coalition between black and gay civil rights activists.

As it happens, the development of a postracist right-wing nativism was predicted in the mid-sixties by Peter Viereck, one of the giants of postwar intellectual conservatism (and one of the first former conservatives to turn against the movement). "Manifestations of ethnic intolerance today tend to decrease in proportion as ideological intolerance increases," he wrote in 1965, referring to the McCarthy-Goldwater right. He coined the term "transtolerance" for "this curious interplay between the new tolerance and the new intolerance. Transtolerance is ready to give all minorities their glorious democratic freedom—provided they accept McCarthyism or some other mob conformism of Right or Left."

> *Transtolerance is the form that xenophobia takes when practiced by a 'xeno.'* Transtolerant McCarthyism is partly a movement of recent immigrants who present themselves (not so much to the world as to themselves) as a 200 percent hate-the-foreigner movement. And by extension: Hate "alien" ideas. Transtolerance is also a sublimated Jim Crow: against "wrong" thinkers, not "wrong" ideas. As such, it is a Jim Crow that can be participated in with a clear conscience by the new, non-segregated flag-waving Negro, who will be increasingly emerging from the increased egalitarian laws in housing and education. In the same way it is the Irishman's version of Mick-baiting and a strictly kosher anti-Semitism. It very sincerely champions against anti-Semites "that American Dreyfus, Roy Cohn"; simultaneously it glows with the same mob emotions that in all previous or comparable movements have been anti-Semitic.

Viereck speculated about the form transtolerant American patriotism would ultimately take: "Won't it be a 'team' (as they will obviously call it) of 'buddies' from 'all three religions' plus the significantly increasing number of Negro McCarthyites, all 'cooperating' in the 'common task' of burning books on civil liberties or segregating all individualists of 'all three' religions?"[77]

The new nativist strategy of transtolerance is apparent in right-wing attacks on the so-called new class (this infinitely elastic term comes from ex-Trotskyite neoconservatives, and means any college-educated group that does not share Republican views). During the 1988 presidential campaign, Vice-President Dan Quayle blended neoconservative and Wallaceite rhetoric in a denunciation of a "cultural elite" using its alleged control of television and other media to destroy "traditional family values."*

As a sinister, demonic enemy, the new class/cultural elite suffers from being vague. Gay and lesbian Americans—though invisible in most classes and in most of the country for fear of persecution—offer a concrete target for nativist attacks that might otherwise be directed at Wall Street. Marvin Liebman, a founder of the conservative movement and an acknowledged homosexual, explains the continuities between today's Republican gay-baiting and conservative strategy in the past:

> The Berlin wall came down, communism fell, and the cement wasn't there anymore. So the conservative movement had to find another enemy—that's how they operate. They couldn't do Jews, though they would have liked to. They couldn't do blacks—too well organized. So they've focused on homosexuals poisoning society. The rhetoric is almost word for word what they used about the communists: schools, Hollywood, media elite. Those code words used to mean Jews, but now they also mean gays.

Even while this new demonology is being purveyed by the far right, however, old-fashioned Protestant nativists continue to vilify Catholics in terms identical to those with which "secular humanists," "the media elite," and homosexuals are demonized. Instead of claiming that secular pagans control the media, one old-style Protestant nativist warns that Catholics are really in charge of the country: "Through its influence in politics and the media, modern Roman Catholicism has become, in fact, the nation's most powerful religious force."[78] Just as the new White American nativists equate secularism or liberal Christianity with sexual debauchery, so the older kind of Protestant nativist is impressed by the supposed depravity of Catholics; one student of Protestant fundamentalist history text notes, "It is interesting how often Catholic faith and sinful, depraved lifestyles are seen as synonymous."[79] The Catholic Church itself is accused of humanism: "the Roman Catholic church in its long

---

*In 1965, it is worth noting, Peter Viereck criticized similar rhetoric by the pseudo-conservative Goldwaterites of his day, noting: "The real kings (the cultural elite that would rank first in any traditional hierarchy of the Hellenic-Roman West) are now becoming declassed scapegoats: the eggheads." (Peter Viereck, *Shame and Glory of the Intellectuals*, New York: G. P. Putnam's Sons, 1965, p. 320.)

history has given increasing importance to the traditions of man at the expense of God's truth."[80] Substitute "new class" or "liberal" or "secular humanist" or "homosexual" for "Catholic" in the above, and you have the script for today's transracial, pan-Christian nativism of the right.

As Peter Viereck suggested, fascism, if it ever came to America, might take the form of transtolerant nativism, with patriots of all races and religions joining together in attacking the designated hate objects of the regime: intellectuals, homosexuals, political heretics. The racial and theological elements of the new white nativism would be played down, in favor of a transethnic and possibly transracial Americanism defined by narrow political, moral and aesthetic conformity. In the wilder nightmares of the left, secular humanists would be purged and persecuted, and women forced to bear unwanted children.

Fortunately we are not likely to see these speculations put to the test. The United States may well experience episodes of authoritarian government in the future but these are unlikely to resemble the mobilizing, chauvinistic dictatorships of interwar Europe, all marching bands and banners. Dictatorship in the United States would most likely be demobilizing, seeking to keep people in their homes, rather than putting them on the streets or in uniform. An American dictatorship would clothe itself in constitutional and legal forms; it would cultivate an aura of nonpartisan technocracy and business expertise, not a feverish cult of the genius-leader and the masses. An American *Fuehrer* would not rant and strut, but crack jokes and adopt the relaxed, ironic, "cool" style of a television host. Individuals resembling Pat Robertson and Pat Buchanan are the *least* likely American dictators imaginable.

Implausible fears of fascism arising on the right only divert attention from the real danger of an American feudalism. A fascist right talks about duty; a feudal right sings the praises of choice. A fascist right wants to take over; a feudal right just wants to opt out. Today's Euro-Christian or pan-Christian nativists, like yesterday's segregationists, do not aspire to take over the federal government, but rather to weaken its authority in order to carve out enclave communities in which they can approach their own communal ideals.

It is not difficult to imagine such subcultural separatism being justified in the language, derived ultimately from the black power movement, of group rights and group victimization. Already white fundamentalists have learned to speak in the language of Multicultural America, claiming that court bans on school prayer or confessional displays in public represent religious discrimination. Some fundamentalists, no doubt, feel uncomfortable with adopting the pose of an aggrieved minority; to do so is to abandon the claim that the religious right speaks for the Christian American nation as a whole, for the moral *majority*. Nevertheless, as the prospects for a triumphalist restoration of something like the old informal Protestant establishment recedes, we can expect the religious right increasingly to mimic the language and strategies of the multicultural left.

Multiculturalism is not an inherently left-wing idea. South African apartheid ("apartness") was multiculturalism, of a sort. During the 1960s, George Lincoln Rockwell's American Nazi Party collaborated with black separatists like Malcolm X. White racists who assumed that nonwhites cannot or will not be assimilated into the white population, and that they are not going anywhere, have often looked favorably on black cultural separatism, which is after all a voluntary form of segregation. In France, the organic-nationalist right of Le Pen favors multiculturalism—*of course,* the multiculturalists of the right argue, French Muslims should have their own, separate schools and institutions. After all, they can never be truly French.

Right-wing multiculturalism in America, should it develop, may well be dressed up as libertarianism. Proposals for school choice, for example, are often presented with libertarian arguments. The Republican party's support for taxpayer funding of church schools, through vouchers, is relatively recent; it originated in Nixon's plan to win the conservative Catholic vote.* Claims by conservatives that the privatization of public education is intended to help poor black ghetto children are hard to

---

*Support for vouchers marked a break with Republican tradition; in 1876, Congressman James G. Blaine (in 1882 the Republican candidate for president) introduced a constitutional amendment, narrowly defeated, that would have banned public support for parochial schools. (Robert T. Handy, *Undermined Establishment: Church-State Relations in America, 1880–1920,* Princeton: Princeton University Press, 1991, pp. 40–41.) Theodore Roosevelt called for "absolutely nonsectarian public schools" and declared it was "not our business to have the Protestant Bible or the Catholic Vulgate or the Talmud read in these schools." (Handy, ibid., p. 160.)

take seriously; the chief beneficiaries would be fundamentalist Bible academies (known as "segregationist academies" in the South) and Catholic parochial schools in the suburbs.

Unlike the public schools, private schools would be able to turn away students whose parents do not make a certain income, or who belong to the wrong religion. The real reason for fundamentalist support for school choice is anything but libertarian, according to "Christian reconstructionist" Gary North:

> So let us be blunt about it: we must use the doctrine of religious liberty to gain independence for Christian schools until we train up a generation of people who know that there is no religious neutrality, no neutral law, no neutral education, and no neutral civil government. Then they will get busy in constructing a Bible-based social, political, and religious order which finally denies the religious liberties of the enemies of God.[81]

The common school was one of the great agents of Americanization in the nineteenth and early twentieth centuries. The decline of American public education, largely as a result of misguided liberal reforms and a sclerotic public education bureaucracy, has led many to wonder whether private schools might do a better job. But the privatization of American education, unless accompanied by strict government controls over the content of curricula to ensure the accurate teaching of natural science and history, would probably accelerate the fissuring of the American population into hostile tribes living in radically separate mental universes. One can only imagine the consequences for American science and technology, and public literacy, if a substantial minority of the white population were to graduate from fundamentalist Bible academies teaching that modern natural science is a diabolical hoax perpetrated by satanic Darwinians. If, at the same time, much of the black American population attended all-black Afrocentric academies, teaching that white people stole their civilization from ancient black Africans, the consequences for American social unity and international competitiveness would be severe. While East Asian students pored over calculus and genetic engineering, ten or twenty or thirty percent of American schoolchildren might be devoting much of their time at school to studying Swahili or "creation science."

Disastrous though it would be, an alliance of multiculturalists and nativists to partition what is left of a common American identity into subcultural fragments is all too easy to visualize. Perhaps support for multiculturalism by the nativist right could be secured by an agreement to include denominations in the group-rights system of Multicultural America. Perhaps, in addition to a black and a Jewish seat on the Supreme Court, there would be a Protestant evangelical seat. Perhaps African-American Studies departments could be joined by Evangelical Studies departments. Perhaps voting districts could be redrawn on denominational lines—Baptist, Episcopalian, Catholic—as well as racial lines. Diversity might be redefined to include denominational and not just racial and gender diversity.

Why not? The spoils system of Multicultural America is flexible and capable of indefinite extension; practically any group can become an object of official recognition and a recipient of federal patronage. Perhaps, as so many liberals fear, the glowering divines will take over the country and force us to listen to endless televised sermons, and bring unwanted fetuses to term. If Multicultural America endures as a political order its leaders may ultimately tame and encapsulate the religious right by encouraging its leaders to redefine it as just one more victim group deserving a comfortable ghetto of its own.

Whether or not religious denominations join the list of protected classes, the development of today's Multicultural America into a right-wing multicultural regime is all too easy to imagine. Indeed, it is the most likely scenario for the future evolution of the United States, if present trends are not reversed.

Multiculturalism II would probably differ from Multiculturalism I in certain respects. For one thing, antiwhite discrimination would be replaced by a straightforward separate-but-equal policy in matters of education, political redistricting, and so on. As officially defined "whites" become the second- or third-largest group in cities like New York and Los Angeles, and then in states like California and Texas, the notion of the white population as simply one more cultural group deserving protection of its own European-American culture and its own proportionate share of the spoils may catch on.

A grand compromise between conservative overclass whites and Hispanics might replace the bargain between white overclass liberals and
the black middle class underlying Multicultural America. Hispanics,
having become the plurality in many if not most of America's most populous cities and states, might become the favored minority of overclass
whites. While Americans of European (and perhaps East Asian) descent
dominated the commanding heights of banking and business, more and
more formal political power would be ceded to Hispanic public figures.
In the military, Hispanics might assume the historic role of white Southerners as the most important source of recruits. A division of labor between a white or Eurasian oligarchy and Hispanic politicians, soldiers,
and police officers might cause problems if the latter ever grew tired of
acting as the security guards for the former. The examples of Fujimori in
Peru, the military-backed champion of those whom he affectionately
calls "the little brown ones" against the white oligarchy, and of Noriega,
the dark-skinned agent, and then master, of light-skinned Panamanian
creoles, might in time seem less irrelevant to American politics.

Despite these differences, Multiculturalism II would resemble Multiculturalism I in its rhetoric of diversity, its careful counting and balancing
of officially designated races, its use of quotas and set-asides. The dynamic of a system like that of Multicultural America was noted in 1947 by
Gunnar Myrdal: "In a society where there are broad social classes and, in
addition, more minute distinctions and splits in the lower strata, *the lower
class groups will to a great extent take care of keeping each other subdued,* thus
relieving to that extent the higher classes of this otherwise painful task
necessary to the monopolization of its power and advantages."[82]

The "Myrdal factor" is clearly at work in the contemporary United
States. In other industrial democracies, the economic stagnation of the
lower half of the population has been translated into political rebellion
against the upper half; this accounts to a large extent for the electoral
annihilation of long-ruling parties in Sweden, Italy, France, and Japan in
recent years. Here, however, racial divisions ensure that the lower-half
Americans waste their energies in zero-sum struggles between races.
Competition and strife between black Americans and other minorities
at the lower end of the socioeconomic scale—Hispanics, new arrivals
from Asia—has the same effect of dissipating reformist energies in con-

flict between groups that might have been allies. The militant peasants can be counted upon to start squabbling among themselves long before they reach the castle gates. This effect of left-wing multiculturalism would simply become the purpose of right-wing multiculturalism.

Manipulation of racial and ethnic antipathies among different groups of Have-Nots, to the benefit of the Haves, is nothing new in English-speaking North America. In the eighteenth century, one Carolinian described the intent of the planters "to make Indians & Negroes a checque upon each other least by their Vastly Superior Numbers we should be crushed by one or the other."[83] After the Civil War, some Southern planters experimented with the importation of Chinese coolie laborers to work in the fields. The Chinese workers, pitted against black workers, were praised for outperforming the latter. According to a southern governor, "Undoubtedly the underlying motive for this effort to bring in Chinese laborers was to punish the negro for having abandoned the control of his old master, and to regulate the conditions of his employment and the scale of wages to be paid him."[84]

During a joint Japanese-Filipino strike in Hawaii in 1920, the Director of the Bureau of Labor of the Hawaiian Sugar Planters' Association called for mobilizing Hawaiian, Portuguese, and Korean strikebreakers against the Japanese and Filipinos: "In order to let the plantation laborers know they are being duped and to make them realize what they are losing by allowing themselves to be misled by the agitating newspapers and strike leaders, we have commenced a program of propaganda. . . . There is absolutely no race so susceptible to ridicule as the Japanese."[85] In the twentieth-century South, some northern employers moved their plants South to undercut white labor: "Hiring black laborers . . . fit conveniently into the antiunion efforts of many industrialists. . . . A labor force divided along ethnic and racial lines poses great difficulties for union organizers."[86] An employment agent for a late-nineteenth-century Chicago meatpacking plant explained why he was trying to hire Swedes: "Well you see, it is only for this week. Last week we employed Slovaks. We change about among the different nationalities and languages. It prevents them from getting together."[87]

Centuries before today's multiculturalists adopted the slogan "Celebrate diversity," William Smith, a slave trader, explained his reasons for celebrating a diversity of cultures:

As for the languages of *Gambia*, they are so many and so different, that the Natives, on either Side of the River, cannot understand each other; which, if rightly consider'd, is no small Happiness to the *Europeans* who go thither to trade for slaves. . . . The safest Way is to trade with the different Nations, on either Side of the River, and having some of every Sort on board, there will be no more Likelihood of their succeeding in a Plot than of finishing the Tower of Babel.[88]

CHAPTER SEVEN

Liberal Nationalism

The Trans-American Melting Pot

After the three partitions of Poland, in 1772, 1793, and 1795, no Polish state existed until one was reestablished in 1919 by the Treaty of Versailles. Nevertheless, the Polish nation continued to exist for a century and a quarter. By contrast, with the breakup of the Yugoslav state there no longer is any group that can be called a Yugoslav people. There never was a Yugoslav nationality, only Croat, Serb, Slovenian, Bosnian Muslim, Kossovar, Albanian, and Macedonian nations dwelling inside a single Yugoslav (South Slav) state.

American liberal nationalism is the theory that America is more like Poland than Yugoslavia. There is a transracial American nation which, like the Polish people, would continue to exist, even if the American nation-state, the United States of America, were wiped off the map. We Americans are more like our neighbors the Mexicans—a racially diverse cultural nation—than like our neighbors the Canadians—a collection of two or more nationalities lacking any common Canadian culture or identity that would survive the breakup of Canada into several states. We Americans, in the liberal nationalist view, are defined by a common language and culture; and as long as these unite us, we will constitute an ethnocultural nation, no matter what the composition of our gene pool, no matter what the political entity in which our people reside, or what its ultimate borders might be. There was an American cultural nation on the Atlantic seaboard before there was a republic called the United States; and, we may hope, there will be a flourishing American cultural nation in its North American homeland when the U.S. Constitution has long been scrapped or amended beyond recognition and when the United States government has gone the way of Nineveh and Tyre.

Liberal nationalism holds, then, that the overwhelming majority of Americans—whatever their arbitrarily defined "race"—already belong, not just to a single citizenry, but to a single people, a single cultural nation, defined by common language, folkways, memories, and mores. Centuries of white supremacy have not prevented the formation of a transracial American culture blending elements of the cultures of many European, African, American Indian, Latin American, and Asian peoples with innovations unique to North America. Nor were white-supremacist laws against miscegenation able to prevent a substantial degree of racial amalgamation, parallelling the fusion of cultures (black Americans are not so much "African-Americans" as "African-European-American Indian-Americans"). The American nation, from the beginning, has had a mixed-race culture. Increasingly it has a mixed-race gene pool.

Almost four centuries of white supremacy, however, have left a pattern of racial separation by social class. Those at the bottom tend to be darker in complexion than those at the top. Even in an America from which racist attitudes were to disappear, the class system by itself would perpetuate the vestiges of slavery and segregation for centuries—perhaps millenia (the correspondence of complexion and class in Hindu society to this day preserves the racial distinction between Indo-European conquerors and their subjects during the Bronze Age). Real integration, in the view of color-blind liberal nationalists, therefore requires a continual churning of the social classes, abetted by a radical (and race-neutral) restructuring of the political, educational, and economic orders that will accelerate the upward mobility of middle-class and working-class talent—as well as hasten the downward mobility of upper-class mediocrity. Liberal nationalism unites the ideal of the transracial melting pot with the tradition of social-democratic egalitarianism. It stands for universal miscegenation and upward-leveling, race-blending, and class-blurring—not in the interest of abstract social equity, but rather with the goal of making the already-existing American nation more integrated and united.

In this chapter I describe the liberal nationalist understanding of the American people as a multiracial/mixed race cultural nation. The multicultural idea that there are five American nationalities—white, black, brown, yellow, red—is rejected by liberal nationalists. So is the cultural pluralist definition of America as a federation of ethnic nationalities, and the superficial universalist claim that we are a nation of individuals (or immigrants) united only by an idea. Liberal nationalism shares, with nativism, the conviction that the United States is a nation-state. But liberal nationalists reject the racialism that tends to inform nativist notions of Americanness; and liberal nationalists also reject the nativist idea of Americanism, which blends political conformity with a narrow sectarian morality, like the conservative version of the "Judeo-Christian" tradition. The philosophy of liberal nationalism provides a basis for an American national identity that is more inclusive than the nativist definition, and at the same time more concrete than the common American identity envisioned by multiculturalism, universalism, and cultural pluralism.

In the chapter that follows this one, I sketch out a possible Fourth American Republic that would be built upon the liberal nationalist vision of the transracial melting pot as Multicultural America has been built upon the dogma of the five official races. The book concludes, in Chapter 9, with a discussion of the "national story" of a new liberal nationalist America, the story of a new ethnocultural nation emerging in this continent from the fusion of groups of many ancestries.

AMERICAN LIBERAL NATIONALISM

Liberal nationalism is a philosophy relevant everywhere in the world. Its predecessors include Rousseau and Herder, Mazzini and J. S. Mill. Liberal nationalists believe that language and culture—not biology—define nationality; that sovereign states, insofar as is possible, ought to coincide with linguistic-cultural nations; and that nation-states, in their constitutional organization, should be liberal (respecting codified rights of property, association, religion, and speech) and, where social conditions permit, democratic. As a political doctrine, liberal nationalism is opposed both to illiberal nationalism (racist or authoritarian nationalism) and to liberal globalism (the belief that a world government, or a world of a few supranational blocs, is preferable to a world organized into strong nation-states).

Liberal globalists often deny that there can be such a thing as liberal nationalism. Nationalism as such, they argue, is inherently racist and xenophobic. In public discourse, the word nationalism is hardly ever found without the prefixes atavistic or dangerous or xenophobic and the synonyms tribalism and racism. Mention nationalism abroad, and Americans tend to think of Serbs, Croats, and Bosnian Muslims butchering each other; mention nationalism in America, and many Americans shudder, picturing a cynical or fanatical politician standing in front of a flag and exhorting the country to a trade war or real war. The very term nationalism seems alien, somehow, in the United States. Compared to patriotism (which is acceptable, as long as it is not qualified by the prefixes super- or ultra-), nationalism evokes the Old World of traditional American caricature, monocles and flags and the crunch of boots in unison. Nationalism equals militarism equals totalitarianism equals racism.

In reality, the correlation between nationalism and other constellations of thought and value is very complex. Consider the frequently encountered equation of nationalism and militarism. The Hapsburgs and Romanovs managed to be quite militarist, without being nationalist; indeed, they considered nationalism the gravest threat to multinational empires like theirs held together by the principle of dynastic autocracy. The multinationalism of the Soviets was as murderous and thorough in its regimentation of life as the racist nationalism of the Third Reich.

Although Johann Gottfried Herder, the father of modern cultural nationalism, is often blamed for later German illiberalism, his conception of a plurality of national cultures was anything but illiberal. The eighteenth-century German philosopher not only championed the value of German culture against the false universalism of the then-hegemonic French culture, but also championed the cultures of the Slavic nations against their detractors, including his fellow Germans. Nor did Herder's nationalism have anything to do with chauvinism, as his remarks in his 1772 "Essay on the Origin of Language" show:

Have we Germans not learned most of what we know as a "civilized nation" from other peoples? Indeed we have. In this and in many other such cases nature has forged a new chain of transmission, from nation to nation. Arts, sciences, languages, the totality of social cultures, have been developed and refined in a powerful progression in this very manner. This international transmission of social cultures is indeed *the highest form of cultural development which nature has elected.*

We Germans would, like the Indians of North America, still be living contentedly in our forests, waging cruel wars as heroes, if the chain of foreign cultures had not pressed in upon us and, with the impact of centuries, had not forced us to join in. Roman civilization hailed from Greece; Greece owed its culture to Asia and Egypt; Egypt to Asia, China perhaps to Egypt, and so on; thus the chain extends from its first link to the last and will one day encircle perhaps the entire world. . . . Let the nations freely learn from one another, let one continue where the other has left off. . . .[1]

In the nineteenth century, nationalism and liberalism often overlapped; liberals like J. S. Mill supported national self-determination as a qualified principle, while nationalists like Mazzini believed that nations liberated from foreign imperial rule should have liberal and democratic constitutions. In the world wars, the liberal democracies were allies of national self-determination movements in Europe, and after World War II the western left supported anticolonial national liberation movements. Hitler's racist nationalism was defeated by counter-nationalisms—by the United Nations, not by the United Individuals; and the Soviet empire was destroyed by a rebellion of "captive nations," not by a rebellion of dissident humanitarians. In the successful European revolutions of 1989, as in the failed European revolutions of 1848, liberalism and nationalism fought as allies against the despotisms of aristocracy or nomenklatura, disguised by the dogmas of religious or ideological universalisms. Indeed, if one takes a long view from 1789 to the present, nationalism has more often been associated with the left than the right—in part, because in domestic politics nationalism often takes the form of a movement for greater political, social, and economic equality among all members of the national community.

Far from demonstrating that nationalism is a threat to liberalism, history shows that the two political philosophies are compatible and sometimes

mutually reinforcing. Liberalism, the theory of the best internal organization of a political community and the relations between political communities, is united with nationalism, the theory that the nation should be the
basis of the political community, in the synthesis of liberal nationalism.

Although the cultural pluralist philosopher Michael Walzer rejects
the idea that the United States is a nation-state, his description of the
philosophy of liberal nation-states takes it for granted that nationalism
can be liberal:

> Their governments take an interest in the cultural survival of the majori-
> ty nation; they don't claim to be neutral with reference to the language,
> history, literature, calendar, or even the minor mores of the majority. To
> all these they accord public recognition and support, with no visible anx-
> iety. At the same time, they vindicate their liberalism by tolerating and
> respecting ethnic and religous differences and allowing all minorities an
> equal freedom to organize their members, express their cultural values,
> and reproduce their way of life in civil society and in the family.[2]

If, unlike Walzer, we conceive of the United States as a liberal nation-
state, then we must reject the idea that liberty in America requires what
might be called a separation of nation and state. There is no analogy between state neutrality, with respect to religion, and state neutrality, with
respect to nationality. There is not, and should not be, an established religion in the United States; but there is, and should be, an established
nationality—that is, a language, culture, and folkways, which are privileged above those of other nationalities that happen to reside in U.S.
territory (German-speaking Amish, unassimilated Chinese and Poles
and Nigerians). With respect to religion, the United States is neutral,
not tolerant; with respect to nationality, the United States is tolerant,
not neutral. From the perspective of minority nationalities, the United
States is a tolerant liberal nation-state, not a neutral non-nation-state.
Enclave nationalities, foreign residents, and unassimilated immigrants
should be treated with respect, but they should not be given a veto over
the loose but real identification of the American state with the American cultural nation.

Of all the elements of a national culture, language is by far the most important. To be a member of a cultural nation is not merely to speak the

language—foreigners can learn that; it is to speak it idiomatically, without a significant accent, with the fluency of a native, to be alive to all the subtle nuances in intonation and vocabulary, to recognize the allusions that make any nation's language a repository of its past. It is possible for foreigners to become not merely citizens of the state, but members of the majority cultural nation; but such acculturation is very difficult, particularly for adult immigrants, requiring years of immersion in the national language and the complex of conceptions and sentiments to which the vernacular language grants access.

Linguistic nationalism, in the U.S. context, provides a rough guide to the definition of American nationality: a cultural American is any North American whose mother tongue, or acquired primary tongue, is one of the dialects of North American English. This excludes German-speaking Amish, but includes almost all white, black, Hispanic, and Asian-Americans as well as assimilated American Indians whose tribal identities are more symbolic than real. As a result of racial intermixture between Europeans, Africans, and American Indians in the Americas, Theodore Roosevelt complained in *The Winning of the West*, "the lines of cleavage of race are so far from coinciding with the lines of cleavage of speech that they run at right angles to them."[3] To which the liberal nationalist replies: Thank God.*

There is more to the national culture than the national language, though the language is both the primary index of nationality and its major means of transmission. In addition, there are folkways—not abstract moral codes, but particular ways of acting, ways of dressing, conventions of masculinity and femininity, ways of celebrating major events like births, marriages, and funerals, particular kinds of sports and recreations, conceptions of the proper boundaries between the secular and religious spheres. And there is also a body of material—ranging from historical events that everyone is expected to know about to widely shared but ephemeral knowledge of sports and cinema and music—that might be called common knowledge. Common language, common folkways, common knowl-

---

*The communications revolution, far from leading to a decline in national identity, will probably reinforce it. There is nothing like being confronted with unintelligible languages to strengthen one's sense of nationality. Americans will no longer need to travel to undergo this experience, when, in a few decades, most homes have access to dozens or hundreds of channels in Spanish, Chinese, Japanese, Russian, and German.

edge—these, rather than race or religion or political philosophy, are what identify a member of the American cultural nation.

The national culture is not fixed, like the canon of an established religion; on the other hand, it is not as ephemeral as the most superficial manifestations of popular culture. It is neither carved in stone nor writ in water; rather it is embedded like boulders in a glacier that moves over time, altering the landscape as it flows, but so slowly that at any given moment it seems to be frozen and still. A national culture is like the national language that tends to be its most important element. Contemporary Polish is different in many ways from eighteenth-century Polish, but the one has recognizably evolved from the other. Because the national culture changes relatively slowly, it is possible to describe it in some detail, even though, like a dictionary, any lexicon of shared traditions is doomed to leave out many new usages and include much that is already obsolete.

Anyone who wants to understand America's common culture cannot go wrong by beginning with the artist Saul Steinberg. A 1976 Steinberg drawing shows a dining room with two pictures on the wall—one of a stereotypical Plains Indian, the other of Niagara Falls. Seated at the dinner table (is it Thanksgiving? the Last Supper?) are, in order, the Easter Bunny, Santa Claus, Abraham Lincoln, the Statue of Liberty, George Washington, and a Halloween witch. It is not clear whether the six American archetypes are gazing at the viewer, or at the peacock tiptoeing rather than strutting in the foreground, looking exotic and somewhat out of place (an immigrant? an artist?) in this familiar, *echt*-American setting.

Steinberg, who emigrated to the United States from Romania, depicts American society as it is experienced by an immigrant—not neatly sorted into political idealism and popular culture, but all mixed up, Santa Claus and the Gettysburg Address and trick-or-treat. One can quibble with Steinberg's iconography (where are Elvis and Huck Finn and Louis Armstrong and John Wayne?). Still, his six mythic figures capture the proportions of American national culture just about right—one-half Anglo-American political idealism (Washington, Lincoln, Lady Liberty) to two-sixths Anglo-Celtic custom (Halloween, Easter) and one-sixth Dutch-American folk tradition (Santa Claus).

American folkways vary enormously among regions, races, and classes. Nevertheless, there is a set of folkways shared by most Americans.

American manners—the plain just-folks style, the handshake, the friendliness that foreigners, including British visitors, find aggressive, the dislike of ostentation—have been shaped disproportionately by the influence of Quakers on the culture of the American Midwest, which since the Civil War has shaped the national culture more than any other region. The American taste for simplicity and straightforwardness in demeanor and style owes less to the New England Puritans than to William Penn and the Society of Friends.

What people eat, and how it is prepared, is an important part of their vernacular culture. Many American foods and drugs, from potatoes and corn, or maize, to tomatoes and tobacco and chocolate, are products of this hemisphere, first cultivated by American Indians. American cuisine—fried chicken, barbecue—also reflects heavy Southern and Southwestern influences, with the latter growing in importance as Mexican-derived dishes become more common on the American menu. To European immigrants we owe the bagel, the pizza, and the food item that McDonald's has made a symbol of America around the world. To date Chinese and Japanese food have remained restaurant specialties, like French cuisine.

The most "American" holidays, Thanksgiving and the American Christmas (a secular folk festival as well as a religious holiday), are legacies of colonial New England and New York. In 1621, Governor William Bradford of the Massachusetts Bay Colony, after a good harvest, ordered a celebration with roast turkeys. In 1863, President Lincoln (following Revolutionary War and French and Indian War precedents), formally set aside the fourth Thursday in November "as a day of thanksgiving and praise to our beneficent Father who dwelleth in the heavens." In the late nineteenth century, the Plymouth Pilgrims rather than the Massachusetts Bay settlers became identified with Thanksgiving. Today it is a family festival. The American Christmas customs of decorating fir trees, caroling, and exchanging gifts derive from Dutch and German settlers in the seventeenth and eighteenth centuries. Santa Claus was adopted from the St. Nicholas of the Dutch in New York (formerly New Amsterdam). In "A Visit from St. Nicholas" (1823), Clement Moore fixed the American Santa Claus myth, while the German immigrant artist Thomas Nast gave the "right jolly old elf" his trademark costume, the red, fur-trimmed coat, in 1863 in *Harper's Illustrated Weekly*.

The only two successful federal or patriotic as opposed to national or customary holidays are the Fourth of July and Memorial Day—the former festive, the latter solemn. Labor Day is nothing but an excuse for a last excursion to the beach before autumn. Washington's and Lincoln's birthdays have been combined in a generic "Presidents' Day," which really has no purpose and should be abolished. At present, the only individual whose birthday is a federal holiday is Martin Luther King, Jr. King Day is widely considered a "black" holiday by nonblack Americans and appears destined to remain an ethnic holiday, like Columbus Day or St. Patrick's Day or Mardi Gras.*

While America's major popular holidays have a Northeastern origin, the musical culture of Americans is disproportionately Southern in its origins, mingling black American and Scots-Irish influences. The black influence is perhaps the major one, flowing into mainstream music generation after generation, in the form of minstrel tunes, spirituals, ragtime, jazz, blues, rock and roll, rap. Not only characteristic American rhythms, but a characteristic American instrument, the banjo, are of African derivation.

If American music is largely Southern and black in its ancestry, American sports are disproportionately Northeastern in their provenance. Football and baseball and basketball are New England sports, codified in their present forms by Eastern gentry in the Ivy League at the turn of the century. They have now been adopted in all parts of the country, and by all classes.

Then there is common knowledge. What "every American knows" when it comes to widely shared recognition of celebrities, show tunes, historical events, and figures is different in 1993 than it was in 1893; but the fact that the common knowledge that marks one as a member of the American cultural community changes over time does not mean that it does not, at any given time, have a status that is almost established. Es-

---

*Missing from the American holiday calendar is a spring holiday (Easter is too sectarian and spring break too profane). There is no holiday celebrating the peopling of North America over the millennia, as opposed to the formation of the federal government of the United States. Perhaps May Day, with its fertility-ritual and common-man associations, would be a good date for an Origins Day, celebrating the blending of diverse populations into a single English-speaking North American nation. As Burke noted in his *Reflections on the Revolution in France,* "People will never look forward to posterity who never look backward to their ancestors."

tablished, but not official; indeed, much of the established national culture consists of an awareness of the kinds of contemporary vernacular slang, folklore, and popular entertainment that have always horrified the prudish guardians of political, religious, and aesthetic orthodoxy.

The fund of common knowledge that most Americans share, like common folkways and the common language, shows the blending of diverse cultures into a new national culture in the United States. The most important kinds of knowledge are those accessible to the widest public, not just to the highly educated elite. This means that sophisticated historical and constitutional information is less important than widely shared Biblical references—and equally widely shared pop-music references. Evangelical preaching and popular entertainment, Moses and Elvis, loom large in the collective memory shared by masses of the population whom scholars and elite journalists will never reach.

One could go on, but the point should be clear. There is a common, inherited American national culture, quite apart from the inherited liberal, democratic, and constitutional political tradition. The common culture is not a mere combination of racial or ethnic cultures maintaining their purity despite their proximity, like tubes of paint arrayed side by side. Rather, the colors are smeared and blended together on the palette, beyond any hope of reconstitution in their original hues.

The term melting pot, trite though it has become, really does express the nature of the American national culture much more accurately than do metaphors like mosaic or salad bowl or quilt or orchestra. The common culture of the American nation is a unique blend of elements contributed by Algonquian Indians and Midwestern Quakers and black Americans and Mexican mestizos and New England patricians. The national culture is not a white culture; black Americans have shaped it far more than the most numerous white immigrant group, German-Americans. Nor is it middle-class; black-derived musical forms like jazz, soul, gospel, and R&B, as well as country and western music, have been frowned upon by the respectable middle classes of every generation. It most certainly is not merely European culture transplanted overseas without alteration; the national culture of English-speaking North America is just as distinctly a product of the Western Hemisphere as is the hybrid European-African-Indian culture of Portuguese-speaking Brazil. Orlando Patterson captures the syncretic nature of America's common culture when he writes that it "is neither a salad bowl nor a static, received tradition, but an ever-evolving national process which selects, unrepresentatively, from the market-place of raw, particular identities those that everyone finds it useful and gratifying to embrace and transform into their own."[4] Albert Murray had it right when he wrote in 1970 that in America the "mainstream is not white but mulatto."[5]

A mere list of ingredients—English, African, Algonquian, Chinese, German, Mexican, Italian—makes American culture sound much more open to novelty than it really is. Precisely because it is so often selective, cultural borrowing does not necessarily represent openness to genuine novelty on the part of a nation. Indeed, members of a nation often borrow only those aspects of foreign cultures that can be easily fitted into the preexisting pattern of their own. It is surely no accident that the ritual-loving Japanese have borrowed the most rigidly rule-governed American games, baseball and golf, rather than football or basketball; that the French, with their tradition of "reasoning drama," have adopted American *film noir* (the detective story being a cousin of the realist novel and the social satire); that the Singaporeans have adopted the skyscraper (that symbol of modernity and hierarchy) while repudiating American ideas of civil liberty.

In America, too, borrowing has always been selective. Other cultures have been raided for items that reinforce rather than undermine the grammar of Americanness. The term *boss,* lifted from the New York Dutch, passed into universal usage in the antebellum United States as an alternative to the English *master,* because white Americans felt uneasy about working for masters (particularly in a country that had slaves). We Americans are even more prudish in our attitudes about power and influence and hierarchies of excellence than about sex, and find it difficult to discuss these subjects in plain American English without blushing or giggling or getting angry. This unease about hierarchy explains why we Americans so often discuss it euphemistically or ironically, with the help of foreign words: head honcho (the term is Japanese, not Spanish), chiefs and Indians, sachems, movie moguls, a baseball czar who presides over sultans of swat.

Selective borrowing permits a society to be outwardly experimental and yet profoundly conservative. The real continuity of a national culture, therefore, must be sought in its "grammar," not its "idiom." Like the national idiom, the national grammar changes, but much more slowly— over centuries, rather than decades or generations. The ultimate source of the grammar in most countries is found in centuries-old premodern political and religious mentalities that are passed down from parents to children, outside of the official lines of transmission like public schools and the quasi-official mass media. Mere political revolutions, even radical social revolutions, often leave the underlying national grammar relatively unchanged. The French Revolution replaced a Catholic-monarchical version of the centralized, bureaucratic state with a secular republican version of bureaucratic centralism, in which presidents are kings and intellectuals are courtiers. The Russian Revolution and seventy years of Communist tyranny and terror merely altered the ideology and the elite while leaving intact the spirit of Russian nationalism and the mindset of Muscovite despotism ("The new official ideology is democracy," one of Yeltsin's officials explained). Successive liberal and socialist revolutions in Mexico have scarcely altered the mentality inherited from the days of Spanish colonial rule. In all of these cases, revolutionary ideologies ended up imitating what they displaced: a "Catholic" version of deism in revolutionary France, complete with secular saints and secular festivals; in Soviet Russia, the mummification and display of Communist saints, after the manner of incorruptible Orthodox holy men; a hortatory, neo-Baroque public art in revolutionary Mexico, with nationalist murals painted on the walls of colonial churches.

The American national grammar is just as conservative. The American Revolution changed the government and its iconography without fundamentally altering the inherited Anglo-American culture. By way of Euro-America we have inherited a culture which, in its deep structure, remains "Anglomorph" (I owe the term to Richard Grenier) and "Protestantoid." It must never be forgotten that the greatest influence on the American mentality has not been the mass media (whose messages, at any rate, are filtered differently by members of different cultures) but rather four centuries of Protestant preachers irrigating the continent, week after week, with sermons and prayers. After the preacher, the county judge, for centuries, was the second great intellectual force in American society. Generations of European immigration, and now immigration from other parts of the world, have not changed this as much as one might expect; America has a way of turning Greeks, Mexicans, Swedes, Chinese, and Polish Jews into reincarnations of seventeenth-century Englishmen.

Calvinism and the common law together have produced what is, perhaps, the most biblicist national culture in the world. For Americans, all moral revolutions begin with reading or rereading some set of scriptures—the True, Uncorrupted, Ancient Gospel—and all political revolutions are presented, in seventeenth-century English Whig fashion, as a return to the True, Uncorrupted, Ancient Constitution. This text-obsessed mentality is shared even by would-be American radicals. Every national grammar contains within it an understanding of how revolutions are made. In Mexico, you put on a bandana and issue an ephemeral manifesto named after a particular town (the Plan de Whatever). In Russia, you stage a coup in Moscow or St. Petersburg. In China, idealistic young scholars sacrifice themselves in protest against abuses of power by imperial ministers. Only in the United States, which is unique in this respect even in the English-speaking world, do radicals—true to the spirit of John Knox and Edward Coke—think that the way to start a revolution is to revise the curriculum of public education, the "canon" (the very term evokes the Protestant Reformers). Apart from the substitution of Maya Angelou for Julia Ward Howe in classroom recitation, what could be more Anglomorph, more Protestantoid?

Black American separatist nationalism is even more traditional, in its conformity to the American grammar, than contemporary American academic leftism. From its beginnings in the Revolutionary era, black nationalism has been addressed to an audience that is not only white, but white American. It has sought to prove that black Americans have a noble tradition, *as white Americans define tradition*. Thus, there is a neoclassical past (Egyptian, instead of Greco-Roman); a "true" or "uncorrupted" religious tradition (Black Christianity, or Black Islam, as the answer to pure Saxon Protestantism); and a pantheon of male political heroes (Martin and Malcolm, instead of Washington and Lincoln; black women, like white women, get short shrift in American iconography). What is the black nationalist talk of "the Plan" by whites to destroy blacks, other than the old white Protestant anti-Catholicism and anti-Masonry transposed? Far from being radical, black nationalists are as quaintly anachronistic, as quintessentially American as the small-town

Shriners with whom they share *faux*-Egyptian imagery inherited from eighteenth-century Europe.

What Americans borrow from other cultures, then, tends to be something that is already compatible with the deep grammar of Americanness. The cultural import then becomes Americanized, that is, sanded down, disinfected, bleached, and made presentable, harmless, nice. European intellectuals who do not understand America have tended to blame the blandness of American culture on capitalism, but capitalism can encourage the raw as well as the cooked. American "niceness," in fact, has more to do with centuries-old codes of Protestant gentility and republican manners than with the modern mass marketplace or the mass media.

There is almost nothing which cannot be made nice in America. Bits of wild Hindu philosophy were domesticated by the Boston Brahmin Transcendentalists, and a century later the beatniks trivialized Zen. In the 1920s, Mexican muralism—at its best, heroic, savage, profound—traveled north and turned into the mild Currier & Ives Regionalism of Thomas Hart Benton and Grant Wood. Punk culture, divorced from its British working-class roots, became a harmless fad among wholesome suburban American teenagers, as did Jamaican-derived rap a decade later.

Even radical political ideologies become nice in the United States. American Communists claimed to be One Hundred Percent Americans, with alarming accuracy. The neo-Nazis in the United States tend to drop the anti-Christian and antibourgeois parts of the original message for a churchliness and moralism rather like that of the Klan. In America, even Hitler becomes a Methodist with a mean streak.

Just as all radical political ideologies imported into the United States tend to turn into tame variants of Anglo-American Whig liberalism, so all religions become Protestant sects in America. They are bleached of foreign ethnicity and transformed into modest "denominations." Judaism, a nationality in Central Europe, became a set of denominations in the United States. As Richard Rodriguez and John Murray Cuddihy have observed, Catholicism—a civilization elsewhere—has also been reduced to the trivial status of a denomination in the United States. Islam may eventually be Americanized, in the same way. With its puritanism, iconoclasm, and lack of priestly hierarchy, this religion of Prophet and Book is tailor-made for America; the similarity between black Protestant evangelicals and Black Muslims is no accident. It is doubtless only a matter of time before the colonial-style brick-and-white-trim First Church of American Islam appears beside the Reformed Temple, with its American flag and stained-glass windows, and the Catholic Church where, in most un-Catholic fashion, parishioners debate what Scripture teaches them about foreign policy, economics, and sex.

The American national vernacular culture—American English and a living tradition that has its own slowly changing grammar as well as its own rapidly fluctuating idiom—is what defines the majority nationality in the United States, a uniquely American nationality that largely overlaps with, but is distinct from, the class of United States citizens, a nationality that today includes people whose ancestors lived on every populated continent. If ethnicity can be defined by language and culture, there is a multiracial and multireligious but unicultural American ethnic nation. We might speak, without contradiction, of the Ethnic American.

But perhaps the word "ethnic" should be avoided. The term ethnicity as used in American discourse is hopelessly ambiguous. It can refer to biological race, Old World national ancestry, language, and even religion—practically *any* social characteristic, except for region (though some might argue there is a Southern ethnicity). Elsewhere in the world, ethnicity typically refers to nationality, defined as language and culture (though sometimes, as in the Levant, the Indian subcontinent and the Balkans, ethnic groups are defined by religion). In the American context, it would be best to drop the term ethnicity altogether, and refer only to nationality. Once the term nationality is substituted for ethnicity, it becomes clearly preposterous to think of white Americans of Irish, Polish, and German descent as members of different nationalities. How many of them, if parachuted into Ireland, Poland, or Germany, could pass undetected as members of the local population?

American nationality is shared by Americans of all races. Black Americans, for example, are not Africans in America. The black American subculture is a unique blend of European and African elements, with the British-derived elements—the English language, Protestant religion—predominant (black English is a variant of Lowland Southern English, itself a relative of the seventeenth-century dialect of southwestern England). Phillip Gay, denouncing the pseudo-ethnicity implicit in the term African-American, points out that there is "a distinctly Black American cuisine of low-cost edibles more indigenous to Europe and the New World than to Africa, a distinctly Black American patois firmly rooted in the English language, relatively distinct Black American patterns of familial organization and . . . religious practices grounded in Christianity, a non-African religion."[6] To use the term African-American is to denigrate the uniqueness and value of the Western Hemisphere culture of black Americans. The soundest tradition among black American thinkers is that of intellectuals like Ralph Ellison, John Hope Franklin, and Charles T. Davis, who saw black American culture as a local synthesis of European and African cultures. Davis criticized DuBois for "finding the roots of the cultural gifts of the Negro within the bounds of inherited characteristics and disclaiming any influence of the white man upon the development of black culture."[7] Not only is black American culture the product of a transcultural melting pot, but most black Americans are themselves of mixed race, with European and American Indian as well as African ancestors. Ishmael Reed has observed that if Alex Haley, author of *Roots*, had traced back his mother's ancestors, he would have ended up in Ireland, not in Gambia.[8]

The contribution of black Americans to the common national vernacular culture is the strongest defense against the charge that the kind of American cultural nationalism I am advocating represents an "organic" or crypto-racist nationalism, or a covert form of white supremacy or middle-class hegemony. The fact is that the universalist conception of American identity is much "whiter" than the liberal nationalist conception. The official culture of the United States political and legal tradition, along with its literary high culture, owes far more to high-toned Anglo-Americans than does our "mulatto" or "mestizo" common culture. Far from being excessively Eurocentric, liberal nationalism is the *only* conception of American nationality that incorporates the elements of American culture contributed by nonwhite Americans into its very definition of American national identity. There is more respect for the cultural influence of black America in the melting-pot ideal of liberal nationalism, with its populist emphasis on the vernacular culture, than there is in Afrocentrism, which *accepts* snobbish dismissals of black (and other) American vernacular subcultures, and which therefore has to struggle to prove that European and American *high cultures* were purloined from ancient Egyptian-Africans.*

It can be argued that black Americans are the *most American* people in this country. Descended from the peoples of three continents, black Americans have far fewer ties to any modern or recent African society than whites, Hispanics, and Asians do to Europe, Latin America, and Asia. In showing the way to a mixed-race American future, it can be suggested, black Americans are the true "model minority."

The liberal nationalist definition of American identity extends it to anyone whose primary, or adopted, culture is America's "mulatto" mainstream. This is an extremely inclusive conception. It is therefore hard to understand why so many American liberals, influenced by democratic universalism, would want to define American nationality solely in terms of political citizenship or subjective opinion. After all, if American identity is bestowed by the government, then the government can take it away. If American identity is bestowed by public opinion, then public disrespect can dis-bestow it. If to be American is to be a U.S. citizen, then black Americans only became American with the enactment of the Fourteenth Amendment. If to be American is to be considered American by the American majority, then one's very identity depends on the prejudices of other people. What is so liberal about these notions? According to the linguistic-cultural test of nationality, from the very earliest years of the colonial period, English-speaking, North American–born black Americans were members of the American cultural nation, even when most were slaves and not citizens, even when most white Americans considered black Americans, wrongly, to be another people.

An older American liberalism knew better than to make a cult of dif-

---

*In correcting for Anglo-American bias, it is important not to go to the other extreme. For example, Carl N. Degler writes, "In fact, the history of African Americans alone would provide a remarkably apt framework (for a common American history), certainly more apt than the experience of any other single national group, including the English. The presence of Africans has helped to shape the law, the Constitution, the politics, and the economy of America, not to mention the greatest single event of all, the Civil War." (Carl N. Degler, "In Search of the Un-Hyphenated American," *New Perspectives Quarterly*, Summer 1991, p. 51.) It is one thing to acknowledge the importance of black Americans and another to minimize the central importance of the Anglo-Americans, who founded the nation-state, whose culture, as modified, is the dominant culture, and who were the overwhelming numerical majority until the twentieth century.

ference. John Dewey is sometimes misleadingly described as a cultural pluralist. He is better described as a melting-pot liberal nationalist:

> Such terms as Irish-American or Hebrew-American or German-American are false terms, because they seem to assume something which is already in existence called America, to which the other factors may be hitched on. The fact is, the genuine American, the typical American, is himself a hyphenated character. It does not mean that he is part American and that some foreign ingredient is then added. It means that . . . he is international and interracial in his make-up. He is not American plus Pole or German. But the American is himself Pole-German-English-French-Spanish-Italian-Greek-Irish-Scandinavian-Bohemian-Jew—and so on.[9]

In the liberal nationalist view, there already exists a common American cultural identity, which—to modify Dewey's explanation—is defined by the English-Dutch-African-Algonquian-German-Irish-Italian-Mexican-Chinese culture shared by various Americans of Latin American and Asian and African and western European descent.

The dramatic figures about the approaching time when nonwhites are a majority in the United States look much less significant, when one realizes that the American *cultural majority* is much larger than the white *racial majority*. This transracial American ethnic group is continually growing, even if the proportion of its members of exclusively European descent is slowly diminishing. The gradual diminution in the relative numbers of Americans of British and European descent need not mean a diminution of the *real* American majority, whose members include black Mississippians, Californians of Asian descent, and Texans of Mexican ancestry, and growing numbers of mixed-race people whose very existence renders our racial categories obsolete.

Call this emergent transracial American ethnocultural majority the Trans-American nationality. Its members—dark and light, tall and short, Christian and Jewish and Muslim and secular—might define a fourth American republic: Trans-America.

CIVIC FAMILISM

Each of the successive American republics, I have argued, has had a common ethic of some sort in addition to a prevalent ethnocultural identity and a political creed. In Multicultural America, the common ethic is the ideal of authenticity. A duty-based morality has been replaced by a rights-based, self-centered morality, in which personal fulfillment is identified with conformity to this or that racial or sexual community. The ideal of authenticity promotes the segmentation of the nation, to the benefit of political elites (which prefer to deal with well-defined, separate, and co-optable client groups) and commercial elites (which can differentiate their products among diverse consumer subcultures).

As an alternative to the secular ethic of authenticity, many conservatives propose a return to the common ethic of Euro-America, a generalized Christianity or Judeo-Christianity.* Even if it were desirable, however, it is too late to promote an informal Judeo-Christian establishment of religion. For one thing, by some estimates there are now more Muslims than Jews in the United States. Out of deference to the feelings of Muslim Americans, are we to speak of the Judeo-Christo-Muslim tradition? If great numbers of Buddhists immigrate to the U.S., are we to speak of the Buddhaeo-Christian tradition? A quadruple or quintuple religious establishment would be cumbersome, to say the least. Even more important, completely secular Americans may outnumber Jews. According to one recent survey, only 82 percent of the population belongs to a Christian denomination; even this number probably includes a great many people who are only nominally Christian. Should an atheist proselytizer be invited to address high school commencements, along with the traditional trio of preacher, priest, and rabbi of post–World War II America?

Conservatives do not recognize how much the nation has changed since the fifties in its religious attitudes. It may be that the religion of most nominal Christians in the United States can no longer be described as traditional trinitarian Christian. The scholarly term for their

---

*The use of the term Judeo-Christian is promoted for reasons of etiquette, rather than theology; in 1976, for example, a *New York Post* columnist suggested, "In this ecumenical age, it might be more tactful for Governor Carter to cite the Judeo-Christian ethic rather than attributing all his talk of love and humility to the teachings of Jesus." (Harriet van Horne, "Good Omens," *New York Post*, June 21, 1976, p. 21.) As Talmudic scholar Jacob Neusner observes: "theologically and historically, there is no such thing as the Judeo-Christian tradition. It's a secular myth favored by people who are not really believers themselves." (Quoted in Kenneth L. Woodward, "Losing Our Moral Umbrella," *Newsweek*, December 7, 1992, p. 60.)

beliefs is *henotheism,* the belief that all ethnic groups and cultures have, and should have, their own gods and rites. In Christian theology, this is the heresy of indifferentism. Robert Linder and Richard Pierard have described the evolution of American civil religion: "Its umbrella has changed from evangelical consensus to Protestantism-in-general, to Christianity-in-general, to the Judeo-Christian tradition in general, to deism-in-general."[10] The decline in belief in Christianity as the only true religion has been extraordinarily rapid in the United States. In a poll taken in 1924 in Muncie, Indiana, 94 percent of high school students agreed that "Christianity is the one true religion and all peoples should be converted to it." By the late 1970s, merely 38 percent of respondents in a later poll in Muncie agreed that Christianity was the only true faith. Two-thirds of the respondents in a 1991 poll agreed that Christians, Jews, Muslims, and Buddhists "pray to the same God."[11]

This sentiment no doubt appalls Christian and Jewish theologians. From the point of view of those concerned with national unity, however, it is an encouraging development. It lessens the chances that religious discord will produce civil strife. Of the policy of ancient Rome, Edward Gibbon wrote: "The various modes of worship which prevailed in the Roman world were all considered by the people as equally true; by the philosophers as equally false; and by the magistrates as equally useful."[12] In the United States, "Potomac piety" has been promulgated by states-men taking the side of the magistrates, from George Washington, who thought that Christianity was useful in protecting "property," that is, the rich minority, from attacks by populists, to President Dwight D. Eisen-hower, who declared: "Our government has no sense unless it is founded on a deeply religious faith, and I don't care what it is." Tocqueville noted: "An American sees in religion the surest guarantee of the stability of the State and the safety of individuals. . . . Much the same may be said of the British."[13] Will Herberg noted that in the United States Christian and Jewish "denominations" are less religious institutions than instru-ments of social integration.[14]

The new, semi-official American religion of indifferentist theism (there is one God and many equally true religions) does not solve the problem of a common ethic. On the contrary, it makes it all the more pressing. Indifferentism necessarily leads to a divorce between religion and ethics, for the simple reason that there is no single, authoritative generic-theist table of commandments.* Fortunately, moral consensus does not require theological consensus. As the neoconservative scholar James Q. Wilson has pointed out, "Religion is for many a source of solace and for a few a means of redemption, but if everyday morality had depended on religious conviction, the human race would have destroyed itself eons ago."[15] Somehow Japanese classrooms manage to be orderly without a copy of the Ten Commandments on every classroom wall (a goal of American fundamentalists). Indeed, outside of North America, the most prosperous, least crime-ridden and most educated countries are the post-Protestant societies of Northern Europe, in which traditional Christianity is in serious long-term decline, and the highly secular Confucian societies of East Asia. Conversely, the parts of Europe and the Americas in which institutional Christianity has been strongest in recent centuries, the Catholic and Orthodox countries, have been characterized by poverty, tyranny, and political instability, which exist to an even greater degree in the Muslim world. The most religious part of the United States, the South, has long been the poorest, most violent, and most illiterate section of the country.

Neither a supposed Judeo-Christian ethic nor a pan-Christian ethic, then, are plausible alternatives to Multicultural America's inadequate ideal of authenticity. The public interest in having certain assumptions accepted as moral givens does not require the reimposition of theological orthodoxy, even by informal means. The members of the Trans-American nation can differ widely in their metaphysical views, while sharing a nonsectarian common ethic. What might be the substance of that ethic?

American universalists and pragmatists like John Dewey have often speculated about a democratic ethic or a religion of democracy: we will have democratic manners, democratic morals, a democratic faith, and so forth. Simply substituting "democratic" for "Christian" or "Judeo-Christian" wherever the latter term is found clarifies nothing. Indeed, it confuses matters to refer to democracy as a way of life, instead of limit-

---

*During the second Parliament of the World's Religions, meeting in Chicago in September 1993 (the first such parliament was also held in Chicago, a century before), leaders of more than 125 faiths adopted a "Declaration of a Global Ethic" with four commandments—You shall not kill, steal, lie, or commit sexual immorality. The price of ecumenical consensus was not only shortening the list of commandments from the biblical ten, but avoiding any mention of God.

ing the term to a procedure for selecting leaders (and, in the case of referenda, passing laws).

A genuine social ethic, instead of restating political ideals like democracy and obvious legal norms (like the norm against pickpockets), must primarily be composed of norms that have nothing to do with politics and are not enforced by law. It must define conduct that is immoral, even if—especially if—it is legal. And it must prescribe duties based on social status, even if—especially if—those duties are not mandated by law.

Most Americans, I have argued, are simultaneously citizens of a liberal polity, the United States, and members of a cultural nation, the Trans-Americans (the Amish and the Navajos being citizens but not Trans-Americans). The organizing principle of the liberal polity is the idea of individual rights. The organizing principle of the nonliberal national community, by contrast, is the idea of social duties, duties which vary among individuals, depending on their ascriptive communal roles: grandmother or grandchild, husband or wife, neighbor or employer. Discriminations based on sex and age have little place in the sphere of the polity; but they are the very basis of the organization of the community. The federal polity is constituted of abstract "persons"; the national community, however, is composed of men and women, husbands and wives, grandparents and grandchildren, young and old, siblings and cousins, godfathers and godchildren. Most of communal life is organized around ritual celebrations of status changes: bar mitzvahs, confirmations, weddings, graduations, fraternity initiations, anniversaries, retirements, and so forth, which are considered important by the community, even if they have—and should have—no consequences for one's standing as a citizen in the eyes of the impersonal liberal government.

The life of the family, the most important community, is based on duties assigned strictly by categories of status: kinship, age, and gender. The culture into which one is born and which will survive long after one dies defines what those family duties are; individuals are given little choice in the matter. The duties of one spouse to another and of the middle-aged to the young and the elderly, are not primarily matters of personal choice or legal compulsion, even though there is some room for individual discretion and even though government may sanction moral failures (requiring child support payments, for example). Most communal duties are defined by custom and enforced by opinion, that is, honor and shame, which are more powerful than positive law.

This common ethic, this communal morality, might be called the *constitution of honor* of the nation. To attempt to define the best constitution of honor for the Trans-American nation would require another book, if not a series of tomes; and the very effort might be foolish, inasmuch as genuine ethical systems are as much the result of evolving practice as of theory. Even so, a few observations are in order.

The constitution of honor of a liberal nationalist American community would not be an otherwordly ethic praising withdrawal from the world, in which the hermit/saint is considered the highest example of the human type. Nor would it be an aristocratic or military ethic, disdaining commercial life and mundane administration and glorifying heroic struggle. The public virtues it would cultivate would be those favored by the bourgeois and the bureaucrat alike—sobriety, knowledge, discipline, responsibility, punctuality, self-control.

Even more than these unexciting but all-important middle-class virtues, the notion of civic familism, I think, must be at the core of a nonsectarian ethic for twenty-first century America. The term *family values* has been abused by conservative ideologues and politicians seeking to accuse their opponents of being "antifamily." This nothwithstanding, the fact remains that the family—defined to include grandparents and grandchildren, siblings and cousins, as well as parents and children—is the most important and enduring community for most people, heterosexual or homosexual, happily married or divorced or permanently single. Healthy and intact families are in the interest of the larger community as well as the individual, inasmuch as broken families have a disproportionate tendency to send their members into poverty, lives of crime, or dependence on private charity or the public dole.

The observation of the British legal historian Henry Maine that history is progress from status to contract is true only in the political realm, and in the sphere of the economy and voluntary private associations. It does not apply to the family which remains, and will always remain, a community of customary status. A government that is organized like a community will be oppressive; a national community that is organized like a polity will collapse in dissension and anomie. The state is not a family (the authoritarian error), and the family is not and cannot be a little democracy (the libertarian error). A family whose members think of their relations in terms of the inappropriate model of citizens jealously vindicating their individual rights, or of entrepreneurs maximizing their individual profit through sharp practice, will not be a happy one.*

The contractual or libertarian notion of the family, the reduction of all marriages to marriages of convenience, as it were, results in a family that is too weak for the good of its members and the nation. On the other hand, families can be too strong for the good of the larger society. The old European-Christian patriarchal family, the Confucian family, the extended family of feuding Ozark clans and Sicilian mafiosi—these may deny the individuality of their members and discourage association between families, making individual creativity and a flourishing civil society impossible. The ideal of civic familism is a family stronger than the bohemian "Hollywood" family but looser and more individualistic than the "Mafia" family. Something like the "companionate" or "bourgeois" nuclear family, with a mild division of labor between the sexes, is probably the form that best reconciles the imperatives of individuality and social order.†

A new civic familism would add, to the familiar emphasis on the duties of parents to their children, a new emphasis on the duties of adult children to their elderly parents—something that will be ever more important, as technology permits people to live longer. The period of caring for aged parents may come to take as much of a person's life as the task of raising children; in practice, because women live longer, aging women will increasingly need to devote years of their lives to taking care of aged mothers. The nurturing of the old by their children where possible, rather than by the state or by private-sector nursing-home employees, should be both expected and praised.

The promulgation of a nonsectarian ethic of civic familism, even by

---

*John Locke never made this mistake. The social contract, according to Locke, was established as a contract between the patriarchs of political clans, who virtually represented their dependents—wife (or wives), children, and servants or slaves. Even Lockean liberalism, in other words, assumed a preexisting stateless or tribal cultural community defined by custom, like that of the ancient Hebrews or early modern American Indians, with their rigid age and gender distinctions.

†The legitimate demands of gay and lesbian couples for some kind of legal recognition and protected testamentary rights can be met without awkwardly trying to treat heterosexual and homosexual couples as variants of the same category.

private means alone, might be resisted by religious fundamentalists of various persuasions. They will maintain that a nonsectarian morality is nothing but a secular morality in disguise; in either case, religious believers, arguing in favor of public policies, would be limited to providing secular reasons for them that could persuade people who do not share their religious views. Indeed, this is the case; privately held religious reasons for particular public policies are acceptable, but not public religious arguments. No doubt this exacts a price from religious believers, who must think one thing in private and say another in public. However, it is difficult to imagine an alternative that would not result in a stalemate between various groups, each angrily shouting passages from its own scriptures at the other. The public square, in a country of many faiths, must remain naked—not to symbolize the triumph of secularism, which may well remain the creed of a minority, but to prevent politics from becoming the arena of interreligious warfare.* The more religious the people in a country of many faiths, the more necessary it is to insist on strict separation of church and state. (The British can tolerate a state church only because its members do not take it seriously.)

Some feminists might attack civic familism—for being too conservative, not too liberal. Civic familism might also be challenged as an ideal by radical libertarians. There is nothing comparable in other advanced countries to the exaggerated libertarian ethic that is so influential in today's America; even highly secular, progressive societies like the Scandinavian take for granted a far greater degree of authority in social relations than do libertarian Americans. American libertarian ethics, it might be suggested, is based on a fundamental mistake—the misapplication, to every realm of social and moral life, of a rights-based way of thinking that is legitimate only in a relatively narrow realm of law and politics. Earlier generations of Americans were Lockean liberals when it came to government, but the thought that individualistic liberalism, rather than deference to legitimate authority, could be the organizing principle in families, schools, universities, corporations, and associations

---

*For similar reasons, one must reject the right's argument in favor of generalized government support of "religion" at the expense of "irreligion." In practice, this too would degenerate into interreligious conflict as the majority religions sought to deny the label of religion to faiths radically unlike their own in form and content.

would have struck them as nonsense. It *is* nonsense, which could sub-vert any effort to reconstruct a nonsectarian consensus morality just as surely as could the zealotry of religious fundamentalists; even the most benign norms could be attacked as oppressive by anarcho-libertarians of the left and right.

If America must have a minimal ethical consensus, let it be civic familism—not the relativist ideal of authenticity, or Judeo-Christian fundamentalism, or radical libertarianism. The next America might best be thought of as a predominantly theist nation with a secular govern-ment and a nonsectarian ethic of civic familism.

A NATION OF IMMIGRANTS?

In the liberal nationalist perspective, then, the United States, despite the genetic and religious diversity of its population, is a conventional nation-state with a majority ethnocultural nation. The majority, the Trans-American nationality, is defined by a common language (American English) and a common culture, rather than by common race or religion. Though in these respects the predominant American nation is more in-clusive than other nations that are more homogeneous in descent and re-ligion, the Trans-American people constitute an ethnocultural nation nonetheless; and like other nations the Trans-Americans can legitimately require a high degree of acculturation as a condition of immigration to their territory.* One of the classic human-interest stories of American journalism has a group of immigrants, from all over the world, represent-ing diverse races and religions, being sworn in as naturalized U.S. citizens. Invariably the story concludes: "And now they are Americans." To which the obvious but never stated coda is, "Well, sort of." The newly natural-ized immigrants are now United States *citizens*, with political and legal rights equal to those of the haughtiest Mayflower descendant; but they

---

*Alan Wolfe has called for recognition that assimilation to a common culture by earlier generations of immigrants is an achievement, not a loss: "Those who made themselves into Americans have every right to insist that their identity as Americans be taken seriously, even if it is an identity root-ed in white bread and suburban tract housing. Americanism is a continually evolving identity that changes with each new group that arrives—but only by insisting that all new groups share in its pre-requisites." (Alan Wolfe, "The Return of the Melting Pot," *The New Republic*, December 31, 1990, p. 30.)

are not members of the predominant American cultural *nation*, though they may acquire its culture, after many years of residence.*

The distinction between political naturalization (which really should be called "citizenation") and national acculturation, far from being a sinister nativist idea, is in fact critical to any *nonracist*, nongenetic conception of cultural nationality. Liberal nationalism, in abandoning race as the basis of nationality, must put more emphasis, not less, on the common language and the common culture. Where one nation has conquered another and is attempting to impose its own language and culture by force, there might be valid objections to acculturation. But there can be no objection to acculturation and the maintenance of a common language and shared traditions where immigration to a nation-state has been voluntary on the part of individuals and families.

Common sense on this subject tends to be warded off by ritual invocation of the cliché that we are "a nation of immigrants." In fact, the United States is not a nation of immigrants, and never has been. At no point in American history have people born abroad constituted more than a minority of the U.S. population. If "the immigrant experience" defines what it means to be an American, then the overwhelming majority of Americans, sad to say, have missed out on the experience. In the real world, as opposed to the realm of the Fourth of July cliché, the United States, from 1776 to the present, has been a nation of native-born Americans, with significant influxes of immigrants in some eras (the 1850s, the early 1900s, and today) and little immigration at others. Most Americans, in every era, have never known any homeland other

---

*As Tzvetan Todorov observes, "nationality that is acquired on the political level by the power of a simple decree requires long years of apprenticeship on the cultural level." (Tzvetan Todorov, *On Human Diversity: Nationalism, Racism, and Exoticism in French Thought*, Cambridge, Mass.: Harvard University Press, 1993, p. 228.) Todorov adds that "we cannot change our culture from one day to the next (as we can change citizenship, by an act of naturalization)": "How does one learn a culture? By mastery of the language, above all; by familiarization with the country's history, its landscapes, and the mores of its original population, governed by a thousand invisible codes (it would obviously be a mistake to identify the culture with what is found in books). Such an apprenticeship takes years and years . . . but we do not have to have been born into a culture to acquire it: blood has nothing to do with it, nor even genes. Furthermore, not all native-born citizens necessarily possess the culture of their country." (Todorov, *supra*, p. 387.)

than the American homeland, and have spoken one or another dialect of American English as their mother tongue.

Of course for many Americans the term nation of immigrants conjures up poignant memories of immigrant parents or grandparents, rather than personal experience of immigration. Nostalgia among white Americans for the "New Swedens" and "Little Bohemias" and "Little Italys" of yesteryear, for example, is natural. But it is misguided. Even the largest European enclave communities in the United States in earlier generations were culturally impoverished, compared to their national homelands and to the greater American nation—any claim to the contrary is pure sentimentality. Minority enclaves are too small to be national communities in their own right, and too remote from the national homeland to participate fully in the cultural and intellectual life of the parent nation (even today, watching foreign broadcasts and talking on the phone just is not the same). The greatest enclave community, before today's Mexican-American community, was that of the Germans. Germany-in-America is now forgotten, even by German-Americans. At best, such diaspora enclaves are like television sets, receiving transmissions from the mother country but unable to transmit messages in return. At worst, they are mere curiosity shops, preserving intact customs and usages of the migrant generation which have long fallen out of fashion in the national homeland. Second- and third-generation immigrants who grow up in such ghettos are cut off from two living societies—that of their ancestors, and the broader community in which they live.

While acculturation is a legitimate goal of public policy, coercive and repressive methods—such as the outlawing of instruction in the German language by several state legislatures after World War I—must be abjured by any liberal nationalist state. The best compromise is to put no limits on the right of different immigrant nationalities to perpetuate themselves as distinct cultural communities on American soil—on the condition that they do so through purely voluntary and private means. If an immigrant culture cannot be perpetuated without government support, then it is right and just that it wither away and that its members become assimilated to the dominant, transracial American cultural nation.

G. K. Chesterton spoke of the American "experiment of a democracy of diverse races which has been compared to a melting pot. But even that metaphor implies that the pot itself is of a certain shape and a certain substance; a pretty solid substance. The melting pot must not melt."[16] The United States, like any liberal nation-state, must tolerate voluntary ethnic divisions among its population. It should not formalize, sponsor or celebrate them. An immigrant group that does not plan to merge with the majority, but seeks to create its own separate nation-within-a-nation within the borders of the United States, should receive no encouragement from the government.

THE NEXT AMERICAN MELTING POT

In viewing the United States as a nation-state, rather than as a federation of ethnic or racial nations, liberal nationalism resembles the consensus in Anglo-America and Euro-America—and breaks with the five-race/five-culture orthodoxy of Multicultural America. Liberal nationalism departs from earlier Anglo-American and Euro-American forms of American nationalism, and from contemporary nativism, however, in rejecting any racial or religious component to national identity. Although one's biological ancestors may have been in China or Poland or Jamaica in the seventeenth century, one's cultural ancestors were in North America—the Anglophone American community, including acculturated, English-speaking black Americans. Americans share common national ancestors, whatever their genetic ancestors. Even if our genetic grandparents came from Finland or Indonesia, as Americans, we are all descendants of George Washington—*and* his slaves.

It cannot be denied that in most of the world there tends to be a *correlation* between linguistic-cultural ethnicity and common descent. The Japanese, the Swedes, the Thais—these nations really are extended families. However, there is less difference between these genetically homogeneous nations and "immigrant nations" like the United States than is generally supposed. The fact that assimilated members of the nation may not share common ancestors is less important than the fact that *they will share common descendants*. It does not matter if you and your neighbor share common grandparents—as long as you will have grandchildren in common. A nation does not have to be a homogeneous genetic community. But there must not be legal or customary barriers against the possibility of its eventually *becoming* a homogeneous genetic community.* Cultural fusion should be a way station to amalgamation. The cultural melting pot can, and should, become a racial melting pot.

The older melting-pot philosophy limited the ingredients of the alloy to European groups. Recall that Israel Zangwill envisioned a melting pot in which the ingredients were old-stock white Americans and immigrant Europeans—"Germans and Frenchmen, Irishmen and Englishmen, Jews and Russians." His amalgamationism was limited to the offspring of Europeans, as was that of his forerunner, Hector St. John de Crèvecoeur in *Letters From An American Farmer:* "I could point out to you a family whose grandfather was an Englishman, whose wife was Dutch, whose son married a French woman, and whose present four sons have now four wives of different nations." Neither Zangwill nor Crèvecoeur, it appears, imagined America as a crucible for melting not just shades of white, but all the colors of the population—a melting pot not just of Europe's ethnic groups, but of the world's races.

In a caste system, socioeconomic class and race are closely correlated. There are two ways to overcome a caste society. The first might be called class-mixing or integration. "Racial" communities can persist, but with members distributed through every socioeconomic class in roughly equivalent proportions, so that the correlation of race and class become confused. The second process is race-mixing or amalgamation. Racial boundaries can become so blurred that the caste system simply collapses. The two strategies are not incompatible—class-mixing may, and should, lead in time to an increasing degree of race-mixing. Racial amalgamation should be the end, of which racial integration is the means.

Many skittish white liberals over the years have hoped that social integration can be achieved without intermarriage. In the early twentieth century George Washington Cable, one of the boldest Southern white

---

*Today it is often assumed that humanity is evolving toward a common physical type, as the result of a sort of global melting-pot amalgamation. Most countries already restrict immigration, however, and restrictions will probably increase in the future. This means that presently diverse populations (like those of the Americas and Oceania) will gradually become more homogeneous, as a result of intermarriage, while already-homogeneous populations (for example, in East Asia, Western Europe, and West Africa) will become ever more closely related. Regional differences in physical characteristics are likely to be *more* pronounced in the future than they are now. The advent of genetic engineering is not likely to alter this trend toward outward differentiation.

liberals of the time, suggested as much: "Nationalization without racial confusion is ours to profess and to procure. . . . To make national unity without hybridity—the world has never seen it done as we have got to do it."[17] Even Martin Luther King dared dream, at least in public, only of black and white children playing together in the red hills of Birmingham, Alabama, instead of dreaming of weddings of mixed-race couples in the churches of Birmingham. In this view, integration will be achieved when whites, blacks, and browns mingle on perfectly equal terms in schools, locker rooms, offices, churches, and theaters, even if they continue to separate into pairs, like the animals marching into Noah's Ark, for marriage and childbearing—white-white, black-black, brown-brown.

Surely this conception of racial integration without ultimate intermarriage is confused. If people discriminate on the basis of physical race when it comes to the most fundamental matters—sex and reproduction—they can hardly be expected to overlook physical race in a thousand lesser areas of social life. They will not forget they are white or black when it comes to voting or hiring, only to suddenly remember they are white or black when it comes to sex and marriage. Race-consciousness cannot be turned on and off, depending on the circumstances; either it is very strong, or it is very attenuated, with respect to *all* matters, intimate and public, profound and trivial.

For these reasons, Calvin C. Hernton argued in 1965 that assimilation cannot be complete, ultimately, without racial amalgamation:

> "Assimilation" is the process of interpenetration and fusion of the habits, customs, traditions and historical backgrounds of different ethnic groups in such a way that their major cultural distinctions become synthesized into one culture, and the groups become more or less one people mutually sharing the privileges and responsibilities of a common society. This process has been going on throughout the entire span of human history. Not once, to my knowledge, has it happened without intermarriage ultimately taking place. In fact, intermarriage is perhaps the crucial test in determining when a people have completely won their way into the mainstream of any given society.[18]

The same logic has led Morton Kondracke to recently conclude that maintaining American democracy in good working order "would be a lot easier if each of us were related to someone of another color and if, eventually, we were all one color."[19] Thinkers in other countries have come to the same conclusion. Tzvetan Todorov points out that "the plurality of races does pose a serious problem, as soon as it is superposed— and this is usually the case—on a very real social stratification. The solution involves racial mixing, that is, the disappearance of physical differences."[20] The Brazilian novelist Jorge Amado has also arrived at the same verdict: "It is necessary to repeat that only one solution exists to the racial problem: the mixture of races. All the rest, whatever it may be, leads irremediably to racism."[21]

These speculations have been anticipated over the generations by leading Americans who envisioned a racial melting pot. Many white Americans, including Thomas Jefferson, who were hostile to black-white amalgamation advocated intermarriage between whites and American Indians.* Few white Americans, however, have advocated racial amalgamation between whites and blacks. One of them was the abolitionist Wendell Phillips. At a speech in 1863 in Framingham, Massachusetts, Phillips called for race-mixing as the ultimate solution to the American race problem:

> Amalgamation! Remember this, the youngest of you: that on the 4th day of July, 1863, you heard a man say, that in the light of all history, in virtue of every page he ever read, he was an amalgamationist, to the utmost extent (applause). I have no hope for the future . . . but in that sublime mingling of races, which is God's own method of civilizing and elevating the world (loud applause). Not that amalgamation of licentiousness, born of slavery—the ruin of both races—but that gradual and harmonizing union, in honorable marriage, which has mingled all other races, and from which springs the present phase of European and Northern civilization.[22]

---

*One of these advocates of Indian-white intermarriage was Thomas J. Morgan, commissioner of Indian Affairs for President Benjamin Harrison. Predicting that most Indians "will become merged in the . . . mass of our population," he speculated that having an Indian pedigree would one day be "almost as desirable as to belong to New York's 'Four Hundred.'" Asked by the American Press Association on the occasion of the 1893 Chicago World's Fair to predict what America would be like in a century, Morgan speculated that the commander of the U.S. armed forces in 1993 might be an Indian (instead, the Commander—General Colin Powell—was a member of another racial minority). (Cited in Michael Rust, "Then on Now: Optimism was Strong in 1893 Essays," *Insight*, March 29, 1993, p. 22.)

In 1873 another abolitionist, the Northern Methodist bishop Gilbert Haven, mused after a visit to Charleston: "What exquisite tints of delicate brown; what handsome features; what beautiful eyes, what graceful forms. No boorish Hanoverian blood here, but the best Plantagenet. . . . It is an improved breed—the best the country has today."[23]

Such thinking, always marginal, became extremely unpopular in the late nineteenth and early twentieth centuries, when extreme forms of pseudoscientific racism contributed to pessimism about the prospects of nonwhites and justified the assembling of formal Jim Crow institutions at home and in the American empire in Cuba and the Philippines. Indeed, in this era the major defenders of transracial amalgamation were found among intellectuals in Latin America—Jose Vasconcelos in Mexico, the philosopher of *mestizaje* or race-mixing, and the Brazilians Manoel Bomfim and Alberto Torres.* In the United States, when the great American anthropologist Franz Boas, a Jewish immigrant from Germany, challenged white supremacy and defended amalgamation in the early twentieth century, he was almost alone among white Americans. In "The Problem of the American Negro," published in the *Yale Review* in 1921, Boas argued that amalgamation through intermarriage was the only way to forever overcome racial prejudice. As mestizo and mulatto Americans proliferated, he predicted, "the consciousness of race would necessarily be weakened. In a race of octoroons, living among whites, the color question would probably disappear."[24] Boas, one of the early champions of the idea of the sophistication of Indian cultures, also believed that most American Indians should ultimately be absorbed through amalgamation into the majority population.[25]

Many black Americans have rejected the idea of amalgamation. In the early 1920s, Marcus Garvey wrote, "There are hundreds of thousands of colored people in America who desire race amalgamation and miscegenation as a solution of the race problem." He denounced "this

---

*Bomfim and Torres were themselves heretics in Brazil, where until recently the major approach to the problem of a multiracial society was the doctrine of "whitening"—the hope (based on outmoded Lamarckian theories of heredity) that black intermarriage with whites would gradually eliminate the African genetic heritage. Though a milder form of racism than the North American version, the ideology of whitening was still white-supremacist, and must be distinguished from an ideal of amalgamation based on the premise of racial equality. See generally Thomas E. Skidmore, *Black into White: Race and Nationality in Brazilian Thought* (Durham: Duke University Press, 1993).

dangerous 'race destroying doctrine'" as a perpetuation of "the mongrel-ization of the race" caused by slavery. He attacked black leaders who sought not only assimilation but amalgamation:

> Such leaders believe that by the amalgamation of black and white, a new type will spring up, and that type will become the American and West Indian of the future.
>
> This belief is preposterous. I believe that white men should be white, yellow men should be yellow, and black men should be black . . . .[26]

The early black nationalist Alexander Crummell also denounced the idea of amalgamation in terms identical to those of white racists. "Races, like families, are the organisms and ordinances of God; and race feeling, like the family feeling, is of divine origin," Crummell wrote in 1888.[27] Crummell's argument that racial amalgamation was not only unlikely but probably physiologically impossible rested on the pseudoscience of his day, according to which the separate European nationalities were races. No one, Crummell wrote, 'can anticipate the future dissolution of this (black) race and its final loss; and so, too, of the other races of men in America."[28] According to Crummell, writing in the late nineteenth century, the Anglo-Americans of his day were "men of as direct Anglo-Saxon descent as the men of Kent or the people of Yorkshire." Irish and French immigrants, "although kindred in blood, temperament, and religion . . . have avoided both neighborhood of locality and marital alliance. . . ." The Germans, according to Crummell, were equally a pure race: "And yet where can one discover any decline in the purity of German blood, or the likelihood of its ultimate loss in the veins of alien people?"[29] Crummell answered in the negative to the question: "Has a *new* race, the product of our diverse elements, sprung up here in America? Or, is there any such a probability for the future?"[30] The answer, as we have seen, is actually yes—Anglo- and German- and Irish- and French-Americans *have* mingled, losing their identity, for the most part, in a new, generic white American population. It may be, of course, that the barriers to the amalgamation of white and nonwhite Americans are much greater than the obstacles to the intermixture of Anglo-Americans and European immigrants. Still, the fact that the traditional black nationalist case against amalgamation depended to such a great degree on a belief in the unassimilability of European immigrants suggests that skepticism about racial fusion may also be quickly refuted.

A number of black American thinkers, including Frederick Douglass, have rejected the black nationalist emphasis on racial separatism. Black abolitionist Henry Highland Garnet (1814–1881) attacked both emigrationists and "the old doctrine of the natural inferiority of the colored race, propagated in America by Mr. Thomas Jefferson." He prophesied, *"This western world is destined to be filled with a mixed race."*[31]

The process of racial amalgamation in America is already well underway in Hawaii. Sixty percent of the babies born in Hawaii in 1991 were of "mixed" race. Conventional categories promise to become increasingly meaningless, as whites, Asians, and Hispanics intermarry in the Pacific-oriented America of tomorrow. Almost one of three Hispanics marry non-Hispanics.[32] Half of all Asian-Americans born in the United States marry outside of their official racial "nation." Such Pacific Rim blending was anticipated in 1850, by a writer in the *Southern Quarterly Review,* who speculated that one day the inhabitants of California "promise to exhibit, at no distant day, the fusion of all the European, Asiatic, and American races." The mixture would be enlarged: "The African may be gradually blended with the mass, by uniting with the Asiatics and Indians."[33]

The prospects for amalgamation between whites, Hispanics, and Asians are no doubt better than the prospects for fusion between black Americans and other groups. Looking back on his advocacy of black-white amalgamation in the 1960s, Calvin C. Hernton recently concluded that he had underestimated the social bias that exists against black-white unions—not least the bias in the black community: "Ultimately, like whites, the vast majority of blacks really feel deep down inside that sex across the color line is morally wrong and somehow sinful."[34] As a result, he predicts, "interracial sex will never be more than tolerated in America; it will never be desired and valued in and by this society and culture; it will only be exploited and employed for pornographic titillation."[35]

In spite of opposition by nonwhites as well as whites, interracial marriage in the United States continues to increase. Children born to black and white parents quintupled from 9,600 in 1968 to 51,000 in 1988, while the general population grew only by 12 percent.[36] Even if black-white amalgamation remains a distant goal, there is no reason to believe that the fusion of the other American racial castes will not steadily proceed. The number of mixed-race Americans, products of unions between whites, East Asians, South Asians, Latin mestizos, and black Americans, is expanding rapidly. The phenomenon has even produced two new "multiracial" magazines, *New People* (circulation 2,500) and *Interrace* (circulation 25,000).[37] We should hope that this trend leads to a mixed-race American majority, just as a generic European-American group has formed from the merging of Anglo-, German-, Celtic-, Italian- and Slavic-Americans.

After World War II, Theodore G. Bilbo, U.S. senator from Mississippi, published a book entitled *Separation or Mongrelization: Take Your Choice.* Despite residual racism, government race-labeling, multicultural separatism, and the enduring legacy of class inequality between races, Americans, two by two, are making that choice. A mongrelized population will eventually complement our already-mongrelized culture—and not a moment too soon.

The increase in interracial marriage is rapidly undermining the five-race theory of American identity that has been official policy since Statistical Directive 15 was promulgated in 1977. In anticipation of the 2000 Census, so-called mixed-race Americans are agitating for the inclusion of a mixed-race category on the Census form. This would break with the "just one drop" theory of nonwhite status shared by yesterday's white supremacists and today's multiculturalists alike. For precedents, the new mixed-race lobby might look to other traditions of race-labeling in this hemisphere. The seventeenth- and eighteenth-century British Caribbean caste system recognized eight categories: negro, sambo (mulatto/negro), mulatto (white man/negress), quadroon (white man/mulatto woman), mustee (white man/quadroon or indian), mustiphini (white man/mustee), quintroon (white man/mustiphini), octoroon (white man/quintroon). Spanish Americans counted (in theory) 128 racial combinations, each with its own place in the colonial status hierarchy. This was simplicity in itself, compared to the caste system in premodern Brazil where, at one point, there were 492 categories of individuals by descent.[38]

Replacing today's arbitrary five-race classification system with an even more complicated, but equally arbitrary, system identifying mixed-race combinations of the five races would only transform the baroque into the rococo. Beginning with the first census of the twenty-first century in 2000, American law should be brought into line with the reality of the transracial cultural majority, by altogether eliminating race as a category from law and politics. In the next chapter, I explore the implications of this long-delayed reform.

Ancestral identities are important—so important, in fact, that every American should have several of them. At the same time, Americans should think of themselves as belonging to only one race—the human—and to only one nationality—the American.

In 1934, the American writer Jean Toomer wrote an essay entitled "The American Race." In that essay, the great novelist and poet—a man of mixed white and black descent, the grandson of P. B. S. Pinchback, the mulatto governor of Louisiana during Reconstruction, equally at home among white American and European intellectuals and the writers of the Harlem Renaissance—set down his mature thoughts on race, culture, and nationality in the United States:

> From my early years I have felt and known I was a member of the American people and of the American race, the new race that is gradually forming in this country owing, not only to the various strains, but to the geography of the North American continent and to the effect of the social and psychological conditions which exist here. . . . This realization is coming to more and more people of all groups; and when it finally becomes a dominant thing, something of great social value is going to happen in this country.

Toomer speculated "that a new type of man was arising in this country—not European, not African, not Asiatic—but American. . . ."

In a letter to the black writer James Weldon Johnson, Toomer rejected the central notion of what is today known as multiculturalism: "My view of this country sees it composed of people who primarily are Americans, who secondarily are of various stocks or mixed stocks. . . ." To express this vision, he turned to poetry: "I wrote a poem called 'The First American,' the idea of which was that here in America we are in the process of forming a new race, that I was one of the first conscious members of this race."

"The First American" became the poem "The Blue Meridian" (1936). A blend of Whitmanian democratic idealism and Asian-influenced mysticism, "The Blue Meridian" envisions the birth of a new democracy and a new race in the continent watered by "The Mississippi, sister of the Ganges/Main artery of earth in the western world." The god known as the Blue Meridian, a symbol of Toomer's "New American" or "First American" consciousness, appears in the conclusion of the poem:

Blue Meridian, banded-light,
Dynamic atom-aggregate,
Awakes upon the earth;
In his left hand he holds elevated rock,
In his right hand he holds lifted branches,
He dances the dance of the Blue Meridian
And dervishes with the seven regions
    of America, and all the world.

A vision like Toomer's of a new American people arising from the blending of races and cultures in our North American homeland is the perception at the core of the philosophy of American liberal nationalism.

North of the Rio Grande, an amalgamated American population can be held forth as an ultimate ideal (if not an immediate goal) without any mystical notions like the claim of the early-twentieth-century Mexican intellectual and reformer Jose Vasconcelos that the Mexican mestizo people were a "cosmic race" with a messianic mission. For messianism of this kind (as of others) there are ample precedents in the U.S. In 1854 George Bancroft (thinking no doubt only of the mingling of white American groups) declared:

The commonwealth of mankind, as a whole, was not to be constructed in one generation. But the different peoples are to be considered as its component parts, prepared, like so many springs and wheels, one day to be put together . . . In this great work our country holds the noblest rank. . . . Our country stands . . . more than any other, as the realization of the unity of the race.[39]

In a similar spirit, Ben Wattenberg recently declared: "In substantial numbers and proportions, Americans can now be said to come from everywhere. No other nation, ever, could have made that claim."[40] This kind of talk is unnecessary, as well as inaccurate; the inhabitants of Surinam or Trinidad and Tobago—many of them of mixed Dutch, East Indian, American Indian, Chinese, and African ancestry—probably have a better claim than anyone else in the Western Hemisphere to having "come from everywhere." Cultural hybridization and racial amalgamation can be justified without invoking extravagant messianic notions about America as a "universal nation." It would be a mistake to substitute the petty race-mysticisms of white supremacists and Afrocentrists with a grandiose American mestizo race-mysticism. Racism and messianism are two things that America has had too much of already.

It is enough to hope, with Emerson, that a new American nation will emerge which in its cultural accomplishments is the equal, not necessarily the superior, of any in the world:

> As in the old burning of the Temple at Corinth, by the melting and intermixture of silver and gold and other metals a new compound more precious than any, called Corinthian brass, was formed: so in this continent,—asylum of all nations,—the energy of Irish, Germans, Swedes, Poles, and Cossacks, and all the European tribes,—of the Africans, and the Polynesians,—will construct a new race, a new religion, a new state, a new literature, which will be as vigorous as the new Europe which came out of the smelting-pot of the Dark Ages .[41]

Liberal nationalism is the idea of the American nation as a melting pot—a cultural melting pot, and ultimately a racial melting pot. The creation of a common national culture, from the cultures of Anglo-Americans, Africans, Algonquians, Dutch, Germans, Irish, Ashkenazim, Mexicans, and many others has already taken place. The extension of the melting-pot ideal from white Americans to Americans of all races is a slow process, but one that is indisputably occurring, despite the opposition of racists of all complexions. To paraphrase Israel Zangwill, God is *still* making the American.

CHAPTER EIGHT

National Democracy and the Fourth Republic of the United States

Liberal nationalism provides the most convincing answer to the question of American identity. To be a member of the American nation is to be not merely a citizen of the United States but a member of the Trans-American majority—a transracial nation united by American English, the slowly changing but identifiable American national culture, and a common ethic of civic familism. The real American majority is not the "white" or "non-Hispanic white" majority, but the Trans-American cultural nation, which, by definition, includes almost all of the U.S. population (so-called non-Hispanic whites plus all black, Hispanic, and Asian-Americans whose mother tongue is American English). The conventional races are not genuine ethnicities, that is, nationality groups, but merely arbitrarily defined castes within the Trans-American nation.

This is not a prophecy, but an observation. The Trans-American nationality is not something that will come into being; *it already exists*, and has for a very long time. The centuries-old cultural unity of Trans-Americans of all ancestries has been obscured, however, by even older race-consciousness. Multiculturalism, as I have argued, is profoundly conservative; it rejects the white-supremacist ranking of the races, but accepts and indeed reinforces the old white-supremacist definition of the races, with only the most minor substitution of terms (for example,

"Asian" or "Asian and Pacific Islander" for "Oriental" or "Mongoloid"). While race-consciousness remains powerful, transracial American identity is as yet weak and uncertain.

Until now, only a few visionaries like Jean Toomer have become *self-conscious* members of the Trans-American community. Self-conscious Trans-Americans are the prophets and pioneers of a new, more inclusive community, in the same way that pan-German and pan-Russian and pan-Italian intellectuals in the nineteenth century were forerunners of nationalisms that seemed alien at first to people accustomed to thinking of themselves as members of tiny, parochial peasant communities. They are harbingers of the next stage in the development of American society: the national awakening.

A national awakening is the spreading *subjective* awareness of an *objective* cultural unity. It transforms an anthropological category—a group of people united by language, culture, and custom—into a self-conscious community.* A national awakening is a phenomenon with political implications. Among other nations in recent centuries, national awakenings have been accompanied by powerful pressures for political consolidation and egalitarianism. When the circle of "us" is expanded from a region or race to the entirety of the cultural nation, formerly accepted inequities become intolerable. Norman poverty that might not bother a Provençal patriot might be intolerable to a patriot who identifies his *patria* as France in its entirety.

The liberal nationalist perception, then, evolves quickly, when translated into politics, into egalitarianism, in the interest of national solidarity. In other countries the egalitarian sentiment that is the natural corollary of liberal nationalism might take different forms; in the United

---

*The philosophical opponents of modern nationalism—a category that includes aristocratic conservatives as well as members of the cosmopolitan left—often argue that modern nationalisms are "invented," in which case national awakenings are really hoaxes perpetrated by nationalist intellectuals and politicians. However, some sort of protonational community must exist for nationalist ideology to have any plausibility; French nationalists failed to persuade Alsatian Germans that they were "French" in the same way as Normans and Provençals, and Spanish nationalists were never able to find Basques (as opposed to, say, Catalonians) who thought of themselves as Spaniards first. Furthermore, the supranational communities which antinationalists have favored—dynastic states like the Holy Roman Empire, socialist commonwealths like the Soviet Union and Yugoslavia—are far more fictive or "invented" than ethnocultural nation-states.

States, for the relevant future, the overriding goal of Trans-American liberal nationalist reform must be to address the enduring legacy of centuries of white supremacy: racial separation by class. Minor reforms of American society will not succeed in truly integrating this country. Nothing less than a radical reconstruction of the American class hierarchy is required to reduce the diminished but still significant correlation between class and color that is the enduring legacy of three centuries of caste law and caste politics.

Liberal nationalism as a political movement in the United States would take the form of an egalitarian assault on the unjust and inequitable political institutions of Multicultural America—the political creed of multicultural democracy and the political practice of the new feudalism. The political creed of a possible Fourth Republic of the United States—call it Trans-America—would be national democracy. The ideal of national democracy is a government that, without being oppressive, is powerful and competent enough to address problems that can only be addressed at the level of the nation as a whole.

Alexander Hamilton described a version of this ideal as "energetic" government. Herbert Croly's explanation of the Hamiltonian persuasion, in *The Promise of American Life* (1909), has never been surpassed: "The central government is to be used, not merely to maintain the Constitution, but to promote the national interest and to consolidate the national organization. . . ."[1] Croly conceded that, as an expression of this basic philosophy, Hamilton's version of Federalism had been inadequate because of its excessive distrust of democracy: "He and his fellow Federalists did not understand their fellow countrymen and sympathize with their purposes, and naturally they were repaid with misunderstanding and suspicion." The basic conception of an activist national government promoting the common good, however, is as compatible with egalitarian as with aristocratic notions of a good social order. The greatest Hamiltonians in the twentieth century have been progressive conservatives or social-democratic liberals like the two Roosevelts, Truman, and Johnson.[2] The link between the Old Hamiltonianism of Clay, Webster, and Lincoln and the New Hamiltonianism of the Progressives and mid-century liberals was Theodore Roosevelt. The liberal nationalists of the twenty-first century can find inspiration in Theodore Roosevelt's Osawatomie, Kansas, speech in 1910:

The American people are right in demanding that New Nationalism, without which we cannot hope to deal with our new problems. The New Nationalism puts the national need above sectional or personal advantage. It is impatient of the utter confusion that results from local legislatures attempting to treat national issues as local issues. It is still more impatient of the impotence which springs from over-division of government powers, the impotence which makes it possible for local selfishness or for legal cunning, hired by wealthy specialists, to bring national activities to a deadlock.

Realizing the ideal of national democracy in the United States, at the beginning of the twenty-first century, would require a generation-long, bloodless Fourth American Revolution. Its first goal would be to accomplish what today's racial preference lobby says must not under any circumstances be done—namely, to turn back the clock in civil rights. The clock can and should be turned back to the mid-sixties—before the ideal of a color-blind America was replaced by an America organized by racial and gender quotas, and before the New Deal alliance between white and black wage earners was replaced by a New Politics/New Left coalition of the black voting bloc with white overclass liberals and a volatile, free-floating group of alienated white middle-class voters.

Renewing the mid-century tradition of color-blind liberalism in twenty-first century America, the tradition of FDR, Truman, and Johnson, of King and Rustin, will require more than a return to the original project of completely eliminating race as a legitimate category in American law and politics. It will require, as well, a genuine democratization of our money-dominated political system and a commitment to the kind of social democratic reforms that the color-blind integrationists of the sixties envisioned as the next logical step after the eradication of formal white supremacy. In the Fourth American Republic, the nation-dividing mixture of racial preference, plutocratic politics and free-market capitalism that defines the politics of Multicultural America would be replaced by a nation-uniting synthesis of color-blind individualism in civil rights, equal voting power, and social market capitalism.

In this chapter I describe each of these elements of the ideal of national democracy. My descriptions are necessarily schematic; they are not intended to be dogmatic. This chapter is a sketch, not a blueprint. If a liberal nationalist reform movement does emerge and succeed in the United States, then it will be as the result of events that cannot be foreseen and it will take particular forms that cannot be anticipated in detail. Even so, exercises like the one that follows have value, if only to serve as inspiration to further thought and principled action. Twentieth-century progressive and liberal reforms accomplished much of what had first been envisioned in utopias like Edward Bellamy's *Looking Backward* and polemics like Herbert Croly's *The Promise of American Life*, even though the prophetic precursors got the details wrong. The details of a reform program can be easily changed, in light of new knowledge or changing circumstances, as long as the principles are sound. What follows is a first attempt to translate Trans-American liberal nationalism into a political program. If we are fortunate, it will not be the last.

INDIVIDUAL RIGHTS

Each republic of the United States to date has had its own political creed. The political creed of Anglo-America was federal republicanism; even before the Civil War inaugurated the Euro-American republic, this was giving way to federal democracy, as class-based restrictions on suffrage (at least among white men) were abolished. In Multicultural America, federal centralization has been combined with the co-optive system of racial preferences; in effect, territorial federalism has been replaced by racial federalism. The ideal of racial federalism is democracy *within* races, not democracy *across* races; its symbol is the racially gerrymandered majority-minority district, an institution legitimated by the theory that only black politicians can represent black constituents (and, by implication, that white voters can only be represented by white officials).

National democracy would be the political creed—the principle of legal and political organization—of Trans-America, as multicultural democracy is the creed of Multicultural America, as federal democracy was the creed of Euro-America, and as federal republicanism was the creed of Anglo-America. National democracy, as I define the term, has three elements: individual rights, equal voting power, and the social market. In subsequent sections I discuss equal voting power and the social market; here the focus is on the principle of individual rights.

Every American republic to date has embodied its conception of the American nation (or nations) in civil rights law. In Anglo-America and Euro-America, to be a "real" American one had to be white, and the laws requiring or permitting racial segregation reflected this idea. Today's racial preference laws are based on two quite different notions; first, that America is a federation of five racial nations and second, that it is just and reasonable to discriminate against members of the "non-Hispanic white" category in the interests of the other four.

The liberal nationalist definition of American identity, as explained in the previous chapter, is completely at odds with this idea. Liberal nationalists reject not merely racial preferences, but the very definitions of the races themselves. The lines of culture and the lines of race do not coincide in the United States; and nationality, properly understood, is a matter of culture, not race. The division of humanity into three, or five, or sixteen "races" is an inherently arbitrary activity; in the United States, the arbitrary is joined by the absurd when dubious categories are linked to real government-enforced benefits and disabilities.

If liberal nationalism in the United States has one nonnegotiable demand, it is this: Racial labeling by the government must be ended, as soon as possible. The U.S. government should no longer give any official sanction to arbitrary color-coded identities—white, black, brown, yellow, red—that do not correspond to the way that Americans actually think about themselves.* Nor should the federal government make a bad situation worse by adding new official races (like the "multiracial" category that is promoted by some mixed-race Americans). Even less should the government substitute a linguistic-cultural criterion, distinguishing Trans-Americans of all races from culturally different but genetically related groups (though such a system would approximate reality better than our present official categories).

The time for racial classification schemes like the five-race pattern

---

*According to a recent study sponsored by the Ford Foundation, most "Hispanics" prefer to be identified by their country of origin—Mexico, Cuba, or Puerto Rico—rather than as "Hispanics" or "Latinos." The same survey revealed that English is the primary language for most U.S.-born Hispanics, and that Mexicans, Puerto Ricans, and Cubans think better of "Anglos" than of other Hispanic national-origin groups. Most, furthermore, are indifferent to Latin America and oppose increased immigration. ("Latinos: Speaking in Their Own Voices," *News From the Ford Foundation*, December 15, 1992.)

promulgated by the OMB in Statistical Directive 15 is past. The color-blind liberals were right, in the early 1960s, to favor the complete elimination of government racial labels. The U.S. government should no more classify native-born American citizens as whites, blacks, Hispanics, or Asians, or for that matter as mixed-race, than it classifies white Americans as Swedish- or Irish-Americans. There should no longer be an ominous-sounding Division of Racial Statistics at the Census Bureau. If people are to be labeled for record-keeping purposes, it should be solely on the basis of country of *personal* (not ancestral) national origin. For government record-keeping, there should be only two categories of U.S. citizens—native-born citizens, and naturalized immigrants (the two groups, of course, would have absolutely identical rights). Only naturalized Mexican-born immigrants to the United States would be described as Mexican-Americans. As far as the U.S. government is concerned, their children, born and raised in the United States, would be Americans.

The government should not be hostile to subcultural identities within the Trans-American nation, but it should exhibit a principled indifference toward them. If self-described Asian-Americans wish to perpetuate themselves as a distinct population by limiting marriage among themselves to Americans of Chinese, Indian, Filipino, Korean, and Malaysian descent, and by teaching their children a fabricated Sino-Indo-Filipino-Korean-Malaysian tradition, similar to the fake African-American and pan-Hispanic traditions, they are welcome to do so—but this should be a purely private matter, like the perpetuation of Polish- or Italian-American identities (and mythologies). Complete obliviousness to race is not necessary for national integration, merely the decline of powerful racial identities into "symbolic ethnicities," so that Americans eventually think of themselves as black or white or Asian in the same way that white Americans now think of themselves as Irish or Anglo or Polish. Conventionally defined race would be one of the facts people note about each other, like height and build, but it would have lost its social connotations and emotional valence. If this seems utopian, recall that only a few generations ago even thinkers on the left like Horace Kallen thought that the white "races" of America—the Germans, the Italians, the Irish—were immutable groups that would forever define the identities of individual Americans.

It might be objected nonetheless that for many generations to come the public would continue thinking in terms of traditional racial distinctions, even if the government ceased labeling citizens by race. The argument from popular prejudice to government policy is unconvincing. Suppose that a majority of Americans were misguided enough to believe that Jews are a race. Should the pseudoracial category of Hispanics be joined by a pseudoracial category of Hebraics? In the nineteenth century, many thought that the Irish formed a distinctive Celtic race. Does the need to overcome the legacies of anti-Irish prejudice justify labeling Irish-Americans as Celts and putting Anglo-, German-, and Scandinavian-Americans together in the category of Teutons?

Four centuries of racial labeling are enough. Let the U.S. Census of 2000 A.D. be the first in American history that does not ask citizens to identify themselves by quasi-fictive categories of race.

The end of racial labeling should be accompanied by the abolition of all racial preference policies, whether carried out by the government or private-sector institutions. Subnational racial group entitlements should be replaced by individual rights and entitlements that are the same for all members of the American citizenry, no matter what their ancestries. The civil rights laws of the Fourth Republic of the United States should be founded on a principle rejected by the drafters of the first three American republics: absolutely color-blind law.

In his dissent in *Plessy v. Ferguson* (1896), the case that legitimated Jim Crow segregation, Supreme Court Justice John Marshall Harlan summarized the color-blind ideal of individual rights:

> There is no caste here. Our Constitution is color-blind and neither knows nor tolerates classes among citizens. In respect of civil rights all citizens are created equal before the law. The law regards man as man and takes no account of his surroundings or of his color when his civil rights as guaranteed by the supreme law of the land are involved.

Three quarters of a century later, another Justice, William O. Douglas (one of the most influential liberals ever to sit on the Court, it should be noted) denounced the emerging system of racial preferences in his dissent in *Defunis v. Odegaard* (1974) as passionately as Harlan had denounced the emerging system of Jim Crow in his day:

The Equal Protection Clause commands the elimination of racial barriers, not their creation in order to satisfy some theory of how society ought to be organized. The purpose of [the university] cannot be to produce Black lawyers for Blacks, Polish lawyers for Poles, Jewish lawyers for Jews, and Irish lawyers for the Irish. . . . A segregated admissions process creates suggestions of stigma and caste no less than a segregated classroom, and in the end it may produce that result despite contrary intentions.

The color-blind ideal was repudiated by the governing class in both Euro-America and Multicultural America. Let Trans-America be the first republic of the United States in which a citizen's race has no legal consequences whatsoever.

All racial preference programs should be consigned to the junkyard of history. Racial gerrymandering to produce "majority-minority" districts by carving up electorates that happen to be the wrong color should be outlawed. All minority set-asides should be eliminated. Busing in order to achieve racial balance should be forbidden by law. Giving preference to individuals on the basis of their race in hiring, promotion, or college admissions, for whatever purpose, should be banned by federal law. Colleges and universities should be forced to end scholarships limited to members of one race, on pain of losing their federal tax-exempt status and federal funding and being subject to antidiscrimination suits. The present amendments to the Voting Rights Act of 1965 that force the racial gerrymandering of districts are scheduled to expire, unless renewed, in 2007. That year should be set as the date by which all race-conscious provisions of American law and public policy are repealed or allowed to lapse. Whether racial preference is eliminated by federal law or by a constitutional amendment is a matter of expedience. However it goes, it must go.

The objections of old-fashioned, seventies-style liberals to the replacement of group rights by race-neutral individual rights are well-known. Without racial quotas, they ask, how will poor black and Hispanic Americans ever move out of poverty? And how will upwardly mobile middle-class and upper-middle-class nonwhites be able to overcome the almost invisible but strong and resilient webs of nepotism and inherited advantage that link members of the white overclass?

In answering this objection, it must be stressed that one goal of liberal nationalists—a greater distribution of black and Hispanic Americans across the entire range of income categories and occupations—is the same as that of multicultural liberals. What is more, liberal nationalists, like multicultural liberals, and unlike conservatives, favor government efforts—social engineering, if you will—to promote this result. The chief difference is that liberal nationalist social engineering, unlike multicultural liberal social engineering, might actually work.

Five hundred years of racial preference will not integrate the United States. At most, it will enlarge new black and Hispanic overclasses, dependent on government patronage and white overclass paternalism, while doing little or nothing for most black and Hispanic Americans. The social mobility of many black and Hispanic Americans is impeded by three quite different kinds of obstacles—active racism, barriers to entry in the economy and politics, and acquired disabilities. No single strategy is appropriate for all three obstacles. Active racism against individuals must be neutralized by rigorous enforcement of antidiscrimination law. Barriers to entry in the economy and politics have to be dismantled by sweeping legislative reforms of how business is done and how elections are carried out in the United States. Acquired disabilities—by which I mean the very real culture of poverty that equips many children of the ghetto and barrio with attitudes making them unfit for the mainstream, workaday community—are the most difficult, because the most subtle, of all obstacles. Nothing less than a program to liberate denizens of the ghettos and barrios from those environments, family by family, is likely to succeed.

To the solution of all these problems, racial preference is irrelevant. Indeed it is dangerous, to the extent that the proliferation of racial preference programs lulls white liberals into the comforting belief that, after all, something serious is being done to alleviate the enduring separation of race by class. Most white conservatives simply do not care.

A serious attempt to integrate American society, then, would consist of coordinated efforts in different spheres—the judicial (antidiscrimination law), the political (legislative reform of education, the professions, electoral methods, and government structures) and the economic (targeted programs to liberate the hereditary poor, as well as broader programs like universal health care and public education benefiting all wage-earning Americans). This argument is not original—it was made by Rustin and Moynihan, among others, in the sixties, and it has recently been restated by William Julius Wilson. The logic of the argument leads away from a narrow focus on civil rights and toward a broader conception of social policy. For this reason, I will discuss efforts to reduce barriers to entry and antipoverty programs below, as part of the discussion of the social market. In the remainder of this section I limit my remarks to antidiscrimination law—the only element of the complex liberal nationalist strategy for racial integration that resembles the conventional understanding of civil rights as a matter of courts and lawsuits.

Under a new, color-blind legal regime of individual rights, there would continue to be redress in the courts for individuals who suffer as individuals from actual discrimination. The abolition of government racial labeling need not affect antidiscrimination law at all; it is already against the law for employers to discriminate against people on the basis of religion, even though employers are not required to keep records of the religious status of their employees. However, in all cases where racial discrimination has been proven redress should be victim-specific, not collective. If an employer discriminates against a black American in promotion, then only the victim of the discrimination should be entitled to redress. The employer should not be required to go beyond ceasing to discriminate against blacks to promising to promote other blacks in some arbitrary quota fixed by a judge, just as an employer who discriminates against one Catholic should not be compelled to hire other Catholics according to some mathematical formula. Such collective justice is dehumanizing. It assumes that all members of a particular group of the population are interchangeable, identical units.*

The abolition of racial preference, then, need not affect antidiscrimination law at all. Indeed, even as group preferences are being abolished, the scope of individualistic antidiscrimination law should be expanded to protect (not favor) new categories of individuals. To name one example, the federal government should strike down all remaining sodomy

---

*The analogy between civil rights cases and class-action lawsuits is false and misleading. The members of a class-action product liability lawsuit have, presumably, suffered actual harm *as individuals* because of a manufacturer's or distributor's negligence. The class action simply bundles together a number of individual claims for redress. That is not the case, where an employer found guilty of discriminating against a particular individual is forced to hire a fixed number of members of that individual's category who never applied for the job earlier and never suffered any individual harm.

laws and prohibit public or private discrimination against homosexuals in all areas outside of family law (a complex area where even the rights of heterosexual citizens are far from absolute or simple). It should be against the law to refuse to hire, or to fire, or to refuse to rent to any American citizen on the basis of sexual orientation.

Not only "liberal" sexual privacy rights, but "conservative" property rights should be extended by federal legislation, too—when it comes to important matters, property owners and businesses should not be at the mercy of local governments and state legislatures. As the United States has increasingly become a single continental society, rather than a confederation of regional subsocieties, the argument in favor of permitting extreme variation in basic individual rights from state to state is weaker than ever. Why should restrictions on abortion vary between New York and Nevada? Why should a company have to deal with entirely different rules for tax assessment in Florida and Maine? Why should a homosexual employee of IBM be considered a law-abiding citizen in Massachusetts and a felon in Alabama, to which he is transferred by the corporation he works for? What is the point of national citizenship at all, if one's most basic personal rights—not just those touching on sex and marriage and parenthood, but also property rights—depend on the territorial jurisdiction in which one happens, perhaps temporarily, to live?

The argument that state legislatures are closer to the people begs the question—*which* people? When it comes to one's individual rights as a citizen, the only relevant population is the American nation as a whole. Perhaps the conclusion would be different if the states corresponded to actual social units, like the German-, French-, Italian- and Romansch-speaking cantons in Switzerland. Most state lines, however, are purely arbitrary, cutting across more natural geographic, cultural, and economic regions. State populations are not genuine moral communities. There is no "Louisiana" morality, no "Massachusetts" morality. A social conservative in Louisiana has more in common with a social conservative in Massachusetts than with a libertarian who happens to be a fellow citizen of Louisiana.

No one, in proposing a constitution for new democracies today—say, in Eastern Europe—would be demented enough to propose that the basic sexual and property rights of citizens should depend on the accident of their residence in a particular state or province. Some forms of federalism are justifiable, but civil rights federalism is an evil anachronism. The more basic the right, the more important that it be protected by the national government from bigoted or misguided local majorities that are national minorities. The twentieth century has seen a gradual nationalization of civil rights in the United States. In the twenty-first century, the process should be completed. Congress, with the help of the federal judiciary, should preempt and codify state legislation in many areas, imposing uniform basic rights laws in place of fifty separate state legal codes, in matters of racial equality, sexual privacy, family law, and the rights of property and business. The basic individual rights of all American citizens should be exactly the same, everywhere on American soil.

Defenders of group preferences often point out that these have always existed in the United States; for generations, civil and political rights were limited to white men. The evolution of notions of citizenship, however, was in the direction of universal individual rights, before the tragic perversion of the color-blind Civil Rights Revolution into a racial and gender preference revolution. Insofar as there is not a single consequence of white-supremacist racial preference that cannot be best addressed by color-blind socioeconomic reforms of the kind I describe later in this chapter, we are justified in trying to make Justice Harlan's dissent the new consensus: *There is no caste here.*

EQUAL VOTING POWER

After color-blind individual rights, the ideal of equal voting power is the second element of the liberal nationalist creed of national democracy. Equal voting power means more than formal equality in voting for candidates who have been preselected by a small group of wealthy donors. It means the substantive realization of the one-person, one-vote ideal. In the United States, realizing this ideal requires success in three major reforms: the separation of check and state, the promotion of multiparty democracy, and the transformation of the malapportioned federal Senate into a new, national Senate.

SEPARATION OF CHECK AND STATE. Today's U.S. government is democratic in form but plutocratic in substance. The American campaign finance system could not work better if it had been deliberately designed to ensure government of the rich, by the rich, and for the rich. In a misguided 1976 decision, *Buckley v. Valeo,* the Supreme Court held that Congress could not limit spending by rich Americans promoting their own candidacies. This decision was to the equalization of voting power what *Dred Scott* was to abolitionism. In *The Yale Law Review,* Jamin Raskin and John Boniface have argued that political candidates in the United States must win a "wealth primary." Candidates without enormous amounts of money, either from their own fortunes or from rich individuals and special interest groups, cannot hope to win party primaries—much less general elections. Indeed, the *Buckley* decision is one reason why more than half of the members of the Senate today are millionaires.[3] The bias toward the rich embodied in American campaign finance practices makes a mockery of America's democratic ideals. Genuine democracy requires not only juridical equality among races when it comes to individual rights, but also political equality among the different socioeconomic classes of citizens.

It is time to build a wall of separation between check and state. Curing the disease of plutocratic politics requires a correct diagnosis of its cause: the costs of political advertising. The basic problem is that special interests buy access and favors by donating the money needed for expensive political advertising in the media. Elaborate schemes governing the flow of money do nothing to address the central problem: paid political advertising. Instead of devising unworkable limits on campaign financing that leave the basic system intact, we should cut the Gordian knot of campaign corruption by simply outlawing paid political advertising on behalf of any candidate for public office. The replacement of political advertising by free informational public service notices in the electronic and print media would level the playing field of politics and kill off an entire parasitic industry of media consultants and spin doctors.

An outright ban on paid political advertising and the imposition of free time requirements on the media are radical measures, but nothing less is necessary if we are to prevent our government from continuing to be sold to the highest bidders. The argument against strict public regulation of money in politics is based on a false analogy between free spending and free speech protected under the First Amendment. The analogy is false, because limits on campaign finance do not address the *content* of speech—only its volume, as it were. It is not an infringement on free speech to say that, in a large public auditorium, Douglas will not be allowed to use a microphone unless Lincoln can as well.*

Indeed, the separation of check and state might permit us to re-create, in modern conditions, something like the American democracy of a century ago. When Illinois voters had to choose between Abraham Lincoln and Stephen A. Douglas, they were not treated to different thirty-second spots—an "image" commercial for Lincoln showing a slave in chains and then cutting to a blurry, idealized log cabin, an "attack" commercial by Douglas showing quotes from Lincoln opposing the Civil War, taken out of context to make him look like a traitor. Instead, nineteenth-century Illinois voters could see Lincoln and Douglas debate for several hours. Today, television technology permits such debates without requiring candidates to travel from town to town. Our televised public debates, sponsored by nonpartisan bodies like the League of Women Voters, represent the best part of our campaign system; the paid political advertisements are the worst. The advertisements should go, the debates remain.

Campaign finance reform is not properly described as a free speech issue at all; it is, first and foremost, a civil rights issue. The progressive exclusion of monetary advantage from the civic sphere, and its confinement to the marketplace, is one of the clearest signs of political progress. When the ideal of popular democracy has triumphed over plutocratic democracy, future generations will look back on the practice of buying access and votes from politicians by means of campaign contributions with the same amazement, horror, and disgust with which we regard the

---

*A much more compelling analogy would be between the electoral process and the judicial system, with the electorate playing the part of the jury. In our system of trial by jury, there are elaborate rules governing the presentation of evidence to the jury by plaintiff and defendant (the "candidates"). If our judicial system were organized the way our electoral system is, then rich candidates would be allowed to buy time before the jury. Texas senator Phil Gramm, in one Senate election, outspent his opponent by 300 to 1; the equivalent, in the judicial system, would be allowing a rich defendant to buy, say, six months to present his side of the case, while the poor plaintiff might be able to purchase only twenty minutes for his side.

poll tax, the selling of exemptions from the draft to the sons of wealthy families during the height of the Civil War, or the college-student exemption to the Vietnam draft. Today progress means, in the words of E. J. Dionne, making sure "that the votes of majorities matter more than the dollars of minorities."[4]*

MULTIPARTY DEMOCRACY. The United States is one of the few democracies in the world that retains the archaic plurality system for electing legislators.† Under the plurality system—sometimes known as "first past the post" or "winner take all"—a representative is elected by a plurality of voters in a single district. The drawbacks of this system are obvious. A candidate who gets 40 percent of the vote, as long as he gets more votes than any other candidate, can be elected—even though sixty percent of the voters voted against him. In what sense is that 60 percent majority represented by the candidate thus elected? Even worse, the plurality system encourages a two-party monopoly, because votes for third parties are wasted.‡ Finally, plurality systems reward the gerrymandering of single-member districts to give parties (or, in the United States, particular racial groups) built-in advantages.

Proportional representation (PR) is free from these defects. In the most common form of PR, the party-list system, a country, or subunit like a state, county, or city, is divided into multimember districts. Several parties present lists of candidates within each multimember district. The voters vote for the parties, rather than the candidates. Seats are allocated among the parties, on the basis of the proportion they receive of the total vote.

---

*The separation of check and state is also a litmus test that separates genuine populists from their imitators. Conservatives who pretend to be populists but oppose outlawing the financing of campaigns by the rich are clearly frauds.

†The United States inherited the plurality system from eighteenth-century Britain. Australia and New Zealand have joined most other First World democracies in moving toward proportional representation; growing numbers support scrapping plurality elections in favor of PR in Britain and Canada as well.

‡For example, a vote for a Libertarian candidate incapable of being elected takes a vote away from the Republican, helping the Democrat, even though the Libertarian voter would prefer the Republican to the Democrat as his second choice.

The kinds of distortions that take place routinely in plurality systems are impossible in PR systems. Under a PR system, a party that wins 40 percent of the vote in a multimember district will win only 40 percent of the seats. PR encourages multiparty democracy, because it permits even small parties to elect representatives (in order to discourage tiny, extremist parties, most democracies with PR now require that parties pass a minimum threshold of the total vote; in Germany, extremist parties have been checked by a 5 percent threshold). PR also reduces the incentives to engage in partisan or racial gerrymandering. Under PR, in multimember districts every significant party or voting bloc will be represented more or less in proportion to its strength in the entire electorate, regardless of how the district lines are drawn. Only in "winner-take-all" plurality systems, in which the voters in an area of several blocks may make the difference between losing everything and winning everything by a few percentage points, is there an incentive to gerrymander.

In the United States, proportional representation would permit us to do away with both partisan and racial gerrymandering, while, at the same time, increasing the political options (as new parties formed) and making it easier for members of minority groups—not only racial, but religious and cultural—to elect at least one member of multimember delegations. PR achieves the goal of the Voting Rights Act—greater voting power for black and Hispanic Americans—but by color-blind, nonintrusive means that benefit members of numerical minorities in general. Under PR, black and Hispanic voters would find it much easier to elect black and Hispanic candidates, if they chose. They would not, however, be maneuvered into such a choice by being electorally ghettoized in safe minority-majority districts. They would not have to live in minority neighborhoods in order to enjoy a greater range of options, and to wield greater individual power at the polls.*

PR could be easily adopted for city councils, county commissions, and state legislatures simply by changes in state law. Furthermore, although

---

*It is important to note that this argument for PR is the opposite of Lani Guinier's argument for cumulative voting. For Guinier, alternate electoral methods are of interest only to the extent that they reinforce other race-based "remedies" like racial gerrymandering. I am arguing, to the contrary, that proportional representation allows us to *abolish* racial gerrymandering with a clear conscience.

many people believe mistakenly that winner-take-all plurality elections and their inevitable result, the two-party monopoly, are enshrined in the U.S. Constitution, nothing more than an act of Congress would be required to establish the election of members of the House of Representatives by PR.*

Our archaic first-past-the-post plurality electoral system preserves a two-party monopoly rejected by a growing number of alienated American voters, forces many Americans to waste their votes, and effectively disfranchises substantial numerical minorities. There are practically no arguments in its favor, other than the fact that it is more than two hundred years old. The Founding Fathers, however, did not so much choose the plurality method as take it for granted. They were not able to consider the merits of proportional representation as an electoral method, because it had not been invented yet. Noting that "the highly cultivated members of the community" find it difficult to be elected under a winner-take-all plurality system, John Stuart Mill wrote, "Had a plan like Mr. Hare's [for proportional representation] by good fortune suggested itself to the enlightened and patriotic founders of the American Republic, the Federal and State Assemblies would have contained many of these distinguished men, and democracy would have been spared its greatest reproach and one of its most formidable evils." The Founding Fathers did not know of alternatives to the inherited electoral system. We do not have that excuse.

THE NATIONAL SENATE.   It would be relatively easy to begin electing representatives by PR from new multimember districts in the fifty states. PR would not work for elections to the U.S. Senate, as it is now designed. All the more reason, then, to redesign the U.S. Senate.

---

*Article I, Section 4 of the Constitution provides: "The Times, Places and Manner of holding Elections for Senators and Representatives shall be prescribed in each State by the Legislature thereof; *but the Congress may at any time by Law make or alter such Regulations,* except as to the Places of chusing Senators" (emphasis added). Congress, then, has the power to preempt all state electoral laws governing the election of members of the House and to mandate a system of multimember districts and PR. For a more detailed discussion of how PR elections to the U.S. Congress might work, see Michael Lind, "A Radical Plan to Change American Politics," *The Atlantic,* August 1992, pp. 73–83.

The Senate has been the most defective branch of American government. In the Anglo-American republic, the Southern planter class,
thanks to the informal compromise embodied in the sectional balance
between slave states and free states, was able to exaggerate its political
power. Had there been no Senate, or had the Senate been elected on the
basis of population, slavery probably would have been abolished in the
United States by the northern majority much sooner. In late-nineteenth-
century Euro-America, the Senate became the favorite branch of government of the new industrial plutocracy. The only major structural
change in the Constitution in more than two centuries was that effected
by the Seventeenth Amendment, which provided for the direct election
of senators, who had formerly been elected by state legislatures whose
members auctioned off senatorial seats to corporations and trusts. The
Seventeenth Amendment did not alter the malapportionment built into
the Senate; it merely gave small-state populations, instead of small-state
legislatures, an unfair weighted vote in federal policymaking.

That weighted vote grows heavier with every passing year, as I noted
in Chapter 5. Today, thanks to Senate malapportionment, 16 percent of
the nation can elect half the Senate—and thwart the senators representing the 84 percent of the public who live in the twenty-five most
populous states. Since most population growth, as a result of replacement and immigration, is taking place in a few populous states, the disparity can only grow over time. Will 10 percent of the public elect half
the Senate in 2010? 5 percent in 2020? 2 percent in 2050? If the Constitution is not amended, by the middle of the twenty-first century a tiny,
almost exclusively white minority of the U.S. population, living in the
largely empty states of the continental interior, may control a majority of
the seats in the Senate. As it happens, small-state whites tend to be political allies of reactionary members of the white overclass in the large
states. A few generations from now, conservative small-state whites may
use their weighted vote to consistently block every program beneficial to
the mixed-race or nonwhite majority, most of whose members will live in
a few populous coastal states like California, Texas, and New York. This

---

*For a good discussion of this problem, see Tom Geoghegan, "The Infernal Senate," in *The New Re-
public*, November 21, 1994, pp. 17–23.

trend is already ominously apparent, in the way that public-spending programs that would benefit nonwhites and whites alike in the populous states are routinely killed by small-state senators in the Senate, after having been passed by the more responsive and representative House.

How are black and Hispanic Americans—to say nothing of big-state whites—going to react, when it becomes evident that the policies they favor are being consistently thwarted by senators representing a tiny number of mountain and prairie state whites? If the U.S. Congress is perceived to be held in a choke hold by a shrinking sliver of a white population that is itself shrinking, pressures will grow for the presidency or the courts to circumvent a deadlocked Congress altogether and take urgent policymaking tasks into their own hands. That way lies presidential dictatorship or government by judiciary.

Sooner or later, in some manner, Senate malapportionment must be eliminated. The best approach would be to sever the Senate from the states altogether. That senators represent the interests of state constituencies is already a fiction, inasmuch as most senators today depend more on out-of-state campaign contributions than on money raised at home. Our corrupt campaign finance system has already, in effect, nationalized the Senate. Let us formally nationalize it, clean it up, and, while we are at it, democratize it. Let senators be elected by proportional representation, in national elections, and serve four years, concurrent with the president.* Members of the House, elected from small multimember districts by PR, would adequately represent local interests; senators, with their national constituencies, would tend to be more concerned with the nation as a whole.

These reforms may sound radical. In fact, they are conservative. Their purpose is to conserve the essence of our constitutional system, by eliminating the factors—campaign finance abuses, unfair electoral methods, and malapportionment—that are alienating an ever-growing number of Americans from the political process. In the words of Tennyson, "That

---

*A related reform might replace the electoral college with direct national elections for the president, with run-off elections where no candidate wins an absolute majority of the nationwide popular vote.

man's the true conservative/Who lops the moulder'd branch away." The legitimacy of the United States Congress is at an all-time low. If it is not restored by timely reforms that restore the confidence of the American people in the institution, people will turn away from Congress and look for leadership elsewhere—in a quasi-dictatorial presidency; even, if they despair enough, in a military strongman. If the historic succession of Republics of the United States is not to be replaced by a succession of pseudo-democratic executive regimes—Protectorates, Directories, Consulates, Empires—we must, sooner rather than later, realize the ideal of equal voting power: not one dollar/one vote, nor one acre/one vote, but one citizen/one vote.

THE SOCIAL MARKET CONTRACT

Social mobility in twenty-first century America will require good jobs for unskilled and low-skilled Americans at good wages with good benefits. All of this, in turn, requires a new social contract—the social market contract—between the national government, employers, and workers, to replace the New Deal system, which has been breaking down since the sixties. A post–New Deal social market contract must promote high wages for American workers without bankrupting either employers or the government, or imposing excessive rigidity in the labor market.

A new social market contract might have the following features. Benefits which are now linked to employment and paid out of payroll taxes, like Social Security and most health care, should be completely severed from any connection with a particular job (though a requirement of work of some kind should be enforced to prevent the development of a class of idle parasites). Employer mandates would be replaced by direct government-to-citizen transactions, financed out of progressive income taxes and consumption taxes (from which staples would be excluded). Higher wages could be encouraged, by ending the influx of unskilled immigrant labor, by passing laws against reliance on temporary workers instead of full-time employees, by discouraging teens from working (they should be studying), and by encouraging caregivers, male or female, to leave the job market or enter it only part-time in order to care for children or aged relatives.

The most promising way to quickly raise wages at the bottom of the income ladder in the United States is to restrict immigration. In the furor over California's Proposition 187, much of the overclass press has attempted to smear all proponents of immigration restriction as immigrant-bashing nativists. No doubt prejudice against the new immigrants—against Hispanic immigrants, in particular—accounts for opposition to immigration on the part of some Americans. Concern about high levels of immigration, however, cannot in itself be dismissed as racism. A sober look at the numbers might be enough to make a restrictionist of the most humanitarian liberal.

Thanks to ever-growing legal immigration, the U.S. Census Bureau has revised its estimate of annual immigration upward *by 50 percent* to 880,000 per year, and now predicts growth from 252 million in 1991 to 383 million in 2050. Largely as a result of the post-1965 immigration wave, the population in 2050 is projected to be 82 million greater than it would have been if immigration had ended in 1991. The U.S. rate of 1.1 percent per year, though it sounds low, is enough to double the U.S. population in sixty-four years.[5]

In addition to enlarging the U.S. population much more rapidly than may be desirable, mass immigration, by increasing the availability of low-wage labor, may have retarded the progress of automation in the United States by making it cheaper for corporations to hire immigrant workers rather than invest in labor-saving technology. Even worse, the continual enlargement of the low-wage labor pool in the United States by immigration since the sixties is probably one of the reasons that wages have stagnated or declined at the bottom of the American class system, as I argued in Chapter 5. Cutting off the competition of native-born or naturalized Americans with new immigrants for jobs could have salutary effects for the bottom half of the American population. Although the ethnic basis of early-twentieth-century U.S. immigration restrictions was objectionable, the overall effects of the restriction of immigration in the 1920s were positive. Immigration restriction helped black Americans by opening up good entry-level jobs that would otherwise have gone to newly arrived Europeans. The postwar American economic boom could hardly have occurred if immigration levels had continued at their turn-of-the-century levels, with impoverished and illiterate Europeans crowding into the big cities, and employers using immigrants in sweatshops to evade labor laws and break American unions. If immigration restriction had these beneficial effects once, why not once again?

The restriction of legal immigration should not be limited to low-wage workers who compete with the native-born poor and working poor for a limited number of unskilled jobs. The United States has benefited, and one hopes will always benefit, from a moderate influx of foreign scientists, scholars, journalists, and other educated immigrants. Furthermore, no immigration policy that turns away people in danger of genocide would be acceptable. Even so, there must be some limit to the number of skilled immigrants who are admitted, if educated Americans, along with low-skilled Americans, are not to see their incomes dragged down. Today many college-educated Americans are being forced to settle for noncollege jobs. Since 1970, the proportion of college graduates taking jobs that do not require college degrees has doubled to 20 percent.[6] From 1990 to 2005 the growth of job openings for college graduates will diminish while the number of bachelor's degrees awarded grows.[7] When growing numbers of college-educated Americans cannot find work worthy of their training, why should they have to compete with skilled immigrants for a diminishing number of places in good universities and desirable jobs? If we must import well-educated foreigners to be scientists and engineers, clearly we are failing to equip native white, Hispanic, black, and Asian-Americans with the necessary skills or necessary attitudes. The East Asian countries managed to create first-rate science and engineering professionals by educating their own people, rather than by bringing in great numbers of Americans and Western Europeans; why can't we, too, raise up the bottom half of the population?*

One can debate how much immigration should be reduced, in order to create a tight labor market, boost American wages, and increase opportunities for upward mobility. The best policy might be one of "zero

---

*The media has spread the myth of Asian academic superiority and economic success—something that is true only of *some* Asians. As Ronald Tagaki points out, Asian-American family income is high only because more family members work; average personal income of Asian-Americans remains below that of white Americans. What is more, all Asian-Americans are not graduate students at Caltech; great numbers form an exploited proletariat in the sweatshops of Chinatowns. (Ronald Tagaki, *A Different Mirror: A History of Multicultural America*, Boston: Little, Brown, 1993, pp. 415–416.)

net immigration"—limiting the number of legal immigrants to the number of people who voluntarily emigrate from the United States each year,
around 200,000 (down from 7–800,000 today), and reducing the number of illegal immigrants to as near zero as possible.*

One result of immigration restriction might be to encourage the flight
of U.S. manufacturing abroad. If immigration restriction denied U.S.
business access to an ever-growing pool of cheap, nonunionized labor
within U.S. borders, more businesses might follow the precedent of
transferring production abroad to countries where wages and benefits
are kept low by inherited poverty, overpopulation, or tyrannical governments that suppress workers. Immigration restriction therefore should
be accompanied by checks upon the expatriation of American industry.
A social tariff, in the amount of the difference between American and
foreign wage rates, might deter American employers in some industries
from responding to rising wages in a tight American labor market by
transferring production abroad. Any price advantage that, say, Motorola
gained by manufacturing in Malaysia rather than in California would be
eliminated by the imposition of a social tariff on imports from Motorola's
Malaysian factories. Since the same social tariffs would be imposed on
all imports, American businesses would not be penalized in competing
with foreign manufacturers seeking to sell to the American market.

Social tariffs imposed to deter the relocation of production by employers seeking to evade generous wage and labor laws need not wreck the
world economy, if they are adopted by most or all of the advanced industrial democracies. For example, the United States, Canada, and the EC
might create a common high-wage trading bloc—a common social market—with a common social tariff. American or German corporations
transferring production to low-wage countries would be penalized, if they
tried to export to the common social market. Within the common social

---

*This pro-worker rationale for immigration restriction is not to be confused with nativist hysteria
about the supposed dilution of American culture or white predominance in the United States by
"Third World immigrants." The kind of immigration restriction I am suggesting would limit the annual numbers of immigrants, but it would not seek to favor particular countries as sources of immigration (as the regime of the 1920s favored Northwestern Europe). Most of the immigrants under a
zero net immigration policy would still come from Latin America and Asia; they would simply come
in smaller contingents.

market, however, trade barriers might be progressively eliminated, so that trade flows increased, say, between the United States and Germany. Unlike free trade between a First World and a Third World country, free trade between First World countries tends to be an unalloyed good, inasmuch as companies derive their advantages from superior quality, organization, or technology, rather than from a particular country's low wages or low regulatory standards. As a general rule, then, free trade should be encouraged between high-wage countries but trade between high-wage and low-wage countries should be regulated in order to prevent mobile transnational corporations from using the poverty of available workers in the latter to drive down wage and benefit levels in the former.

The most compelling argument for the adoption of a common social tariff by the high-wage industrial countries is the preservation of middle-class living standards in the First World. The goal of U.S. economic policy is to raise the living standards of ordinary Americans; whether the pursuit of high incomes for Americans happens to promote global welfare is a matter of secondary importance. A common social tariff, protecting a common social market, might, however, have an incidentally beneficial effect, insofar as it encouraged Third World countries to develop by creating well-paid workforces and large domestic markets, instead of by treating the poverty of their people as a resource in a never-ending competition to host offshore production facilities owned by American, European, and Japanese corporations. The common social tariff would not affect investment from the developed countries, as long as that investment was limited to transplant factories making goods for local consumption. While American investors would be discouraged from making computers in, say, India for the American market, they would be free to grow rich by investing in Indian factories producing for the local Indian market. The United States, Japan, and Germany developed on the basis of production for protected domestic markets, with the help of foreign investment. The claim of free-market globalists that the successful development by protectionism of the three leading capitalist countries of our day can never be repeated, and that Third World countries can only hope to develop by specializing in low-wage piecework for foreign-owned companies and foreign markets, finds no support in history.

The point is not to promote protectionism in the abstract against free trade in the abstract, but to promote pragmatism in trade and investment policy. We do not assume that a single tax policy is best, for all countries, at all levels of development, in all phases of world history; why should we assume that a single trade policy should be the *only* trade policy? Trade-building is like road-building; the dogma that we always need more roads, and it does not matter where they are or where they go, would be a poor guide to rational decisions about building a national infrastructure. We must be pragmatic and experimental in our national and multinational economic strategy, not guided by abstract rules that purport to be the best for all times and all places. *Realpolitik* in military and diplomatic strategy needs to be joined by a pragmatic policy of economic realism promoting the interests of the salaried majority in the United States and similar high-wage countries: *Realekonomik*.

The combination of immigration restriction with a social tariff, by dramatically reducing the effective labor pool for corporations selling goods and services in the United States, would tend to drive up the average American wage. Employers would have a choice between paying higher wages—thereby arresting the economic decline of the least fortunate Americans—or moving toward automation, something that, however disruptive in the short term, would promote the long-term evolution of the U.S. economy as a capital-intensive and technology-intensive rather than labor-intensive economy. The low-wage, low-investment strategy that American business has followed since the sixties, a strategy made possible by a constantly renewed supply of cheap immigrant labor and low-wage overseas production sites, would be replaced by a high-wage, technology-intensive strategy. Robots in American factories, yes; immigrant workers in America and workers in American-owned or funded sweatshops abroad, no.

This would not be a "Luddite" strategy, because it would welcome, even encourage, the replacement of workers by machines. Automation is already destroying not only traditional blue-collar industrial jobs but "pink-collar" secretarial and clerical jobs. The high-wage strategy would accelerate this new version of what the economist Joseph Schumpeter called creative destruction. Within a few generations, thanks to automation, the number of Americans engaged in factory work and routine office work may be as small as the number engaged in agriculture. If

handled properly, this transition from a labor-intensive industrial economy to an automated industrial economy could usher in a new age of
widespread affluence.

The potential for disaster, however, is high. America's ghettos are full
of the children and grandchildren of rural Southern agricultural workers
displaced by technology in the early twentieth century. The public housing estates of Europe and the shantytowns of Latin America, like the
favelas of Brazil, are crowded by the white and mestizo urban underclasses similarly created by the dispossession of peasantries by mechanized
agriculture. Prudent action by government will be required to prevent
the decline of technologically obsolete blue-collar and pink-collar workforces into new hereditary urban or suburban underclasses composed of
the alienated, the ignorant, and the unemployable.

In today's political climate, shaped by the antigovernment tax revolt
of the rich, it is unpopular to talk about new obligations for government.
Like it or not, though, the government in the twenty-first century United States, if it wishes to preserve the American middle class, will have to
ensure that the American population as a whole, and not just a small
elite of shareholders, managers, and professionals, benefits from the
gains in productivity that automation will produce in a "skeleton crew"
industrial economy. This means not retraining, that oversold and inef-
fective panacea of the neoliberal Clinton administration, but unsubtle,
crude, old-fashioned redistribution of wealth, through taxation and public spending. In the absence of redistribution of the economic gains from
automation, a neo-Victorian social order might evolve, with a small
number of "robot barons," the equivalents of the oil and railroad magnates of yesteryear, providing employment for armies of underpaid workers in luxury industries, while alienated and violent underclasses fester
in ghettos, barrios, and slums (surveyed and policed, perhaps, by computers and robot police). We do not want the middle-class century in
the United States to be followed by a new Gilded Age in which most
people work as the equivalent of butlers, footmen, maids, nannies,
valets, chefs, gardeners, governesses, and dancing masters for a tiny,
largely hereditary oligarchy that owns or controls the quietly humming
automatic factories and communications networks.

Governmental redistribution of the gains from automation, then, will be necessary to prevent the further polarization of society. This new redistributionism might take the form of increased spending on public services and amenities or subsidies to enable more people to obtain basic services and amenities in the private sector. The very distinction between the "public" and "private" sectors might become blurred, in a system of "voucher capitalism," in which citizens were given consumption vouchers not only for basic necessities like housing and transportation but for amenities like recreation and entertainment. Thanks to such consumption subsidies, the most important market for the services of middle-class workers would be other middle-class workers, not the wealthy few.

What would those middle-class service careers be? Many would be familiar in-person service jobs: teaching, nursing, cleaning, police and fire protection, janitorial work. Today these are poorly paying and low-status occupations. In a high-wage, high-tech economy, however, they might be transformed into respectable middle-class vocations, that not only command higher wages but demand higher skills. Tomorrow's nurses, police officers, and janitors may not be menial laborers; they may oversee complex robots and computers, which will perform many of the routine or degrading or dangerous tasks done by people today. Already, as "smart" or computer-controlled buildings become more common, the blue-collar "super" is giving way to a new breed of building superintendent or "resident manager" skilled in computer electronics as well as business and personal diplomacy.[8]

The War on Oligarchy

Will janitors be members of the solid, educated middle class in 2050? The idea seems strange today, but for the past few centuries formerly despised vocations have consistently moved upward in social status. Few people in 1850 could have imagined that despised mechanics like unionized auto workers would be the very model of middle American affluence in 1950, just as few in 1750 could have dreamed that merchants and lawyers—at that time the insecure, ridiculed members of the middle rung of an aristocratic social order—would be at the top of the status hierarchy in countries like the United States in 1850. Since the industrial revolution, as if they were on an escalator, the lower rungs of society have consistently moved up, in affluence and status, with one era's lower class becoming the next era's middle class.

The corollary trend has been the disappearance, or at least the marginalization, of a series of upper classes. In the Euro-American world, the landowning elite gave way to a proprietary industrial bourgeoisie, which then gave way, in the late nineteenth and early twentieth centuries, to the dominant professional classes of managers, lawyers, and financiers. As James Burnham and others were realizing as early as the 1930s, modern industrial organization, with its separation of ownership and control, has created a class of managers of large economic enterprises who tend to fuse with accredited professionals in a managerial-professional elite. The term "new class" originally referred to this elite, before it was distorted by conservative polemicists. The contemporary credentialed managerial-professional elite will not be automatically or painlessly transformed or replaced by the mere operation of economic processes. That will take the equivalent, for the upper class, of the war on poverty—a war on oligarchy.

The war on oligarchy would be the class-war strategy of a post-Marxist egalitarianism. Post-Marxist egalitarians would recognize that, in a managerial society, the ownership of the means of production may take many forms: concentration in the hands of a few families or trusts; decentralized private ownership by vast numbers of small shareholders (say, through pension funds); even government ownership (where enterprises are allowed to pursue profits in a more or less rational way). All of these different patterns of ownership are compatible with the same monopolization of the best positions in the managerial-professional elite by a hereditary or quasi-hereditary social class. If the United States government nationalized all of the banks tomorrow, *and that were the only reform*, the class backgrounds of bank officials would be utterly unchanged. CEOs and professionals would, at least nominally, be civil servants, but in this new socialist United States the children of the white overclass would still predominate in the higher reaches of the economic bureaucracy and black and brown Americans would be concentrated disproportionately in the lower tiers.

My point in discussing this hypothetical scenario is not to give any credence to socialism. Democratic socialism is a contradiction in terms, not for reasons of political economy (in theory, a socialist economy might work, with the proper quasi-private incentives) but for reasons of politics; socialism increases the scope of potential tyranny while reducing the barriers to its exercise. My point is that *in addition* to breeding political tyranny, socialism can (and often has) either preserved or reinforced existing class and caste divisions (there have been few black Cubans in Fidel Castro's elite, and few Central Asians made it to the top in the defunct Soviet Union). If the goal is to reconstruct the class system in the interests of greater social mobility, then communism—paradoxical though it sounds—may be too conservative.

Real radicalism is not compensating the losers of a crooked game, but rewriting the rules of the game itself, so that more people can play and so that there are more opportunities to score. The rules of the class game in America revolve primarily around professional licensing and education. In a country where control of the means of production is more important than ownership of them, and where access to that control depends on credentials, the *real* class war must take the form of struggles over credentialing.

James Fallows, among others, has proposed that the professions be disaggregated into small subfields, each of which would have lower (and less expensive) barriers to entry. Medicine need not be monopolized by M.D.s, if nurse-practitioners were permitted to write some simple prescriptions; the J.D., who now must have four years of undergraduate education and three years of law school in addition in most states, could be replaced by a variety of legal-services specialists—say, conveyancers, who could make valid wills and trusts on the basis of an eight-month study course. A Ph.D., that nineteenth-century Germanic credential, would no longer be required for college teaching (much of which, anyway, is now done by underpaid graduate student teaching assistants). Brain surgeons, corporate lawyers, and distinguished academics would continue to meet high standards and command high fees, but much of what is now done by doctors and lawyers would be done by New Professionals, to the benefit of middle-class and working-class Americans (who would move into these newly multiplied trades) and of consumers of all classes (who would pay lower fees).

This is merely carrying the logic of capitalist rationalization of efficiency through the division of labor through to its conclusion. The professional generalist would continue to give way to the professional specialist. The legal profession would become the legal services industry, divided into dozens of specialized functions. Professional management would become management services. The professoriate would be replaced by the higher education services industry. The medical profession would give way to the medical services industry. In every case, subdivision would open up new jobs with lower entry requirements—that is, new opportunities for working-class and middle-class Americans.

A national debate over professional educational and licensing practices is long overdue. The federal government has no business trying to determine fair compensation for CEOs, lawyers, or doctors. It can, however, assume the task of professional regulation from the fifty state governments, and investigate and proscribe attempts by the great guilds of management, law, and medicine to artificially drive up salaries and fees by prevailing on state legislatures to write monopolistic guild regulations into law. What is more, the federal government has the right, and the responsibility, to determine not only what the requirements for entry into the professions should be, but how the professions are defined in the first place. A reform like dividing the Great Guilds of law, medicine, management, and the professoriate into dozens of modest vocations is the sort of thing that democratic legislatures are supposed to do. The professions, after all, are artificial creatures of statute; new professions can be formed from old ones and existing professions broken down with the stroke of a pen.

The final redoubt of oligarchy in the managerial-capitalist United States, after the great professions like law, management, medicine and the professoriate, is our caste-like educational system. Without diluting standards of intellectual excellence, the rules of the educational game, as well as the rules of professional accreditation, need to be rewritten to make social mobility easier in America—to the benefit not only of black, Hispanic, and Asian-Americans but of a majority of white Americans as well.

For generations, Americans have perceived the link between universal public education and social mobility. That link needs to be restored, by efforts that revitalize the public school system—for example, by equalizing funding for all public schools (a reform underway in a number of states) and imposing statewide and national standards to measure how much students actually learn. Experiments with vouchers and stu-

dent choice might be worthwhile, as long as their purpose is to reinvigo-
rate public education, not destroy it.

We should also give some thought to turning higher education from a
largely private luxury into a universal entitlement and a regulated public
utility. The rationing of access to higher education by parental income
and wealth—the chief means by which inherited money is converted into
managerial-professional credentials—should be brought to an end. One
way to achieve this goal might be the adoption, from some health care
schemes, of a universal, single-payer system for higher education. Here
is how it might work. Colleges and universities would be banned from
accepting any payments from students or their parents except for government higher education vouchers, on pain of losing their federal tax-exempt status. All young adults in America would be entitled to a voucher,
though the amounts would vary based on academic achievement, mea-
sured by achievement tests (which are less biased than IQ and aptitude
tests) and other race-neutral and gender-neutral measures. Most Americans might receive two- or four-year vouchers; the top 10 or 20 percent,
in terms of academic achievement, would get six- or eight-year vouchers.
The vouchers would not be loans. They would be free of any obligation,
except the obligation to adequately finish a course of study.

In order to prevent the costs of this new middle-class entitlement
from spiraling out of control, the federal government would have to impose tuition caps on all colleges and universities, private or state, that
accept the vouchers (and the tax-exempt status that comes with it). The
tuition at Yale and Harvard would be exactly the same as the tuition at,
say, the University of Nebraska—say, a few thousand a year. Would this
tend to erase the difference between the expensive Ivy League schools
and other colleges and universities? Naturally—and about time, too.
The abolition of private financing of higher education, along with the
outlawing of alumni preference, would force the Ivy League to abandon
its historic role as a credentialing institution for a social oligarchy. The
prestige of a college in the new system would depend on its attracting
the brightest students, of all backgrounds, not on coaxing funds from
rich alumni parents in return for warehousing their mediocre children
for four years.

These suggestions seem radical now. But tuition cost inflation (driven
by our inequitable system of loans, rather than grants, to middle-class

students) is rapidly pushing American higher education toward bankruptcy. At some point in the twenty-first century, this design defect of our present system of financing higher education will have to be dealt with, if the college experience is not, as in the nineteenth century, to be limited to the children of the rich. Wealthy Americans have many advantages over middle-class Americans; the ability to buy a first-rate education for their children should no longer be one.

Even in the absence of sweeping reforms like these, equalizing access to higher education requires the outlawing, by the federal government, of one of the pillars of social oligarchy in America: legacy preference in college admissions. In an industrial, bureaucratic society in which access to wealth and power depend on educational credentials, alumni preference in university admissions is the managerial-professional equivalent of primogeniture. Legacy preference is affirmative action for the Haves.

The arguments in favor of legacy preference are so obviously specious that they need only be mentioned to be refuted. There is, for example, the argument that, in return for lower admissions standards for their offspring, wealthy alumni contribute money that goes to scholarship students. By this logic, it might save time and trouble simply to sell diplomas for their children to rich alumni parents through the mail.

The argument that outlawing legacy preferences would be a sort of sinister socialistic interference with private institutions is just not convincing. Private colleges and universities are chartered by government, the agent of the democratic citizenry, and they are bound to follow any regulations that the citizenry sees fit to impose—the ban on racial discrimination today, a ban on the class discrimination represented by alumni preference tomorrow. Eliminating legacy preference in college admissions would open up as much as a fifth of the spaces at elite schools for talented Americans of all races who are now passed over in favor of less-qualified students with family connections.

Democratizing the professions, making higher education a universal civic entitlement rationed by demonstrated ability rather than by parental income, and outlawing the oligarchic institution of legacy preference—all of these can be seen as the latest in a series of historic reforms intended to realize the American ideal of a society in which individuals compete, sometimes fiercely, on the basis of their talents, not their family wealth or connections. The abolition of titles of nobility and primogeniture and entail, during the American Revolution; the elimination of property restrictions on citizenship, in the Jacksonian period; the elimination of the ability to buy exemption from military service in wartime; the extension of civil rights to non-Christians, nonwhites, and women—all of these have pushed America a little closer to the goal of a meritocratic social order. The products of affluent and educated families will always derive indirect and informal benefits from their origins; they should not derive any direct and formal benefits. Family advantage may put one ahead at the starting line, but one should still be required to clear the hurdles all by oneself, at every point along the track, before reaching the finish line.

The social market contract would create a floor for wage earners; the war on oligarchy would create a new and more accessible ladder, or staircase. Neither can be taken advantage of by members of the American underclasses, as long as they are, metaphorically, in another room.

There are several hereditary underclasses in the United States. There is a rural white underclass, concentrated in the Appalachians and the Ozarks, and the makings of Hispanic underclasses in the barrios. As important as it is not to neglect these groups, it is even more important to rehabilitate, employ, and integrate the black ghetto underclass of the major metropolitan areas.

The goal must not be to reupholster the ghetto, but to eliminate it completely, through the assimilation of its inhabitants to mainstream American norms, and their gradual dispersal throughout metropolitan suburbs. The rehabilitation of the black underclass, however, must come before its dispersal. Residential class integration should have as its purpose the dispersal of the solid working class—not the underclass. There is no better way to doom a program of mixed-income class integration than to turn it into a program for sending the most desperately poor members of the urban underclass into middle-class neighborhoods. Working-class Americans will resent any program that gives the poor subsidies to live in housing better than theirs. And middle-class and upper-middle-class Americans will have ample reason to oppose programs that bring violent or criminal youth into their neighborhoods.

The decades-long argument about the culture of poverty, sparked by the Moynihan report, is over. The culture of poverty is real. Children who grow up adjusted to the environment of the ghetto grow up maladjusted to workaday America. The ghetto poor are not so much immoral, as moral according to norms governing sex, work, violence, and honor that the larger society rejects. The morality of the ghetto is not a black morality, since most black Americans reject it. It is not dissimilar from poverty cultures among the white poor of today, or among residents of white ghettos in the past (for example, the Irish and Italians of Hell's Kitchen a few generations ago).

It is difficult to imagine a successful program for dispersing the ghetto poor that would not have an intermediate stage of education and acculturation and, if necessary, rehabilitation. That stage would have to involve a period of separation from the ghetto environment and incentives for learning standard English, mainstream manners, and useful skills. The government, perhaps working through charitable or religious institutions, would have little choice but to assume moral as well as material tutelage of its poorest wards, in the hope of making them productive members of the national community. The model might be something like the settlement houses for European immigrants of Jane Addams and other turn-of-the-century social reformers. James Q. Wilson has suggested a revival of the orphanage and the boarding school. A government effort along these lines would combine idealism with a freedom from romantic illusions, like the fantasies of white overclass liberals about ghetto gangsters as romantic countercultural revolutionaries, or the equally romantic fantasies of laissez-faire conservatives about ghetto entrepreneurs. It would be paternalistic, in the best sense of the term. Instead of "maximum feasible participation," the ideal of the romantic countercultural liberals of the sixties, the ideal would be "maximum feasible paternalism."

The old-fashioned left, sounding like a broken record, denounces such notions as racism. Neither the left nor the libertarian right, however, can offer a credible alternative. Referring the problem to the black community is not an answer. Middle-class and affluent black Americans do not, collectively, have either the resources or the authority to help the ghetto poor. The white majority, in the nineteenth and twentieth centuries, had the political power and economic clout to drive the black poor into the ghettos; only the Trans-American majority, in the twenty-first century, will have the collective political power and economic resources to free the ghetto's fourth- and fifth-generation prisoners. If the effort is undertaken at all, it will be not because of an identification between Trans-Americans of all races and the old white supremacists (liberal guilt) but because of an identification between Trans-Americans of all races and the disadvantaged members of their transracial community (liberal nationalism).

The reforms I have suggested here are intended as examples, not as an exhaustive enumeration of all possible liberal nationalist proposals. In discussing reforms, it is important not to lose sight of the basic perception of color-blind liberal nationalism—namely, that the answer to the problem of racial separation by class is not tokenism that chiefly bene-fits affluent nonwhite Americans but the weakening of class barriers and increasing mobility between classes, to the benefit of the transracial American majority. Greater movement from the lower ranks naturally corresponds to an accelerated eviction rate at the top; those moving up should be given a hand, and the skids should be greased for those going down. The goal is not to eliminate the abstract categories of rich and poor—there will be high- and low-income people in any capitalist society (and, in practice, in any noncapitalist society). The goal, rather, is to minimize the correspondence between income categories and *social classes*—to ensure that the rich do not tend to share a common upper-class accent and habits, and that the poor do not tend to have a similar complexion. To put it another way, the goal is a society in which the middle class, as a distinct social class, not merely an economic group, is overwhelmingly dominant. The rich would rise out of the middle class, but their offspring would quickly fall back into it; the ranks of the poor would be made up, for the most part, by unfortunates who had dropped out of the middle class temporarily, rather than by hereditary underclasses whose members are cut off more with each generation from middle-class customs and norms.*

---

*At the beginning of the twentieth century, Herbert Croly summarized the meritocratic ideal in *The Promise of American Life* (1909). His words remain an adequate description of the goal that we have approached in the intervening decades, but have yet to reach: "A democracy, not less than a monarchy or an aristrocracy, must recognize political, economic, and social distinctions, but it must also withdraw its consent whenever these discriminations show any tendency to excessive endurance. The essential wholeness of the community depends absolutely on the ceaseless creation of a political, economic, and social aristocracy and their equally incessant replacement."

Since the 1960s, middle-class, color-blind, social-mobility liberalism has been deserted by the New Left and defeated by the New Right. Now, after the failure of both multicultural tokenism and conservative free-market radicalism, color-blind liberalism should be given a try.

Liberal nationalist reformers who reject the nostrums of the laissez-faire, antistatist right can look for inspiration to one of the right's own heroes: Adam Smith. As Gertrude Himmelfarb notes, Smith "was the first to offer a systematic, comprehensive rationale for high wages" as part of a progressive economy. Smith would have had contempt for the present-day American business elites who, while raising their own compensation to unprecedented levels, argue that wages are too high in the United States: "Our merchants and master-manufacturers complain much of the bad effects of high wages in raising the price, and thereby lessening the sale of their goods both at home and abroad. They say nothing of the bad effects of high profits. They are silent with regard to the pernicious effects of their own gains. They complain only of those of other people." While Smith generally favored the free market, he was willing to countenance government intervention in the domestic economy and trade in the interest of the working classes: "Whenever the legislature attempts to regulate the differences between masters and their workmen, its counsellors are always the masters. When the regulation, therefore, is in favour of the workmen, it is always just and equitable; but it is sometimes otherwise when it is in favour of the masters." A social tariff would certainly seem to fall into Smith's approved class of mercantilistic regulations "in favour of the workmen."

Smith, who was deeply suspicious of guilds and professions, would probably have supported attempts to lower the artificial barriers to entry into professional services that have been erected by our politically powerful professional guilds like the ABA and the AMA in order to boost the fees of lawyers and doctors: "People of the same trade seldom meet together, even for merriment and diversion, but the conversation ends in a conspiracy against the public, or in some contrivance to raise prices." The system of single-payer higher education I have proposed might also find a precedent in Smith's thinking. After all, the Scottish philosopher favored a system of universal public education that was truly radical for its time: "Having spent the better part of two volumes arguing against government regulation," Himmelfarb notes, "he now advanced a scheme requiring a greater measure of government involvement than anything that had ever existed before."⁹ Without the intervention of an enlightened and paternalistic government, Smith feared, the working poor would degenerate into an ignorant and alienated underclass: "in every improved and civilized society this is the state into which the labouring poor, that is, the great body of the people, must necessarily fall, unless government takes some pains to prevent it." Smith dismissed the argument—now being revived by neohereditarian theorists of eugenics like Charles Murray and Richard Herrnstein—that the differences in ability between people of different classes are primarily the result of differences in innate ability: "The difference between the most dissimilar characters, between a philosopher and a common street porter, for example, seem to arise not so much from nature, as from habit, custom, and education. . . . By nature a philosopher is not in genius and disposition half so different from a street porter, as a mastiff is from a greyhound."

With regard to taxes, Smith held what are nowadays considered "liberal" positions. Unlike modern conservatives, who favor a regressive flat tax that affects the poor much more than it does the rich, Smith favored progressive taxes on individuals "in proportion" to their ability to pay. Furthermore, he thought that the "luxuries" of the rich should be taxed while the "necessaries" of the poor should be exempt from taxation. He even favored what might be called a "progressive user fee," arguing that highway tolls on "carriages of luxury" like expensive coaches should be higher than on "carriages of necessary use" like carts and wagons. (The Singaporeans have finally implemented this sensible approach, with an ingenious computer-aided highway toll system that automatically charges the owners of expensive cars higher tolls.)

The true heirs of Adam Smith today, it can be argued, are not free-market libertarian radicals, much less the politically influential business elites that he despised, but rather those who support government interference in the economy to support high wages, reforms that break up the guild-like professions in the interest of consumer savings and social mobility, and inexpensive, universal, quality public education (including higher education)—with the costs of these programs paid for not only by progressive income taxes, but by progressive user fees and sales taxes on the affluent (of a sort that computer technology now makes possible).

As they attempt to repair the damage done to the broad American middle class by market-worshipping conservatives and neoliberals, the liberal nationalists of the twenty-first century would be justified in wearing Adam Smith neckties.

LIBERAL NATIONALISM AND THE FOURTH GRAND COMPROMISE

Dismantling Multicultural America and replacing it with Trans-America would require a generation-long Equal Rights Revolution as sweeping as the Civil Rights Revolution. Opportunities for such sweeping renovation come rarely, usually during or after some major international upheaval; as I showed in Chapter 3, the Civil Rights Revolution itself was triggered in large part by the Cold War. It would be foolish for liberal nationalists to speculate about a timetable for the fourth American revolution. But it is not too early to speculate about the politics of a liberal nationalist movement.

The reconstruction of the American class system, by such means as a new social market contract and a war on oligarchy, would require a broad if diffuse political majority transcending the arbitrary bureaucratic categories of the post-seventies five-race system, a transracial coalition devoted to purging American society of oligarchy and plutocracy, as American law was earlier purged of white supremacy. No stable transracial egalitarian coalition can emerge, however, as long as differential treatment based on race sets Americans labeled as whites, blacks, Hispanics, and Asians against one another in zero-sum struggles for government favors. It is self-defeating to tell non-Hispanic whites (to use the government's absurd term for an enormously diverse population) that morality requires costly discrimination against them on behalf of officially recognized minorities, and then to call upon the very same non-Hispanic whites to join in a "rainbow coalition" promoting the common economic interests of the common man. Either most non-Hispanic whites are the enemy of nonwhite Americans, or they are potential allies in a just crusade for reform; they cannot be enemies for purposes of racial preference programs and at the same time be allies in the voting booth. It is difficult enough to persuade voters to support programs that benefit members of groups other than their own *disproportionately;* it is practically impossible to gain their support for programs that benefit

other groups *exclusively*. This is the reason that advocates of racial preference prefer to have policies promulgated by fiat by judges and bureaucrats, instead of enacted into law by responsive legislatures. But this is
shortsighted. No ambitious program of increasing social equality and social mobility can succeed in any democracy if the majority of the electorate does not consider itself the primary beneficiary. And in this
democracy the majority of the electorate for the foreseeable future will
be the Americans defined by the government as white.

Liberal nationalists have much to learn from the mistakes of their predecessors, the liberal integrationists of the sixties. Both the Kennedy and
Johnson administrations and the conventional color-blind civil rights
leaders acted in such a way as to make any such coalition all but impossible. In the form of "community action," the White House sponsored
what looked very much like black counter-machines backed by affluent
white Episcopalians and Jews trying to destroy Irish- and Italian-domi-
nated city halls—not the way to preserve or extend an alliance. And
color-blind civil rights leaders like Martin Luther King, Jr., in his later
years, and George Wiley came up with a truly terrible idea—mobilizing
the desperately poor as an interest group and getting them to march to
demand their welfare rights. Even the most convinced egalitarians must
have misgivings about completely removing the stigma from living at the
expense of others; Populists, Fabians, and Marxists alike have had no tolerance for shirkers ("He that does not work, neither shall he eat" was a
Populist slogan aimed at beggars as well as rentiers). And there can be no
quicker and more effective way to scare the wits out of the economically
insecure lower middle class, of all races, than to call for marches by the
angry poor culminating in tent cities in public squares.

While many wage-earning black Americans might be enthusiastic recruits to a transracial liberal nationalist movement, even though most of
its beneficiaries would be middle-class and working-class white Americans, it seems unlikely that the conventional college-educated black
elite would easily give up their commitment to racial preferences and
multicultural democracy. The new black overclass, as I argued in Chapter 4, is heavily dependent on affirmative action and government employment, and many black elected officials owe their positions to racial
gerrymandering. Conventional black leaders can therefore be expected
to denounce color-blind liberal nationalism as "white hegemony" or

metaphorical "lynching" or something to that effect. But such ritualized rhetoric on the part of members of the black elite is no longer taken seriously, even by their would-be allies.

For a generation after the Civil Rights Revolution, the black elite had immense moral capital. It squandered that capital, by turning itself into a rigid pressure group with a singleminded devotion to erecting legal privileges for its own members. Liberalism, in the meantime, has been crippled by being identified with a patronage system for black Americans every bit as corrupt as the ethnic machines of previous generations. There are signs that the era in which white liberals uncritically indulged black particularism is approaching an end. In the twenty-first century, American liberalism, if it is to survive, must jettison racial preference and the ideological baggage of multiculturalism and diversity that accompanies it. If black liberals object, then white liberals may have no choice but to break with them and seek allies among Americans of Hispanic and Asian descent.

What incentive would there be for members of the college-educated black overclass to repudiate the racial preference system that benefits them as individuals (even when it does not help disadvantaged members of their categories)? The answer, I think, is recognition of the divisive effect of racial preference. Already Hispanics and blacks are engaged in fierce conflicts across the country as they contest control of city councils, government jobs, government contracting, congressional districting. Sooner or later, it will occur to the losers in these struggles—black leaders here, Hispanic leaders there—that they might be better off in the long run if they devoted their energies to enlarging opportunities as part of a transracial middle-class coalition instead of fighting potential allies. The peasants should stop fighting over the property lines between their tiny plots in the village and direct their united attention to the castle and its fields.

The mass constituency of liberal nationalism, then, would be the transracial American majority—the four fifths of the population whose members lack a four-year college degree and who work as insecure salaried employees. Though it represents the majority of the American population, this group is not adequately or honestly represented by any contemporary American elite. Members of the transracial middle class are not represented directly by the old unions, which represent a dwindling percentage of the workforce, mostly in industries doomed to obsolescence by automation. They are not represented in either party; the Democrats are scarcely less devoted to the narrow short-term interests of big business and the elite professions than the Republicans. Business elites themselves, in an earlier era, took an interest in the well-being of their fellow Americans; but that was before a misguided (though fortunately reversible) policy of free-trade globalism permitted the economic interests of American business to be detached from the well-being of the American majority.

In other countries, a patrician elite or a high civil service with a paternalistic sense of noblesse oblige might act as a countervailing influence checking the subordination of American government to the American business class, but no such "Tory" elites exist in the United States. The closest approximation is found in the federal judiciary; but in practice federal judges tend to exercise their power to promote the material interests, or realize the moral and political ideals, of the tiny white overclass from which most of them come. Nor can intellectuals, as a group, act as spokesmen for the interests of the many. American intellectuals tend to be snobs, deeply disdainful of the culture of middle-class and working-class Americans and hostile to their moral values. Even worse, the American intelligentsia is still colonial in its attitudes, concentrated on the East Coast and looking to London or Paris or Prague for validation, turning its back on Harlem and Nashville and New Orleans and Los Angeles and Seattle. Even if they were not alienated from their own national community, American intellectuals would be unable to speak the language of their countrymen, now that most members of the American intelligentsia have withdrawn to university campuses and become academic bureaucrats communicating with one another in an impenetrable scholastic patois.

If there is to be a liberal nationalist counter-elite, capable of rallying the leaderless Trans-American majority and opposing the white overclass, it would be most likely to coalesce around Congress and the military. That is because the U.S. House of Representatives is the body most responsive (or least unresponsive) to ordinary wage-earning voters, and because the U.S. military recruits more heavily from the white, black and Hispanic wage-earning classes than does the civilian executive or the federal judiciary. An individual president might lead a liberal nationalist movement, but the contemporary presidency, as an institution, is insulated from middle-class pressure and dependent on business (for campaign contributions) and white overclass advisors and appointees. Over time, increasing numbers of dissident members of the white overclass might join a coalescing liberal nationalist counter-elite, as it becomes clear that the present combination of multicultural democracy and plutocracy is leading the country to ruin.

A fourth Grand Compromise, then, might link a new, nationalist counter-elite with the transracial wage-earning majority. The new elite, for its part, would aggressively promote rising living standards for the wage-earning majority; the members of the Trans-American majority, in turn, would support a reformed constitutional system instead of supporting the demagogic would-be strongmen who could otherwise be expected to appear with increasing frequency. The price of this new bargain would be paid in part by the nonwhite overclasses, whose members would lose their racial-preference privileges, but mostly by members of the white overclass, whose political power would be curtailed, and whose taxes would go up.

The political majority based on this new extraconstitutional bargain would resemble the New Deal coalition of Late Euro-America rather than the New Politics/New Right coalitions of Multicultural America. To be successful, a liberal nationalist movement would probably have to take the form of a political party. This is because it will be impossible to dismantle the racial preference system and the built-in structural class biases of Multicultural America overnight. It will take a generation or more to repeal or overrule the major laws, executive decrees, and judicial rulings that have cemented the racial-preference system into American society. Overhauling our corrupt, money-dominated political system will be an effort as difficult as those now underway in Japan and Italy. So will purging overclass privilege from higher education and the professions. These efforts cannot be undertaken by a single heroic president, notwithstanding the fantasy of many Americans that some great Oval Officer, a super-Lincoln or mega-FDR, can miraculously solve problems that were generations, even centuries, in the making. Revolutionary and enduring structural reform must be undertaken gradually by a new political coalition in control of Congress as well as the executive and judiciary.

Of the three, Congress is most important. Unless the United States becomes a presidential dictatorship, all major changes in public policy must be initiated or ratified by federal legislation, and that requires a stable congressional majority. As long as the United States retains its archaic English electoral law instead of proportional representation, the two-party system will probably endure, so that such a liberal nationalist coalition, at least initially, would have to be either Republican, Democratic, or bipartisan.

A bipartisan coalition, like the conservative coalition of Republicans and Southern Democrats that was so important in Congress between the late 1930s and the 1960s, seems quite unlikely. The Solid South had a single overriding goal—preserving segregation—and the monopolization of electoral office and longevity of its members was based on corrupt political practices which have been outlawed. Without such an artificially sustained political base, it is difficult to see how a faction within one of the two major parties could have enough independence of the leadership to function year after year as a de facto third party frequently in alliance with members of the other major party.

Neither of the two national parties today is hospitable to liberal nationalism, as I define it. The Democrats—under FDR, Truman, and LBJ the great champions of the national state and national integration—since McGovern have been identified with the multicultural conception of America as a coalition of groups. The alienation of Democrats from the national sentiments of the American majority accounts, in large part, for the Democratic party's loss of both houses of Congress to the Republican party in the mid-term elections of 1994. Post-sixties Republicans, while they have almost monopolized the language and imagery of American patriotism, have lost contact with the older Republican tradition of strong national government and civil rights (Goldwater, the father of the modern Republican party, voted against the Civil Rights Act of 1964). Jacob Javits, in *Order of Battle* (1964), his defense of the Hamiltonian tradition in the GOP against Goldwaterite conservatives of the South and West, got it right: "This is the spirit which has represented the most dominant strain in Republican history. Hamilton-Clay-Lincoln and Theodore Roosevelt: they represent the line of evolution embodying this tradition."[10] No one of any influence in today's GOP thinks this way. The Democrats, it might be said, believe in the State but not the Nation, while the Republicans believe in the Nation but not the State. Neither party unites the two halves of Hamiltonian nationalism into a theory of the strong and integrated American nation-state.

The particular party or parties used as a vehicle for a liberal national-ist movement—populist Democrats, centrist Republicans, or a new re-form party—is of secondary importance. What is important above all is the mobilization of an electoral majority around the liberal nationalist agenda, to arrest the slow decay of the United States into a pseudo-mul-ticultural oligarchy and renovate it as a meritocratic, melting-pot na-tion-state under a government no longer dominated by the rich and their agents. Liberal nationalism, if successful, would redefine the con-sensus as to what constitutes American identity. Liberal nationalist con-cepts would define the terms of debate for *all* parties in the twenty-first century, in the same way that Appomattox and the Civil Rights Act of 1964 altered the meanings of conservatism and liberalism for genera-tions afterward. The Trans-American "left" and "right" would debate the extent of civil rights for individuals, but both sides would agree that group preferences are illegitimate. Trans-American liberals and conser-vatives would disagree over the details of a new social market contract, not over the everlasting need for a third way between laissez-faire capi-talism and unworkable socialism. If liberal nationalism were to succeed, talk of America as a multicultural society will sound as archaic and grotesque to the ears of twenty-first century Americans as talk of "the Anglo-Saxon mission" and Social Darwinism does to us today. Indeed, in the Fourth Republic, any politician or journalist who claimed that America is not a nation-state, but a collection of American peoples, would disqualify himself from being taken seriously. There might contin-ue to be multiculturalists, of course, just as there are still democratic so-cialists and white supremacists, but they would be on the margins of American political and intellectual life. They would have sects and newsletters, but they would lack the power and influence to do further harm to the country.

LOOKING BACKWARDS

The United States at the end of the twenty-first century was far more dem-ocratic, unified, and prosperous than it had been at the end of the twen-tieth. A hundred years earlier, in the 1990s, the United States had been slowly fissuring along class lines, while its two-hundred-year-old electoral system and thirty-year-old racial preference politics confounded attempts at reform. More than a million immigrants a year, most of them poor, many of them illegal, were crowding into a few cities in a few states. As wages fell in a labor pool increased by immigration and the expatriation of industry, American business elites inflicted further blows on the work-force, scaling back benefits, downsizing, coercing workers into longer hours for less pay. An angry and confused public, failing to realize that the oligarchic structure of American society and obsolescent constitu-tional arrangements were the chief cause of decline, turned from one demagogue and panacea to another.

The crisis came to a climax in the early twenty-first century, when the Senate—by then controlled by a tiny minority of white voters and wealthy national and foreign donors—thwarted the latest of a series of reform packages passed by a House of Representatives responsive to the emerging transracial majority living in the coastal states. When the mili-tary refused to fire on rioters during the riots that followed, the conserva-tive-dominated government was thrown into turmoil. The Fourth American Revolution had begun.

In the decade and a half of instability that followed, the legal and polit-ical structure of the United States was transformed, as the reactionary white conservatives who had dominated the country for so long were fi-nally routed. Racial preferences, a source of interethnic division in states where Hispanics and blacks were now the majority, and government racial labels, which were increasingly inaccurate given the growing num-bers of mixed-race Americans, were abolished forever. The Constitution was reformed, to eliminate the private financing of political campaigns, and to create a new Senate elected by the people of the United States. The adoption of proportional representation destroyed the old Democrat-Republican duopoly and produced a flourishing multiparty system in the United States. The re-invigoration of congressional democracy meant that the American people were now less likely to look anxiously for salva-tion by a dictatorial president.

Campaign finance reform and Senate reform removed the greatest barriers to broader social reform, by drastically diminishing the clout of wealthy whites and small-state whites. Long-overdue reforms that had been killed by free-spending special interests or bottled up in the malap-portioned Senate for decades passed into law at last. Means-testing of federal subsidies and tax breaks brought money pouring into the Federal

Treasury. So did the elimination of special benefits for private interests using federal lands. The Federal Land Grant University Act set aside revenues from the development of federal lands to help defray the costs of the new system of single-payer higher education.

Mass immigration was brought to an end, though a small number of legal immigrants continued to move to the United States under the family reunification program, a small skilled-immigrants program, and humanitarian asylum laws. As the low-skill labor pool shrank and wages went up, corporations began to move their production overseas. Congress, however, put an end to expatriation, by imposing a social tariff, as part of a concerted effort by the governments of the high-wage countries to replace global free trade with a new system of trade based on social-market blocs. World trade declined, but living standards and global productivity rose, as multinational corporations, thwarted in their effort to pursue a cheap-labor strategy, began to invest worldwide in state-of-the-art transplant factories producing goods for local markets and paying good wages to stimulate local demand. In the United States, thanks to rising wages, such factories were soon almost completely automated. Consumption vouchers, funded by income and profits taxes, redistributed buying power from the wealthy few to the burgeoning new middle classes in the personal service industries: health care, teaching, police, entertainment, fashion, marketing.

Though pockets of poverty remained in the United States in the 2090s, the urban ghettos of the twentieth century had long since vanished. Most of the ghetto poor had been successfully integrated into the wage-earning majority, by a combination of workfare and residential deconcentration. In time social integration promoted racial amalgamation. Intermarriage across racial lines was rapidly effacing the old caste distinctions. The typical American of the twenty-second century, the U.S. Census predicted, would have ancestors of several races. Trans-Americans celebrated their diverse racial heritages in the relaxed spirit in which white Americans, at the end of the twentieth century, had indulged a more or less meaningless pride in Irish or German or Polish ancestry.

The mixed-race American population was older, better educated, more prosperous, and more equal than ever before. Thanks to the high-wage, high-tech strategy, the United States led the world in the new frontiers of artificial intelligence and robotics (something that gave

America a welcome edge in never-ending geopolitical rivalries). The elimination of parental income as a factor in access to education at all levels had produced a scientific and cultural Renaissance, as talented Americans who might have languished in underclass ghettos or barrios a few generations before had the opportunity to develop their innate talents to the fullest. Nobel Prizes in the sciences and humanities began to go to the descendants of the twentieth century's white, black, and Hispanic poor.

To be sure, the United States, on the eve of the twenty-second century, was not a utopia. The evils of caste and class continued to exist, though in more subtle forms. Politicians lied, spouses cheated, criminals robbed and murdered and raped. Merit often languished unrecognized while charlatanism was praised; justice was delayed at times and denied at others. The Trans-American republic was not heaven on earth. But it was the closest approximation of the good society that the North American continent had yet seen. Three centuries after the American Revolution, and five centuries after the first English settlement at Jamestown, the promise of American life was finally being fulfilled.

This is not, we can be certain, what histories composed in the twenty-second century will record. The actual development of the United States in the future will depend largely on events that cannot be foreseen. The exercise above is useful, nevertheless. You cannot decide the best way to get there, until you have some idea in your mind of where you want to go.

The difficulties confronting proponents of national renewal should not be underestimated. Machiavelli warns in *The Prince*: "It must be considered that there is nothing more difficult to carry out, nor more doubtful of success, nor more dangerous to handle, than to initiate a new order of things. For the reformer has enemies in all those who profit by the old order, and only lukewarm defenders in all those who would profit by the new."[11]

Cynics may argue that plans to radically improve American society and government are utopian projects that are doomed to fail. History suggests another conclusion. American society has been transformed dramatically for the better every few generations since 1776. When one considers the differences between the United States of 1800 and 1900 and

2000 A.D., then dramatic change seems much more thinkable. Less than a century ago, Americans reformed the Constitution to provide for direct election of senators and an income tax; only sixty years ago, the New Deal assured all Americans of basic economic security; and it was only thirty years ago that the three-century-old white-supremacist caste system was torn down. Again and again in our history, Americans have re-created their state and their society, to reflect new ideals, or to embody old ideals in a better way. A noble but misguided piety should not prevent us from distinguishing what is green and living in the country we have inherited from what is dangerous deadwood. By the same token, excessive skepticism should not paralyze us when action needs to be taken. Sometimes cynical "realists" are less realistic than hardheaded "idealists."

Against the aggressive imperialisms of the partial communities of race and gender and class, liberal nationalism reasserts the complementary ideals of the Nation and the Individual. In the effort to replace Multicultural America with Trans-America, the example of the modernizing American nation-builders a century ago can be a guide. Progressives at the end of the nineteenth century faced problems remarkably similar to those that we face at the end of the twentieth—the decline of the dominance of a superpower that had policed the world and promoted international free trade (Britain in their case, America in ours); the emergence of a new, multipolar world order based on regional military and economic blocs; massive immigration overburdening the institutions of assimilation; corrupt urban political machines and patronage systems; an unrepresentative Senate; the manipulation of politics by free-spending corporate interests and rich individuals; the coexistence of dreadful squalor with plutocratic opulence. Now, as then, renewing the American republic will require a new generation of bold leaders, no longer fighting the battles of the sixties and seventies, a generation of men and women sharing the vision and confidence of Secretary of State John Hay in his eulogy for the murdered President McKinley almost a century ago:

> The past gives no clue to the future. The fathers, where are they? and the prophets, do they live forever? We are ourselves the fathers! We are ourselves the prophets![12]

CHAPTER NINE

The National Story

The ideal of liberal nationalism, as I have described it in the previous two chapters, is an American nation defined by a melting-pot culture, living under a strong, genuinely democratic government that intervenes in the economy to protect and raise the living standards of the wage-earning majority. Liberal nationalism combines individualism in civil rights with transracial fusionism in culture, equal voting power in politics with worker-friendly social market capitalism. The liberal nationalist conception of the United States is uncompromisingly opposed to the multiculturalism of the left and the religious nativism of the right. The goal of liberal nationalism is simple and radical: to peacefully and legally abolish the Third American Republic in a bloodless Fourth American Revolution, and replace Multicultural America with a Fourth Republic of the United States: Trans-America.

Though liberal nationalism is neither liberal nor conservative as those categories are today defined, it has many precedents in American tradition. In its philosophy and program, it is the heir, in many ways, to the great state-building and nation-uniting movements of the American past—Hamilton's Federalists and Lincoln's Republicans, the Progressives of Theodore Roosevelt and the New Deal liberals of Franklin Delano Roosevelt, the abolitionists and the suffragettes and the crusaders against segregation, the champions of the melting pot against the nativists, and the color-blind integrationists. The last major figures in this broad tradition were Lyndon Johnson, the third of the great New Deal presidents, and Martin Luther King, Jr.

Why did this tradition fail? Why did New Deal egalitarianism and color-blind integrationism die in the sixties, to be replaced by McGovernite liberalism and Reaganite conservatism? Why are King and Johnson today symbols of the road not taken, instead of the venerated founding fathers of a post-racist, social-democratic American republic? Why did the civil rights philosophy of James Farmer and Stokely Carmichael, and the political economy of Barry Goldwater, prevail? The answer, I have argued in previous chapters, has a great deal to do with the capture of both the Democratic and Republican parties by the white overclass. But it also has something to do with a failure of vision on the part of the liberal integrationists of the sixties—a failure that is painfully apparent, when contrasted with the success of the New Deal liberals.

The New Deal redefined American identity so successfully that its Late Euro-American conception continues to be the predominant conception, in the absence of a popular multicultural alternative. The pantheon of the presidents considered great, the romanticization of Ellis Island as a symbol of a nation of immigrants, artistic monuments like Gutzon Borglum's Mount Rushmore and Aaron Copland's *Fanfare for the Common Man*—all of these continue to resonate in the public mind, long after the political and economic projects of the New Deal have been taken for granted or forgotten. One can speak of the imagery, the mythology, of New Deal America and be understood. But the imagery of the Great Society? The monuments, the sculptures, the symphonies, the songs and stories? The very term Great Society merely evokes the image of a middle-aged white politician or bureaucrat, wincing, perhaps, at rock song riffs or antiwar chants in the background.

The color-blind phase of the Civil Rights Revolution, it is true, produced an enduring mythology—but it is a divisive mythology. The archetypal image of the Civil Rights Revolution was the scene of protesters being set upon by police dogs. The image is powerful—so powerful, in fact, that every subculture or interest group in the United States since the sixties, from the gay rights movement to the evangelical fundamentalist counterculture, has tried to write itself into that scene. What blacks were in the sixties, we are today, claim the born-agains and the environmentalists and the handicapped, the feminists and the members of the men's movement. Behold us set upon by the dogs; pity us; pass laws on our behalf. The perversion of our political culture by victimology arises from this effort to deny the uniqueness of the black experience with segregation, and to generalize it as a model for all struggles of value or interest, no matter how minor.

This is, as I have said, a powerful imagery—but it is also inflammatory and divisive. Everyone wants to be the protest marchers, but somebody has to play the role of the police with the dogs. One American's Martin Luther King is another's Bull Connor. The evangelicals claim they are being persecuted by the powerful secular humanists; no, no, reply the secular humanists, see how powerful the fundamentalists are, they are Bull Connor, we are King! Black Americans, one might think, would have an objection to this appropriation of the memory of their struggles. But the black political establishment, as we have seen, itself keeps the sixties mythos alive, insisting on seeing a policeman with a dog in every judge who questions a further extension of racial preference.

An American legal-political regime, of the sort I am calling a republic, can be established and can endure without a settled imagery. The Anglo-American republic, in spite of a common fund of Anglo-Saxonist, Protestant, and Whiggish traditions, never really acquired its own distinctive iconography. The Euro-American republic did, but only very late in the day, during the New Deal era from the thirties to the sixties. Multicultural America's iconography is bitterly contested. It would be possible to dismantle Multicultural America and to assemble the institutional framework for a fourth American republic, Trans-America, along the lines described in the last chapter, without having settled on an agreed-upon version of history, an iconography, a pantheon.

Even so, there must, I think, be some guiding conception not only of what the American nation is today (something answered by the liberal nationalist idea of the Trans-American cultural nation) but how it is related to the past. The Trans-American nation so far lacks not only a self-conscious communal identity as something other than a mere citizenry and more than an aggregate of people of different colors, it also lacks its own national story, its own understanding of its origins and its possible future. The American historian William H. McNeill, speaking of "mythistory," has written: "A people without a full quiver of relevant agreed-upon statements, accepted in advance through education or less formalized acculturation, soon finds itself in deep trouble, for, in the absence of believable myths, coherent public action becomes very difficult to improvise or sustain."[1] He concludes, "To be a truth-seeking mythographer is therefore a high and serious calling, for what a group of people knows and believes about the past channels expectations and affects the decisions on which their lives, their fortunes and their sacred honor all depend."[2]

In this chapter I describe what I understand to have been the "believable myths" of the first three American republics. None of these various ways of understanding the origins and destiny of the American nation is wholly adequate for the Trans-American nation-state of the twenty-first century. The chapter, and the book, conclude with speculation about what form might be taken by a liberal nationalist mythistory and pantheon of venerable Americans.

THREE MUSEUMS

Each of the first three republics of the United States has had its own national story or mythistory. The mythistories of Anglo-America, Euro-America, and today's Multicultural America might be illustrated by the device of imaginary museums.

A museum of Anglo-American mythistory—call it the Ceramicus, in neoclassical fashion, after the garden of heroic statuary in ancient Athens—would take the form of a marble temple, in the austere Palladian style favored by Thomas Jefferson for the style of the young republic. Entering through the Doric colonnade, you find yourself in a dim, cool space, the interior of a bisected drum. To the right, the wall curves from a marble-maned statue of Moses to a Christ as white as wool, and on to the cold figure of one of the British Reformers—Wycliffe, or Tyndale, or Knox. To the left, the progression of true religion is paralleled by the progress of republican liberty. The sequence begins with Horatius Cocles symbolizing republican virtue, and ends with one of the heroes of the seventeenth-century English parliamentary revolution against Stuart tyranny. The young John Adams, who was later to be the second president of the United States, wrote in 1765 that contemporary British tyranny would permit American patriots to become "Brookes, Hampdens, Vanes, Seldens, Miltons, Nedhams, Harringtons, Nevilles, Sidneys, Lockes."[3]

Between Horatius and Hampden or Pym stands Alfred the Great, who symbolizes the tradition of Anglo-American constitutionalism. The founding generation, you will recall from Chapter 1, was deeply influenced by the enthusiasm for the Anglo-Saxons of the radical English Real Whigs of the mid-eighteenth century (Catherine Macaulay, author of a famous contemporary history of England arguing that modern British liberty had Saxon roots, visited one of her admirers, George Washington, at Mount Vernon). David Hume, who wrote his own Tory history of England to refute Macaulay's Whig history, thought that attempts to trace modern liberal civilization to ancient Germanic tribal customs were nonsense. He would have looked with disdain and amusement on Thomas Jefferson's enthusiasm for the Anglo-Saxons. The prolific Virginian in fact banned Hume's books from the University of Virginia—Jefferson thought that the skeptical Scottish Tory might be a bad influence on young republicans.

The dominant Anglo-American ideology, inherited from the English Real Whigs, assigned the mission of demonstrating liberty for mankind to the Anglo-Saxon race—whether in Britain or North America—not to any particular *government* of Anglo-Saxons. It was the race that provided the continuity in Anglo-Saxon-American history—from the forests of Germany, to post-Roman Britain, to the Protestant Reformation in England and Northern Europe, the war of Parliament against the Stuarts, the Glorious Revolution, and at last the American War of Independence.

Jefferson took Whig Anglo-Saxon mania further than any of the other founders. Hamilton had little use for Anglo-Saxonism or the cult of neoclassical republicanism: he thought it "as ridiculous to seek for models in the simple ages of Greece and Rome, as it would be to go in quest of them among the Hottentots and Laplanders."[4] Jefferson planned to resurrect Anglo-Saxon institutions in America like "the hundreds of your Saxon Alfred" in the form of wards within counties. He even wrote a grammar of Anglo-Saxon and included it in his curriculum for the University of Virginia, in the hopes that Anglo-American students "will imbibe with the language their free principles of government." As Jefferson wrote, "The battle of Hastings, indeed, was lost, but the natural rights of the nation were not staked on the events of a single battle. Their will to recover the Saxon constitution continued unabated."[5] Bizarre as the idea seems today, for an Anglo-American like Jefferson, the American War of Independence was part of a greater historic effort by Anglo-Saxons in Williamsburg, Philadelphia, New York, and London alike to restore the ancient constitution of the Saxon race. Here is Jefferson, writing in 1776: "Has not every restitution of the antient Saxon laws had happy effects? Is it not better now that we return at once into that happy system of our ancestors, the wisest and most perfect ever yet devised by the wit of man, as it stood before the 8th century?"[6]

Shortly after writing the Declaration, Jefferson served on a committee of the Continental Congress charged with designing a Great Seal of the United States. John Adams wrote his wife, "Mr. Jefferson proposed the children of Israel in the wilderness, led by a cloud by day and pillar of fire by night; and on the other side, Hengist and Horsa, the Saxon chiefs from whom we claim the honor of being descended, and whose political principles and form of government we have assumed."[7] In this view, the American continent, after Saxony and Britain, constituted the *third* and most promising historic homeland of the nomadic and ever-westering Anglo-Saxon nation. A mural on the wall of the Ceramicus, inspired by Jefferson's rejected design for the Great Seal, shows the Saxon migration to formerly Roman and Celtic Britain in the sixth century A.D. In the background are the dragon-prowed ships, in the foreground are hardy barbarian pioneers strolling alongside covered wagons, horses, cattle, and oxen. Looming in front, gazing westward toward the ultimate homeland of their people, are two blond-bearded Germanic warriors, dressed in mail and animal skins, armed with battle-axes and swords—Hengist and Horsa, the earliest Founding Fathers of the Anglo-American nation.

The parallel triumphs of Protestant Christianity and Anglo-Saxon liberty intersect in the alcove that is the focus of this American pantheon. Here the luminous figure of George Washington seems to condense from the ambient shadow, a benevolent demigod as cold as ice and as pure. The *genius locus* of the Anglo-American republic stares down at you with a gaze that commands respect while forbidding intimacy. The deification of the Virginia planter practically invites ridicule, like the nineteenth-century humorist Artemus Ward's description of George Washington: "G. Washington was about the best man this world ever set eyes on. . . . He luved his country dearly. . . . He was a human angil in a 3

kornered hat and knee britches."[8] But laughter is sacrilege in this echo-
ing well of marble and darkness.

Turning, at last, from the grave patriarch, you see for the first time the
frieze that decorates the wall above the pillared entrance. Cincinnatus,
ploughing his field, looks up as a messenger informs him that the Senate
has chosen to make him temporary dictator, in order that he may lead in
the defense of Rome from its enemies, the Volsci and Aequi. In the next
scene, Cincinnatus in armor leads the attack; a triumph through the
streets of Rome follows, not a debauched revel but a sober and stately
pageant. In the final scene, the gentleman-soldier, having renounced a
prerogative that was deed him in trust by the republic, has returned to
the plough, a humble citizen whose arms hang idle on a tree. You look
back at Washington, and see him as did his contemporaries in the era of
Iturbide, and Bolivar, and Bonaparte.

The national story of Anglo-America told how an offshoot of the
Anglo-Saxon race was destined to conquer North America and set an
example for the world of liberal government and true (Protestant Christian) religion. This myth of Anglo-Germanic racial destiny was superseded, in Euro-America, by the quite different conception of a unique
American ethnogenesis—the formation of a new Caucasian nation from
the blending of European immigrant groups in the United States. The
American nation would be, not an English diaspora, but a population of
generic Europeans. The Second Republic of the United States, Euro-
America, was particularly successful in producing a widely shared vision
of American history, with exemplary figures like the Pilgrims, the Founding Fathers, the Western Pioneers, and a corresponding set of symbols—
the neo-Roman buildings and monuments of Washington, D.C., the
Statue of Liberty, Mount Rushmore, the cowboy mythology. The Euro-
American account of national history, like the Anglo-American, took it
for granted that there was an extrapolitical American ethnic nation, indeed, a racial nation, which had a history that could not be reduced simply to the history of its liberal and democratic institutions of government.

The monument to Euro-America's mythistory is classical in inspira-
tion, but its classicism has little in common with the austere style of the
Anglo-American Ceramicus. The manner is Imperial Roman, or rather,
Imperial American, the self-important Beaux-Arts *Romanitas* of the
White City at the Chicago World's Fair and the great white fleet of

McKim, Mead, and White flagship office towers on the boulevards of new metropoli. Inside, the first sight you behold are three great marble statues: Jefferson, author of the Declaration of Independence, patron saint of democratic idealism; James Madison, remembered for his contributions to the Constitutional Convention and partial authorship of the Federalist, a symbol of constitutional unionism; and finally the figure who symbolizes the synthesis of Liberty and Union, Abraham Lincoln. Here Lincoln is portrayed as the Great Commoner, a favorite uncle or a friendly neighbor, an average man the size of Paul Bunyan. Lincoln is not only a god of democracy, but a democrat among gods.

Of Lincoln, Robert Lowell wrote: "For us and our country, he left Jefferson's ideals of freedom and equality joined to the Christian sacrificial act of death and rebirth."9 A similar sentiment moved Boston's early twentieth-century Mayor James Michael Curley, during a visit to the Lincoln Memorial in 1923, to exclaim that when the "struggle and sacrifice for human rights and the blessings of liberty and equality were about to be lost, He sent us a savior—Lincoln."10 In a tribute to the sixteenth president by the constitutional scholar Martin Diamond, the divinization of Lincoln reaches a point that has yet to be exceeded:

> He was *of* us, and he was *for* us, but he was not *by* us. . . . His greatness of soul and mind belong not to us, but to man as man. He transcended the conditions of any society as such. But what we can everlastingly claim is that we did accept this prince of men, we gave ourselves to him, we let him lead us, and we have the sense to love him.11

Beyond Lincoln, at the far end of the gallery, glows a mural. European immigrants, idealized, heroic, gaze up at the Statue of Liberty as their boat nears Ellis Island. The promise of the melting pot seems realized already in their features; they might be German or Irish, Polish, perhaps even Italian or Jewish. America, the mural seems to say, is the Promised Land of the generic European.

In the other murals that decorate the gallery, American history is reduced to a few emblematic scenes. The familiar scene of the First Thanksgiving stands for the colonial era; Indians and Pilgrims dine in amity on turkey, pumpkin, corn. No Indians can be seen in the mural that shows a party of westering pioneers at the mouth of a mountain gap, though the vigilance of the buckskinned men and the anxiety of their bonnetted brides suggests that the land has not been wholly secured for their kind. Of black Americans, there is not a sign; the Civil War mural shows the surrender at Appomattox, a scene that symbolizes the reconciliation of white Americans; a coda, as it were, to the mural of the signing of the Declaration of Independence on the facing wall.

On reaching the far end of the gallery, you look back and see the mural over the entrance: Columbus, wading ashore on Hispaniola. Hispaniola/Ellis Island. . . . The concept behind the iconography suddenly becomes clear. The American people are not Anglo-Saxons, and American history does not begin with Sir Walter Ralegh or Captain John Smith. The American people are Europeans-in-America.

In the Third Republic of the United States, Multicultural America, the very idea of a common national ethnocultural identity is rejected. Much of the public political symbolism of an older America remains, though many inherited public symbols have been reinterpreted (the Lincoln Memorial, for example, now means civil rights, rather than white egalitarianism or national unity). Still, the Third American Republic has not come up with its own, extrapolitical national story. Indeed, by its own terms, it cannot. In a multicultural society, while there might be an agreed-upon civic iconography, representing the ideals and institutions of the common government, there must be as many national stories and as many high cultures as there are official racial nationalities.

Multiculturalists, if they were true to the logic of their own ideologies, would support parallel histories for separate racial and ethnic groups. Instead of the history of the American nation, we would have the history of white Americans, the history of black Americans, the history of Hispanic Americans, and so on. Instead, multiculturalism and pluralism are usually represented, in debates over public-school history texts, by advocates demanding greater representation of individuals and episodes from the history of a particular group in a general history—not a separate Hispanic history, but more Hispanics in a general American history.

Such tokenism is evident in successive revisions of Todd and Curti's popular high school history text, *Triumph of the American Nation*. In 1950, the text did not mention Crispus Attucks, the obscure black stone-thrower (he may not even have been black) killed in the so-called Boston Massacre; in the 1986 version (which does not mention the sinking of the *Lusitania*) Attucks gets half a page as the first martyr of the American Revolution. In the same 1986 edition, a painting of the *Bonhomme Richard* of John Paul Jones has been replaced by a painting of Deborah Sampson, a woman who disguised herself as a man to fight in the Continental Army. However well-intentioned, this kind of thing is ultimately patronizing to those it intends to benefit. Somehow, many women were able to choose careers in the U.S. military on their own, without the example of Deborah Sampson to inspire them. The American Indian writer Vine Deloria, Jr., has poked fun at this "All-American Platoon" concept: "Under this theory members of the respective racial minority groups had an important role in the great events of American history. Crispus Attucks, a black, almost single-handedly started the Revolutionary War, while Eli Parker, the Seneca Indian general, won the Civil War and would have concluded it sooner had not there been so many stupid whites abroad in those days."[12] This approach replaces one kind of pious fraud with another. Deborah Sampson, however valiant, was hardly typical of patriot women, whose contributions took more conventionally feminine forms (like that, say, of Betsy Ross). And from all the attention given Crispus Attucks, one would never guess that the overwhelming majority of black Americans who fought in the War of Independence fought *against* the United States on behalf of their freedom—and the first Great Emancipator, King George III of England. Rather than reflecting a really fresh look at American history, the tokenist approach parallels the Multicultural regime in co-opting representatives of aggrieved groups—a black American here, a white woman there—to shore up an otherwise unchanged structure.

Let us follow a second-grade class at a multicultural school, as they leave their studies of ancient Egyptian medicine and non-Western mathematics for a field trip to a Multicultural Heritage Center in that harmonious mosaic metropolis, Los Angeles. The Multicultural Heritage Center is housed in a ring, as befits an essentially cyclical view of history as Paradise, Paradise Lost, Redemption, and Paradise Regained.

PARADISE. In the first gallery, multimedia installations—dioramas, nature films, folk art, postmodern performance art—evoke a pre-Columbian Arcadia, in which indigenous Americans lived in perfect harmony with each other and the abundant wildlife. (The Aztecs are not shown.)

PARADISE LOST. Scenes of horror and subjugation following the European invasion of the Americas. The teachers lead their frightened charges through a labyrinthine House of Horrors, as a disturbing sound track rolls on: screams, gunfire, the crackle of flames, the crack of whips. This gallery, like Madame Tussaud's, features lurid waxwork atrocities. Columbus's debauched crewmen are borne on litters by enslaved Arawaks. North American Indian villages lie deserted, laid waste by disease. The Middle Passage is shown, with dead Africans mingled with the living in the ship's fetid hold; and then there is the auction block. A female white indentured servant is publicly flogged; company goons attack workers, in a turn-of-the-century strike. Cherokee elders collapse, along the Trail of Tears; the baffled Nisei stare through barbed wire. This is American history as Arnaud's Theater of Cruelty, as Grand Guignol. Though it is not the whole truth, it is true.

REDEMPTION. Screams and groans are replaced by inspiring anthems, as the children are led into a gallery devoted to scenes of emancipation. Although some white males are given their due—Garrison, Sumner— for the most part the exhibits glorify the self-emancipation of blacks and other nonwhite ethnic groups, women, workers. Frederick Douglass, Sojourner Truth, Harriet Tubman, Booker T. Washington, W. E. B. DuBois, Malcolm X, and Martin Luther King, Jr., are joined by Susan B. Anthony, the leaders of the American Indian Movement (AIM) and Cesar Chavez, the Wobblies, and Jesse Jackson's Rainbow Coalition.

PARADISE REGAINED. The final chamber, a great drum-shaped space, shows a new Arcadia, pre-Columbian America re-created in a modern setting. The room, with anthropological dioramas around its edges, symbolizes a continent in which separate but equal tribes live in harmony. Here, African-Americans celebrate Kwanzaa, there, Euro-Americans celebrate Christmas, Hispanics celebrate Cinco de Mayo, Chinese-Americans celebrate the Chinese New Year. And in the center of the spacious gallery there is nothing, nothing at all; for Multicultural America *has* no center.

THE TRANS-AMERICAN STORY

Those who reject the fabrication of a multicultural history to support modern American racial preference in public policy tend to settle for one of two alternatives. The nativists of the extreme right wish to simply restore the pieties of the older Euro-American and Anglo-American past; some conservative journals actually carry advertisements for complete facsimile reprints of the original *McGuffey's Reader.* More moderate conservatives and centrist liberals, realizing that there is much validity in accusations that the older American consensus history was full of unexamined assumptions about race and sex, do not fantasize about simple restoration. Rather, as we have seen, they put their faith in a democratic universalist reading of American history, hoping to minimize disputes over the conflict by redefining American history as the progressive realization of a few, mostly procedural, civic ideals on which everyone, or almost everyone, can agree in principle—equal rights before the law, the right to vote: America as a political convention in the making.

None of these approaches is adequate as a basis for the shared memory of the Trans-American nation. The multicultural version must be rejected, along with the cultural pluralist, because the American people are a nation, not a collection of racial nationalities or ethnic groups. Euro-American and Anglo-American history cannot be simply recycled, as the nativists would prefer; they are too implicated in white supremacy. Universalist idealism in history must be rejected, because there is more, much more, to the history of the American people than a series of extensions of the franchise. What is needed is an account of America's origins and history from a liberal nationalist perspective, selecting what from that perspective is most important to us, without alteration or elision of unpleasant fact.

Is the enterprise conceivable? Fears of the abuse of history by ideology are well-founded. The term "national history" can evoke the image of schoolchildren at their desk, reciting the same passages at precisely the same hour, according to the directives of some Napoleonic Ministry of Education or Ministry of Culture. Such old-fashioned enlistment of culture in the service of bureaucratic regimentation, though quite bad enough in itself, was relatively benign compared to the abuses of the idea of national culture by modern dictatorships. To be sure, the frequent abuse of national history for tendentious political purposes makes many suspect of the very enterprise. Nationalist historians are not always as candid in revealing their purposes as was the West Indian politician Eric Williams in 1962, describing his goal in writing a history of Trinidad and Tobago: "The aim was to provide the people of Trinidad and Tobago on their Independence Day with a National History, as they have already been provided with a National Anthem, a National Coat of Arms, National Birds, a National Flower, and a National Flag."[13] This kind of crudely propagandistic history inspired the English philosopher Michael Oakeshott to dismiss all national history: "We may be offered 'A History of France,' but only if its author has abandoned the engagement of an historian in favor of that of an ideologue or a mythologist shall we find in it an identity—*La Nation* or *La France*—to which the differences that compose the story are attributed."[14] One might reply that there is far more lasting evidence of something called France than of something called Michael Oakeshott.

An allergy to the very idea of a national history is an understandable reaction, but it is mistaken—as mistaken as the idea that nationalism in politics is, by its very nature, the ally of intolerance and tyranny. Just as there is an inclusive and enlightened liberal nationalism distinct from illiberal nativism, so there can be a conception of national history that is not simply a tool of political regimentation or a weapon in the arsenal of a dominant class, race, or ethnic group. Indeed, liberal nationalism in politics can scarcely exist without the belief that the cultural nation has an existence, and hence a history, distinct from that of the government, however much the two may partly blend. What is more, to the extent that American liberal nationalism de-emphasizes race, religion, and political belief as the criteria that define nationhood, it becomes necessary to put more weight on a common public memory, as well as a common national language and culture, as the most important elements defining and uniting Americans.

A Trans-American national story would resemble the Euro-American in being the story of the formation of a new American people through the mingling of many; it would differ inasmuch as it would not be limited to Americans of European descent. It would not be a cheerful Disneyland costume pageant, but a story of race war and racial amalgamation,

of culture war and cultural synthesis, a tragedy of feuding and intermarrying families, a tragedy whose conclusion is far from certain.

As the epic of the making of a concrete, historic nation, defined by
language, custom, and values, the Trans-American national story would
concentrate less on political ideology than on the fundamentals of history: the conquest and peopling of a national territory. Conquest comes
first, for the simple reason that there cannot be a nation-state without a
settled nation, and there cannot be a settled nation without a national
territory—a territory which, in most cases, and certainly in the case of
the United States, was won from rival nations by war.

There have been four great formative wars in the history of the American nation: the French and Indian War, the Revolutionary War, the Mexican War, and the Civil War (the War of 1812 was very limited in its
effects and consequences). Two of these major struggles, the French and
Indian War and the Mexican War, can be described as *homeland* wars;
they determined what regions of North America would be inhabited by
English-speakers. The Revolutionary War and the Civil War were *sovereignty* wars; at stake in them were issues of political governance—independence from London, unity under Washington, D.C.

The influence of democratic universalism is responsible for the widely
held conception among Americans that the Revolutionary and Civil
Wars were "good" wars—that is, wars over high principle—while the
Mexican War was a "bad" war, with ignoble motives—territorial aggran-
dizement, relative national power. As for the French and Indian War, it is
forgotten, thanks to the influence of the absurd fallacy that the American
nation, and not merely the American federal government, was "created"
in 1776.* The obvious objection to the de-emphasizing of the homeland
or territorial wars is that the acquisition of the territory precedes disputes
over how it is to be governed. Even the most ethereal "idea-state," even
the most exemplary liberal democracy, must have a material base in the
form of a distinct territory or territories, in which a particular population
resides. A people united by an idea must have an address.

From a liberal nationalist perspective, then, the state-extenders and

---

*The implication of the anti-expansionist, purely idealistic reading of American history is that the
only "good" wars are civil wars in which we Americans kill one another.

state-preservers are if anything more important, as a matter of logic as well as a matter of fact, than the constitution-drafters and constitution-reformers. The greatest of the state-extenders are the commanders who defended and extended the territory of English-speaking North Americans: General James Wolfe, conqueror of French North America; General Sam Houston, hero of the Texas war of independence, which turned a region the size of Germany into part of the American homeland; and General Winfield Scott, conqueror of Mexico. Looking on are their political masters: Prime Minister William Pitt; Andrew Jackson, the covert supporter of the Texan war; and the most successful of imperial presidents, James K. Polk. The great rivals (not villains) are the great warriors of the adversary nations—the French General Montcalm (who died, along with General Wolfe, in the battle of Quebec) and the Mexican general and dictator Santa Anna (defeated both by Houston in 1836 and Scott in 1847). Wolfe, Houston, and Scott—soldiers of the British Empire, the Texas Republic, and the United States, respectively—are the greatest military heroes of the homeland wars. They are equaled, not surpassed, in importance by the heroes of the sovereignty wars, by Washington and his generals, who won American independence, and Lincoln and his generals, who ensured that the United States would remain united.

In a liberal nationalist history of the American cultural *nation,* as opposed to a democratic universalist history of the U.S. federal *government,* the struggles of Wolfe and Montcalm for the interior of the continent, and of Scott and Santa Anna for the West, would receive as much attention as the rivalry of Grant and Lee, or the struggle of Washington with Cornwallis. The question of *how much* of the North American continent was to be conquered and colonized by the English-speaking population obviously is as important, if not more important, than the question of *whether* that territory, or parts of it, would be governed from London, Washington, Ottawa, Austin, or Richmond. Whether we approve or disapprove of their deeds is irrelevant; a contemporary Englishman may denounce William the Conqueror all he likes, that will not alter the fact that he is in some way William's work. Just as modern Latin Americans need not praise the rapacious conquistadors who founded their societies, so we need not venerate the conquerors whose legacy we have inherited; but in order to understand our origins we have no choice but to remember them.

After the conquerors of the national homeland, the culture-founders deserve the greatest priority. In an 1802 address commemorating the Pilgrims, John Quincy Adams recalled the "Founders"—Raleigh, Calvert, Penn, Bradford, Winthrop.[15] Today, a typical list of "Founders" would include names like Washington, Jefferson, Madison, and Hamilton—a result of the confusion of founders of the American nation with founders of the U.S. federal government. We should distinguish between state-founders (the drafters of the Constitution) and culture-founders, who bequeath the ideologies and norms that shape a nation for generations afterward. Only the latter, the culture-founders, are actually like "legislators" in the classical sense—individuals who led large groups of people to a new home in North America, or who reformed the mores and religion of a substantial population. Compared to such Lawgivers, mere Constitution-drafters and elected legislators are of secondary importance. Framers improve the government of a people; Founders *created* the people in the first place.

The real Founders of our nation, in this sense, were, among others, the great colonial impresarios, responsible not only for settling large tracts of the core of Anglophone America, but for settling them with certain selected populations with particular characteristics, and promulgating certain laws and social codes. We also find, among exploited populations like black Americans, leaders who shaped the consciousness of a major subculture and created institutional structures to mobilize the collective strength of its members. Much more than the later political-legal Framers, the white and black founders of the basic American regional subcultures tended to be driven by intense Christian faith.

Here are a few of the *real* founders of the Trans-American nation:

JOHN WINTHROP (1558–649). A Suffolk lawyer, Winthrop was the governor of the Massachusetts Bay colony for much of its early history. He was one of the major leaders of the great migration which brought 80,000 Puritans to New England during the 1630s, when Charles I, ruling England without Parliament, sought to purge the Anglican church of dissenters through his instrument, Archbishop William Laud (later executed during the English Civil War). The populous and fecund Bay colony itself sent out colonists to settle Connecticut and the rest of New

England. Everywhere the Puritans settled, they established a regiment-ed, vicious Calvinist regime, with strict Sabbath-keeping and sumptuary laws, and a list of capital offenses lifted directly from the Pentateuch—witchcraft, idolatry, blasphemy, and even rebelliousness by children all merited the death penalty. The Puritan religious authoritarians not only engaged in witch-hunts but tortured and executed male and female Quaker missionaries and other non-Calvinist Christians. John Winthrop's statement (borrowed from the Sermon on the Mount), "We shall be as a City upon a Hill, the eyes of all people are upon us," has become a staple of American political rhetoric, but modern Americans can only look back with horror on the New England Puritans. While the sinister Puritan code has long been repudiated, some New England cultural innovations remain part of North American national culture: baseball, football, Thanksgiving, and right-wing Protestant fundamentalism, which has found a new home in the Southern and Western states.

SIR WILLIAM BERKELEY (1606–1677). More than any other individual, Sir William Berkeley is responsible for shaping the Old South, with disas-trous results that linger to this day. An Oxford-educated courtier and playwright, Berkeley became Royal Governor of Virginia in 1642 and governed the crown colony with an iron hand for 35 years. Under his rule, Virginia ceased to be a struggling outpost and became a prosperous and highly stratified plantation society. The population rose from 8,000 when Berkeley took over to 40,000. The governor granted vast estates and political favors to other Royalist cavaliers, fleeing from civil war and Puritan rule in England. His allies formed an interlocking network of rich families that dominated Virginia politics and society for centuries. The monopolization of power and wealth by this oligarchy helped pro-voke Bacon's Rebellion, an uprising of backwoodsmen, in 1676. The re-bellion was savagely crushed. Berkeley's authoritarianism—aristocratic, rather than religious—was expressed in Anglican intolerance of other Christian denominations in Virginia (today's southern evangelical Protestantism has northern ancestors), and the ancient Southern hostil-ity toward public education. Berkeley declared in 1671: "I thank God there are no free schools nor printing, and I hope we shall not have these (for a) hundred years; for learning has brought disobedience, and heresy, and sects into the world, and printing has divulged them, and libels against the best government. God help us from both!" The slave-planter oligarchy established by Berkeley, after helping to create and govern the early United States, tried to destroy the United States in 1860; reconstituted as the Bourbon oligarchy of the New South, these rich families blighted the lives of nonelite white and black southerners well into the twentieth century.

SIR WILLIAM PENN (1644–1718). If New England and Virginia represent two kinds of illiberalism, religious and aristocratic, in early Pennsylvania anticipations of modern American tolerance and pluralism can be found. The Society of Friends was founded in England by George Fox (1624–91), a Protestant visionary who began teaching his doctrine of the Inner Light in 1646. William Penn, the Oxford-educated son of a rich naval officer, became a soldier himself before converting to "Quakerism" as Fox's sect became known. Imprisoned several times, Penn wrote *The Great Case of Liberty of Conscience* while confined, and impressed many people, including his friend and benefactor King Charles II. The king, who owed Penn's father money, repaid the debt by granting the largest of three Quaker colonies—West Jersey, Delaware, and Pennsylvania—to Penn as Lord Proprietor (legend has it that Charles II himself wrote in "Penn" before the proposed name "Sylvania"). The Pennsylvania colony, located in the Delaware Valley at a place that George Fox, visiting, had urged on Penn, became a place of refuge for Quakers, German Pietists, and other dissenting Christians. Today's mainstream American accent owes a great deal to the English Midlands speech, modified by German influence, of the Pennsylvanian colonists, just as American plainness in dress and speech, religious tolerance, political democracy (Penn, a Whig, helped save John Locke from prison), and egalitarian dislike for aristocracy owe much to the Quaker ethos. American Quakers, like their British counterparts, led the way in both industrialization and the abolition of slavery.

RICHARD ALLEN (1760–1831). Allen has been called "the Father of the Negro." A slave who bought his freedom with money he had earned, Allen moved to Philadelphia and organized the Bethel African Methodist

Episcopal Church in 1794. That same year, along with another black minister, Absalom Jones, Allen issued a pamphlet denouncing slavery and racism. He opened a day school for children and a night school for adults. In 1800, Allen and other black Philadelphians petitioned Congress to end slavery; the anticolonization movement, defending the right of black Americans to stay in their American homeland, was launched at Allen's Bethel AME church in Philadelphia in January 1817. In his later years, Richard Allen was elected president of the first national black convention in 1830. Allen can truly be considered a Lawgiver for the black American population; combining religious evangelism with civil rights activism, he acted as a model for successors like Martin Luther King, Jr.

BRIGHAM YOUNG (1801–1877). Raised in New York, Young converted to the Church of Jesus Christ of Latter-day Saints (the Mormons) in 1832. He became an Apostle in 1835 and traveled to Britain as a missionary in 1840–41. Assuming command of the Mormons after Joseph Smith was lynched in 1844, Young organized the migration of 16,000 Mormons from Illinois to Utah in 1846–52. He also established a Perpetual Emigrating Fund Company, which brought 80,000 converts from Britain, Scandinavia, and western Europe to Utah and 350 other Mormon settlements in the West between 1852 and 1877. A prolific preacher—over 500 of his sermons survive—Young was one of the great organizing geniuses of American history. He contracted to build sections of the transcontinental telegraph lines and railroad. Governor of the Utah territory from 1851–58, Young used his influence to give Utah women the vote in 1870. Among his other monuments are the Mormon Tabernacle in Salt Lake City, Brigham Young University, and the University of Utah (formerly the University of Deseret). The bee, a symbol of industry the Mormons adopted from the utopian Fourierists of the early nineteenth century, evokes the hive-like, communitarian ethos of the Mormon West—an ethos which, in a more liberal form, is more relevant to the crowded urban and technological America of the twenty-first century than the frontier individualism of the Old West.

These visionaries and others helped to plant sections of North America with settler populations, or (like Allen) to mold the character of populations already here. By selecting immigrants who shared certain values—whether aristocratic, as in the case of Berkeley, or modest and egalitarian, as in the case of the Quaker William Penn—the impresarios established regional cultures that shape American society to this day. One need not share their religious enthusiasms to adopt their ethics. Their values come in secular as well as Christian forms: there are, it can be argued, a Puritan secularism, a Cavalier secularism, a Quaker secularism. They are more important than the Patriots of 1776 and the Framers of the Constitution; while the Framers founded the nation-state, the impresarios founded the nation.

Only after the conquerors and the culture-founders have been enumerated should we turn to the political founders of the American nation-state and their illustrious emulators. Here, too, the absurd overemphasis on the eighteenth-century Founding Fathers in conventional American discourse would be corrected. Those who improve the Constitution by amending it in the light of greater experience and sounder analysis surely deserve credit along with those responsible not only for its virtues but for its defects. In the history of Trans-America, the Constitution-framers of the Philadelphia Convention will have to make room on Parnassus for the Constitution-repairmen: the Reconstruction Republicans, the turn-of-the-century Progressives, and the leaders of the New Deal and the color-blind phase of the Civil Rights Revolution, Franklin Roosevelt and Harry Truman and Lyndon Johnson and Hubert Humphrey, who amended the Constitution in spirit rather than in the letter. A certain amount of room needs to be left; revising the U.S. Constitution, formally or informally, will be one of the urgent challenges confronting the ablest leaders of twenty-first century America.

Sharing honor with the drafters and amenders of the federal constitution are great renovaters of the republic who never exercised political power, political and social reformers who have enlarged our conception of citizenship and nationality. First among these is Frederick Douglass, surrounded by the great black and white abolitionists: Henry Highland Garnet, William Lloyd Garrison, Sojourner Truth, Wendell Phillips, Samuel Ringgold Ward, Thaddeus Stevens, Charles Sumner. Here, too, are Elizabeth Cady Stanton and Susan B. Anthony, A. Philip Randolph and Martin Luther King, Jr., and Bayard Rustin; here is Franz Boas, the greatest of the Jewish-American intellectuals and activists who helped to destroy the philosophical and political foundations of white supremacy; here are Horace Mann and Jane Addams, representing countless anonymous Americans whose labors on behalf of literacy and civility and a humane standard of living for all are less dramatic but no less important than the conquest of countries or the drafting of government charters.

THE TRANS-AMERICAN PANTHEON

From among the members of the Trans-American pantheon, a few might be selected, to serve as emblems of the principal values of liberal nationalism, as totems, as tutelary spirits. The figures would be different, I think, from the trinity of late Euro-America: Jefferson, Madison, and Lincoln.

Thomas Jefferson presents us with the most remarkable example, to my knowledge, of a figure who is venerated for sentiments which for the most part he did not possess. His views have been consistently (and, in some cases, no doubt deliberately) misconstrued, much to the benefit of his contemporary reputation. The Jefferson quoted by Democrats and Republicans alike, by Chinese demonstrators and Eastern European dissidents, is a kind, benevolent, republican philosopher-prince, a figure at once timeless and up-to-date, the patron saint of radical democracy, a kind of Tom Paine without an edge to his voice. It is this Jefferson—this pseudo-Jefferson, one might say—who with Washington and Lincoln is the only American statesman to be honored with his own memorial in Washington, D.C.

The real Thomas Jefferson was a figure far different, and infinitely less attractive, than the Jefferson of the Memorial and the speechwriter and the pro-democracy dissident. He was the patron saint, not simply of a vague conception of liberal democracy, but of a particular, narrow, and to, most of us, repellent, version of liberal democracy—a version based on pseudoscientific racism, white supremacy, states' rights, and anti-industrial agrarianism. Far from being a humane prophet, a saint who belongs to the world, like Tolstoy or Gandhi, this rich Virginian planter-politician was in many ways the greatest southern reactionary, in a tradition of southern parochialism that flows from him, through John C. Calhoun and Jefferson Davis, to its final miserable estuary in the careers of mid-twentieth century Dixiecrats like Theodore Bilbo and Strom Thurmond.

The real Thomas Jefferson, as I have shown elsewhere in this and other chapters, was a fervent believer in white supremacy and the superiority of the Anglo-Saxon branch of the white race. His Anglo-Saxonism and racism were not tangential to his thought and career; neither his views on the colonization of black Americans nor his elaborate political and economic theories can be understood except as elements of a single project of preserving the purity of the Anglo-American race. Jefferson was obsessed, in particular, by the fear that his precious Anglo-Saxon nation would be corrupted by intermarriage with nonwhites. Fear of miscegenation was perhaps the most consistent aspect of his thought, from his youth to his old age. During the American Revolution, Jefferson, as a member of a Virginia legislative committee charged with revising state law, helped to tighten the slave codes and forbid free blacks from becoming citizens—even as rules governing the immigration of whites were liberalized. The Virginia legislature rejected, as too harsh, another proposal of Jefferson's, which would have banished from the state any white woman bearing "a child by a negro or mulatto," on pain of the enslavement of the child.[16] Jefferson supported the Northwest Ordinance, which banned slavery in the northwest territories; later, however, he changed his mind, arguing during the Missouri debates in 1820 in favor of the "diffusion" of slavery through all of the states, north and south (a fact that is never taught in civics classes). Jefferson, it is true, favored emancipation in principle, but only if "*expatriation* could be effected."[17] In 1814 we find Jefferson in retirement counseling a fellow slave owner not to free his adult slaves for fear that this would encourage their "amalgamation with the other color," that is, whites.[18] Jefferson practiced what he preached; of the several hundred slaves he owned in his lifetime, he freed only eight, bequeathing the rest to his heirs to work to pay off his exorbitant debts (around two dozen of Jefferson's slaves escaped, during the American Revolution, to fight on the side of the British). Jefferson's record looks all the shabbier when it is contrasted with that of George Washington, who refused to buy or sell slaves, and who arranged for the liberation, after his wife's death, of his own.

Even if Jefferson's racism, which he shared with generations of white

Americans, might be forgiven him, there remain his other views. He was opposed to cities. He was opposed to factories. He was opposed to standing armies. He was opposed to conventional diplomacy. He was opposed to all but the most minimal authority on the part of the federal government. Every major feature of the modern United States—from racial equality to Social Security, from the Pentagon to the suburb—represents a repudiation of Jeffersonianism. Taking the racism, antistatism and agrarianism out of Jefferson's thought is like taking the class analysis, the dialectic, and the call for revolution out of the thought of Marx. What, in either case, remains except for vague and unobjectionable aspirations to better mankind? Though everyone today claims to be a Jeffersonian, the only genuine contemporary Jeffersonians are cranky, reactionary conservatives, who think the country went wrong with the North's victory in the Civil War, or industrialization, or desegregation. The rest of us should be honest enough to let them have *their* Jefferson; he happens to be the real one.

For these reasons, Jefferson cannot be an important figure for liberal nationalists—unless, perhaps, he is to symbolize the major fallacies and evils that we in the United States have overcome. The place of Jefferson, in today's pantheon, should be taken, in a Trans-American pantheon, by his arch-rival, Alexander Hamilton.

There is no great Hamilton Monument in Washington, D.C., to compete with the Lincoln and Jefferson Memorials and the Washington Monument, only a modest statue in front of the Treasury Department. Only five thousand visitors a year go to the Grange, Hamilton's modest home in Harlem, compared to the 500,000 who visit Jefferson's luxuriant Monticello. Now and then Hamilton is invoked by those seeking to justify policies of economic nationalism or realism in foreign policy. To all but a few historians, however, Hamilton remains unknown. This, despite the fact that his life—from his years as a child prodigy in the Caribbean through his tempestuous tenure as President Washington's prime minister, threatened by his scandalous affair with Mrs. Maria Reynolds, to his death at 47 in a duel at the hands of Aaron Burr—is as dramatic as any in the annals of the American republic. And Hamilton's influence on the United States can be seen everywhere. As Washington's aide-de-camp, he played a vital role in American independence. Later he helped initiate the move toward a more centralized union that resulted in the Philadelphia convention of 1787 and the federal constitution. As Secretary of the Treasury, he established the fiscal infrastructure of the new republic; his Bank of the United States was the precursor of the Federal Reserve. Hamilton not only articulated the theory of tariff-based industrial policy that would later inspire American, German, and Japanese modernizers, but organized The Society for Useful Manufactures (SUM), the first American research institute and industrial conglomerate, sited on 38 acres by the Passaic River falls at Paterson, New Jersey. He founded the New York *Post*, the oldest surviving newspaper in New York, and defended freedom of the press in *People v. Croswell*. He helped to found the Bank of New York. The U.S. military academy at West Point grew out of another Hamiltonian project (though he and Washington were frustrated in their desire to found a National University for civilian administrators). His interpretation of the federal constitution became prevalent, thanks to his admirers and students John Marshall, Joseph Storey, and Daniel Webster, while his conception of expansive presidential war and foreign policy powers would prevail in the twentieth century. In many ways, the contemporary United States itself—a relatively centralized nation-state, with a military second to none in the world, a powerful presidency, a strong judiciary, and an industrial capitalist economy—is a monument more important than Hamilton's portrait on the ten-dollar bill, or the statue on the steps of the Treasury Department.

In the late twentieth century, however, Hamilton is missing from the American pantheon, a victim of the rather devious effort of New Deal propagandists in the thirties and forties to paint FDR as an heir to the Jefferson-Jackson Southern Democrats and disguise the actual roots of New Deal statism in the Federalist-Whig-Republican-Progressive tradition. Today the consensus, shared by the left as well as the right, holds that Noah Webster was just when he described Alexander Hamilton as "the evil genius of this country."[19] Most often Hamiltonianism, by which is meant a blend of plutocracy and authoritarianism, is invoked as a foil to the democratic idealism of his lifelong political rival Thomas Jefferson (Jefferson placed a bust of Hamilton on the right side of the entrance hall at Monticello, across from his own portrait on the left; he explained to visitors: "Opposed in death as in life.") The few who remember the mastermind of the young American republic tend to know only a caricature of him as a champion of the rich—a prototypical Wall Street wizard like Andrew Mellon or Michael Milken.

Ironically, it is Jeffersonianism—the poisonous amalgam of white supremacy, states' rights, and antigovernment rhetoric, which has come in both agrarian and pro-industrial forms—that has legitimated or promoted the grossest forms of racial and class inequality for centuries in the United States. Though often maligned as a champion of plutocracy, Hamilton favored luxury taxes on the rich as a way of "taxing their superior wealth," praised inheritance laws that would "soon melt down those great estates which, if they continued, might favor the power of the few," and denounced poll taxes—a version of the regressive flat tax favored by Jeffersonian conservatives—in order "to guard the least wealthy part of the community from oppression."[20] Though Hamilton was not alarmed by a moderate deficit, he would have been shocked by deficits produced, like Reagan's, by an unwillingness to levy taxes to match spending. In his Second Report on the Public Credit (1795), he wrote that runaway debt is "the natural disease of all governments" and that it is difficult "to conceive anything more likely than this to lead to great and convulsive revolutions of empire."[21] The first and greatest Secretary of the Treasury, who during the Whiskey Rebellion helped President Washington to mobilize the militia to collect excise taxes, would not have smiled upon the tax revolt rhetoric of Howard Jarvis and Ronald Reagan. Hamilton, who had seen the consequences of feeble government during the Revolutionary War and the years of the Articles of Confederation, would have been appalled by Reagan's assertion that "Government is not part of the solution; it is the problem." Indeed, during the French Revolution, Hamilton contemptuously dismissed the "pernicious system" that maintained "that but a small portion of power is requisite to Government . . . and that as human nature shall refine and ameliorate by the operation of a more enlightened plan, government itself will become useless, and Society will subsist and flourish free from its shackles."

Like his rival Jefferson, Alexander Hamilton was a theorist as well as a statesman. He was the superior thinker, because he was the more practical—while Jefferson wasted his time on deluded projects like searching for the origins of American liberty among Anglo-Saxon barbarians and rewriting the New Testament to free it of miracles, Hamilton was thinking about practical measures to render American republicanism secure and solvent. His death at the hands of Aaron Burr prevented him from writing the "full investigation of the history and science of civil government and the various modifications of it upon the freedom and happiness of mankind," to which he had planned to devote his later years, according to his admirer Chancellor Joseph Kent, an early Chief Justice of the Supreme Court of New York. Though he never wrote his treatise on government, Hamilton lived to see the republication of *The Federalist* and his polemical *Pacificus* letters defending presidential authority in foreign affairs. These and other occasional writings, together with the three great reports he made to Congress as Secretary of the Treasury—the Reports on the Public Credit (1790), on the Bank of the United States (1790), and on Manufactures (1791)—constitute a substantial body of work explicating the principles of Hamiltonianism.

Like Jeffersonians, Hamiltonians are liberal, constitutional republicans, but Hamiltonians have believed from the beginning that both individual liberty and constitutional government are easier to secure in a strong nation-state with a stable government and a diversified economy than in a weak, decentralized, economically backward confederacy which, pursuing utopian schemes in foreign policy and domestic governance, would inevitably be dominated, in fact, by parochial politicians and foreign powers. For Hamiltonians, the United States is and should be, not a weak confederacy of petty, squabbling republics, but a relatively centralized nation-state in which the states are clearly subordinated to a strong but not oppressive federal government. The federal government must possess the military force not only to secure America's interests abroad but to quickly and effectively suppress domestic insurrection—a lesson taught not only by the Civil War but by the Whiskey Rebellion that President Washington, with Hamilton's aid, suppressed in 1794. The success of the federal government, for Hamilton and his followers, requires an efficient and competent executive branch and a powerful federal judiciary, both insulated to a degree from the popularly elected legislature. "The test of good government," in Hamilton's words, "is its aptitude and tendency to produce a good administration." Good administration requires first-rate officers with long tenure; Hamiltonians do not share the naive Jeffersonian belief that a great and powerful state can be administered by amateur politicians and short-term, inexperienced appointees dependent on the guidance of lobbyists.

Hamilton is best understood, not as a lawyer-politician or an economic policymaker in the contemporary sense, but rather as an intellectual military officer, an idealistic colonel of a sort not unfamiliar in postcolonial regimes in our own century, who went into democratic politics, law, and business to promote his nationalist convictions. In foreign policy, he is the patron saint of the tradition of American realism, which stresses particular national interests rather than utopian world-order goals. Hamilton saw political economy, as well, as an instrument of nationalist statecraft, unlike modern academic economists who treat economics and world politics as separate, self-contained realms, and urge policymakers to ignore the relative status of their nation in the world economy in order to concentrate on the utopian goal of promoting the absolute well-being of the world as a whole.

Hamilton is not usually thought of as one of the precursors of the civil rights movement, though one might have expected the leaders of the Civil Rights Revolution to have looked to him for inspiration. After all, the Civil Rights Revolution, in both its legitimate color-blind phase and the later perversion of it into a racial preference movement, was largely carried out in the name of federal authority by federal judges, whose power and independence Hamilton strenuously defended (notably in *Federalist* No. 76). What is more, Hamilton was one of the most ardent opponents of slavery and racism among the Founding Fathers. When he was aide-de-camp to Washington, Hamilton, in a prefiguring of the Emancipation Proclamation, wanted to give blacks their freedom and citizenship and arm them as soldiers: "The contempt we have been taught to entertain for the blacks, makes us fancy many things that are founded neither in reason nor experience. . . . The dictates of humanity and true policy equally interest me in favour of this unfortunate class of men." After the war, Hamilton—who had grown up in the slave society of the Caribbean island of St. Kitts—helped organize the Society for Promoting the Manumission of Slaves.[22] Jefferson, by contrast, opposed emancipation if it could not be accompanied by the immediate colonization of black Americans abroad, and his speculations about alleged black racial inferiority in his *Notes on the State of Virginia* made him one of the heroes of generations of pseudoscientific racists. Nevertheless, the modern habit of attributing everything good in American life to the inspiration of Jefferson alone has resulted in his being given credit for convictions about universal equality and freedom that are actually those of Hamilton. Today a few black Americans, recognizing this, have fittingly enough tried to make Hamilton's historic house in Harlem, the Grange, a symbol of black capitalism.

John Marshall, the first Chief Justice of the Supreme Court, who did so much to fix Hamilton's expansive view of federal authority in law, thought that Hamilton and his mentor Washington were the greatest of the Founders. One contemporary acquaintance, Judge Ambrose Spencer, who had clashed with him went so far as to declare: "Alexander Hamilton was the greatest man this country ever produced. . . . He, more than any man, did the thinking of the time." The great French diplomat and statesman Talleyrand, who worked with Hamilton during the Revolution and the early years of the republic, singled out for praise among the Founding Fathers "General Hamilton, whose mind and character placed him, I thought, on a par with the most distinguished statesmen of Europe, not even excepting Mr. Pitt and Mr. Fox."[23]

In the words of Clinton Rossiter, Hamilton "was conservative and radical, traditionalist and revolutionary, reactionary and visionary, Tory and Whig all thrown into one. He is a glorious source of inspiration and instruction to modern conservatives, but so is he to modern liberals."[24] Henry Cabot Lodge, Sr., wrote a biography of Hamilton, in which he predicted "so long as the people of the United States form one nation, the name of Alexander Hamilton will be held in high and lasting honor, and even in the wreck of governments that noble intellect would still command the homage of men."

Not only Jefferson, but Madison, would be expelled from a Trans-American Parnassus. Only in the forties and fifties was James Madison elevated to the status of the great mastermind of American constitutionalism, partly because New Deal Democrats sought to downplay the role in the writing of the Federalist Papers of Hamilton (whom they thought of, anachronistically, as an Andrew Mellon Republican), and partly because Madison's Federalist Number 10 could be interpreted (or misinterpreted) by mid-century liberal political scientists to support their theory of interest-group, broker-state liberalism. Before this mid-century revival of "little Jimmy Madison," the fourth president had been remembered chiefly for his incompetence as commander-in-chief during the disastrous War of 1812, symbolized by the image of his wife Dolley fleeing the presidential mansion with paintings and furniture as British troops approached to burn it down. The earlier image of Madison as a relatively inconsequential figure was accurate.

For liberal nationalists, the most important figure in the American political tradition, after Hamilton, might be Franklin Delano Roosevelt. This might come as a surprise—why FDR, rather than Lincoln? The answer is that Lincoln, though he saved the Union, did not change notions of the proper relationship between American government and American society in the same lasting way that FDR did. Some conservatives, to be sure, try to find the origins of New Deal statism in the Civil War, but this is anachronistic. Lincoln and FDR were both Hamiltonians (though each, with varying degrees of sincerity, painted himself as the true successor to the ever-popular Jefferson): but Lincoln was an Old Hamiltonian, of the school of Webster, Clay, and Hamilton himself, whereas FDR was the greatest of the New Hamiltonians, of the school of Herbert Croly and Theodore Roosevelt. Lincoln, and the Republican presidents who succeeded him, at least until McKinley, seem almost as remote now as most of the antebellum politicians. Only during the reign of FDR do we begin to recognize our America.

Reign is the right word. In his four terms, FDR, for better and worse, shaped our notions of the presidency even more than he shaped our ideas of the proper scope and authority of the federal government. Some of his legacies, like the imperial presidency in foreign policy, have proven dangerous, when the man is not worthy of the office; others of his bequests, like his pragmatism in economics, are undervalued in this age of doctrinaire free-market ideology. Even his detractors must concede his importance. Our only four-term president looms above the other American statesmen of the century, including his cousin Theodore, like a whale above porpoises. Truman and Johnson were footnotes to the testament of FDR; Reagan, a quibble in the margin.

FDR's strength, like that of Washington and Lincoln, was less the quality of his mind than the quality of his temperament. It was, on the evidence, a temperament more stoic than theirs. One wonders whether the irritable Washington or the melancholy Lincoln could have led the country through twelve years of Depression and four years of global war with such equanimity—all of this, after having been crippled for life by polio. FDR lacked the intellectual brilliance of his great allies Churchill and de Gaulle; on the other hand, he was free from their self-deceptions. He did not, like Churchill, fancy himself a strategist greater than his generals, and unlike de Gaulle he never mistook himself for his nation, though no American statesman since Washington would have been so easily forgiven for that mistake. His conservative detractors claim that the New Deal did not cure the Depression, which is true, and that he was a dupe of Stalin, or the British, or both, claims which are false. The former Secretary of the Navy who replaced Henry Wallace with Harry Truman as his potential successor, and in dying bequeathed him access to the worldwide markets and bases of the British empire, a UN based in America and rigged in favor of U.S. allies and Latin American auxiliaries, and, of course, the atomic bomb, looks, from this distance in time, like the most successful practitioner of *Realpolitik* since Bismarck (Nixon and Kissinger, whose schemes, when they were not oversold like the opening to China, usually ended in failure, were amateurs compared to the more cunning, and quieter, FDR).

Half a century after his death, we are still too close to see FDR in proper perspective. It is my suspicion that Americans of the twenty-first century will consider his importance to be surpassed only by that of Washington and Lincoln; and perhaps not even by theirs. Our descendants will gratefully remember "Dr. New Deal," the eclectic social democratic liberal who described himself as "slightly left of center," on occasions when they painfully learn again, as we are learning again in the aftermath of Reaganism, that a middle-class standard of living is not an inevitable by-product of the operations of a free market. And when the United States faces ruthless, determined great-power adversaries in the future, as it almost certainly will, Americans will think back to the cheerful man in the wheelchair, serene and wise in the midst of an unprecedented catastrophe, calmly guiding the ramshackle coalition that saved the world.

If Hamilton symbolizes the nation-state for liberal nationalists, and FDR the modern social-market version of the nation-state, Frederick Douglass, more than any other American figure, is the appropriate symbol of the multiracial/mixed-race Trans-American nation. Frederick Douglass was, at the very least, the foremost of the champions of American individual liberty. A case can be made that he was the greatest American of all time.

"It was said long ago," the *Boston Commonwealth* observed before the Civil War, "that the true romance of America was not in the fortunes of the Indian, where Cooper sought it, nor in New England character, where Judd found it; nor in the social contrasts of Virginia planters, as Thackeray imagined, but in the story of the fugitive slaves."[25] If to be an American is to be a self-made man, then there has never been anyone more American than the slave born in 1817 as Frederick Augustus Washington Bailey who escaped in 1838 and took the name of the hero of a romance by Sir Walter Scott: Frederick Douglass. The self-emancipated slave who became one of the greatest orators of the English language and did as much as any single individual to destroy the millennia-old evil of slavery was certainly far more of a self-made man than the Abraham Lincoln of Euro-American mythology, the "Great Commoner," whose efforts at self-improvement took him only from middle-class origins to upper-middle-class affluence as a railroad lawyer. Lincoln was a great man; but Douglass was a greater man, because he went further, against greater odds. He saw further as well. Douglass thought more deeply about American nationality than all but a few American leaders, of any race, in his day or ours.

In the 1880s, Douglass predicted that the black American "will not be expatriated nor annihilated, nor will he forever remain a separate and distinct race from the people around him, but that he will be absorbed, assimilated, and will only appear finally . . . in the features of a blended race."[26] Even under slavery, Douglass pointed out, an enormous amount of amalgamation had taken place: "If this blending of the two races were impossible we should not have at least one-fourth of our colored population composed of persons of mixed blood, ranging all the way from a dark-brown color to the point where there is no visible admixture." Douglass dismissed those who argued that black pride would prevent race-mixing, even if white prejudice did not: "The opposition to amalgamation, of which we hear so much on the part of colored people, is for most part the merest affectation, and will never form an impassable barrier to the union of the two varieties." Taking the long view, he pointed out: "It was once degradation intensified for a Norman to associate with a Saxon, but time and events have swept down the barriers between them, and Norman and Saxon have become Englishmen."[27]

Far from being a crypto-racist notion, the idea of racial amalgamation in America, an idea rejected by Jefferson and Lincoln alike, was the very center of the vision of the future expressed by the greatest black American of the nineteenth century, perhaps the greatest American, of any race, of any century:

> Of course this result will not be reached by any hurried or forced process. It will not arise out of any theory of the wisdom of such blending of the two races. If it comes at all, it will come without shock or noise or violence of any kind, and only in the fullness of time, and it will be so adjusted to surrounding conditions as hardly to be observed. I would not be understood as advocating intermarriage between the two races. I am not a propagandist, but a prophet. I do not say that what I say *should* come to pass, but what I think is likely to come to pass, and what is inevitable. . . . Races and varieties of the human family appear and disappear, but humanity remains and will remain forever.[28]

Douglass believed that "the Negro and the white man are likely ever to remain the principal inhabitants of this country," because the black American's "tawny brother, the Indian, dies, under the flashing glance of the Anglo Saxon," and Asians would be excluded by the whites who "have attempted to slaughter Chinamen."[29] The post-1965 immigration, however, ensures that Hispanics and Asians as well as white and black Americans, in the twenty-first and twenty-second centuries, are likely to help realize Douglass's vision of a racially amalgamated nation under a color-blind legal and political order.

Because the goal of an amalgamated American nation-state was ever in his mind, Douglass refused to make any concessions, no matter how minor or seemingly benevolent, to racial preference or racial pride. Of his contemporary, the black nationalist Martin Delany, Douglass remarked, "I thank God for making me a man simply; but Delany always thanks him for making him a black man."[30] When Delany proposed that blacks be assigned quotas in federal jobs according to their proportion in the population, Douglass mocked him, asking whether there would be

German and Irish quotas too. Douglass would be appalled by today's racial preference system.

He would be equally appalled by Afrocentric ideology, a revival of hoary fallacies that were old even in his day. While he perpetuated the fallacy (believed by many white anthropologists of his day) that "a direct relationship may be claimed by the Negro race, to that grandest of all the nations of antiquity, the builders of the pyramids,"[31] he repudiated those who sought to minimize European and Euro-American achievements in order to enhance black self-esteem:

> If we had built great ships, sailed around the world, taught the science of navigation, discovered far-off islands, capes and continents, enlarged the boundaries of human knowledge, improved the conditions of man's existence, brought valuable contributions to art, science, and literature, revealed great truths, organized great States, administered great governments, defined the laws of the universe, formulated systems of mental and moral philosophy, invented railroads, steam engines, mowing machines, sewing machines, taught the sun to take pictures, the lightning to carry messages, we then might claim, not only potential and theoretical equality, but actual and practical equality. Nothing is gained to our cause by claiming more for ourselves than of right we can establish belongs to us.[32]

Without demeaning Africa, Douglass rejected the definition of black Americans as an African diaspora. "No one idea has given rise to more oppression and persecution toward the colored people of this country," Douglass wrote in 1859, "than that which makes Africa, not America, their home."[33] He denied that black Americans form a nationality distinct from the larger American community: "A nation within a nation is an anomaly. There can be but one American nation under the American government, and we are Americans. . . . Our policy should be to unite with the great mass of the American people in all their activities, and resolve to fall or flourish with our common country." Separate black-only institutions were at best a temporary measure in the face of white racism. Consistent with his integrationism, Douglass repudiated the idea that black Americans had a moral duty to buy from other black

Americans: "A colored newspaper maker has no higher claim upon us for patronage than a colored carpenter, a colored shoemaker, or a colored bricklayer. . . . Our people should not be required to buy an inferior article offered by a colored man, when for the same money they can purchase a superior article from a white man."[34]

In his 1963 book *Why We Can't Wait*, Martin Luther King, Jr., who matched Douglass's moral courage but not his perspicuity, made the mistake of calling for a "Negro bloc," on the grounds that "by forming a bloc a minority makes its voice heard." King reasoned from a false analogy between a racial bloc and the fact that "labor, farmers, businessmen, veterans, and various national minorities have voted as blocs on various issues" to the conclusion that a black-only bloc could be "a wholesome force on the political scene."[35] The black political class since the sixties has followed his advice; as a result, the black leadership is now seen by many if not most white Americans as an entrenched special interest of a kind with the peanut and tobacco lobbies, while the Republican right has profited from the weakening of transracial liberalism (and even collaborated with King's "Negro bloc" in corralling black voters into electorally segregated congressional districts). Generations earlier, Douglass criticized "the error that union among ourselves is an essential element of success in our relations to the white race" and that "if we were only united in one body, under wise and powerful leaders, we could shape the policy of both political parties, make and unmake parties, control the destiny of the republic, and secure for ourselves a desirable and happy future." Douglass demurred: "I hold that our union is our weaknesss. . . . When we thus isolate ourselves we say to those around us: 'We have nothing in common with you,' and, very naturally, the reply of our neighbors is in the same tone and to the same effect; for when a people care for nobody, nobody will care for them."[36] Douglass wrote, "We cannot afford to draw the color line in politics, trade, education, manners, religion, fashion, or civilization. Especially, we cannot afford to draw the color line in politics. No folly could be greater. A party acting upon that basis would be not merely a misfortune but a dire calamity to our people."[37]

Indeed, Douglass denied that there was a "Negro problem," as opposed to an American problem: "The Negro is of inferior activity and power in the solution of this problem. He is the clay, the nation is the potter." Douglass conceded that "while he may hold that primarily and fundamentally it is an American problem and not a Negro problem, he may materially assist in its solution" by self-cultivation.[38] While stressing the need for a transracial coalition, Douglass was suspicious of white paternalism. "I think the American people are disposed often to be generous rather than just. . . . What I ask for the Negro is not benevolence, not pity, not sympathy, but simply *justice*." By justice Douglass meant color-blind procedural justice: "Everybody has asked the question . . . 'What shall we do with the Negro?' I have had but one answer from the beginning. Do nothing with us! If the apples will not stay on the tree of their own strength, if they are wormeaten at the core, if they are early ripe and disposed to fall, let them fall! I am not for tying or fastening them on the tree in any way . . . ."[39] He was confident that black Americans, if treated fairly, without special treatment, in time would become "educated and prosperous" and would "rise in the social scale."[40]

For too long we Americans have falsely attributed the color-blind ideal to Thomas Jefferson and Abraham Lincoln, great but limited politicians who believed that nonwhite Americans would never fit into the American nation and should emigrate. The credit properly belongs to the abolitionists, Douglass foremost among them. A consistent defender of civil rights in every form, Douglass was not only an abolitionist, but an early champion of equal rights for women. A man of mixed race who married a white woman and predicted the eventual blending of white and nonwhite in a new American ethnic nation, a descendant of Africans who embodied the best of the Euro-American Enlightenment and biblical traditions, a consistent and rigorous critic of white bigotry and black racial mysticism alike, a man who braved ridicule to fight for women's rights, a proponent of an American legal order that excludes no citizen on the basis of race or gender, Frederick Douglass must be the central figure in the pantheon of a new American liberal nationalism. Ahead of his time in the age of segregation, and still ahead of ours in this era of racial preference and multicultural race-mysticism, Douglass more than anyone else deserves the title of the First Trans-American.*

---

*It is an anomaly, if not a disgrace, that Washington, D.C. contains monuments to the colonizationists Jefferson and Lincoln while there is no great memorial for Frederick Douglass. Congress should establish a Douglass Memorial on or near the Mall in Washington, at least as splendid and prominent from a distance as the Lincoln and Jefferson Memorials.

THE VISION OF TRANS-AMERICA

The museum of Trans-American history is somewhere west of the Mississippi, where the majority of Americans live today. Its cubic contours and earth tones evoke a southwestern adobe mission, a parallel made complete by the belfry that contains a facsimile of the Liberty Bell. The southwestern ambience is even stronger within. The statues that command the gallery are not neoclassical specters, cold and colorless, but polychrome sculptures reminiscent of the saints in a Mexican church or the luridly colored figures—half Baroque, half comic-book—created by the contemporary American artist Luis Jimenez.

The first emblematic figure is a slender, boyish man in the uniform of a Revolutionary War Colonel—Alexander Hamilton, portrayed in his youth as the trusted aide-de-camp of George Washington. Beyond him, leaning in his wheelchair like a monarch upon a comfortable throne, FDR smiles jauntily at you.

From the mastermind of the American nation-state and the patron saint of the American social market contract, you turn to the third ghost who dominates the hall. The giant figure is that of a striking man in his twenties, dressed crisply in an antebellum suit. His handsome features are a blend of African and European, framed by a shock of black hair and a thin fringe of beard. Brow wrinkled in concentration, he gazes down, as though at an expectant audience. Frederick Douglass prepares to speak.

Turning, you see the wall above the entrance to the chamber. Here is a mural symbolizing the origins of the Trans-American nation, a mural you see for the first time. The two core populations in the United States are portrayed here, the Anglo-Americans and black Americans. With these, from a very early date, many American Indians, chiefly of the East and South, have merged by assimilation and intermarriage (the extent of the historic amalgamation between American Indians and black Americans is still not acknowledged by leaders of both groups). Around the Anglo-American/black/Indian core, the nation has grown from the influx first of European immigrants, and now of immigrants from Latin America and Asia and the Middle East. Scots-Irish frontier farmers and Angolan slaves, Dutch merchants and Cherokee elders, Mexican *campesinos* and Jewish garment workers, New England Yankees and Salvadoran refugees, Chinese and Swedes and Lebanese—all of these are shown here, transforming the transracial American nation even as it transforms and absorbs them.

Your eyes are now drawn away fom the origins mural to the mural that dominates the gallery's far wall. It is unlike anything in conventional American iconography; it possesses not a trace of the serene acceptance of surfaces to be found in Currier & Ives or Norman Rockwell or Thomas Hart Benton. The painter has tried to give plastic form to the collective unconscious of the American mind, a mentality shaped most profoundly not by classical republicanism or Whig liberalism but by seventeenth-century English Protestantism. Dreams and nightmares blend in this American Revelation, this American Apocalypse.

First, the American Eden: the North American wilderness as a garden, as a place of pilgrimage and play. Here are the wise innocents of American literature, Huck Finn and Dorothy, on a raft with their non-human guides, the chthonic spirits of the American landscape from Indian and African lore—Bigfoot, a gentle shaggy giant, the Pan of the American woods and fields, and Br'er Rabbit the trickster, whose native cunning complements Bigfoot's benevolent strength. The river carries the four past miniature versions of North American natural wonders, as in a Disney theme park: a waist-high Niagara Falls empties into a doll-size Grand Canyon, its waters reemerging as a Yellowstone Geyser in the Painted Desert. The land, for Americans, is not the land of georgic, or even (despite the cowboy mythos) of pastoral; it is not something that is worked, and that in turn works its effects on the countryman. There is something of the Puritan rejection of pagan fertility rituals and Catholic calendrical cycles in the resolute preference of Americans for the untouched Wilderness over the cultivated landscape, for the untrod mountain rather than the slope terraced and quilted by farms, for the country as a vista and not as a home. Here Wilderness is seen as a sublimity that hides no threat, a human-scale wilderness without fat black flies or blizzards or tornadoes or ticks, and Huck and Dorothy behold its splendors as tourists secure in their identity who after their excursion will return to Hannibal or the Kansas farm utterly unchanged by what they have seen. Only the Indian arrowhead that Huck spies on the riverbank introduces a hint of mortality, of loss, to this American pastoral—*Et in Arcadia ego*. But the arrowhead is a symbol as well of successful appropriation, and it is all the more reassuring because it is not a prophecy. Huck and Dorothy will return to this sunny backyard every day, forever.

Next, the painter shows the American Babylon, the antithesis of the innocent Garden. A mountain screen of skyscrapers and spewing smokestacks and neon signs and palm trees thrusts up into the belly of the early morning above a saloon where Marilyn Monroe or Mae West or Little Egypt dances the hootchy-kootchy before a leering audience: chalk-striped gangsters, stubbly Western outlaws, Frankie and Johnny, tipsy and starting to squabble. In the alley outside, where Sam Spade lingers and smokes as he waits for an informant, a tout tries to lure sailors on leave and farm boys and immigrants, but their attention is diverted to the Fair, a Midway full of the newest whizzing gizmos patented by the Wizard of Oz, who is visible on a large-screen TV, a sort of combination of Edison and Rockefeller, a Prospero gone to seed.

Babylon is just a front, a facade like a Hollywood set. Behind it the real masters can be seen. Caesar is the embodiment of the military-industrial complex dreaded by the left and right alike, the Money Power, Leviathan, the State, the Merchants of Death; the generalissimo sports a uniform paneled with medals and a black mustache accentuating his scowl; he is Hitler, Stalin, Saddam, Santa Anna, Napoleon. And at his side, his mentor and advisor, "that old deceiver," not the goat-legged satyr with a sunburn or the goateed circus magician mocked by the village atheist, but the fallen prince dreaded by generations of Calvinist divines, a handsome upper-class Englishman in a tux with a cigarette in his fingers and a smirk on his lips: Beelzebub as James Bond.

Babylon must be destroyed. Luxury and tyranny must be annihilated. The painter shows the Big Sky, the American firmanent, unscrolling like a curtain, as in a Dürer print, to reveal the American Christ. He is not the patiently suffering Man of Sorrows of the Latins, cradled by a weeping Madonna, nor is he a prince sitting at the right hand of a royal father, an Orthodox Cosmocrator. He has no mother and no father, this American Jesus. His manner is that of a solemn young gunslinger, deputized by the desperate faithful, riding into a town run by Satan and Caesar and the Whore and the Wizard. He is going to clean it up and shut it down and put a stop to this foolishness *right now*.

And I saw heaven opened, and behold a white horse; and he that sat upon him was called Faithful and True, and in righteousness he doth judge and make war. . . . And out of his mouth goeth a sharp sword, that with it he should smite the nations: and he shall rule them with a rod of iron: and he treadeth the wine press of the fierceness and wrath of Almighty God.

The American Jesus is every implacable American reformer and every ferocious reactionary. He is Wyatt Earp at the OK Corral and George Washington crossing the Delaware and Carrie Nation raiding a saloon and John Brown advancing on Harpers Ferry and Eliot Ness breaking into a brewery and Douglas MacArthur attacking the Bonus Army and Woodrow Wilson ordering the bombing of Veracruz and Sherman in Georgia and a federal agent busting up an illegal Catholic bingo game. He is the FBI and the Black Panthers and the Klan and the Vice Squad and the Sons of Liberty and the U.S. Cavalry and the Guardian Angels and the Texas Rangers and the DEA and the Untouchables and the Marines. He is the fundamentalist preacher, and he is the fundamentalist atheist whose uncompromising iconoclasm is more Protestant than he knows. He is not just on a mission from God, he *is* God, and this is God's country—or will be, once he takes it back. By the time the hosts of football-player angels arrayed in their flying saucers above him have finished their energy-beam strafing raids from the High Frontier, the American Babylon will look like Hiroshima or Dresden or Baghdad or Veracruz, a waste of eyeless smoke-striped towers and comb-black neon signs and tubes of cinders that were boulevard palms.

Beyond the smoking rubble rises the American Jerusalem, the *New* Jerusalem, the New Atlantis, the New Republic, the New Deal, the New Frontier, the New Birth of Freedom, Morning in America, *novus ordo seclorum.* As in an allegory by Cole, the artist limns a monumental city rising in the Midwest, the distillation of all old-time virtue and all ancient good—Greek temples, Egyptian obelisks, Roman Senate. Strolling down the Capitol steps, engaged in quiet and earnest conversation with one another, like Raphael's philosophers in the *Stanza della Segnatura* in the Vatican, are the patron saints of the City on a Hill: the stern Roman in his nylon toga, Cincinnatus or Cato; the Founding Father, in woolly wig and buckled shoes; the bearded Hebrew patriarch with sandals and staff; and, beside him, conversing with him with the incongruity of dream, the sage Negro Pharaoh of black American myth, resplendent in his glittering headdress. Their midwestern town of gold and jasper and pearl will never be complete, and the American Babylon will never be entirely destroyed; but in the foreground the American Garden will always glow beyond the river's bank, as untouched as the world on creation's first day.

Notes

Introduction

1. Cokie Roberts, "Good Old-Fashioned Public Servants," *The Washington Post*, October 28, 1992, p. A25.
2. Paul Starobin, "Did God Bless America?" *National Journal*, December 10, 1994, p. 2930.
3. Paul Johnson, "God and the Americans," *Commentary*, January 1995, p. 45.

Chapter 1. The First Republic

1. Thomas Jefferson to James Monroe, Nov. 24, 1801, in Andrew A. Lipscomb and Albert E. Bergh, eds., *The Writings of Thomas Jefferson*, 20 vols. (Washington, DC: Thomas Jefferson Memorial Association, 1905), vol. 10, p. 296. Jefferson also wrote in 1786 that "our Confederacy must be viewed as the nest from which all America, North and South, is to be peopled." In Julian P. Boyd, ed., *The Papers of Thomas Jefferson* (Princeton: Princeton University Press, 1950), vol. 9, p. 218.
2. Thomas Jefferson to John Jacob Astor, Nov. 9, 1813, in Lipscomb and Bergh, supra, vol. 13, p. 432.
3. Dickinson W. Adams, ed., *Jefferson's Extracts from the Gospels* (Princeton: Princeton University Press, 1983), pp. 405–406, 409.
4. Reginald Horsman, *Race and Manifest Destiny: The Origins of American Racial Anglo-Saxonism* (Cambridge, MA: Harvard University Press, 1981), pp. 19–20.
5. Richard Hakluyt, "Pamphlet for the Virginia Enterprise," 1602, in E. G. R. Taylor, ed., *The Original Writings and Correspondence of the Two Richard Hakluyts*, 2 vols. (London, 1935), vol. 2, p. 331.

6. David Hackett Fischer, *Albion's Seed: Four British Folkways in America* (New York: Oxford University Press, 1989).

7. Quoted in Alexander DeConde, *Race, Ethnicity, and American Foreign Policy* (Boston: Northeastern University Press, 1992), p. 10.

8. Quoted in Gerald Stourzh, *Benjamin Franklin and American Foreign Policy* (Chicago: University of Chicago Press, 1969), p. 81.

9. John M. Murrin, "Beneficiaries of Catastrophe: The English Colonies in America," in Eric Foner, ed., *The New American History* (Philadelphia: Temple University Press, 1990), p. 21.

10. John Richard Green, *History of the English People* (New York: George Munro, 1880–1881), vol. 4, book 9, p. 31.

11. Quoted in Francis Parkman, *Montcalm and Wolfe*, in *Francis Parkman's Works*, Frontenac ed. (Boston: Little, Brown, 1906), vol. 13, p. 250.

12. Winthrop D. Jordan, *The White Man's Burden: The Historical Origins of Racism in the United States* (New York: Oxford University Press, 1974), pp. 132–133.

13. Jedediah Morse, *The American Geography: or, a View of the Present Situation of the United States of America* (1789, reprint ed., New York: Arno, 1970), p. 63, quoted in Horsman, *Race and Manifest Destiny*, supra, p. 94.

14. Alexis de Tocqueville, *Democracy in America*, 2 vols. (New York: Alfred A. Knopf, 1951), vol. 2, p. 36.

15. Quoted in D. W. Meinig, *The Shaping of America*, vol. 1, *Atlantic America* (New Haven: Yale University Press, 1986), p. 43.

16. Lewis Henry Morgan, *Ancient Society, or Researches in the Lines of Human Progress from Savagery through Barbarism to Civilization* (1877; reprint edited by Eleanor Burke Leacock, Cleveland, OH: World Publishing, 1963), pp. 11–12.

17. Ralph Waldo Emerson, *English Traits*, edited by Howard Mumford Jones. (Cambridge, MA: Harvard University Press, 1966), p. 547.

18. Quoted in Reginald Horsman, *Race and Manifest Destiny*, supra.

19. Orson S. Fowler, *Hereditary Descent: Its Laws and Facts* (New York, 1843), p. 47.

20. Orson S. Fowler, ibid., pp. 301–317.

21. Charles B. Boynton, *Oration: Delivered on the 5th of July, 1847 . . . in Cincinnati* (Cincinnati, 1847), vol. 10, quoted in Dale T. Knobel, *Paddy and the Republic: Ethnicity and Nationality in Antebellum America* (Middletown, CT: Wesleyan University Press, 1986), p. 5.

22. Henry F. May, *The Enlightenment in America* (New York: Oxford University Press, 1976); H. M. Morais, *Deism in Eighteenth Century America* (New York: Columbia University Press, 1934).

23. Jean N. Matthews, *Toward a New Society: American Thought and Culture, 1800–1830* (Boston: Twayne, 1991), p. 29.

24. Paul Goodman, *Towards a Christian Republic: Antimasonry and the Great*

Transition in New England, 1826–1836 (New York: Oxford University Press, 1988); S. M. Lipset and E. Raab, *The Politics of Unreason* (Chicago: University of Chicago Press, 1970).

25. Henry M. Brackenridge, "A Vindication of Civil Rights for Jews," in *Annals of America* (Chicago: Encyclopedia Britannica, 1968), vol. 4, p. 559.

26. *Vidal v. Girard's Executors*, 43 U.S. 2 How. 127, 198 [11:205, 234] (1844), quoted with approval in *Church of the Holy Trinity v. United States*, 143 U.S. 457 (1926).

27. Quoted in J. H. Elliott, *The Old World and the New, 1492–1650* (Cambridge: Cambridge University Press, 1970), p. 94.

28. Quoted in Winthrop S. Hudson, *American Protestantism* (Chicago: University of Chicago Press, 1962), p. 62.

29. Quoted in William Haller, "John Foxe and the Puritan Revolution," in *The Seventeenth Century*, Richard F. Jones et al. (Stanford, CA: Stanford University Press, 1951), p. 220.

30. John Adams, "A Dissertation of the Canon and Feudal Law" [1765], in *Works of John Adams* (Boston, 1865), vol. 3, p. 447, quoted in Ernest Lee Tuveson, *Redeemer Nation: The Idea of America's Millenial Role* (Chicago: University of Chicago Press, 1968), p. 21.

31. Horace Bushnell, "The Principle of National Greatness," An Oration Pronounced Before the Society of Phi Beta Kappa, 1837, quoted in Tuveson, supra.

32. Michael Felberg, *The Turbulent Era* (New York: Oxford University Press, 1980).

33. Alexis de Tocqueville, *Democracy in America*, edited by J. P. Mayer and Max Lerner, (New York: Harper & Row, 1966), p. 315.

34. Eric Foner, "From Slavery to Citizenship: Blacks and the Right to Vote," in Donald W. Rogers, ed., *Voting and the Spirit of American Democracy* (Chicago: University of Illinois Press, 1990), pp. 57–58.

35. Lerone Bennett, Jr., *Before the Mayflower: A History of Black America*, 5th ed. (New York: Penguin, 1982), pp. 256, 181.

36. Henry Clay, "On African Colonization," January 20, 1827, *The Life and Speeches of Henry Clay*, 2 vols. (Philadelphia, 1855), vol. 1, p. 270.

37. James M. McPherson, *Abraham Lincoln and the Second American Revolution* (New York: Oxford University Press, 1991), pp. 12–13.

38. Marshall Smelser and Joan R. Gundersen, *American History at a Glance*, 4th ed. (New York: Harper & Row, 1978), p. 86.

39. James Oakes, *Slavery and Freedom: An Interpretation of the Old South* (New York: Vintage, 1991), pp. 75–76.

40. Thomas Jefferson to Joseph Priestley, Jan. 18, 1800, in Paul Leicester Ford, ed., *The Works of Thomas Jefferson*, Federal Edition (12 vols.) (New York, 1904–5), vol. 7, p. 406.

41. Clement Clarke Moore, *An Inquiry into the Effects of Our Foreign Carrying*

Trade upon the Agriculture, Population, and Morals of the Country . . . (New York, 1806), pp. 11–12, quoted in Drew R. McCoy, *The Elusive Republic: Political Economy in Jeffersonian America* (New York: W. W. Norton & Company, 1980), p. 213.

42. Thomas Jefferson to General Thaddeus Kosciuszko, June 28, 1812, in Lipscomb and Bergh, supra, vol. 13, p. 170.

43. Quoted in Arnaldo DeLeon, *They Called Them Greasers* (Austin, TX: University of Texas Press, 1983), p. 12.

44. Quoted in Alexander DeConde, *Ethnicity, Race, and American Foreign Policy*, supra, p. 33.

45. Quoted in Adrienne Koch, *Jefferson and Madison: The Great Collaboration* (Gloucester, MA: P. Smith, 1970), pp. 244–245.

46. Quoted in Winthrop D. Jordan, *The White Man's Burden*, supra, pp. 191–192.

47. Jefferson to Governor William Henry Harrison, February 27, 1803, in Lipscomb and Bergh, supra, vol. 10, pp. 370–373.

48. Jefferson to Andrew Jackson, February 16, 1803, in Lipscomb and Bergh, supra, vol. 10, pp. 357–359.

49. Chilton Williamson, *American Suffrage: From Property to Democracy, 1760–1860* (Princeton: Princeton University Press, 1960), p. 266.

50. Quoted in Maldwyn Allen Jones, *American Immigration*, 2nd ed. (Chicago: University of Chicago Press, 1992), p. 72.

51. Jones, supra, p. 75.

52. Thomas Jefferson, *Notes on the State of Virginia* (New York, 1964), p. 84.

53. Quoted in Charles A. Beard, *The Idea of National Interest: An Analytical Study in American Foreign Policy* (New York: Macmillan).

54. Charles A. Beard, *The Idea of National Interest*, supra, p. 353.

55. Alexander Hamilton, *The Works of Alexander Hamilton*, Henry Cabot Lodge, ed., 12 vols. (New York: G. P. Putnam's Sons, 1904), vol. 8, p. 217.

56. Jones, *American Immigration*, supra, p. 79.

57. Ibid., p. 106.

58. Ibid., p. 100.

59. Congressional Globe, June 20, 1856, p. 1413.

60. Quoted in A. James Reichley, *The Life of the Parties* (New York: The Free Press, 1992), p. 120.

61. Congressional Globe, 29th Cong., 2nd Sess., Washington, 1847, Appendix, 317.

62. Abraham Lincoln to Joshua Speed, Aug. 24, 1855, in Basler, supra, vol. 2, p. 323.

63. Quoted in Tyler Anbinder, *Nativism and Slavery: The Northern Know Nothings and the Politics of the 1850s* (New York: Oxford University Press, 1992), p. 10.

64. Cited in Stephen Steinberg, *The Ethnic Myth: Race, Ethnicity, and Class in America* (Boston: Beacon Press, 1989), p. 178.

65. Quoted in David Hackett Fischer, supra, p. 620.

66. Dale T. Knobel, supra, p. 90.

67. Alexander DeConde, supra, p. 39.

Chapter 2. The Second Republic: Euro-America

1. Alexander DeConde, *Ethnicity, Race, and American Foreign Policy* (Boston: Northeastern University Press, 1992), p. 140.

2. Thomas Paine, *Common Sense* (Harmondsworth and New York: Penguin, 1986).

3. James Russell Lowell, "Condescension in Foreigners," *Writings*, vol. 3, p. 246.

4. Claudia D. Goldin and Frank D. Lewis, "The Economic Costs of the American Civil War: Estimates and Implications," *Journal of Economic History*, vol. 35, no. 2 (June 1975), pp. 299–326; Claudia D. Goldin, "The Economics of Emancipation," *Journal of Economic History*, vol. 33, no. 1 (March 1973), pp. 66–85.

5. C. Vann Woodward, *Origins of the New South* (Baton Rouge: Louisiana State University Press, 1951), p. 111.

6. James M. McPherson, *Abraham Lincoln and the Second American Revolution* (New York: Oxford University Press, 1991), p. 13.

7. Robert T. Swaine, *The Cravath Firm and its Predecessors, 1819–1947* (New York: privately printed, 1947); cited in Philip H. Burch, Jr., *Elites in American History*, vol. 3, *The Civil War to the New Deal* (New York: Holmes and Meier, 1981), p. 52, n. 40.

8. Philip H. Burch, Jr., supra, pp. 25–26.

9. Henry James, "Hawthorne," in Edmund Wilson, ed., *The Shock of Recognition* (New York: Doubleday, 1943), p. 460.

10. Arthur N. Applebee, *Tradition and Reform in the Teaching of English: A History* (Urbana, IL: National Council of Teachers of English, 1974), pp. 30, 36.

11. Walt Whitman, *Democratic Vistas* (New York: Liberal Arts Press, 1949), p. 52.

12. Quoted in Paul C. Nagel, *This Sacred Trust: American Nationality, 1798–1898* (New York: Oxford University Press, 1971), p. 262.

13. Stephen Steinberg, "How Jewish Quotas Began," *Commentary*, September 1971, pp. 67–76.

14. Thomas J. Schlereth, *Victorian America: Transformations in Everyday Life, 1876–1915* (New York: HarperCollins, 1991), pp. 169–175, 297–298.

15. Thomas Sowell, *The Economics and Politics of Race* (New York: William Morrow, 1983), pp. 100, 152.

16. Roger Daniels, *Coming to America: A History of Immigration and Ethnicity in American Life* (New York: HarperCollins, 1991), p. 25.

17. John MacDonald, May 12, 1882, in Canada, House of Commons, *Official Debates, 1882* (Ottawa: Maclean, Roger, and Co., 1882), vol. 12, p. 1477.

18. Paul Gordon Lauren, *Power and Prejudice: The Politics and Diplomacy of Racial Discrimination* (Boulder: Westview Press, 1988), pp. 38, 53–54.

19. Quoted in Alexander DeConde, supra, p. 46.

20. Quoted in DeConde, ibid., p. 46.

21. George M. Fredrickson, *White Supremacy: A Comparative Study in American and South African History* (New York: Oxford University Press, 1981), p. 224.

22. Frederick Merck, *Manifest Destiny and Mission in American History: A Reinterpretation* (New York: Vintage Books, 1963), p. 243.

23. Ellis Cose, *A Nation of Strangers: Prejudice, Politics, and the Peopling of America* (New York: William Morrow, 1992), p. 45.

24. Quoted in Lerone Bennett, Jr., *Before the Mayflower: A History of Black America* (New York: Penguin, 1982), pp. 179–180.

25. *American Federationist* (September 1905), vol. 12, pp. 636–637.

26. *American Federationist* (February 1898), vol. 4, pp. 269–271.

27. George M. Fredrickson, supra, pp. 224–225.

28. Douglas S. Massey and Nancy A. Denton, *American Apartheid: Segregation and the Making of the Underclass* (Cambridge, MA: Harvard University Press, 1993), p. 28.

29. John Morton Blum, *The Republican Roosevelt*, 2d. ed. (Cambridge, MA: Harvard University Press, 1977), p. 34.

30. Quoted in Thomas G. Dyer, *Theodore Roosevelt and the Idea of Race* (Baton Rouge: Louisiana State University Press, 1980), p. 135.

31. Theodore Roosevelt, *The Winning of the West*, in *The Works of Theodore Roosevelt*, 20 vols. (New York: Scribner, 1926), vol. 9, pp. 57–58.

32. Walt Whitman, in *Brooklyn Daily Eagle*, 7 July 1846, quoted in Alexander Saxton, *The Rise and Fall of the White Republic*, p. 153.

33. Walt Whitman, in *Brooklyn Daily Eagle*, May 6, 1858, quoted in Saxton, supra, p. 154.

34. Lance E. Davis et al., *American Economic Growth* (New York: Harper & Row, 1972), p. 126.

35. *Statistical Abstract of the United States*, 1992.

36. Maldwyn Allen Jones, *American Immigration*, 2d ed. (Chicago: University of Chicago Press, 1990), p. 195.

37. American Social History Project Staff, *Who Built America? Working People and the Nation's Economy, Politics, Culture and Society*, vol. 2, *From the Rise of Industrial Capitalism to the Contemporary Era* (New York: Pantheon, 1991), p. 308.

38. Christopher J. Kauffman, *Faith and Fraternalism: The History of the Knights of Columbus, 1882–1982* (New York: Harper & Row, 1982).

39. Thomas J. Schlereth, supra, pp. 225–229.

40. Harold F. Gosnell, *Machine Politics: Chicago Model* (Chicago: University of Chicago Press, 1937), pp. 71–72.

41. Maldwyn Allen Jones, supra, p. 199.

42. A. James Reichley, *The Life of the Parties: A History of American Political Parties* (New York: The Free Press, 1992), p. 314.

43. Howard Penniman, *Sait's American Parties and Elections*, 5th ed. (New York: Appleton-Century-Crofts, 1952), p. 283.

44. James O'Kane, *The Crooked Ladder: Gangsters, Ethnicity, and the American Dream* (New Brunswick, NJ: Transaction Publishers, 1992).

45. Madison Grant, *Passing of the Great Race, or, the Racial Basis of European History* (New York: Ayer, 1970 [1918]), pp. 77–79.

46. Quoted in Maldwyn Allen Jones, supra, p. 204.

47. John R. Hersey, *A Bell for Adano* (New York: Knopf, 1944).

48. Finley Peter Dunne, *Mr. Dooley on Ivrything and Ivrybody*, Robert Hutchinson, ed. (New York: Dover Publications, 1963), p. 19.

49. U.S. Congress, House of Representatives, "Emancipation and Colonization," H. Report 148, 37th Cong., 2nd Sess., 1862, 14.

50. Barbara Miller Solomon, *Ancestors and Immigrants: A Changing New England Tradition* (Cambridge, MA: Harvard University Press, 1956), pp. 75, 79, 117.

51. Quoted in Ronald Takaki, *A Different Mirror* (Boston: Little, Brown, 1993), p. 164.

52. Quoted in Takaki, ibid., p. 161.

53. Richard D. Alba, *Ethnic Identity: The Transformation of White America* (New Haven: Yale University Press, 1990), pp. 186, 312.

54. Theodore Roosevelt, "History as Literature," in *The Works of Theodore Roosevelt*, supra, vol. 14, pp. 27–28.

55. Maldwyn Allen Jones, supra, p. 297.

56. Jones, ibid., p. 255.

57. James Davison Hunter, *Culture Wars: The Struggle to Define America* (New York: Basic Books, 1991), pp. 199–200.

58. Randall Balmer, *Mine Eyes Have Seen the Glory: A Journey into the Evangelical Subculture in America* (New York: Oxford University Press, 1989), pp. 32–37.

59. Quoted in Peter N. Carroll and David W. Noble, *The Free and the Unfree: A New History of the United States*, 2d ed. (New York: Penguin, 1988), p. 294.

60. H. L. Mencken, "On Being An American," in James T. Farrell, ed., *Prejudices*, (New York: Random House, 1958), p. 105.

61. Richard Hofstadter, *The Paranoid Style in American Politics* (Chicago: University of Chicago Press, 1964), pp. 73–74, n. 4.

62. Justin D. Fulton, *The Fight With Rome* (1889, reprinted New York: Arno, 1977), pp. 1–2.
63. *Church of the Holy Trinity v. United States*, 143 U.S. 457, 472 (1892).
64. Lord Bryce, *The American Commonwealth*, 2d ed. (London: Macmillan, 1891), vol. 2, pp. 2, 576–577.
65. Quoted in Robert T. Handy, *Undermined Establishment: Church-State Relations in America, 1880–1920* (Princeton, NJ: Princeton University Press, 1991), pp. 25–26.
66. Alfred Haworth Jones, *Roosevelt's Image Brokers: Poets, Playwrights, and the Use of the Lincoln Symbol* (Port Washington, NY: Kennikat Press, 1974), pp. 27–28.
67. Jones, ibid., p. 64.
68. Jones, ibid., p. 65
69. Jones, ibid., p. 71.
70. Jones, ibid., pp. 66–67.
71. Richard Polenberg, *One Nation Divisible: Class, Race, and Ethnicity in the United States Since 1938* (New York: Penguin, 1980), p. 24.

Chapter 3. The Third Republic: The Making of Multicultural America

1. Quoted in Robert Dallek, *The American Style of Foreign Policy: Cultural Politics and Foreign Affairs* (New York: Oxford University Press, 1983), p. 142.
2. Wendell L. Willkie, *One World* (New York: Simon & Schuster, 1943), pp. 192–194.
3. Quoted in Paul Gordon Lauren, *Power and Prejudice: The Politics and Diplomacy of Racial Discrimination* (Boulder, CO: Westview Press, 1988), p. 173.
4. Lauren, ibid., p. 195.
5. Lauren, ibid., p. 197.
6. Lauren, ibid., p. 173.
7. *Brown v. Board of Education of Topeka*, 347 U.S. 783 (1954); *Bolling v. Sharpe*, 347 U.S. 497 (1954). *Brown* applied to state law, *Bolling* to federal law.
8. Richard Polenberg, *One Nation Divisible: Class, Race, and Ethnicity in the United States Since 1938* (New York: Penguin, 1980), p. 24.
9. Bayard Rustin, "From Protest to Politics: The Future of the Civil Rights Movement," *Commentary* (February 1964).
10. *Public Papers of the Presidents: Lyndon B. Johnson, 1965* (Washington, DC: U.S. Government Printing Office, 1966), vol. 1, p. 636.
11. Hugh Davis Graham, *The Civil Rights Era: Origins and Development of National Policy, 1960–1972* (New York: Oxford University Press, 1990), pp. 104–106.
12. Graham, ibid., p. 111.
13. Graham, ibid., p. 106.
14. Graham, ibid., p. 110.

15. Graham, ibid., p. 62.

16. Thomas Byrne Edsall with Mary D. Edsall, *Chain Reaction: The Impact of Race, Rights, and Taxes on American Politics* (New York: W. W. Norton, 1991), pp. 50–51.

17. Stokely Carmichael and Charles V. Hamilton, *Black Power: The Politics of Liberation in America* (New York: Vintage, 1967).

18. Carmichael and Hamilton, ibid., pp. 53–54.

19. Stokely Carmichael, "What We Want," *New York Review of Books*, September 22, 1966, p. 5.

20. Gene Roberts, "Dr. King Declares Rights Movement Is Close to a Split," *New York Times*, July 9, 1966, p. 1.

21. Alfred Blumrosen, *Black Employment and the Law* (New Brunswick, NJ: Rutgers University Press, 1971).

22. *Green v. County School Board*, 391 U.S. 430 (1968); *Swann v. Charlotte-Mecklenburg Board of Education*, 402 U.S. 1 (1971).

23. Archibald Cox, *The Warren Court: Constitutional Decision as an Instrument of Reform* (Cambridge, MA: Harvard University Press, 1968).

24. Richard Neely, *How Courts Govern America* (New Haven: Yale University Press, 1981), p. 6.

25. Daniel Patrick Moynihan, "The New Racialism," in Moynihan, *Coping: Essays on the Practice of Government* (New York: Random House, 1973), pp. 204–205.

26. Thernstrom, Abigail, *Whose Votes Count? Affirmative Action and Minority Voting Rights* (Cambridge, MA: Harvard University Press, 1987), p. 51.

27. Russel B. Nye, *This Almost Chosen People* (East Lansing, MI: Michigan State University Press, 1966), p. 340.

28. David A. Hollinger, "Postethnic America," *Contention*, vol. 2, no. 1 (Fall 1992), p. 85.

29. Lawrence Wright, "One Drop of Blood," *The New Yorker* (July 1994), pp. 46–55.

30. Quoted in Tony Snow, "Professor Nietzsche's Blackboard Jungle," *The Washington Times*, January 4, 1990, p. F2.

31. Walter E. Williams, "Lying About Race Becoming Common Because of Quotas," *Gazette Telegraph* (Colorado Springs), January 25, 1991, p. B9.

32. *The New York Times*, December 11, 1988.

33. Terry Eastland and William J. Bennett, *Counting by Race: Equality from the Founding Fathers to Bakke and Weber* (New York: Basic Books, 1979), pp. 168–169.

34. Guy B. Johnson, "Personality in a White-Indian-Negro Community," in Alain Locke and Bernhard J. Stern, eds., *When Peoples Meet* (New York: Progressive Education Association, 1942), p. 577.

35. Melvin J. Lasky, "Race, Press, and Chromatic Deceits," *Encounter* (April 1986), p. 75.

36. David Rosner and Gerald Markowitz, "Race and Foster Care," *Dissent*, Spring 1993, p. 235.

37. Shane C. Perry, Letter, *Reconstruction*, vol. 2, no. 1, 1992, p. 109.

38. Mona Charen, "The Color of Love and Longing," *The Washington Times*, March 22, 1993, p. E4.

39. Abigail M. Thernstrom, *Whose Votes Count?*, supra, pp. 187–189.

40. Lani Guinier, "The Triumph of Tokenism: The Voting Rights Act and the Theory of Black Electoral Success," 89 *Michigan Law Review*, pp. 1077, 1102–1103.

41. Joane Nagel, "The Ethnic Revolution: Emergence of Ethnic Nationalism," in Leo Driedger, ed., *Ethnic Canada: Identities and Inequalities* (Toronto: Copp Clark Pitman, 1987), p. 40.

42. Felix and Padilla, "Latino Ethnicity in the City of Chicago," in Susan Olzak and Joane Nagel, eds., *Competitive Ethnic Relations* (Boston: Academic Press, 1986), pp. 153–172.

43. Ben L. Martin, "From Negro to Black to African American: The Power of Names and Naming," *Political Science Quarterly*, vol. 106, no. 1 (1991), p. 98.

44. Martin, ibid., p. 83.

45. Michael Novak, *The Catholic Ethic and the Spirit of Capitalism* (New York: The Free Press, 1993), p. 177.

46. Cedric McClester, *Kwanzaa: Everything You Always Wanted to Know But Didn't Know Where to Ask* (New York: Gumbs & Thomas, 1985).

47. Molefi Kete Asante, *Afrocentricity: The Theory of Social Change* (Buffalo: Amulefi Publishing Co., 1980), p. 9.

48. "Democrats Pick Non-Hispanic in Third Houston Vote," *The Washington Post*, July 29, 1992, p. A11.

49. Bill Keller, "Gorbachev Urges Minority States," *New York Times*, April 18, 1987, p. A5.

50. Toni-Michelle C. Travis, "Boston: The Unfinished Agenda," in R. P. Browning, D. R. Marshall and D. H. Tabb, eds., *Racial Politics in American Cities* (New York: Longman, 1990), p. 117.

51. *United Jewish Organizations of Williamsburgh, Inc.* v. *Carey*, 430 U.S. 144 (1977).

52. Owen M. Fiss, "Groups and the Equal Protection Clause," *Philosophy and Public Affairs*, vol. 5, no. 2 (Winter 1976), pp. 108, 148, 157, 159–160.

53. Ronald Dworkin, "The Bakke Case: An Exchange," *New York Review of Books* no. 18 (November 10, 1977), pp. 11–15; Dworkin, "Reverse Discrimination," *New York Review of Books* no. 21 (January 26, 1978), pp. 42–44.

54. Ronald J. Fiscus, *The Constitutional Logic of Affirmative Action* (Durham, NC: Duke University Press, 1992), pp. 13–14.

55. Ellis Cose, *A Nation of Strangers: Prejudice, Politics, and the Peopling of America* (New York: William Morrow, 1992), p. 108.

56. Cose, ibid., p. 105.

57. Quoted in Paul Gordon Lauren, supra, p. 228.

58. Lyndon B. Johnson, "The State of the Union—Address of the President of the United States," *Cong. Record*, Jan. 8, 1964, H113.

59. Hearings Before Subcommittee No. 1 of the Committee on the Judiciary, U.S. House of Representatives (Washington, DC: U.S. Government Printing Office), p. 418.

60. Hearings, ibid., pp. 2–3.

61. "The Immigrants," *Business Week*, July 13, 1992, p. 114.

62. Ellis Cose, supra, p. 11.

63. "State of America: Census Report," *Washington Post*, March 3, 1991.

64. Daniel Patrick Moynihan, *Pandaemonium: Ethnicity in International Politics* (New York: Oxford University Press, 1993), p. 100.

65. Takashi Oka, "A High School Tosses An American Salad," *The Christian Science Monitor*, April 10, 1992, p. 19.

66. Quoted in Lawrence Auster, "America: Multiethnic, not Multicultural," *Academic Questions* (Fall 1991), vol. 4, no. 4, p. 76.

67. David A. Hollinger, "Postethnic America," *Contention*, vol. 2, no. 1 (Fall 1992), p. 85.

68. September 1988 Census Bureau Report, quoted in Alexander DeConde, *Ethnicity, Race, and American Foreign Policy* (Boston: Northeastern University Press, 1992), p. 159.

69. Katherine Tate, *From Protest to Politics: The New Black Voters in American Elections* (Cambridge, MA: Harvard University Press, 1993), p. 173.

70. John Mintz, "Perot's War: Viet Vets' 'Tombstone'," *The Washington Post*, July 7, 1992, p. A1.

Chapter 4. The White Overclass and the Racial Spoils System

1. "Zoe's Child Care Lessons," editorial, *The Wall Street Journal*, January 26, 1993, p. A14.

2. Paul Seabury, "HEW and the Universities," *Commentary* (February 1972), p. 44.

3. David Hackett Fischer, *Albion's Seed: Four British Folkways in America* (New York: Oxford University Press, 1989), p. 758.

4. Michael T. Jacobs, *Short-Term America: The Causes and Cures of Our Business Myopia* (Boston: Harvard Business School Press, 1991), p. 82.

5. Jacobs, ibid., pp. 201–202.

6. "Executive Pay: It Doesn't Add Up," *Business Week*, April 26, 1993, p. 122.

7. Jacobs, *Short-Term America*, supra, p. 204.

8. "Executive Pay," supra, p. 122.

9. Donald L. Bartlett and James B. Steele, *America: What Went Wrong?* (Kansas City, MO: Andrews and McMeel, 1992), pp. 99–101.

10. The University of Michigan's National Election Study (NES), quoted in Frank J. Sorauf, *Inside Campaign Finance: Myths and Realities* (New Haven: Yale University Press, 1992), p. 29.

11. William Greider, *Who Will Tell the People? The Betrayal of American Democracy* (New York: Simon & Schuster, 1992), p. 248.

12. *Hidden Power: Campaign Contributions of Large Individual Donors, 1989–1990* (Washington, DC: Citizen Action, 1991), p. 18.

13. Donna F. Edwards and Peter Nye, "Campaign Finance Reform: Change or Rhetoric?" *Public Citizen* (March/April 1993), p. 12.

14. Edwards and Nye, ibid., p. 10.

15. Larry Makinson, *The Price of Admission* (Washington, DC: The Center for Responsive Politics, 1991), p. 10.

16. Charles R. Babcock, "Hill Fund-Raising: Better Safe than Sorry?" *Washington Post*, September 26, 1990, p. A23.

17. Edwards and Nye, supra, p. 12.

18. Richard L. Berke, "Pragmatism Guides Political Gifts," *The New York Times*, September 16, 1990, p. 26.

19. John Judis, "The Pressure Elite," *The American Prospect* (Spring 1992), p. 24.

20. Thomas Byrne Edsall with Mary D. Edsall, *Chain Reaction: The Impact of Race, Rights and Taxes on American Politics* (New York: W. W. Norton, 1992), p. 182.

21. Cited in Walter Dean Burnham, "Elections and Democratic Institutions," *Society*, vol. 24, no. 4 (May/June 1987), p. 39.

22. V. O. Key, *Southern Politics in State and Nation*, 2d ed. (Knoxville, TN: University of Tennessee Press, 1984), p. 307.

23. Quoted in E. Digby Baltzell, *The Protestant Establishment Revisited*, Howard G. Shneiderman, ed. (New Brunswick, NJ: Transaction Publishers, 1991).

24. Bart Landry, *The New Black Middle Class* (Berkeley: University of California Press, 1987), p. 212.

25. Landry, ibid., p. 148.

26. Morton Kondracke, "The Two Black Americas," *The New Republic*, February 6, 1989, p. 18.

27. Edsall with Mary D. Edsall, supra, p. 162.

28. Augie Meier, "Civil Rights Strategies for Employment," in Arthur M. Ross and Herbert Hill, eds., *Employment, Race and Poverty* (New York: Harcourt, Brace and World, 1967), p. 198.

29. William B. Gould, *Black Workers in White Unions* (Ithaca, NY: Cornell University Press, 1977), pp. 345–351.

30. "Nixon Urges 'Black Ownership' to Help Solve Racial Problems," *New York Times*, April 26, 1968, 27:1.

31. Philip H. Burch, Jr., *Elites in American History*, vol. 3, *The New Deal to the Carter Administration* (New York: Holmes and Meier, 1980), pp. 184–185.

32. California Legislature, Joint Committee for Review of the Master Plan for Higher Education, *California Faces . . . California's Future: Education for Citizenship in a Multicultural Democracy* (1989), pp. 20–21.

33. Lewis R. Jones, "Admissions Omissions," *The American Prospect* (Winter 1993), p. 153.

34. Kimberley Naahieula, "Admitting Goals," *The Virginia Advocate* (University of Virginia), April 1991, p. 7, quoted in Thomas Sowell, *Inside American Education* (New York: The Free Press, 1993), p. 280.

35. Lino Graglia, "Racial Preferences in Admission to Institutions of Higher Education," in Howard Dickman, ed., *The Imperiled Academy* (New Brunswick, NJ: Transaction Publishers, 1993), p. 134.

36. Timothy Maguire, "My Bout With Affirmative Action," *Commentary*, April 1992, pp. 50–52.

37. Quoted in Barbara A. Perry and Julia A. McDonough, "Affirmative Action in Higher Education: Bakke to the Future" (Paper delivered to the American Political Science Association, Atlanta, 31 August–3 September 1989), p. 14.

38. U.S. Commission on Civil Rights, "Civil Rights Issues Facing Asian Americans in the 1990s" (February 1992), pp.106–107.

39. Alexandra K. Wigdor and John H. Hartigan, "The Case for Fairness," *Society* (March/April 1990), p. 4.

40. Thomas Sowell, supra, p. 282.

41. Linda Chavez, "Demystifying Multiculturalism," *National Review*, February 21, 1994, vol. 46, no. 3, p. 26.

42. *Commentary*, May 1978, p. 27.

43. Derek Bok, "Admitting Success," *The New Republic*, February 4, 1985, p. 14.

44. Andrew Hacker, "An Affirmative Vote for Affirmative Action," *Academic Questions*, Fall 1992, vol. 5, no. 4, p. 25.

45. John Larew, "Why Are Droves of Unqualified, Unprepared Kids Getting into Our Top Colleges?," *The Washington Monthly* (June, 1991), pp. 10–14.

46. 110 Cong. Rec., p. 12723.

47. Nathan Glazer, *Affirmative Discrimination* (New York: Basic Books, 1975), pp. 46–47.

48. Alan Farnham, "Holding Firm on Affirmative Action," *Fortune* (March 13, 1989), p. 88.

49. Linda Greenhouse, "Court Bars Plan Set Up to Provide Jobs to Minorities," *The New York Times* (January 24, 1989), p. 1.

50. George R. LaNoue, "Social Science and Minority 'Set-Asides,'" *The Public Interest*, no. 110 (Winter 1993), p. 51.

51. LaNoue, ibid., p. 60.

52. "Shades of Green," *The Economist*, September 22, 1992.

53. David Drier, "'Disadvantaged' Contractors' Unfair Advantage," *The Wall Street Journal* (February 21, 1989), p. A20.

54. Bernard J. Frieden, "The Downtown Job Puzzle," *The Public Interest*, issue 97 (Fall 1989), pp. 80–81.
55. Joel Garreau, "Life on the Edge," *The Washington Post*, May 17, 1992, p. C4.
56. Bernard J. Frieden, supra, pp. 83–84.
57. Eric Mann, "The Poverty of Corporatism," *The Nation*, March 29, 1993, p. 410.
58. Evan Gahr, "FCC Preferences: Affirmative Action for the Wealthy," *Insight*, February 22, 1993, pp. 6–7.
59. Leslie Wayne, "Big Firms Gain Bond Work Set for Minorities," *New York Times*, August 11, 1994, pp. A1, D19.
60. Miles Benson, "Government Lax in Hiring Minorities," *San Francisco Chronicle* (December 1, 1991).
61. Katherine Tate, *From Protest to Politics: The New Black Voters in American Elections* (Cambridge, MA: Harvard University Press, 1993), p. 93.
62. Jeremiah Cotton, "Opening the Gap: The Decline in Black Economic Indicators in the 1980s," *Social Science Quarterly*, vol. 70, no. 4, pp. 803–819.
63. Bayard Rustin, "The Blacks and the Unions," *Harper's Magazine*, May 1971, pp. 73–81.
64. U.S. Bureau of the Census, Current Population Reports, Series P-60, Number 174, Money Income of Households, Families, and Persons in the United States: 1990 (Washington, DC: U.S. Government Printing Office, 1991).
65. Douglass S. Massey and Nancy A. Denton, *American Apartheid: Segregation and the Making of the Underclass* (Cambridge, MA: Harvard University Press, 1993), p. 160.
66. Massey and Denton, ibid., p. 77.
67. See, for example, William Labov, *Language in the Inner City: Studies in the Black English Vernacular* (Philadelphia: University of Pennsylvania Press, 1972); William Labov, "The Logic of Nonstandard English," in Paul Stoller, ed., *Black American English: Its Background and Its Uses, in the Schools and in Literature* (New York: Dell Publishing, 1975), pp. 89–131; John Baugh, *Black Street Speech: Its History, Structure, and Survival* (Austin: University of Texas Press, 1983).
68. William Julius Wilson, *The Truly Disadvantaged: The Inner City, the Underclass and Public Policy* (Chicago: University of Chicago Press, 1987), p. 157.
69. Wilson, ibid., p. 26.
70. Bayard Rustin, "From Protest to Politics: The Future of the Civil Rights Movement," *Commentary* (February 1965), p. 28.
71. Quoted in Hugh Brogan, *The Penguin History of the United States of America* (New York: Penguin, 1990), p. 639.
72. Mary R. Jackman and Robert W. Jackman, *Class Awareness in the United States* (Berkeley and Los Angeles: University of California Press, 1983).

73. Gerald Dillingham, "The Emerging Black Middle Class: Class Consciousness or Race Consciousness?," in *Ethnic and Racial Studies* no. 4 (1981), pp. 432–447; I. A. Lewis and William Schneider, "Black Voting, Bloc Voting and the Democrats," *Public Opinion* 6 (5): 12–15, 59.

74. Katherine Tate, *From Protest to Politics,* supra, p. 43.

75. Massey and Denton, *American Apartheid,* supra, p. 214.

76. Massey and Denton, ibid., pp. 214–215.

77. Bell Hooks, *Black Looks: Race and Representation* (Boston: South End Press, 1993).

78. Quoted in Hugh Davis Graham, *The Civil Rights Era: Origins and Development of National Policy, 1960–1972* (New York: Oxford University Press, 1990), p. 110.

Chapter 5. The Revolution of the Rich

1. "Inequality," *The Economist,* November 5, 1994, pp. 19–20.

2. Heather MacDonald, "The Diversity Principle," *Partisan Review,* vol. 60, no. 4 (1993), p. 621.

3. Quoted in David Remnick, "Day of the Dittohead," *The Washington Post,* February 20, 1994, p. C4.

4. Lee Atwater, "The South in 1984," unpublished memo for the Reagan–Bush campaign, quoted in Thomas Byrne Edsall and Mary D. Edsall, *Chain Reaction: The Impact of Race, Rights and Taxes on American Politics* (New York: W. W. Norton and Company, 1990), p. 221.

5. Guy Molyneux and William Schneider, "Ross Is Boss," *The Atlantic Monthly,* May 1993, p. 92.

6. Mack C. Shelley, *The Permanent Majority: The Conservative Coalition in the United States Congress* (University, AL: University of Alabama Press, 1983).

7. Larry M. Schwab, *The Illusion of a Conservative Reagan Revolution* (New Brunswick, NJ: Transaction Publishers, 1991), p. 221.

8. John D. Ehrlichman, *Witness to Power* (New York: Simon & Schuster, 1982), pp. 228–229.

9. Paul E. Peterson and Mark Rom, "Lower Taxes, More Spending, and Budget Deficits," in Charles O. Jones, ed., *The Reagan Legacy: Promise and Performance* (Chatham, NJ: Chatham House Publishers, 1988), p. 215.

10. Larry M. Schwab, supra, pp. 96–97.

11. Robert McIntyre, *Inequality and the Federal Budget Deficit: 1991 Edition* (Washington, DC: Citizens for Tax Justice, 1991), pp. 10–11.

12. Peter G. Peterson, "Facing Up," *The Atlantic Monthly,* October 1993, pp. 82, 84.

13. Robert McIntyre, supra, p. 15.

14. Paul E. Peterson, "An Immodest Proposal," *Daedalus*, vol. 121, no. 4 (Fall 1992), p. 160.

15. George Gilder, *Wealth and Poverty* (New York: Basic Books, 1981), p. 118.

16. Edward N. Luttwak, *The Endangered American Dream* (New York: Simon & Schuster, 1993), p. 163.

17. Robert McIntyre, supra, p. 16.

18. Frederick R. Strobel, *Upward Dreams, Downward Mobility: The Economic Decline of the American Middle Class* (Lanham, MD: Rowman & Littlefield, 1993), p. 144.

19. Bennett Harrison, "Where Private Investment Fails," *The American Prospect*, Fall 1992, p. 106.

20. Larry M. Schwab, supra, p. 177.

21. Kevin Phillips, *Boiling Point: Republicans, Democrats, and the Decline of Middle-Class Prosperity* (New York: Random House, 1993), p. 111, table 5.

22. Thomas Byrne Edsall with Mary D. Edsall, *Chain Reaction: The Impact of Race, Rights and Taxes on American Politics* (New York: W. W. Norton & Company, 1992), p. 169.

23. Thomas Byrne Edsall with Mary D. Edsall, ibid., p. 193.

24. Robert McIntyre, *Inequality and the Federal Budget Deficit,* 1990 edition (Washington, DC: Citizens for Tax Justice, March 1990).

25. "'Soak the Rich' Fallacy," *Christian Science Monitor,* May 10, 1991.

26. Advisory Commission on Intergovernmental Relations, A Commission Report, *Interstate Tax Competition* (Washington, DC: U.S. Government Printing Office, 1981), p. 63.

27. Kevin Phillips, supra, p. 111, table 5.

28. Larry M. Schwab, supra, p. 104.

29. William Greider, *Who Will Tell the People: The Betrayal of American Democracy* (New York: Simon & Schuster, 1992), p. 100.

30. Greider, ibid., pp. 98–99.

31. "Inequality," *The Economist,* supra, p. 20.

32. "The Global Economy: Who Gets Hurt," *Business Week,* August 10, 1992, p. 52.

33. "What's Wrong? Why the Industrialized Nations Are Stalled," *Businesss Week,* August 2, 1993, p. 59.

34. Ray Marshall and Marc Tucker, *Thinking for a Living: Education and the Wealth of Nations* (New York: Basic Books, 1992), p. 49.

35. Robert Kuttner, "Skills Don't Create Jobs," *The Washington Post,* February 8, 1994.

36. Richard J. Barnet, "The End of Jobs," *Harper's Magazine,* September 1993, p. 48.

37. "What's Wrong?" supra, pp. 56–57.

38. "The Global Economy," supra, p. 50.

39. "The Global Economy," ibid., p. 50.

40. "Clinton's Version of Supply-Side Economics," editorial, *In These Times*, August 23, 1993, p. 2.

41. Richard J. Barnet, supra, p. 48.

42. Herbert Spencer, *Principles of Sociology* (New York: Appleton, 1876–1885, reprinted 1887–1897), quoted in Bernard Semmel, *The Liberal Ideal and the Demons of Empire: Theories of Imperialism from Adam Smith to Lenin* (Baltimore: Johns Hopkins University Press, 1993), p. 107.

43. J. A. Schumpeter, *Imperialism and Social Classes* (New York: Meridian, 1919, reprinted 1974, pp. 84–89, quoted in Semmel, ibid., p. 173.

44. Undelivered speech as summarized by Friedrich Engels, "The Free Trade Congress at Brussels," quoted in Roman Szporluk, *Communism and Nationalism: Karl Marx v. Friedrich List* (New York: Oxford University Press, 1988), pp. 40–41.

45. Karl Marx, "Speech on the Question of Free Trade," in Karl Marx, *Collected Works* (New York: International Publishers, no date available), vol. 6, p. 465.

46. Quoted in William Greider, "The Global Marketplace: Closet Dictator," in *The Case Against Free Trade* (Berkeley: North Atlantic Books, 1993), p. 209.

47. Quoted in Richard J. Barnet and John Cavanagh, *Global Dreams: Imperial Corporations and the New World Order* (New York: Simon & Schuster, 1994), p. 281.

48. "People Protectionism," editorial, *The Wall Street Journal*, June 11, 1984, p. 24; "In Praise of Huddled Masses," editorial, *Wall Street Journal*, July 3, 1984, p. 16.

49. "In Praise of Huddled Masses," ibid.

50. "The Honest Solution," editorial, *The New Republic*, April 1, 1985, p. 20.

51. Malcolm S. Forbes, Jr., "We Need More People," *Forbes*, February 9, 1987, p. 25.

52. Statement of Rep. Barney Frank (D.-Mass.), *Congressional Record*, June 13, 1984, H5726.

53. See George Borjas and Richard Freeman, *Immigration and the Work Force: Economic Consequences for the United States and Source Areas* (Chicago: University of Chicago Press, 1992).

54. Thomas J. Espenshade and Thomas Muller, *The Fourth Wave: California's Newest Immigrants* (Washington, DC: Urban Institute Press, 1985).

55. George Borjas, *Friends or Strangers* (New York: Basic Books, 1990), pp. 18–19.

56. Julian L. Simon, *The Economic Consequences of Immigration* (London: Basil Blackwell, 1989).

57. Thomas Muller, *Immigrants and the American City* (New York: New York University Press, 1993), p. 283.

58. "To Make a Nation," *U.S. News and World Report*, October 4, 1993, p. 52.

59. "Zoe's Child Care Lessons," editorial, *The Wall Street Journal*, January 26, 1993, p. A14.

60. Quoted in Arthur M. Schlesinger, Jr., *The Coming of the New Deal*, vol. 2 of *The Age of Roosevelt* (Boston: Houghton Mifflin, 1958), p. 479.

61. Thomas Muller, *Immigrants and the American City*, supra, p. 282.

62. Susan Headden, "Made in the U.S.A.," *U.S. News and World Report*, November 22, 1993, p. 54.

63. Thomas Jefferson, "Bill for the More General Diffusion of Knowledge," in Paul Leicester Ford, ed., *The Works of Thomas Jefferson*, Federal Edition (12 vols.) (New York, 1904–5), vol. 2.

64. Pilita Clark, "Fortress America," *Sydney Morning Herald*, April 30, 1994, section 5.

65. Edward Luttwak, *The Endangered American Dream* (New York: Simon & Schuster, 1993), p. 197.

66. Robert Reich, *The Work of Nations: Preparing Ourselves for Twenty-First Century Capitalism* (New York: Knopf, 1991).

67. "Private Tolls on Interstates Discussed," *The Washington Post*, October 1, 1993, p. A23.

Chapter 6. Alternative Americas

1. Glenora Croucher, "Flag Waving: Does the Country Need a New Pledge of Allegiance?" *In These Times*, November 30, 1992, p. 7.

2. George Will, "Commencement at Duke," *The American Scholar*, Autumn 1991, p. 498.

3. Quoted in Giles Ginn, "Perception at the Pitch of Passion," *Yale Review*, Autumn 1984, p. 141.

4. Cited in Dennis Farney, "Turning Point: Even U.S. Politics Are Being Reshaped by a Global Economy," *The Wall Street Journal*, October 28, 1992, p. A1.

5. George Weigel, "Catholicism and the American Proposition," *First Things*, May 1991, p. 38.

6. Quoted in C. Vann Woodward, *The Old World's New World* (New York: Oxford University Press, 1991).

7. Allan Nevins, ed., *America Through British Eyes* (Gloucester, MA: Peter Smith, 1968), p. 261.

8. G. K. Chesterton, *What I Saw in America* (New York: Da Capo Press, 1968), p. 7.

9. Address by Margaret Thatcher, March 8, 1991, Washington, DC. Quoted in Everett C. Ladd, "The American Ideology: An Exploration and a Survey

of the Origins, Meaning, and Role of American Values," Conference paper for "The New Global Popular Culture," The American Enterprise Institute, March 10, 1992, p. 29.

10. Robert Penn Warren, *The Legacy of the Civil War: Meditations on the Centennial* (New York: Random House, 1961), p. 78.

11. Allan Bloom, ed., *Confronting the Constitution* (Washington, DC: The American Enterprise Institute Press, 1990).

12. Quoted in Michael Kammen, *Mystic Chords of Memory* (New York: Alfred A. Knopf, 1991), p. 231.

13. *The Economist*, November 30, 1991, p. 18.

14. Abraham Lincoln, "The Perpetuation of Our Political Institutions: Address Before the Young Men's Lyceum of Springfield, Illinois, January 27, 1838," in John Grafton, ed., *Great Speeches: Abraham Lincoln* (Mineola, NY: Dover, 1991), p. 5.

15. Mark Twain, *Life on the Mississippi* (Boston: J. R. Osgood and Company, 1883; reprinted by New American Library, New York, 1961), p. 15.

16. George Santayana, *Character and Opinion in the United States* (Garden City, NY: Doubleday, 1956), pp. 111–112.

17. Henry Steele Commager, *Living Ideas in America* (New York: Harper & Row, 1951), p. 109.

18. C. Vann Woodward, "The Aging of America," in C. Vann Woodward, *The Future of the Past* (New York: Oxford University Press, 1989), p. 107.

19. "Survey America," *The Economist*, October 26, 1991, pp. 25–26.

20. Peter Scott, *Knowledge and Nation* (Edinburgh: Edinburgh University Press, 1990), p. 168.

21. Linda Colley, *Britons: Forging the Nation, 1707–1837* (New Haven: Yale University Press, 1992).

22. Eugen Weber, *Peasants into Frenchmen: The Modernization of Rural France, 1870–1914* (Stanford, CA: Stanford University Press, 1976), pp. 485–486.

23. G. K. Chesterton, *Heretics* (New York: John Luce Company, 1905), pp. 256–257.

24. H. L. Mencken, *Prejudices*, James T. Farrell, ed. (New York: Random House, 1955), pp. 99–100.

25. Ralph Waldo Emerson, "The American Scholar," in Larzer Ziff, *Ralph Waldo Emerson: Selected Essays* (New York: Penguin, 1982), p. 105.

26. Quoted in Hans Kohn, "The Paradox of Fichte's Nationalism," *Journal of the History of Ideas*, vol. 10, no. 3 (June 1949), p. 326.

27. Quoted in Hans Kohn, "Arndt and the Character of German Nationalism," *American Historical Review*, vol. 54, no. 4 (July 1949), pp. 787–803.

28. Ronald Koven, "Muslim Immigrants and French Nationalists," *Society*, vol. 29, no. 4 (May/June 1992), p. 33.

29. "Harper's Index," *Harper's Magazine*, January 1992, p. 13.

30. Herman Melville, *White-Jacket* (New York: Holt, Rinehart and Winston, 1967), p. 150.
31. Conor Cruise O'Brien, *God Land: Reflections on Religion and Nationalism* (Cambridge, MA: Harvard University Press, 1987).
32. Donald Harman Akenson, *God's Peoples: Covenant and Land in South Africa, Israel and Ulster* (Ithaca, NY: Cornell University Press, 1992).
33. John Milton, *Areopagitica,* in Stephen Orgel and Jonathan Goldberg, eds., *John Milton* (Oxford University Press, 1991), p. 244.
34. John Milton, ibid., p. 265.
35. John Adam Cramb, *The Origins and Destiny of Imperial Britain and Nineteenth Century Europe* (New York: E. P. Dutton and Co., 1915).
36. Quoted in N. V. Riasanovsky, *A Parting of the Ways: Government and the Educated Public in Russia, 1801–1855* (Oxford: The Clarendon Press, 1976), pp. 192, 187.
37. Mikhail Petrovich Pogodin, "Letter on Russian History" 1837, in *The Mind of Modern Russia,* ed. Hans Kohn (New Brunswick, NJ: Rutgers University Press, 1955), pp. 66–68.
38. Peter Alter, *Nationalism* (London: Edward Arnold, 1989).
39. E. J. Hobsbawm, *Nations and Nationalism Since 1780: Programme, Myth, Reality* (Cambridge: Cambridge University Press, 1991), p. 22.
40. Cited in Elie Kedourie, *Nationalism,* 4th ed. (Cambridge, MA: Blackwell, 1993), p. 7.
41. Quoted in George Gusdorf, *La Conscience Révolutionnaire: Les Idéologues* (Paris, 1978), p. 174.
42. Quoted in Tzvetan Todorov, *On Human Diversity; Nationalism, Racism, and Exoticism in French Thought* (Cambridge, MA: Harvard University Press, 1993), p. 245.
43. Todorov, ibid., p. 211.
44. Alexis de Tocqueville, *Democracy in America,* ed. Phillips Bradley (New York: Vintage Books, 1954), vol. 1, p. 410.
45. Matthew Arnold, *Civilization in the United States: First and Last Impressions of America* (Boston: Cupples and Hurd, 1888), pp. 159–192.
46. John Bodmar, *Remaking America: Public Memory, Commemoration, and Patriotism in the Twentieth Century* (Princeton, NJ: Princeton University Press, 1992), p. 237.
47. *The Responsive Community,* Winter 1992–1993, p. 80.
48. See generally Bruce Clayton, *Forgotten Prophet: The Life of Randolph Bourne* (Baton Rouge: Louisiana State University Press, 1984).
49. Kallen, ibid., pp. 124–125.
50. Pierre Trudeau, "Against Nationalism," *New Perspectives Quarterly,* Summer 1990, p. 60.
51. Michael Waltzer "Comment," in Amy Guttman, ed., *Multiculturalism and*

"The Politics of Recognition": An Essay by Charles Taylor (Princeton, NJ: Princeton University Press, 1992) pp. 100–101.

52. Kallen, "Democracy *versus* the Melting Pot," supra, p. 116.

53. Randolph Bourne, "Trans-national America," *Atlantic Monthly* (July 1916), vol. 118, no. 1, p. 93.

54. Bourne, ibid., p. 95.

55. Bourne, ibid., p. 96.

56. Kallen, "Democracy *versus* the Melting Pot," supra, p. 124

57. Kallen, ibid., pp. 119–120.

58. Kallen, ibid., p. 122.

59. Kallen, ibid., p. 122.

60. Michael Walzer, *What It Means to be an American: Essays on the American Experience* (New York: Marsilio, 1992), p. 17.

61. Michael Walzer, ibid., p. 74.

62. Michael Walzer, ibid., p. 49.

63. Michael Walzer, ibid., pp. 17–18.

64. Michael Walzer, ibid., p. 47.

65. Diane Ravitch, "A Response to Auster," *Academic Questions*, vol. 4, no. 4 (Fall 1991), p. 86.

66. Nathan Glazer, "Multiculturalism and Public Policy," in Henry J. Aaron, Thomas E. Mann, and Timothy Taylor, eds., *Values and Public Policy* (Washington, DC: Brookings Institution, 1994).

67. John Stuart Mill, "On Tocqueville," in Mortimer J. Adler, Otto Bird, and Robert M. Hutchins, eds., *The Great Ideas Today: 1964* (Chicago: William Benton, 1964), p. 479.

68. Sanyika Shakur, a.k.a. Monster Kody Scott, *Monster: The Autobiography of an L.A. Gang Member* (New York: The Atlantic Monthly Press, 1993), p. 206.

69. "Christian Group Keeping to the Right," *The New York Times*, September 12, 1993, p. A37.

70. John George and Laird Wilcox, *Nazis, Communists, Klansmen, and Others on the Fringe* (Buffalo, NY: Prometheus Books, 1992), pp. 37–38.

71. Quoted in Allen J. Matusow, *Joseph R. McCarthy* (Englewood Cliffs, NJ: Prentice-Hall, 1970), p. 21.

72. Michael Lind, "Rev. Robertson's Grand International Conspiracy Theory," *The New York Review of Books*, February 2, 1995, p. 21.

73. Sidney Blumenthal, "Christian Soldiers," *The New Yorker*, July 18, 1994, p. 37.

74. John George and Leonard Wilcox, supra, p. 245.

75. Stephen Bates, *Battleground: One Mother's Crusade, the Religious Right, and the Struggle for Control of Our Classrooms* (New York: Poseidon Press, 1993), p. 105.

76. Bates, ibid., p. 71.

77. Peter W. Williams, *Popular Religion in America,* rev. ed. (Urbana: University of Illinois Press, Illini Books edition, 1990), p. 193, n. 181.

78. William F. Buckley, Jr., *In Search of Anti-Semitism* (New York: Continuum, 1992).

79. Peter Viereck, "The Radical Right from McCarthy through Goldwater," in *Shame and Glory of the Intellectuals: Babbitt, Jr., vs. the Rediscovery of Values* (New York: Capricorn Books, 1965), pp. 322–323.

80. Raymond A. St. John, *American Literature for Christian Schools,* Book 2, *Realism, Naturalism, and Modern American Literature,* Teacher's Edition (Greenville, SC: Bob Jones University Press, 1991), p. 541, quoted in Albert J. Menendez, *Visions of Reality: What Fundamentalist Schools Teach* (Buffalo, NY: Prometheus Books, 1993), p. 53.

81. Menendez, ibid., p. 52.

82. David A. Fisher, *World History for Christian Students* (Greenville, SC: Bob Jones University Press, 1984), p. 180, quoted in Menendez, ibid., p. 34.

83. Gary North, "The Intellectual Schizophrenia of the New Christian Right," in *Christianity and Civilization,* vol. 1 (Geneva Ministries, 1982), p. 25, quoted in Os Guinness, *The American Hour: A Time of Reckoning and the Once and Future Role of Faith* (New York: The Free Press, 1993), p. 261.

84. Gunnar Myrdal, *An American Dilemma* (New York: Pantheon, 1975), quoted in Daniel Patrick Moynihan, *Pandaemonium: Ethnicity in International Politics* (Oxford: Oxford University Press, 1993), p. 58.

85. Quoted in William S. Willis, Jr., "Divide and Rule: Red, White, and Black in the Southeast," *Journal of Negro History,* no. 48 (1963), p. 165.

86. Quoted in James W. Loewen, *The Mississippi Chinese: Between Black and White,* 2d ed. (Cambridge, MA: Waveland Press, 1988 [1971]), p. 23.

87. Quoted in Ronald Takaki, *Strangers from a Different Shore* (New York: Penguin, 1989), p. 153.

88. Clement T. Imhoff, "The Recruiter," in Marc S. Miller, ed., *Working Lives* (New York: Pantheon, 1974), p. 56.

89. Quoted in Peter N. Caroll and David W. Noble, *The Free and the Unfree: A New History of the United States,* 2d ed. (New York: Penguin, 1988), p. 265.

90. William Smith, *A New Voyage to Guinea* (1744), quoted in J. Dillard, *Black English: Its History and Usage in the United States* (New York: Random House, 1972), pp. 73–74.

Chapter 7. Liberal Nationalism

1. Johann Gottfried Herder, "Essay on the Origin of Language" (1772), in F. M. Barnard, *Herder's Social and Political Thought: From Enlightenment to Nationalism* (Oxford: Oxford University Press, 1965), pp. 173–174. Emphasis in original.

2. Michael Walzer, "Comment," in Charles Taylor, *Multiculturalism and the Politics of Recognition* (Princeton, N.J.: Princeton University Press, 1992), p. 100.

3. Theodore Roosevelt, *The Winning of the West,* in Herman Hagedorn, ed., *The Works of Theodore Roosevelt,* 24 vols. (New York, 1925), vol. 10, p. 9.

4. Orlando Patterson, "Black Like All of Us: Celebrating Multiculturalism Diminishes Blacks' Role in American Culture," *The Washington Post,* Sunday, February 7, 1993, p. C2.

5. Albert Murray, *The Omni-Americans: New Perspectives on Black Experience and American Culture* (New York: Avon, 1970), p. 112.

6. Phillip T. Gay, "A Vote Against the Use of 'African-American,'" *Los Angeles Times,* Metro ed. April 2, 1989, pt. 2, p. 2.

7. Wilson J. Moses, "On Dr. Charles T. Davis," *Reconstruction,* vol. 1, no. 1, 1992, p. 76.

8. Ishmael Reed, "Is Ethnicity Obsolete?" in Werner Sollors, ed., *The Invention of Ethnicity* (New York: Oxford University Press, 1989), p. 227.

9. John Dewey is quoted in Horace M. Kallen, *Culture and Democracy in the United States: Studies in the Group Psychology of the American Peoples* (New York: Boni and Liveright, 1924), pp. 131–132.

10. Robert D. Linder and Richard V. Pierard, *Twilight of the Saints* (Downers Grove, IL: InterVarsity Press, 1978), p. 44.

11. Stephen Bates, "Fundamentally Out of Fashion," *The Washington Post,* September 7, 1993, p. A17.

12. Edward Gibbon, *The History of the Decline and Fall of the Roman Empire* (New York: DeFau, 1906), vol. 1, p. 35.

13. Alexis de Tocqueville, *The Old Regime and the French Revolution* (Garden City, NY: Doubleday, 1955), p. 153.

14. Will Herberg, *Protestant, Catholic, Jew: An Essay in American Religious Sociology* (Chicago: University of Chicago Press, 1983 [1955]).

15. James Q. Wilson, *The Moral Sense* (New York: The Free Press, 1993).

16. G. K. Chesterton, *What I Saw in America* (1922, reprinted New York: Da Capo Press, 1968), pp. 7–8.

17. George W. Cable, *The Negro Question* (Garden City, New York: Doubleday Anchor Books, 1958), pp. 117–118.

18. Calvin C. Hernton, *Sex and Racism in America* (New York: Doubleday, 1988 [1965]), p. 182.

19. Morton Kondracke, "Blenders," *The New Republic* (September 21, 1992), p. 50.

20. Tzvetan Todorov, *On Human Diversity: Nationalism, Racism, and Exoticism in French Thought,* trans. by Catherine Porter, (Cambridge, MA: Harvard University Press, 1993), p. 96.

21. Quoted in Robert Klitgaard, *Adjusting to Reality: Beyond "State versus Market" in Economic Development* (San Francisco: ICS Press, 1991), p. 175.

22. National Anti-Slavery Standard, July 11, 1863, p. 3, col. 2, quoted in

Andrew Kull, *The Color-Blind Constitution* (Cambridge, MA: Harvard University Press, 1992), p. 60.

23. Quoted in Lerone Bennett, Jr., *Before the Mayflower: A History of Black America*, 5th ed. (New York: Penguin, 1982), p. 318.

24. Franz Boas, "The Problem of the American Negro," *Yale Review*, vol. 10 (Jan. 1921), pp. 392–395.

25. Carl N. Degler, *In Search of Human Nature: The Decline and Revival of Darwinism in American Social Thought* (New York: Oxford University Press, 1991), p. 78.

26. Marcus Garvey, "Race Assimilation," in Howard Brotz, ed., *African-American Social and Political Thought, 1850–1920* (New Brunswick, NJ: Transaction, 1992), p. 553.

27. Alexander Crummell, "The Race Problem in America," in Brotz, supra, p. 184.

28. Crummell, ibid., p. 185.

29. Crummell, ibid., pp. 182–183.

30. Crummell, ibid., p. 184.

31. Henry Highland Garnet, "The Past and the Present Condition, and the Destiny of the Colored Race" (excerpt), in Brotz, supra, pp. 200–201 (italics in original).

32. Ben J. Wattenberg, *The First Universal Nation* (New York: The Free Press, 1991), p. 53.

33. *Southern Quarterly Review* 17 (July 1850), cited in Reginald Horsman, *Race and Manifest Destiny* (Cambridge, MA: Harvard University Press, 1981), p. 256.

34. Calvin C. Hernton, *Sex and Racism in America*, supra, p. xvii.

35. Hernton, ibid., p. xix.

36. Mildred Leinweber Dawson, "The Genetic Blending of Afro-Amerasians," Letters, *The New York Times*, December 3, 1992, A24, citing the National Center for Health Statistics.

37. Hanna Rosin, "Boxed In," *The New Republic*, January 3, 1994, p. 12.

38. Edward Braithwaite, *The Development of Creole Society in Jamaica, 1770–1820* (Oxford: Oxford University Press, 1971), p. 167.

39. George Bancroft, "The Necessity, the Reality, and the Promise of the Progress of the Human Race," oration delivered before the New York Historical Society, November 20, 1835, quoted in Liah Greenfield, *Nationalism: Five Roads to Modernity* (Cambridge, MA: Harvard University Press, 1992).

40. Ben J. Wattenberg, *The First Universal Nation* (New York: The Free Press, 1991), p. 54.

41. Quoted in Milton M. Gordon, "Assimilation in America: Theory and Reality," in Norman R. Yetman, *Majority and Minority: The Dynamics of Race and Ethnicity in American Life*, 5th ed. (Boston: Allyn and Bacon, 1991), p. 252.

Chapter 8. National Democracy

1. Herbert Croly, *The Promise of American Life* (Boston: Northeastern University Press, 1989 [1909]), pp. 39–40.
2. Croly, ibid., p. 42.
3. E. J. Dionne, Jr., "Democracy or Plutocracy," *Washington Post*, February 15, 1994, p. A17.
4. Dionne, ibid.
5. Virginia D. Abernethy, *Population Politics* (New York: Plenum Press, 1993), pp. 259–261.
6. "Training Up America," *The Economist*, January 15, 1994, p. 35.
7. John Judis, "Why Your Wages Keep Falling," *The New Republic*, February 14, 1994, p. 29.
8. Mervyn Rothstein, "Meet the New Super Super of the High-End Residence," *The New York Times*, September 25, 1994.
9. Gertrude Himmelfarb, *The Idea of Poverty: England in the Early Industrial Age* (New York: Random House, 1985), p. 59.
10. Jacob K. Javits, *Order of Battle: A Republican's Call to Reason* (New York: Pocket Books, 1966), p. 63.
11. Niccolo Machiavelli, *The Prince*, George Bull, trans. (London: Penguin Books, 1961), p. 51.
12. *Congressional Record*, vol. 35, pts. 3–5, 57th Cong., 1st sess. (Feb. 27, 1902), p. 2202; quoted in Martin J. Sklar, *The Corporate Reconstruction of American Capitalism, 1890–1916* (Cambridge: Cambridge University Press, 1988), p. 440.

Chapter 9. The National Story

1. William H. McNeill, "The Care and Repair of Public Myth," in *Mythistory and Other Essays* (Chicago: University of Chicago Press, 1986), p. 23.
2. McNeill, ibid., p. 22.
3. "Dissertation on the Canon and the Feudal Law," in John Adams, *Works of John Adams*, (Boston, 1865), vol. 3, p. 463.
4. Alexander Hamilton, *Continentalist* Number 6 (1782), in Harold C. Syrett, ed., *The Papers of Alexander Hamilton* (New York: Columbia University Press, 1961–1979), vol. 3 pp. 102–103.
5. Thomas Jefferson, letter, of Oct. 25, 1825, in A. Lipscomb and Albert E. Bergh, eds., *The Writings of Thomas Jefferson*, 20 vols. (Washington, DC: Thomas Jefferson Memorial Association, 1905), vol. 16, p. 127.
6. Thomas Jefferson to Edmund Pendleton, Aug. 13, 1776, in Julian P. Boyd, ed., *The Papers of Thomas Jefferson* (Princeton: Princeton University Press, 1950), vol. 1, p. 492.

7. Charles Francis Adams, ed., *Familiar Letters of John Adams and His Wife Abigail Adams, during the Revolution* (Boston, 1875), p. 211, quoted in Reginald Horsman, *Race and Manifest Destiny* (Cambridge, MA: Harvard University Press, 1981), p. 22.

8. Quoted in Gordon S. Wood, "The Father of Spin Control," *The New Republic*, February 1, 1993, p. 68.

9. Quoted in Robert N. Bellah, *Beyond Belief: Essays on Religion in a Post-Traditional World* (New York: Harper & Row, 1970), p. 178.

10. James Michael Curley, *I'd Do It Again: A Record of All My Uproarious Years* (Englewood Cliffs, NJ: Prentice-Hall, 1957), p. 208.

11. Martin Diamond, in William A. Schambra, ed., *As Far as Republican Principles Will Admit* (Washington, DC: The AEI Press, 1992).

12. Vine Deloria, *We Talk, You Listen* (New York: Macmillan, 1970).

13. Eric Williams, *History of the People of Trinidad and Tobago* (Port-of-Spain, 1962), p. vii, quoted in David Hackett Fischer, *Historians' Fallacies: Toward a Logic of Historical Thought* (New York: Harper & Row, 1970), p. 82.

14. Michael Oakeshott, *On History and Other Essays* (Oxford: Oxford University Press, 1983), p. 100.

15. Samuel Flagg Bemis, *John Quincy Adams and the Foundations of American Foreign Policy* (New York: Knopf, 1949), pp. 111–113.

16. Paul Finkelman, "Jefferson and Slavery," in Peter S. Onuf, ed., *Jeffersonian Legacies* (Charlottesville: University Press of Virginia, 1993), pp. 194–195.

17. Thomas Jefferson to Thomas Humphreys, Feb. 8, 1817, in Paul Leicester Ford, ed., *The Works of Thomas Jefferson*, 12 vols. [Federal Edition] (New York, 1904–1905), vol. 10, p. 77.

18. Thomas Jefferson to Edward Coles, Aug. 25, 1814, in Merrill D. Peterson, ed., *The Portable Thomas Jefferson* (New York: Penguin, 1975), p. 346.

19. Quoted in Robert A. Hendrickson, *The Rise and Fall of Alexander Hamilton* (New York: Van Nostrand Reinhold, 1981), p. xi.

20. *Continentalist* No. 6, July 4, 1782; *Letters from Phocion*, no. 2; *Federalist*, no. 36.

21. Alexander Hamilton, "Second Report on the Public Credit, January 20, 1795," in Samuel McKee, Jr. and J. Harvie Williams, eds., *Papers on Public Credit, Commerce, and Finance* (Indianapolis: Bobbs-Merrill, 1957), p. 151.

22. Quoted in Harvey Flaumenhaft, *The Effective Republic: Administration and Constitution in the Thought of Alexander Hamilton* (Durham, NC: Duke University Press, 1992), pp. 36–37.

23. Charles Maurice de Talleyrand-Perigord, Prince de Benevent, *Memoirs of the Prince de Talleyrand* (New York: AMS Press, 1973), pp. 81–82.

24. Clinton Rossiter, *Conservatism in America*, 2d ed., rev. (Cambridge, MA: Harvard University Press, 1982 [1962]), pp. 109–110.

25. Quoted in Lerone Bennett, Jr., *Before the Mayflower: A History of Black America*, 5th ed. (New York: Penguin, 1982), p. 154.

26. Frederick Douglass, "The Future of the Colored Race," in Howard Brotz, ed., *African-American Social and Political Thought, 1850–1920* (New Brunswick, NJ: Transaction, 1992), p. 309.

27. Frederick Douglass, "The Future of the Negro," in Brotz, ibid., p. 308.

28. Frederick Douglass, "The Future of the Colored Race," in Brotz, supra, p. 310.

29. Both from Frederick Douglass, "The Claims of the Negro Ethnologically Considered," in Brotz, supra, p. 243.

30. Quoted in Lerone Bennett, Jr., supra, p. 170.

31. Frederick Douglass, "The Claims of the Negro Ethnologically Considered," in Brotz, supra, pp. 237–238.

32. Frederick Douglass, "The Nation's Problem," in Brotz, supra, p. 318.

33. Frederick Douglass, "African Civilization and Society," in Brotz, supra, p. 264.

34. Frederick Douglass, "The Nation's Problem," in Brotz, supra, p. 320.

35. Martin Luther King, Jr., *Why We Can't Wait* (New York: Harper & Row, 1963), p. 150.

36. Frederick Douglass, "The Nation's Problem," in Brotz, supra, pp. 318–319.

37. Douglass, ibid., pp. 319–320.

38. Douglass, ibid., pp. 314–315.

39. Frederick Douglass, "What the Black Man Wants," in Brotz, supra, p. 283.

40. Frederick Douglass, "The Future of the Negro," in Brotz, supra, p. 308.

Index